CONQUEST WITHOUT WAR

CONQUEST
WITHOUT WAR

An analytical anthology of the speeches, interviews,
and remarks of Nikita Sergeyevich Khrushchev,
with commentary by Lenin, Stalin, and others

Compiled and edited by

N. H. MAGER and JACQUES KATEL

 A TRIDENT PRESS BOOK

SIMON AND SCHUSTER · NEW YORK

Library of Congress Catalog Card Number: 61-12291

Published simultaneously in the United States and Canada by Trident Press

Distributed by Affiliated Publishers, Inc.

Printed in the United States of America

ACKNOWLEDGMENTS

The editors acknowledge with thanks the unsolicited assistance of Andrei Shevchenko and G. T. Shuisky, ghost writers for Mr. Khrushchev, without whose efforts these words might never have been written.

Of particular help in providing background material were the many studies made for executive agencies and agencies for Congress by individuals, organizations, and the institutes for Russian Studies at Columbia and Harvard Universities. The editors have drawn liberally from this material as well as from the ideas of the many recent writers on the subjects discussed.

Acknowledgment is made to E. P. Dutton & Co., Inc., and Hutchinson and Co., Ltd., of London, for permission to quote from the official translation of Khrushchev's speeches which appear in his work *For Victory in Peaceful Competition with Capitalism*.

Preface

Conquest Without War was designed as a mosaic of the words and ideas of the new force that threatens to change the way of life on this planet. Beginning with Chapter 3, the words are those of Nikita Sergeyevich Khrushchev and his ghost writers. They appear in Roman type. Commentary (which appears in boldface type, such as you are now reading) has been selected from his ideological forebears, Vladimir Ilyich Lenin (né Ulyanov) and Joseph Vissarionovich Stalin (né Dzhugashvili), and from others associated with the world revolution and those who have studied it, together with remarks by the editors to provide a meaningful context for the Khrushchev statements.

Laid end to end, the stream of words spells out clearly the objectives and techniques of Soviet imperialism. The editors feel they have honestly distilled the essence of Mr. Khrushchev's ideas. The seeds of almost every thought were clearly and uninhibitedly laid down in the basic writings of communist dogma. The contemporary interpretations of these ideas are presented here from the mouth of Mr. Khrushchev.

Wherever possible, the editors have used authorized or officially approved translations of Khrushchev's remarks, although at times the English appears somewhat awkward and the text has been somewhat sanitized.* Figures are quoted in pre-1961 rubles for obvious reasons.

Only limitations of space—and the reader's patience—prevented

---

*Thus Khrushchev is quoted as saying: "When I tell my foreign minister to sit on a cake of ice, he sits on a cake of ice." The actual statement began: "When I tell my foreign minister to pull down his pants and sit . . ."

endless repetition of the same themes, which Khrushchev has expounded time and again, and in almost the same words, to different groups in different places. The late French socialist leader Leon Blum is reported to have said, "A politician has no alternatives other than to repeat himself or to contradict himself." Mr. Khrushchev succeeds on both scores.

Contents

ix

PART THREE: METHODS

Contents

PART **1**

THE SCENE

CHAPTER 1

Quest for World Domination

"I have always been impressed at our seeming reluctance to give credence to official statements which are made by political leaders in other countries when we disagree fervently with what they say or when their statements seem at times to be bombastic or unrealistic.

"For example, Hitler's Mein Kampf, written in 1924, had a wide circulation in Germany and left a deep impression on the German people. Over here it received comparatively little attention until after the outbreak of World War II. Yet this book was the blueprint of Hitlerian policy of the superiority of the Herrenvolk, of the manifest destiny of the German Reich, of the anti-Semitic campaigns, and of the whole trend of Hitlerism." —Allen W. Dulles [1]

The contemporary equivalent of *Mein Kampf* is contained in the millions of words uttered in almost every latitude and longitude by the leader of the world communist movement. From this flow of nouns, verbs, adjectives, and epithets, there emerges a Nikita Sergeyevich Khrushchev who considers himself the most powerful man on earth, the head of the most powerful country, the senior member of the most powerful coalition. He parades his power over the whole planet. His pennant flies on the moon.

Khrushchev's speeches, statements, reports, interviews, and impromptu remarks cover a variety of subjects—including advice to farmers on how to milk cows and grow corn, a discussion of the best

3

way to write novels, and major pronouncements on world affairs. They also contain promises and threats, slogans of action, and a way for communist victory.

The slogans—and the actions for which they form the base—unmistakably outline Khrushchev's aims and methodology. He makes no secret of his desire to rule the world. He is committed to trying to establish the Soviet type of communist system in all countries and on all continents.

This is the challenge at the beginning of the seventh decade of this century. To rule, Khrushchev must first conquer. And conquest is the central theme of all he says, the objective of everything he does.

His expressions of peaceful intent, his proposals for peaceful coexistence, are meant to—but, in fact, do not—hide the deadly conflict that is continuously foisted on us by the Soviet leadership.

Khrushchev wants this conflict to appear to be ideological: socialism versus capitalism. He firmly believes, or at least he says he does, that the world is in a period of transition, that history is on his side, and that the victory of socialism is inevitable. "Inevitable" is the key word. Those who try to oppose the forward march of socialism (i.e., Soviet power) are, he says, headed for destruction. To those who wish to follow him on his road to inevitable triumph, he promises a world free from war, poverty, and oppression.

Khrushchev hopes that this victory over "decadent, crumbling capitalism" will still occur in his lifetime. For a man nearing the age of seventy, this is a short-range perspective.

Khrushchev's arsenal seems formidable indeed: intercontinental ballistic missiles capable of delivering nuclear warheads to targets thousands of miles distant from the launching pads; a huge standing army that, if not deterred by threat of massive atomic retaliation, could overrun Europe, Asia, and Africa, where footholds have already been secured; a fifth column of so-called national Communist Parties formed into a disciplined and dedicated apparatus of subversion directed from Moscow; uncounted millions of men and women, a multitude moved by fright, prepared to accept any "compromise," even the most abject surrender, so as to avoid a threatened "nuclear holocaust"; almost a billion men and women who must work for him and cannot escape.

His base is an empire that appears solid and united for the purpose of conquest. Khrushchev has shown that any attempt by a satellite to leave the Soviet orbit is crushed by armed force, and that "neutralism" (which he encourages in the noncommunist world) is a crime in the Soviet empire.

While, in the years following World War II, the Soviet-occupied nations were being welded into this monolithic bloc, the old empires were disintegrating. Nationalism erupted after decades or centuries of discrimination and oppression, generating violent if unreasoned hatred for the former masters. This hatred was fanned by verbal support from Moscow and military aid discreetly provided. Khrushchev proclaimed his attachment to "equality and progress" and offered help to the new nations—economic and military power to protect their freedom and their still-fragile independence.

The center of the empire, the Soviet Union itself, is no longer the country that under Stalin lived on a subsistence level and was prostrated by fear, with no other future in sight than more suffering and deprivation; a country that was being whipped into new efforts and sacrifices in order to prepare for a new war, which Stalin believed necessary in order to enlarge his empire. In Khrushchev's Russia, life is better and the future appears bright, certainly brighter than during the dark years of Stalin's rule.

However, the regime that Khrushchev represents and that, he promises, will bring freedom and plenty to the whole world is totalitarian, different in degree but not in essence from Stalin's dictatorship. All decisions are resolved by one man, assisted by a small, trusted elite. He dominates his country and his empire with the support of a new class of communist aristocrats who produce nothing and control every aspect of Soviet life. The secret police, on which Stalin relied to impose "socialism" in one country and later "socialism" in the empire, is today in the background. But it is still there, keeping its all-embracing files up-to-date for possible future use, for possible purges and liquidations.

The Communist Party, the repository of all power, is expanding

5

its influence, while the so-called representatives of the peoples, the parliaments of the Soviet bloc, still, as under Stalin, unanimously endorse the dictates of the Party leadership.

Like any dictator, Khrushchev can act fast, free from the restraints democracies impose upon their governments. He alone decides that the national effort shall be concentrated on producing more rockets and fewer consumer goods. He is the sole judge over good and evil. He alone determines whether there will be war or peace.

Khrushchev says he wants peace. He wants peace because he knows the risks of a nuclear war. He also knows that all peoples want peace, but perhaps none more than the people of the Soviet Union. Thirty million Soviet citizens died before the Red Army crushed the Nazi invader. The land was scorched, towns leveled. In proclaiming his desire for peace, Khrushchev knows he will receive the genuine, indeed enthusiastic, support of his own nation.

But Khrushchev's concept of peace is not a static one. What he wants is a peace of conquest. Maintenance and consolidation of the status quo as the West knows it would be undesirable for Khrushchev. Retreat is unacceptable. He would rather fight than give up positions the Soviets have acquired. He has made this clear; his own words are unequivocal.

Khrushchev knows that there is only one power on earth capable of resisting him. His propaganda, his threats and smiles, all tend to "neutralize" the United States, to weaken its military power, and to destroy its will to resist.

Khrushchev's speeches and acts clearly show that he regards the retaliatory potential of the United States as the main military restraint to a communist push forward. At present and for the next few years—until the United States' ICBM's are fully operational and available in sufficient numbers—the American deterrent capability is largely dependent on overseas bases. These bases are therefore the first target of the Soviet leadership.

Khrushchev has used many techniques and tactics to obtain or impose American withdrawal from overseas bases. His proposals on disarmament invariably set as the very first condition the liquidation of American airfields and rocket launching pads installed on the

6

territories of its allies. He and his spokesmen have presented proposals ranging from withdrawal of Soviet troops from Eastern Europe to creation of "nuclear-free zones" in exchange for scrapping of American bases and installations in Europe, Asia, and Africa. Such plans alternate with dire threats and verbal abuse. Khrushchev has warned West Germany, France, Britain, Italy, Greece, Turkey, Norway, Denmark, and even Austria that they would be wiped off the face of the earth in any conflict if they remained allied to the United States and allowed United States bases to remain on their soil, or even allowed U.S. rockets to fly over their land.

To further weaken United States power overseas (air and rocket bases are only one of its manifestations) the Soviet leadership has helped foment revolutions in Iraq and Laos and tried to foment them in Iran, has supported guerrillas in the Philippines, nationalists in Africa, and pacifists in Japan. The Soviet (Communist) Party in France supported President de Gaulle when Khrushchev thought that revival of French nationalism would weaken French-American ties. He has bought fish from Iceland and courted the Conservatives in Britain. He proclaimed himself the protector of Cuba after Fidel Castro became the main mouthpiece of anti-Americanism in the Western Hemisphere, and of Lumumba's Congo balancing on the edge of chaos.

United States air and missile bases—essential as they may be at the present time to insure a balance of power and thereby a balance of terror, and through the balance of terror, to discourage military ventures—are not the only signs of the noncommunist world's determination to resist Soviet expansion. The U.S. chain of defensive alliances created since 1948, when the Soviet intentions became evident from the communist coup in Czechoslovakia and the blockade of Berlin, and reinforced since the 1950 aggression in Korea, requires stability and peace within the noncommunist world. The Marshall Plan promised such stability to Europe. It thus became the target of continuous Soviet attack and of violent protests by the local Communist Parties. Aid to underdeveloped nations, designed to help stabilize their new independent regimes, was decried as "neo-imperialism." Stalin's adventure in Korea was ascribed to American aggression, and world-wide fear of an extension of this conflict was effective in spreading neutralism in large parts of Asia and the Middle East.

To weaken the European allies of the United States, Khrushchev encouraged Nasser of Egypt to bring under his control the oil lines from the Arab world. The Soviet interest and stake in Algeria and the Congo are closely tied to the policy of attacking the Western alliance at its weak points. Khrushchev has missed no opportunity to exploit the difficulties of the noncommunist world.

The Khrushchev-provoked crisis over Berlin in the spring of 1960 may go down in history as a classic example of the war of nerves. Tough, very tough pronouncements are followed by not-so-tough acts. Every partial or temporary retreat by the dictator from his maximum demands, or even from the time limit he himself originally imposed, is hailed as a concession and a sign of reasonableness. The fact that Khrushchev, by virtue of valid international instruments, has no right to modify unilaterally the status of Berlin disappears in a maze of statements about the abnormality of the situation prevailing there and of references to the "powder keg" whose explosion would destroy the whole world. Khrushchev's announced intention of violating wartime agreements by concluding a separate peace with East Germany is drowned in a cataract of words that sound sensible and moderate—compared to his irresponsible statements of the previous day.

Unable short of war to destroy the West's defensive arsenal, Khrushchev attempts to destroy the will to use it—in the face of a possible war of planetary annihilation. What Khrushchev wanted and expected on Berlin was surrender—similar to what Hitler obtained in Munich in 1938, after frightening Neville Chamberlain of Britain and Edouard Daladier of France into a so-called compromise that was to preserve "peace in our time."

But the will to resist Soviet demands was stronger than the desire to solve the Berlin crisis on Khrushchev's terms. Khrushchev scuttled the Paris summit meeting, which he had advocated for years as the universal panacea, when it became apparent there would be no

8

basic Western concessions, no surrender of Western rights in the name of "peaceful coexistence."

The threat to Berlin still remains. Khrushchev, although often a man in a hurry, can also be patient. The crisis may erupt anew any day, any minute.

This war of nerves is taking place at a time of extraordinary scientific advances. Beyond accentuating the latent military threat, Soviet scientific achievements have opened a new front in psychological warfare. As heralded by skilled communist propagandists, the successes of Soviet space rocketry are "proving" that industrially— and therefore economically—the Soviet Union has already caught up with and surpassed its capitalist opponent.

What these propagandists do not say, but what is evident even in the Soviet press, is the enormous price the Soviet people have had to pay for shooting the moon. The motherland of the Lunik is still an underdeveloped country as far as the standard of living of its people is concerned. The great mass of Russians still live today as did the European or American workers of the nineteenth century. A few weeks after the Soviet flag was planted on the surface of the moon, Khrushchev had to admit the Soviet people still did not have enough shoes.

Khrushchev knows he cannot win the economic competition in his lifetime. He knows that the figures he cites are distorted and incomplete. He knows that the economic progress he has made has been concentrated in a relatively narrow sphere that provides military capability rather than well-being for the population. His boasts of "economic competition" are not a delusion, however. For the economic competition in which he engages is a competition for political power. Whatever good the populace receives is merely corollary. His "economic competition," like his "peaceful coexistence," is a distraction, a sort of semantic soporific, to provide the time needed for "socialist construction."

But the Soviet leader believes he is winning and will conquer.

He sees his nation grown from a fourth-rate power to the second power on earth. He sees his economy, his scientists, his military, forging weapons such as Russia—even the world—has never seen before. There are weapons of propaganda and weapons of trade, psychological weapons and military weapons. There are marching columns and fifth columns.

In the disintegration of colonial empires, Khrushchev sees not the birth of new freedoms but the downfall of "capitalism in its highest form," the loss of markets and raw-material supplies to the West and an opportunity for Soviet infiltration.

He has seen a small group of dedicated men build a hard-core Party of 33 million, now able to rule a billion people.

Given time, the communist empire will become stronger. In some measure it will provide more for its own people. Undoubtedly, in a changing world, some nations' leaders will succumb to bribery or blandishment, and join the communist sphere of influence. Some of these will be able to free themselves when disillusion sets in; perhaps others will not. But time will undoubtedly tell the whole story to the world. As the Soviet leader so often says, "We can wait; the wind is not blowing in our face."

Rule by the Party of One

Khrushchev is the chief exponent of a regime that is more than a one-party state, and that has been aptly described by Leo Gruliow, an American writer on Soviet affairs, as "the party state."[2]

The Communist Party rules the Soviet Union. All decisions are made by the Party. As under Stalin, the Party remains the instrument of the "dictatorship of the proletariat," which, according to Stalin, is "in essence . . . the dictatorship of the 'vanguard' of the proletariat, . . . [which] is the dictatorship of the Party."[3]

Lenin, the founder of the Party, defined it at the time of its creation, in 1903, as a closely knit group of dedicated militants—professional revolutionaries who unhesitatingly accept the decisions of the leadership. Article One of the constitution of what was to become the Bolshevik Party, defined a Party member as one "who recognizes the Party's progress and supports it by material means and by personal participation in one of the Party organizations." The regime within the Party was based on "democratic centralism."

10

Discussion was permitted until a decision had been reached. This was democracy. But once the decision had been adopted—adopted, that is, by the central organs of the Party—it was binding on all members. At the time of its founding, the Party was an illegal organization striving to overthrow the Czarist regime. Membership was necessarily restricted to a few thousand men and women, ready to sacrifice liberty and often life for their ideas. (In 1905 the Party had 8,500 members, and a few months before the 1917 October Revolution, only 23,000.)

Today, according to the latest available figures, the omnipotent Party of the Soviet Union has a membership of 8,708,000—about four per cent of the population. The Party organization parallels the territorial subdivision of the state, with a Party branch in each jurisdiction. Thus there are fifteen organizations for republics, eight for territories, 167 for regions, thirty-six for areas, 4,886 for districts, and 544 for cities.

Membership is an indispensable steppingstone to advancement in practically any field. Almost one million Party members hold some political office, from head of government to positions in trade unions or regional, provincial, or local administration.

Admission to the Party is a promise of a better future. Khrushchev is probably right when he says:

"If we said, Let anyone who wants join the Communist Party, our Party would now certainly have many tens of millions of members. But we say, We do not need this. In order to become a Communist, one must not only understand communism, but must also be its active soldier. And not everyone who supports the ideas of the Communist Party is able to do this." [4]

Candidates for membership are carefully selected. *Pravda*, the official organ of the Party, comments, "We have limited the Party's growth and accepted only a portion of those wishing to join." [5]

Usually new young members are admitted after serving in the Young Communist League. "Only workers, peasants, and intelligentsia who are enlightened, active, and devoted to communism are admitted." A candidate serves one year, and is then screened again for admission. The initiation fee is two per cent of a month's salary; dues are one-half to three per cent of income, depending on salary.

The four per cent of the population who form the Party represent an "elite," an aristocracy that technically directs the destinies of the remaining 96 per cent of Soviet citizens.

Within the Party itself, it is again a small minority—in this case one man, Khrushchev—that defines, formulates, and insures the execution of decisions binding on the Party, the nation, and the empire. The Party is today what Leon Trotsky, as early as 1904, had predicted it would become: "The Party organization at first substitutes itself for the Party as a whole, then the Central Committee substitutes itself for the organization, and finally a single 'dictator' substitutes himself for the Central Committee." [6]

In practice, the leadership of the Party is not responsible to the membership, which is consulted only when the leadership so desires. Such consultation takes the form of a Party congress. According to Party statutes, the congresses are supposed to be convened regularly, but actually the intervals between them have varied from one to more than thirteen years. (Since Stalin's death two congresses have been held, in 1956 and in 1959. Another, the twenty-second, is scheduled for October 1961.)

At a congress the Party membership, which now numbers almost nine million, is represented by about 1,300 delegates, carefully chosen by local Party Secretariats before being sent to Moscow. The delegates are called on to approve—and they always do so unanimously—the composition of the Central Committee, which has at present 240 members (235 men and five women).

The Central Committee meets twice a year. In theory it selects, but in practice only endorses, the nominations submitted by the leadership for its two executive organs, the Presidium (formerly called Political Bureau or, shortened, Politburo) and the Secretariat. At the Central Committee meeting of May 1960, a six-man Secretariat and an eleven-member (ten men and one woman) Presidium were elected. All members of the Secretariat, headed by First Secretary Khrushchev, are also members of the Presidium.

At the time of the Revolution and for several years thereafter, the more important of these two bodies was the Politburo. It was the Politburo that discussed all important problems affecting the new state and communist doctrine.

But Stalin, once he became Secretary-General, infused real power into the Secretariat—the power to appoint the personnel of the Party machine. And within the Secretariat, the First Secretary supervises all important nominations and promotions. He is thus able to bring into the Central Committee lieutenants loyal to him. Also, he can, by applying the letter of the Party statutes, overrule a decision of the Politburo or Presidium that would be unfavorable to him. (Khrushchev used this power in 1957 to defeat opposition to his policy by a majority of the Presidium.)

Throughout its history, the Communist Party of the Soviet Union— and with it, the world communist movement—has suffered convulsions generally described as "purges." Here again, Lenin's concept of the Party, of its membership, and of its role as the revolutionary vanguard, underlies this permanent feature of communism. Lenin recommended that the Party be kept pure of "petty-bourgeois elements which inevitably attach themselves to it" once it can carry out its work legally. To achieve this he advised the Party to "periodically purge" (re-register) its membership.

Under Stalin, the "purge" was used in order to maintain the "monolithic unity" of the Party and to insure for the Secretary-General the unanimous support of the terrorized Politburo, Central Committee, and membership.

In the twenties, exclusion from the Party, banishment to Siberia, and, in the case of Leon Trotsky, exile were due punishment for deviation from the "general line" laid down by the Secretary-General, Joseph Stalin. In the thirties, Stalin adopted more radical methods against his real or alleged adversaries: a Mauser bullet in the head.

The most clear-cut indictment and the most authoritative explanation of the way Stalin implemented the recommendation to re-register the membership was presented by Khrushchev in what is called officially in the Soviet Union the "Report on the Cult of the Personality and Its Consequences," submitted to the Twentieth Party Congress, in 1956.*

The "party state" has a parliament to enact the decisions of the Party into laws and a government to execute them.

The Council of Ministers, formerly called the Council of People's Commissars, is headed by the Premier, who is theoretically chosen by the Supreme Soviet (parliament). Now, as during the last years of Stalin's reign, the Premier is also the First Secretary of the Party's Central Committee (Khrushchev).

The Supreme Soviet is composed of two houses: a Soviet of Nationalities and a Soviet of the Union. The former consists of twenty-five representatives from each Union Republic, eleven from each Autonomous Republic, five from each Autonomous Region, and one from each National Area. The Soviet of the Union consists of one representative per 300,000 constituents.

Candidates for deputies in the Supreme Soviet are nominated by the Party or by trade unions, cooperatives, youth or cultural organizations, all of which operate under Party control. Moreover, the candidates must be approved by an electoral commission, which may reject a candidate without giving any reason. In practice, one out of each five candidates is not a Party member.

Usually there is one candidate for each office. Soviet citizens over eighteen years of age are eligible to vote. Even citizens passing through an area on a train are permitted to cast their ballot there. Those who do not vote are looked upon with suspicion. In these circumstances, the unopposed candidates receive more than 99 per cent of the total vote.

---

* In the noncommunist world, this report is generally referred to as Khrushchev's "Secret Speech." It was delivered in secret before the 1,436 full delegates and alternates to the Party Congress on the night of February 25, 1956. The "fraternal delegates," representatives of non-Soviet Communist Parties, were excluded from the meeting. But very soon the text of Khrushchev's report began to circulate in the satellite countries and in the West. On June 4, 1956, the U.S. State Department published a version of the speech that the USSR had sent, after editing, to leaders of foreign Communist Parties. All evidence indicates that this text is substantially correct, although Khrushchev may have gone further in his accusations against Stalin than the document from which we are quoting suggests.

14

The Supreme Soviet is theoretically invested with all the powers of a Western parliament. In addition, it selects the procurator general (attorney general), and the Supreme Court, as well as the Council of Ministers. Besides the government, the Supreme Soviet elects a Presidium of 133 members, which together with the Council of Ministers, exercises the legislative power when the Supreme Soviet is not in session.

CHAPTER 2

The First Secretary

Nikita Sergeyevich Khrushchev is the best known and most self-advertised of the rulers of the Soviet state. At the same time he is the least predictable. Millions in the noncommunist world have seen this little man (five feet five, 200 pounds), surprisingly nimble, with very small and very light blue eyes, in person or on television screens, joking, cajoling, clowning, adroitly dodging questions, kissing babies on all continents like a politician on an election tour. They have heard him quote Russian proverbs and invoke God as a witness to his love for peace. They have read about his stumbling after too many toasts. They have also seen him point an accusing finger and shake his fist at "decadent capitalists." The whole world has been stunned by the brutality of his war threats and the coarseness of his insults shouted at Western statesmen, gathered in New York for the U.N. General Assembly.

Noncommunists who have talked with him have been struck by his "strong personality" and describe him as a natural leader, a most remarkable man.

Some communists who know the present number-one man of the communist world appraise him in less flattering terms. Shortly after the bloodless Warsaw revolt against Soviet domination, a Polish official privately called Khrushchev an irresponsible "madman" given to sudden impulses, capable of provoking a major war in a fit of rage.

His life history, however, suggests he is anything but that.

Khrushchev is the first top Soviet leader of real proletarian origin and no revolutionary past. "I am a worker," he says, "the son of a working man, the grandson of a serf." Lenin was an intellectual from the small landed gentry; Stalin, although a cobbler's son, received a higher education in a religious seminary. Both had known Czarist jails and Siberian exile.

Nikita Khrushchev was born on April 17, 1894, in the village of Kalinovka, in the Kursk district of Central Russia, not far from the border of the Ukraine. Little is known about his early years. Some historians assert that until his twenties, Khrushchev was illiterate. This conclusion is probably based on his own remarks, such as this one addressed to Western diplomats: "I never went to school." [1]

However, in April 1960 Khrushchev told French trade unionists that before the Revolution he finished only "an elementary parochial school." Although the academic level of such institutions, run by Greek Orthodox priests before the Bolshevik Revolution, was not high, they did prepare the children for secondary schools. Surely, an "exemplary pupil," as Khrushchev described himself, would have learned to read and write.

Life must have been hard in Kalinovka. The Khrushchev family was poor—"very poor," Khrushchev says. In one of his speeches he gives the following account of his childhood and youth:

"I began working when I learned to walk. Till the age of fifteen I tended calves, then sheep, and then the landlord's cows. I did all that before I was fifteen. Then I worked at a factory owned by Germans and later in coal pits owned by Frenchmen. I worked at Belgian-owned chemical plants." [2]

During the time Khrushchev was growing up socialist propaganda was aimed at "the working class," which was a minority in overwhelmingly rural Russia. He does not seem to have been touched by appeals to his "revolutionary class-instincts" or to have been convinced that he, the underpaid, oppressed proletarian, represented the future. It is not known why Nikita Khrushchev was not drafted into the Imperial Russian Army during World War I; he reached military age in 1914. It is probable that he was kept out of service because he was an industrial worker. Thus he escaped what Lenin and later all communists called the "imperialist war," which it was the workers' "duty" to transform into a civil war against "their own bourgeoisie." (In the heat of his Paris press conference following the collapse of the 1960 summit conference, Khrushchev apparently forgot Lenin's teaching, for he spoke of the "heroism" of Marshal Rodion Malinovsky, Soviet Defense Minister, during the fight against "German imperialism" in World War I. Malinovsky was with the Russian contingent in France.)

Later Soviet historians may "discover" that Khrushchev was always a communist at heart and a communist in deed. Khrushchev has already laid the foundations for additions to his biography that would show he was a revolutionary in his youth. He has claimed that years before he joined the Communist Party, he already understood the nature of international capitalism and was on his way to developing into a communist internationalist. He had discovered, he says, that the owners of the factories and mines, whether German, French, Belgian, or Russian, were all the same: "They wanted us to work more and earn less."

In a conversation with French trade-union leaders he has also asserted that "despite my youthful years, I enjoyed the confidence of the workers, and more than once I was among the workers' delegations in negotiations with the entrepreneurs."

The volume of the "Large Soviet Encyclopedia" containing Khrushchev's official biography was printed in February 1957, at a time when the Soviet Union was still ruled by "collective leadership" and before the assumption of uncontested supreme power by Khrushchev. Since that version, Khrushchev's life history has become vastly more heroic. In April 1959, on the occasion of his sixty-fifth birthday, Soviet Marshals Andrei I. Yeremenko and Vasily I. Chuikov wrote in the most glowing terms about Khrushchev's outstanding role in planning the Battle of Stalingrad, a role previously ascribed to Stalin.

Two months later, in June 1959, the new official history of the Communist Party of the Soviet Union went to press. It contains a list of twenty-three names, in alphabetical order, of Lenin's "comrades-in-arms and disciples hardened in the civil war . . . on whose back lay the burden of liquidating the consequences of the war and constructing a socialist society." Khrushchev is for the first time included in this list as well as Stalin.

Thus, Khrushchev's stature is already considerably greater than it was in 1957. It is not unreasonable to expect further changes, further enlargement of his personality in the future. But for the time being, the official Soviet biographers do not mention Khrushchev's "class struggle" in pre-Revolutionary days; they merely note that he joined the Communist Party in 1918 (probably in February or March), after the Revolution.

Khruhschev received his baptism of fire in the Civil War. He fought on the southern front, he says, in the ranks of the Red Army that drove the Whites into the Black Sea. Since the official biographers give no details of his achievements as a soldier in the Civil War, it is safe to conclude that he played a rather obscure role. They credit him only with "active Party work in the regiment."

Khrushchev returned to the Donbassin (Donets Basin, Ukrainian coal-mining region) mines after the Civil War, where he was again noted for his "active Party work." This time he was rewarded with admittance to the newly created "Workers Faculty" of Yuzovka (to-day Stalino), an industrial center in the Ukraine.

These special Party schools had been established for selected adult workers who were literate and Party members of at least four years' standing. The three years of secondary education in these schools was to prepare them for future employment in industry, for higher training, or, as in Khrushchev's case, for a career in the Party. In the Ukraine, there were eight "Workers Faculties," attended by about 1,500 students.

It was, of course, a privilege to be admitted to a Party school. But it also entailed hard work and living in substandard conditions —in unheated, crowded dormitories and with little food. Long hours of courses in academic subjects were followed by interminable Party meetings, at which the problems of the day were examined in "Marxist" terms and at which the students' attitude toward the power struggle in the Kremlin was carefully scrutinized.

The official biography does not indicate exactly when Khrushchev attended the Workers Faculty, in which, the "Large Soviet Encyclopedia" states, he "conducted active Party work." But he was there in 1924, when, according to his present wife, Nina Petrovna, he

19

married for the second time. Mrs. Khrushchev disclosed that his first wife had died "of famine" and that when he married her his two children by his first wife were six and eight years old. These details of Khrushchev's life became known only in 1959, when Nina Petrovna addressed a press conference in Washington, D.C., during the Soviet leader's trip to the United States.

* * * * * * *

Lenin died in January 1924. The struggle to succeed him started immediately—in fact, it had been going on in the background for nearly two years, while Lenin was limited to almost complete inactivity following a series of strokes.

The Revolution, the Civil War, the famines that followed it, had exhausted the country. They had also exhausted the Party, which was yearning to reap the fruit of its struggles. But according to Marxist doctrine, the teachings of Lenin, and the proclamations of Leon Trotsky, who had led the insurrection and built the Red Army, the battle had only begun. The Russian Revolution was to be the first successful step in the "inevitable" world revolution—provided the Russian communists supported the anticipated upheavals in Germany and the rest of capitalist Europe, and led the colonial peoples in their struggle to oust the "imperialist oppressors." Trotsky demanded new sacrifices, particularly from the "elite."

Stalin realized that the victorious Party wanted peace and power. The Party had already changed in membership and character. It was much larger than the pre-Revolutionary organization. It now attracted not the dedicated revolutionaries, but the ambitious careerists, of which Khrushchev is the archetype. These men understood that Party membership meant privileges and advancement. Stalin promised these, but first he needed support to dispose of the troublemakers calling for "permanent revolution."

Stalin offered a consolidation of the Party's gains. He launched the slogan of "socialism in one country," a socialism that would not be the promised egalitarian society (Stalin denounced such promises as "petty-bourgeois," i.e., "counterrevolutionary," rantings of "left-wing scatterbrains"), but of which the Party and its members would be the main if not the sole beneficiaries.

It became essential to remain in the Party, the sole vehicle of promotion. And to remain in the Party, it was indispensable to accept the new doctrine and obey unquestioningly the leadership that was building this new brand of "socialism" in one country and for a new class. For several years after Lenin's death, this leadership was a "collective," but not a stable one. To eliminate Trotsky, then described as "left-wing," Stalin allied himself with the "right-wingers." Once Trotsky had been beaten and exiled, Stalin turned on the "right-wingers," who were then labeled "petty-bourgeois sentimentalists."

These twists and turns in Kremlin policy were accompanied by continuous large-scale purges—amounting at that time to expulsion from the Party—of all those associated with the "deviationists" of the left- or right-wing variety.

Stalin's support came from the subservient Party functionaries, whom he or his lieutenants selected from among the membership. They constituted the *apparatchiki,* the machine. Their positions (in later years their freedom and later still, their very lives) depended not so much on their efficiency as on their unquestioning acceptance of the "line."

But this was not enough: Stalin's decisions had to be carried out in the country at large. When collectivization of agriculture was decreed, the apparatchiki had to see to it that the peasants were driven into the *kolkhozes* (collective farms), regardless of the price in lives and suffering. A Party man who wavered was ruthlessly eliminated; he endangered the standing of his superior, who was responsible for the conduct of his "men."

On the other hand, every zig or zag, every important new step, led to the elimination of "untrustworthy elements"—those of the apparatchiki whose "leader," the man to whom they owed their position, had fallen from grace as a result of the change in policy. Thus, a purge could originate at the top or at the bottom of the apparat.

This Stalinist concept of the Party insured continuous "vigilance" by the apparatchiki. At every level of the hierarchy, the Party functionaries were closely following each move in the Kremlin, insignificant as it might seem to the uninitiated. They were also watching one another, because "socialist vigilance" required the "uncovering" of "deviations and deviationists," the "unmasking of the class enemy" who might have "wormed his way into the Party."

The pre-Revolutionary Russian aristocracy had conversed in French or German so as not to be understood by the servants and the people, whom they despised. The new aristocracy now developed its own language, its own signs, which were solely for the consumption of the apparatchiki and not intended to be understood by the common mortal. The successful apparatchik was the one who correctly read the signs and correctly understood the hidden meaning of the class language, and was ready to execute at the right moment the decision taken at the top. He had to be an accomplished "Kremlinologist."*

Thus, in the early twenties, Khrushchev must have "correctly" evaluated the situation in Moscow. He must have realized that the Party apparatus, headed by the Secretary-General, Stalin, would in the end overcome the opposition, formidable as the stature of Trotsky might have seemed. Khrushchev's alignment with the Stalin faction was probably also determined by self-interest. He had just become an apparatchik, a member of the Party machine, one year after joining the Yuzovka Workers Faculty. According to some of his nonofficial biographers, Khrushchev became the principal Party Secretary of the school, "in real influence outranking the director of the school and all the teaching staff." [3]

Khrushchev finished the Workers Faculty in 1925 or 1926. His subsequent career indicates that he had probably excelled in Party work and not in science or engineering, which he had set out to study. The Party apparatus was by then firmly in Stalin's hands. Already it had assumed the Stalinist pattern, in which every-

* Kremlinology has also been developed in the world at large, vitally interested in the power struggle in Moscow because its outcome may affect the destiny of the whole planet.

thing from ideology to production depends on the loyal Party functionaries.

Khrushchev was appointed Secretary of a district Party Committee in Yuzovka, already renamed Stalino. In this capacity, he controlled not only the district's Party activity but also its industrial production.

While Khrushchev was Committee Secretary, one of Stalin's lieutenants, Lazar M. Kaganovich, had been sent to the Ukraine to reorganize the Party, to purge from it all "untrustworthy" elements, men who had shown less foresight than Khrushchev when the outcome of the power struggle was not yet clear. After Kaganovich "discovered" the young Stalinist, Khrushchev advanced rapidly. From a district Committee he moved up to the Stalino city Party Committee, where his particular organizational and administrative talents were put to use. In 1927, he took part in the Tenth Congress of the Ukrainian Communist Party and presented proposals designed to strengthen local Party administration.

The years 1927 and 1928 were trying, particularly in the industrial centers of the Ukraine. There was threat of famine, the peasants were not delivering enough grain to feed the urban population. Stalin countered with terror. The Party and the secret police launched a requisition drive, "liquidating" with machine guns the "kulaks," as those peasants who were unwilling to satisfy the demands of the Party agitators were labeled. Khrushchev participated actively in this campaign. He does not seem to have shown any scruples—"petty-bourgeois sentimentality"—or any pity.

And he was rewarded. Before returning to Moscow in 1928, Kaganovich spoke highly to his successor in the Ukraine, Stanislav V. Kosior, of the dependable young man from Stalino. Soon Khrushchev was transferred to Kiev, to the Secretariat of the Party Committee of the largest city in the Ukraine.

In Kiev, says the "Soviet Encyclopedia," Khrushchev engaged in "leading Party work," in contrast to "active Party work," which he had done in Stalino. This new post was a steppingstone to further promotion. Men like Khrushchev—ruthless and with no ideological past or commitments—were needed to replace "deviationists," who were being expelled from the Party and, by now, also arrested by the thousands. Thus in 1929 he was called to Moscow (where Kaganovich was boss of the city Party organization) ostensibly to receive higher education at the J. V. Stalin Industrial Academy. All the official biography says about his higher education is that he was "elected Secretary of the Party Committee of the Academy." His job was to supervise the ideological behavior of the faculty and students, to "unmask" and denounce to the secret police any "anti-Party elements."

Khrushchev apparently justified the trust placed in him by his protectors. After about a year and a half at the Academy, he was graduated and was immediately appointed to the Moscow Party machine, almost certainly by Kaganovich. In the following years, Khrushchev swiftly climbed the hierarchical ladder. Between 1931 and 1934, he rose from Second Secretary of the Moscow city Committee to Second Secretary of the Moscow Regional Committee and was, under Kaganovich, responsible for its organization and personnel.

* * * * * * *

The years 1929 to 1933 are among the most tragic in the entire history of Russia. Khrushchev left the Ukraine as the forced collectivization of agriculture was just beginning. Peasants resisting collectivization were again attacked as kulaks and enemies of the people, and Stalin decreed the "liquidation of the kulaks as a class." Conservative estimates place the number of deaths during these years at about ten million, with another ten million deported to slave-labor camps in Siberia, Central Asia, and the Far North.

The mass terror against the peasants shook the Communist Party and even part, if not the majority, of its leadership. Stalin reacted by demanding the right to execute members of opposition groups within the Party. In an unprecedented move, both the Politburo and the Central Committee refused to accede to his demand. Thus the blood bath was delayed for a few years.

In 1934, Stalin convened the Seventeenth Congress of the Communist Party, hailed as the "Congress of the Victors," to celebrate the completion of the collectivization drive and to endorse a new purge of the Party, involving several hundred thousand members.

During these years, Khrushchev continued to rise in Party ranks. At the 1934 Congress he was elected a full member of the Central Committee. It is thus evident that he showed no hesitation over the mass terror or the mass purges. On the contrary, it is certain he participated in the latter and fully approved of the former. At the 1934 Congress, Khrushchev himself proudly proclaimed that the "rightist deviation" (those who opposed the terror) had been "beaten in the Moscow organization," which, he said, was united behind "our genius leader, Comrade Stalin." He called for the strengthening of "the organs of the dictatorship of the proletariat [the secret police] for the final annihilation of the class enemies."

The final annihilation of the "class enemies" began shortly after the Congress of the Victors. On December 1, 1934, Sergei M. Kirov, a member of the Politburo and boss of the Leningrad Party organization, was killed by a young Party member. At the time there was widespread belief in the noncommunist world that Stalin himself had instigated the murder to convince the Party that the blood purge he had been denied two years earlier was long overdue. In February 1956, Khrushchev confirmed this theory. In the Secret Speech before the Twentieth Congress of the Communist Party of the Soviet Union,[4] he declared: "It must be asserted that to this day, the circumstances surrounding Kirov's murder hide many things that are inexplicable and mysterious and demand careful examination. There are reasons for the suspicion that the killer of Kirov, Nikolayev, was assisted by someone from among the people whose duty it was to protect Kirov [the secret police]."

But in 1935 Khrushchev had no such misgivings. *Pravda* (June 13, 1935) quotes Khrushchev's address to Moscow Communists: "The shot that struck Comrade Kirov showed that our enemies will stop at nothing. Exposed and maddened, they resort to any kind of foul deed, from setting fire to collective-farm sheepfolds, poisoning food in workers' canteens, to murder of the leaders of the people." And eighteen months later: "The Trotskyite scoundrels prepared ter-

25

roristic acts against our leaders. The unforgettable Sergei Mironovich Kirov was assassinated by a treacherous bullet!"

Kirov's murder was the signal for unprecedented terror. The show trials of 1936, '37, and '38 wiped out the Bolsheviks who had led the Revolution, practically all the surviving members of Lenin's Politburo. In the cellars of secret-police prisons, thousands upon thousands of persons who refused to confess to the "crimes" of which they were accused—poisoning workers' canteens, sabotaging kolkhozes and railroads, spying for Nazi Germany and imperialist Japan—were summarily shot. No one was safe during those harrowing years. In his 1956 speech, Khrushchev described what had happened: The "terror was actually directed not at the remnants of the defeated exploiting classes, but against honest workers of the Party and of the Soviet State; against them were made lying, slanderous, and absurd accusations concerning 'two-facedness,' 'espionage,' 'sabotage,' preparations of fictitious 'plots,' etc." Khrushchev added that of the 139 members and candidates of the Central Committee elected by the "Congress of the Victors," 98 (i.e., 70 per cent) were arrested and shot (most of them in 1937–1938). Of the 1,966 delegates to this congress, 1,108 were arrested on charges of anti-Revolutionary crimes.

What was Khrushchev doing while terror gripped the Party, while every apparatchik lived in fear of arrest and death every moment of day and night? According to the official biography, he "carried out organization work of great magnitude in executing the plans projected by the Party and Government for the socialist reconstruction of Moscow, for developing public services in the capital, for the improvement of the living conditions of workers and employees."

This picture of Khrushchev's activities corresponds to the image created at that time by the Moscow press (controlled by the then Secretary of the Moscow Party Committee: Khrushchev). Photographs of Khrushchev supervising the building of the Moscow subway, talking with workers, conversing with Stalin, appeared almost daily in Moscow's papers.

The late thirties were the years of the "Yezhovschina" (named after Nicolai Yezhov, chief of the secret police, who conducted the purges). In his 1956 Secret Speech "On the Cult of the Personality and Its Consequences," Khrushchev charged Stalin with the responsibility for the "degenerate practices" of Yezhov in 1937.

But in 1937, Khrushchev's ire was directed at Yezhov's victims, collectively designated as "Trotskyites." *Pravda* of January 31, 1937, reported that at a Red Square rally Khrushchev had denounced the "enemies of the people" (a concept Khrushchev expressly rejected in his 1956 report because, he said, "it made possible the most cruel repression") in the most unmistakable terms:

"The detestable and base Trotsky degenerates smell of carcass. . . . The traitors and betrayers of the Motherland . . . began by preaching the Trotskyite, anti-Leninist 'theory' of the impossibility of constructing socialism in one country and ended with the betrayal of their country, espionage, diversion, terror, and intervention; they turned into the vilest lackeys of fascism. . . . The Trotskyite skunk is squashed in the Soviet Union."

In the same speech, and despite the assertion that the enemy had been "squashed," Khrushchev called for more purges: "[we] should increase our vigilance, raise even higher the level of our work in all sectors of socialist construction in order to finish off and crush out all remnants of these vile murderers, fascist agents."

The "socialist construction" in which, according to his official biographers, Khrushchev was then engaged, apparently included the building up of Stalin's "cult of the personality":

"By lifting their hand against Comrade Stalin," said Khrushchev in January 1937, "they [the "enemies of the people"] lifted it against all of us, against the working class, against the toiling people! By lifting their hand against Comrade Stalin they lifted it against the teaching of Marx, Engels, and Lenin.

"By lifting their hand against Comrade Stalin they lifted it against all the best that humanity possesses; for Stalin is hope, he is expectation, he is the beacon that guides all advanced and progressive mankind. Stalin is our banner! Stalin is our will! Stalin is our victory!"

The period of the purges coincides with the period of Khrushchev's most spectacular advances: in 1935, in addition to the Secretaryship of the Moscow Party Committee (gained in 1934), he was given the post of First Party Secretary for the entire Moscow region; in January 1938, when the purges reached their peak, Stalin made him an alternate member of the Politburo; soon afterward he was sent to the Ukraine as First Secretary of the Central Committee and member of the Politburo of the Ukrainian Party. He replaced Stanislav V. Kosior, soon to become a victim of the purge, whom Khrushchev now describes as an "eminent Party and State worker" against whom "the case was fabricated." In 1939, when the major purpose of the purges had been achieved, Khrushchev became a full-fledged member of the Politburo. He was now one of the eight most important Party officials in the Soviet Union. Meanwhile he retained his post in the Ukraine.

For nine years, Khrushchev was absolute ruler of the Ukraine, under Stalin. For the Ukrainian Republic, where from 1944 onward Khrushchev was Chairman of the Council of Ministers as well as First Secretary of the Central Committee of the Ukrainian Communist Party, these nine years were a continuous ordeal.

The Yezhovschina, which had spread from Moscow to the provinces, continued in the Ukraine through 1938.

Khrushchev's official biography of 1937 is vague and noncommittal. Khrushchev, it says, "played an outstanding role in rallying the Communists of the Ukraine for the solution of tasks in the sphere of economic and cultural development and raising the welfare of the workers."

A 1938 Soviet history of the Ukraine was more specific: "With the arrival in the Ukraine of the close comrade-in-arms of Stalin, N. S. Khrushchev, the eradication of the remnants of the enemy and the liquidation of wrecking activities proceeded particularly successfully." Khrushchev himself explained his task more succinctly when he addressed the 1938 Congress of the Ukrainian Communist Party: "We will smash their [the enemies of the people] heads in once and for all."

* * * * * * *

By 1939 the Great Purges were over. That September, a few days after signing a nonaggression pact with Stalin, Hitler struck

28

against Poland. By agreement with Germany, the southeastern part of Poland, soon to be named Western Ukraine, was occupied by the Red Army in the last two weeks of September. And Khrushchev moved into Lvov to supervise the Sovietization of the newly acquired territory.

Hundreds of thousands of Polish Ukrainians were deported to the East; they were "bourgeois" landowners, industrialists, government officials, leaders and officials of political parties (including the leaders and militants of the Polish and Jewish Socialist movements), officers of the Polish Army, etc.

Khrushchev undertook similar activities in the Rumanian provinces that were incorporated into the Ukraine in late June 1940. Again trainloads of deportees moved toward the forced-labor camps of Siberia and of the Russian North.

One year later Hitler attacked the Soviet Union. The official biography notes briefly and in stereotyped language:

"During the Great Fatherland war of 1941–1945, N. S. Khrushchev was with the army in the field and carried out work of great magnitude at the front, was a member of the Military Council of the Special Kiev military district, of the Southwestern sector, of the Stalingrad, Southern, and First Ukrainian fronts. N. S. Khrushchev actively participated in the defense of Stalingrad and in the preparation of the destruction of the German Fascist troops at Stalingrad.

"Simultaneously with his work at the fronts, N. S. Khrushchev as Secretary of the Central Committee of the Communist Party of the Ukraine conducted work of great magnitude in the organization of the all-peoples' partisan movement in the Ukraine against the German Fascist invaders."

Khrushchev in his Secret Speech described the defeats of the Soviet armies in the first months of the war and blamed them on Stalin who, he said, planned military operations "on a globe." But Khrushchev did not mention that these defeats were accompanied by large-scale disaffection, particularly in the Ukraine. In many regions of the Ukraine, the Germans were greeted as liberators. The mayor of Kiev offered the traditional bread and salt of welcome to the German general who had conquered the city. Millions of Ukrainian nationalists—peasants who had survived the executions and famines of enforced collectivization, Party members who had endured the bloody terror of successive purges—were only too glad to fraternize with any invader, provided only that he was an enemy of the Georgian dictator in the Kremlin. (The Germans themselves later alienated the Ukrainians by what Joseph Goebbels, the Nazi Propaganda Minister, called "hitting them too hard over the head.")

Stalin, who understood the situation, knew that to rally the Ukrainian people against the invader he had to show that the Germans were worse than the Russians. "War must be cruel," was Stalin's order, and it was Khrushchev's task to make sure war was "cruel" in the Ukraine.

One of Khrushchev's close associates, Secret Police General T. A. Strokach, began organizing partisan units in the fall of 1941. The partisans, who were under Khrushchev's jurisdiction in all German-occupied Ukrainian territories, had a major role to play in the execution of Stalin's order.

According to Russians who participated in the operations behind the German lines, the partisans' first duty was to show the populace of occupied areas that they were not out of reach of Moscow's secret police. Overt or suspected collaborators with the Nazis were executed by Soviet agents parachuted into enemy-occupied territory. Any lack of resistance to the Germans was declared akin to collaboration and was punishable by death.

There was no active resistance in the towns and villages where the German commanders were not Nazi brutes, and partisan units made sure that such commanders disappeared. The Nazi ratio of retaliation was savage: ten Ukrainians murdered for each German soldier killed, up to one hundred for each German officer. War was indeed cruel for the Ukrainians.

* * * * * * *

Khrushchev emerged from the war with his stature undiminished. But his domain, more than any other part of the Soviet Union, was a wasteland, and still in turmoil. Anti-Soviet "partisans" roamed the deep forests, harassing the Red Army, plundering and killing real and assumed communists, spreading terror among the populace.

Khrushchev used his supreme power to restore order. The Red Army, reinforced by secret-police troops, moved against the rebels. Promises of amnesty for those who surrendered were coupled with ruthless repression.

At the same time Khrushchev attempted to rehabilitate the country's economy in accordance with Stalin's first postwar Five-Year Plan. The Soviet people, after their unbelievable sacrifices of the war years, looked for an easing of their lot and expected the government to concentrate its energies on providing the essentials, the bare essentials of life. But Stalin was setting out to prepare for a new war. He geared the government's whole effort toward developing heavy industry and shifting the industrial centers from the exposed Ukraine to the East—behind the Urals.

To the man-made suffering imposed by Stalin, nature added its own. What Khrushchev later described as the worst drought since 1890 struck Russia and the Ukraine in 1946. Again the Soviet Union was on the verge of starvation.

While the country lay exhausted, the power struggle in the Kremlin continued. In March 1947, Khrushchev suffered the only known setback of his career: he was removed from the Party job as First Secretary of the Ukrainian Central Committee and replaced by Kaganovich, although retaining his post as Premier of the Ukraine and his membership in the Politburo. Clearly some faction in Moscow was successfully moving against Khrushchev: Kaganovich brought with him a Second Secretary, apparently intending to groom the new man as Khrushchev's successor.

Khrushchev recovered from this reverse with relative speed. By December 1947, he was reinstated to his position within the Ukrainian Communist Party and Kaganovich returned to Moscow. Stalin seemed to be fully satisfied with Khrushchev's work in the Ukraine. In December 1949 he recalled his faithful "comrade in arms" to Moscow, where Khrushchev became Secretary of the Central Committee of the CPSU (Communist Party of the Soviet Union) and First Secretary of the Moscow Regional Committee. Some experts on

Soviet affairs, such as Boris I. Nicolaevsky, the eminent Russian-born analyst, believe that Stalin, bent on starting the "third round of war and revolution," brought Khrushchev to Moscow for the specific task of strengthening the kolkhozes, a policy "which was nothing else than the preparation of the country" to withstand a new military ordeal. Khrushchev was among Stalin's most trusted assistants at the time (in late 1952 and early 1953) when the dictator was preparing a new series of blood purges—"a second Yezhovschina"—an integral part of which were the anti-Semitic measures, such as the Kiev trial of "Jewish speculators" in November 1952, and the so-called "doctors' plot." [5]

This latter "conspiracy," soon to be exposed as a "fabrication," was directed primarily against Lavrenti P. Beria, chief of the secret police, who, contrary to Khrushchev and Bulganin but with the apparent help of Malenkov and even Molotov, opposed Stalin's war policy.

Khrushchev, in his Secret Speech, gave a vivid picture of the atmosphere in the Kremlin during the last months of Stalin's reign:

"Because of his extreme suspicion, Stalin toyed with the absurd and ridiculous suspicion that [Kliment Y.] Voroshilov [one of the military leaders of the Revolution, later one of Stalin's closest friends] was an English agent. It's true—an English agent. A special tapping device was installed in his home to listen to what was said there. . . .

"Let us consider the first Central Committee plenum after the Nineteenth Party Congress [1952] when Stalin, in his talk at the plenum, characterized Vyacheslav Mikhailovich Molotov and Anastas Ivanovich Mikoyan and suggested that these old workers of our party were guilty of some baseless charges. It is not excluded that had Stalin remained at the helm for another several months, Comrades Molotov and Mikoyan would probably have not delivered any speeches at this Congress.

"Stalin evidently had plans to finish off the old members of the Political Bureau. He often stated that Political Bureau members should be replaced by new ones." [6]

In the hours following Stalin's death, on March 5, 1953, and even before the official announcement that "the heart of Lenin's comrade-in-arms and the inspired continuer of Lenin's cause, the wise teacher and leader of the party and the people, has stopped beating," Stalin's political heirs proceeded to reshuffle the Soviet Party and the government machinery.

A few months before his fatal stroke, Stalin had enlarged the Presidium of the Central Committee to twenty-five members. His heirs restored it to a small body of ten. The Secretariat, which Stalin had enlarged to ten Secretaries, was reduced to five.

Georgi Malenkov emerged from these deathbed deals as the number-one man, combining in his person the functions of both First Secretary and Premier, as had Stalin before him. He was surrounded by four "First" Deputy Premiers—Beria, Minister of the Interior and State Security; Molotov, Foreign Affairs; Bulganin, Defense; and Kaganovich, without portfolio—and one plain Deputy Premier, Mikoyan, Minister of Trade. Voroshilov was named Chairman of the Supreme Soviet, a purely honorary post. Khrushchev became one of the five Secretaries of the Central Committee.

This reorganized Soviet structure lasted scarcely one week. On March 14, Malenkov resigned from his position within the Secretariat, officially to concentrate on government work, while Khrushchev resigned from the Moscow Regional Committee to "concentrate on work in the Central Committee of the CPSU." In fact, if not in title, Khrushchev had become First Secretary. (He officially assumed the title a few months later, on September 7, 1953.) Thus, while Malenkov remained chief of the executive branch of the government, Khrushchev moved into the position of chief executive of the Party.

Events were to show that in the post-Stalin era, just as during the life of Stalin and perhaps even more so, the Party outranked the government.

In March 1953 the Party appeared to be a singularly weak instrument for ascent to supreme power. Under Stalin, it had become no more than a tool in the dictator's hands; frightened functionaries from the lowest to the highest echelon were always eager to give a standing ovation to the Vozhd (leader) for his every pronouncement, willing to denounce or confess, ready to kill in order to stay alive. Khrushchev confirmed in his Secret Speech to the Party Congress what had been apparent before: there was no leadership but only one leader for the Party, the country, the empire.

With the Vozhd dead, the Party apparatus—the privileged bureaucrats hated and despised by the large mass of the people as representatives of tyrannical power and corruption—suddenly found itself a body without a head. And the body was threatening to disintegrate. Khrushchev, who had made his whole career within the Party apparatus, realized this shapeless body had to be revitalized if the regime was to survive.

The "collective" leadership had shown signs of hysteria on the death of Stalin; their very first act had been an appeal to the people not to panic. Now they relied for their protection from the masses they dreaded on the only solid organization Stalin had left the country, the secret police. In and around Moscow a massive concentration of the special forces of the M.V.D. was posted. (Ministry of the Interior was the name then used for the secret police; now it is K.G.B., Committee for State Security.)

Whether it was because secret police chief Beria sensed that he had the power to liquidate the collective leadership and install himself at the head of the country, or because the rest of the collective merely felt threatened by this possibility, the collective arrived at an apparently unanimous decision a few months later: Beria must be removed.

When Beria fell, so did thousands of his appointees. They were replaced with men selected by the Party Secretariat—under the supervision of Khrushchev.

The unity achieved against the common enemy, Beria, had not interrupted the jockeying for position. Although Malenkov had lost his important post in the Party Secretariat a few days after Stalin's death, he still appeared to be the strongest candidate for supreme leadership. He moved strongly to gain popularity by announcing that the country's perennial problem of adequate grain production had been solved, that a solid industrial base had been established, and that the people could now expect an increased flow of consumer goods—in short, a better and easier life.

The First Secretary

Soon afterward Khrushchev, now officially confirmed in his position as First Secretary, gave the lie to the Premier's optimistic assessment of Soviet agriculture. For the first time, the Soviet propaganda line that Khrushchev himself had obediently propounded for many years was discarded. Now Khrushchev admitted publicly that the country did not have enough to eat. His disclosures were followed by announcement of a grandiose plan to cultivate huge neglected territories in Central Asia and Siberia. The plan resulted entirely from Khrushchev's initiative, and the other members of the collective were happy to let the First Secretary undertake the venture, confidently expecting it to fail. Khrushchev threw all his energy into the "virgin lands" program. He whipped the national and local Party bureaucrats into action to mobilize hundreds of thousands of rank-and-file Communists and Komsomoltsy (members of the Communist Youth Organization) for this unique effort, which has been compared with the opening of the American West. Luck was with him: the first harvest from the millions of new acres, the harvest of 1954, was a tremendous success. (Later harvests were not so bountiful, but by that time Khrushchev's power was established.)

Khrushchev now felt sufficiently secure to move against Malenkov on the industrial front. At the end of 1954, the Khrushchev-controlled Party press began a sustained campaign demanding absolute priority for development of heavy industry over production of consumer goods. Within a few months, Khrushchev had discredited Malenkov enough to force him to resign as Premier and admit "lack of experience." On Khrushchev's proposal, the Supreme Soviet replaced him with Marshal Nikolai A. Bulganin.

Khrushchev's insistence on priority for heavy industry may have been motivated by his general outlook on world politics. A Stalin man to the very end, Khrushchev believed a third war inevitable. Malenkov, on the other hand, was the first Soviet leader to declare a new war "unthinkable," predicting it would mean the annihilation of the human race. (Ironically, Khrushchev is today the foremost proponent of Malenkov's thesis of the impossibility of a nuclear war, while the former "Khrushchevite" line—capitalism will perish, socialism survive—is being expounded by the Chinese Communists. But like Stalin, who often adopted the policies of his victims, Khrushchev is unembarrassed by such inconsistencies, which he may not even perceive.)

In 1955, having installed his man Bulganin as Premier, Khrushchev began his exploration of the outside world. In May he was in Belgrade trying to convince Tito that with Stalin dead and Beria liquidated, all obstacles to Soviet-Yugoslav friendship had disappeared. In July he was in Geneva meeting with the Western Big Three. He had wanted this summit meeting ever since he had felt the state power within his grasp, and he had paid the price for it by agreeing to a state treaty with, and withdrawal of Soviet troops from, neutralized Austria. In Geneva he was more in evidence than the stately Bulganin, officially the head of the Soviet delegation. The "B & K," or rather "K & B," team then proceeded to Asia, where Khrushchev vociferously denounced British colonialism in India and Burma and offered a $100,000,000 loan to Afghanistan.

Between these trips, the First Secretary crisscrossed the Soviet Union, calling for new efforts from the collective and state farmers, reshuffling the Party machines in the provinces, and beginning to promise peace and plenty to the Soviet people. In his office in the Central Committee Building in Moscow, the staff he had assembled kept him abreast, hour by hour, of all developments at home and abroad. Khrushchev had succeeded in replacing servility with obedient efficiency. "A friend is a friend, but work is work" was Khrushchev's slogan for his brain trust.

* * * * * * *

"De-Stalinization" was one of the first tasks undertaken by the new leadership after the dictator's death in March, 1953. A few weeks after the solemn burial, the "doctors' plot" was exposed as a fabrication, though not as yet attributed to Stalin's paranoiac mind. Shortly thereafter, amnesties were proclaimed and the gates of the concentration camps opened for millions of slave laborers— political deportees, suspects, former prisoners of war. It became easier to breathe within the Soviet Union and the empire. Soviet writers openly spoke about "the thaw." A relaxation of the almost unbearable tension was visible to any observer, diplomat, casual traveler, or long-time student of Soviet affairs. The leadership itself seemed to be transformed. For the first time in thirty years, the members of the Presidium could be seen smiling or even laughing.

Like everything else in the Soviet Union, de-Stalinization did not follow a straight, even road. There were zigs and zags, ups and downs, advances and retreats. Entrenched bureaucrats believed too much relaxation would lead to the crumbling of the entire apparatus on which their careers and their easy lives depended. However, the pressure for a drastic change and the fear of a return to the past were stronger. It became clear that the Party, the country, the empire, and even the noncommunist world must be told explicitly that the times of terror were gone, that there would be no return to purges by execution, that "Soviet legality" had replaced the arbitrary rule of the Stalin era. Khrushchev was not the only one, nor probably even the first one, to recognize this need. But he felt it was up to him to act. Because of his position (he had inherited Stalin's Party post, although the title of General Secretary had been dropped and he was "only" First Secretary) and his close association with Stalin to the very end, Khrushchev was suspected of wishing to reinstate the rigid dictatorship. In 1955, and perhaps even earlier, insinuations about Khrushchev's intentions of stopping the de-Stalinization trend could be heard in Party circles.

Khrushchev moved to put an end to these rumors and, at the same time, to the Stalin legend. On the night of February 25, 1956, he took the floor before a closed session of the Twentieth Congress of the Soviet Communist Party and told at least part of the truth about the late tyrant.

In the months following the exposure of Stalin's crimes (against the Communist Party, not against the Russian people), the cautious and frightened must have felt that they were justified in their apprehensions. Very rapidly, the Secret Speech became one of the best-known documents of the Twentieth Congress and received world-wide circulation. The disclosures led to upheavals among Communists: anti-Stalinists rose against Stalinists; Stalinists in Georgia rose to protest the attacks on the most illustrious of their countrymen.

The upheavals were particularly marked in the satellite countries. Poland purged its Stalinists. Hungary revolted.

By virtue of Communist logic—there must be scapegoats for every "failure," the Party being infallible—Khrushchev's position was endangered. He reacted with characteristic vigor. In Poland, he failed to impose his will but did succeed in avoiding an irreparable break. In Hungary he demonstrated that his denunciation of Stalinist methods of terror did not prevent him from using these same methods to suppress revolt.

Already within the leading organs of the Party (particularly in the Presidium), a coalition had formed around the slogan "Stop Khrushchev." Malenkov, although now occupying the minor post of Minister of Electric Power Stations, was still a formidable figure in the Communist hierarchy. No less formidable were the old Bolsheviks Molotov and Kaganovich. Khrushchev's handling of the Party and, even more, his apparent determination to substitute personal power for collective leadership united these men in what Khrushchev was later to call the "anti-Party group." In the summer of 1957, the underground struggle broke into the open. Khrushchev, upon being outvoted in the Presidium of the Party, invoked his right as First Secretary to convene the Central Committee. The Central Committee then overruled the Presidium. This was no accident: during the preceding few years Khrushchev had used the administrative machinery of the Party to bring into the Central Committee new members loyal to him.

The bloodless purge that followed eliminated the last obstacles on Khrushchev's road to absolute power. In January 1958, Bulganin, who later confessed to active membership in the "anti-Party group," resigned, and Khrushchev assumed the Premiership. Like Stalin, he now was chief of both Party and government. (It will be remembered that Malenkov had held the two posts for only one week in March 1953.)

* * * * * * *

In less than five years, Khrushchev had established himself firmly at the helm of the country. But his ambition, no less than the original precepts of communism, led him to plan new advances. He felt sure

38

the power of the Soviet Union would enable him to conquer the whole world without war. Soviet science had developed Sputnik, and Soviet engineering, which had concentrated on that particular branch of heavy industry, was now producing long-range and intermediate-range rockets—perhaps not, as Khrushchev boasted, on the assembly line, but at least in sufficient numbers, he hoped, to intimidate possible opponents of his forward moves.

Khrushchev exploited this "great leap forward" in military power to the full. His "either-or"—either you "coexist" (submit to my will) or I will smash you—pronouncements followed one another in rapid succession. With boldness bordering on the improbable, Khrushchev challenged the noncommunist world to compete with him in raising the standard of living of the masses. He vowed to outdistance the United States in per capita production of meat, milk, and butter, and to make the "Soviet toilers" wealthier than the "capitalist slaves." Meanwhile his Five-Year Plan had to be discarded as unrealistic and replaced by a more modest Seven-Year Plan.

But still Khrushchev continues to advocate peaceful competition and to announce that he is winning.

He is continuously on the go. In the space of a few days he can address a mass meeting in Prague, appear briefly in Moscow, board his jet airliner for Peking or New Delhi or Vienna. By now his personal apparatus of speech writers and assistants has been streamlined to such an extent that he can deliver five major addresses during the same day and on the most varied subjects—literature, agriculture, aid to underdeveloped countries, and, always and foremost, peaceful coexistence and peaceful competition, a competition that, he repeats again and again, "the socialist system" is winning.

Since 1958 Khrushchev has been the sole spokesman for Soviet policy on these and all other subjects. (Voroshilov, until he resigned in 1960 as titular head of the Soviet state because of old age, was allowed from time to time to propose ceremonial toasts; Mikoyan has, on rare occasions, permitted himself to voice a few seemingly original thoughts.)

The Party Central Committee, which Khrushchev built up and which saved him in the hour of crisis, has been relegated to a role similar to the one it played under Stalin: it meets to approve Khrushchev's reports, to endorse Khrushchev's proposals, to applaud Khrushchev's policy. The executive organs of the Central Committee, the Presidium, and the Secretariat are entirely composed of "Khrushchev men." There is no longer any danger for him of being outvoted by his "colleagues."

In these circumstances, even the references to collective leadership are becoming less frequent and less emphatic. Khrushchev seems to draw his inspiration from his personal entourage, a sort of enlarged family circle in which his son-in-law Alexei Adzhubey, editor of the government organ *Izvestia*, appears to play a major role. Although no family ties exist with Mr. Ilyichev, whom Khrushchev found in the position of chief of the press section of the Foreign Ministry and promoted to a choice place in the Agitprop (Agitation and Propaganda Department) of the Central Committee, and Yuri Zhukov, presently the chief of cultural relations with foreign countries, these two men are also said to wield great influence with Khrushchev.

When in Moscow, Khrushchev is easily accessible to foreign diplomats and often surprises them by his knowledge of the problems under discussion.

On the basis of the impressions of several Western visitors, an American writer gives the following description of Khrushchev in 1959:

"He has a quick, alert mind that pounces eagerly upon any advantage dropped in verbal exchanges. This alertness serves him especially well in the art of repartee, at which he shows great skill. He loves an argument, and after even eight hours of it can still beam with zest. Change of pace to catch his opponent off balance is a technique he employs cleverly. While in the main more clumsy than polished, he can be fair, courteous, and logical in debate. Contrariwise, he can be abusive to those not present, vain, and deceitful if it suits his purpose. He exhibits a sense of humor—a hearty feeling for the human drama and the trials of everyday folk. By using an old Russian literary device, the proverb, he embroiders his speeches and coins quips with the aim of pointing to life's lessons and to morals he seeks to inculcate." [7]

By the end of 1960 Khrushchev's external appearance had considerably changed; he no longer is the solemn-faced Party functionary of the thirties, the efficient executor of Stalin's orders of the forties, the ebullient First Secretary of the fifties. Now he wants to look the part of an accomplished statesman, or at least the Communist version of one. No longer for him the baggy suits of the Soviet proletarians; a fashionable Italian tailor cuts his clothes to fit his figure. The cloth cap, which since Lenin had been a favorite headgear of the Communists, has been replaced by a diplomat's hat or a close imitation of one. A Western visitor noted that in winter Khrushchev protects himself from the cold with a very bourgeois, indeed aristocratic, sable-lined coat. He attempts to show the proper dignity at official receptions, indulging less and less, so Western observers report from Moscow, in the impromptu jests that were his trade-mark at the time of the "B & K" duet.

For the Soviet citizen, Khrushchev is the man who stopped the terror of the secret police, who emptied the concentration camps, the man who gives the people enough to eat, provides new housing, and the man who promotes international *détente* and promises peace. There is considerable evidence that Khrushchev is genuinely popular with the Soviet people.

But genuine popularity is not enough, even in Khrushchev's Russia. In a totalitarian state, there must be adulation of the leader. The picture that is presented in a biographical film shown in the winter of 1959 to seventy million spectators (no Soviet leader since Lenin has been so honored) emphasizes the closeness to the people of its only star. He is shown in the thirties visiting factories, nurseries, rest homes, talking to the workers building the Moscow subway; he is shown in the forties in uniform at the front. There is almost no reference to his relationship with Stalin. The motion-picture camera accompanies the First Secretary after Stalin's death on visits to the newly built housing developments in Moscow and travels with him on his "triumphs" abroad. (The picture has been carefully edited so that it does not associate Khrushchev with Bulganin, now in disgrace.) Since 1959 the "cult of [Khrushchev's] personality" has been emerging as a feature of Soviet life. In public meetings, "the immense victories of our country won under the leadership of the Leninist Central Committee . . . headed by our dear Nikita Sergeyevich Khrushchev" are being celebrated. The Communist youth is told that Khrushchev's speeches are of "the greatest and [of] priceless value." In the Supreme Soviet the sycophants return to neo-Stalinist phraseology to describe the leader: "The seething energy, the indefatigability of an organizer, the flaming ardor of a propagandist, the firm consistency and the flexibility in policy, the Leninist resolution and sagacity, the tremendous love for the people . . . all these are the noble qualities which our dear Nikita Sergeyevich Khrushchev has." [8]

The Soviet people are repeatedly told about Khrushchev's humble origin (he comes "from the depths of the people's masses"). They are told of his firmness and resolution "in the face of the threats of the bellicose circles of imperialism." The world is asked to admire the "Khrushchevian" smile ("wide, open, catching"), and his eyes are described as "sparkling," and "kind, attentive, intelligent."

Khrushchev's 1959 visit to the United States is the subject of a full-length feature film. A seven-hundred-page book, *Face to Face with America,* by Soviet newspapermen who accompanied him on his trip, tells how, always speaking the "truth without omissions and embellishments," he has been able to dispose of verbal opponents, always to the applause and the enthusiasm of the American masses.

* * * * * * *

To the noncommunist world, Khrushchev remains an enigmatic figure. Statesmen, diplomats, experts on Soviet affairs, newspapermen, have tried to explain his changing moods. He is pictured as fighting "doctrinaire" Chinese Communists bent on world revolution even at the risk of a world war. He is described as struggling against intrigues, cabals, and opposition within his own party. He is said to be resisting pressure from the Soviet Army.

History cautions us not to reject any of these hypotheses out of hand. The continuous wrangling about communist theory, which in the late summer of 1960 erupted into name calling between Moscow and Peking, certainly conveys the impression of a growing tension that may lead to an open break between Khrushchev and Mao Tse-tung. Repeated conferences have brought announcements of agreements in principle—but no effective settlement of the fundamental dispute. The November 1960 meeting of the world Communist leadership does not appear to have solved the Sino-Soviet differences.

But for the present at least, Khrushchev seems to have the support of the great majority of the Communist Parties outside China. There is no solid evidence that the Peking Communists, who believe war inevitable, have any following within the upper strata of Soviet bureaucracy, be it the Party or the Army.

For the present, Khrushchev still appears to be the boss.

The following chapters—in his own words—indicate the direction of his leadership of the Soviet empire.

PART 2

OBJECTIVES

CHAPTER 3

Conquest Without War

The sections which follow set in lightface type are Khrushchev's own words; commentary is set in **boldface** type and *italics* are used for emphasis.

We have climbed up the mountain to a height from which we can already see broad perspectives on the way to our ultimate aim, a communist society.[1]

In the short time I still have to live, I would like to see the day when the communist flag flies over the whole world.[2]

"We will win, we will win," **he told David Susskind after his television interview in September 1960.**

As early as 1906, Lenin made the observation that the road to power required flexibility:

"Marxism is distinguished from all primitive forms of socialism by the fact that it does not tie the movement to any particular form of struggle. It recognizes the most varied forms of struggle. . . . At different moments of economic evolution, and depending on varying political, national, cultural, and other social conditions, different forms of struggle assume prominence, become the chief forms of struggle, and in turn cause the secondary and supplementary forms of struggle to change their appearance." [3]

Communism was conceived as a world philosophy and a world movement. The call of the Communist Manifesto, **"Proletarians of all lands, unite," was based on the contention that social class, not nationality or race, is the important link between men.**

47

"In the *Communist Manifesto* we were told that the proletariat should conquer the whole world. . . ."[4]

Lenin thought the Russian Revolution would spread to Europe first, and then sweep the whole world. "Let us show not only in words but also in deeds that we [the Russian] Bolsheviks are true internationalists,"[5] Lenin said and wrote again and again.

World revolution, Lenin taught, would insure the security of the new Soviet state. Imperialism would be overcome by proletarian revolution, and with this the encirclement of the only socialist country in the world would be broken.

Stalin expanded the communist sphere not only by propaganda but by force of arms. The countries of Eastern Europe became Soviet satellites after World War II, not by internal revolution but through military conquest and occupation by the Soviet Army. (The exception was Yugoslavia, whose communist regime broke with Stalin early because the Yugoslav Communist Party was unwilling to submit to Moscow's dictates.)

Khrushchev adds this:

We have no reason to conceal our aims. The communists openly announced them over a hundred years ago in the famous *Communist Manifesto*. We communists have never concealed that we are convinced champions and active fighters for a society in which there would be no exploitation of man by man, no oppression of some peoples by others, and in which freedom and happiness would be insured to all people and to all nations.[6]

Khrushchev, too, wants to extend Soviet hegemony. He clearly says so, although he never speaks of enlarging the Soviet empire. He speaks only of "socialism." But the difference is only in semantics:

Since the world-wide triumph of 'socialism' would mean that the Soviet Union would become the dominant world power, there is no conflict between Soviet national power considerations and the Marxist-Leninist view of the progress of social transformation of the world so long as 'socialism' is defined, as it is in Soviet ideology, as the rule of the Communist parties acting on common principles and with the discipline of a single camp directed by the Soviet Union.[7]

Continuously Khrushchev sells the "inevitable triumph" of socialism.

Capitalism is a worn-out old mare while socialism is new, young, and full of teeming energy.[8]

Our firm conviction is that sooner or later capitalism will give way to socialism. No one can halt man's forward movement, just as no one can prevent day following night.[9]

Whether you like it or not, history is on our side. We will bury you! [10]

The words "We will bury capitalism" should not be taken literally as indicating what is done by ordinary gravediggers who carry a spade and dig graves and bury the dead. What I had in mind was the outlook for the development of human society. Socialism will inevitably succeed capitalism.[11]

My life would be too short to bury every one of you if this were to occur to me. . . . I said that in the course of historical progress and in the historical sense, capitalism would be buried and communism would come to replace capitalism.[12]

Representatives of bourgeois countries often reproach us, saying that the leaders of the Soviet state declare in their speeches that the communist ideas will triumph throughout the world. Yes, dear gentlemen, we are absolutely convinced of that; we are sure that the people will achieve their aim.[13]

We believe, for example, that there may come a time when the calendar will be based on the day of the October Revolution. But that is a thing of the future. When we speak of the triumph of communism all over the world, we have in mind, first and foremost, the inevitable victory of communist ideas and the triumph of the Marxist-Leninist philosophy.[14]

Marx and Engels proved, on the basis of profound scien-

49

tific analysis, that the collapse of capitalism and the victory of socialism, which would replace it, were inevitable, and they advanced and substantiated the world-historic role of the proletariat as the gravedigger of capitalism and the creator of a communist society, a society without classes, without exploitation and oppression.[15]

We are convinced that sooner or later capitalism will perish . . . All the world will come to communism.[16]

Khrushchev's estimates as to the strength of the capitalist world vary:

The rotten [capitalist] world is collapsing. Friends, let's drink, let's laugh, let's rejoice.[17]

Capitalism is at its ebb, heading for collapse. This does not mean that it is already lying down with its legs stretched out; much work has yet to be done to bring it to such a state.[18]

But:

We do not underestimate the powers of capitalism, for we know that it is still strong.[19]

We are convinced that the peoples of all countries will come to socialism, to communism, but when and how—that is the internal affair of each people.[20]

Khrushchev cites the growth of the communist empire to prove that history is on his side:

Prior to the Second World War, the Union of Socialist Soviet Republics was the only socialist country, with not more than seventeen per cent of the territory, three per cent of the population, and about ten per cent of the output of the world. At present the socialist countries cover about one-fourth of the territory of the globe, have one-third of its population, and their industrial output accounts for about one-third of the total world output.[21]

The socialist countries are inhabited by 1,000 million people out of a world population of 2,500 million. And how many people in other countries adhere to socialist views! [22]

Once upon a time our country was a lone rock in the capitalist world. Now the great Chinese People's Republic and other brotherly socialist countries are marching with us along the road to communism. About one billion people are united by a common goal and help each other. Our monolithic unity, friendship, and cooperation are the guarantee of the invincibility of the communist cause. The world system of socialist countries is growing and consolidating. [23]

Why should we, comrades, lose courage or underestimate our strength at such a time? [24]

Capitalism long ago ceased to be an all-embracing system which used to rule the world. In the last ten years many countries who took to the road of socialism broke away from the capitalist system. In these countries new, socialist relations are being created, great material and spiritual values produced; the international forces of the working class of the whole world and all progressive mankind are uniting still more and more closely. [25]

More and more people are marching under the banner of Marxism-Leninism, and we can already see our ultimate goal appearing on the horizon—the victory of the working class throughout the whole world, the victory of the ideas of communism. [26]

We live at a time when new millions upon millions of people are coming under the great banner of Marxism-Leninism. Marxism-Leninism is our main weapon. We will conquer the capitalist world by using this mighty ideological weapon and not a hydrogen bomb. [27]

Today, hundreds of millions of people are marching under the banner of Marxism-Leninism. Tomorrow, additional tens and hundreds of millions of working people will place themselves under the victorious banner. [28]

Objectives

But it would be contrary to Khrushchev's whole argument to mention the fact that in all countries—except China and to a degree Yugoslavia—"socialism" came only as a by-product of Soviet military conquest. He talks as if economic power, higher productivity, better living conditions, and the hope for a brighter future were the sole ingredients of the growth of "socialism."

The unity and fraternal cooperation of the peoples of the socialist countries make each of them and the camp as a whole strong and impregnable.[29]

We live in a remarkable time when historical development leads inevitably to the final triumph of socialism and communism throughout the world. From a dream, socialism has turned in our day into a great and unconquerable world force that astonishes mankind with its magnificent victories.[30]

I do not want to frighten the capitalists. We don't intend to interfere with their affairs, we don't think to wage war against them in order to set up our system in foreign countries. There is no need to do this. The workers, peasants, and working intelligentsia in the capitalist countries will do this themselves when they see that the people of our country, who were poorer than they, have begun to live a richer life. The working people will take our path, the path shown by Lenin.[31]

The socialist economy is steadily advancing, free of the recessions and crises characteristic of the capitalist economy.[32]

We are confident that we shall conquer capitalism. We shall conquer it not by war, but by demonstrating practically to all that the working class has a great truth—the teaching of Marxism-Leninism. This truth will triumph.[33]

Yes, we have said and still say that in the peaceful competition between the two economic systems, the socialist system will be victorious, for it is the most advanced, progressive system based on the only correct teaching—Marxism-Leninism.[34]

Conversely, Khrushchev sees capitalism as on the decline economically and politically, and believes nothing can save it:

Capitalism digs its own grave because it restrains the development of productive forces, gives birth to crises and poverty; because under the capitalist production system the riches are concentrated in the hands of a small group of exploiters, while millions of working people, who create those riches, remain beggars and are deprived of any rights.[35]

The process of historic development is inexorable. It cannot be stopped by any reactionary forces. Should they try to do so by force of arms and unleash war, they will dig their graves with their own hands. The peoples will no longer tolerate a regime that gives birth to wars and brings to mankind torment and suffering.[36]

It is now becoming increasingly clear that the rule of capitalism is coming to an end in other countries, too, and that capitalism is an outmoded system that is doomed to inexorable death. The future is ours. The future belongs to Marxism-Leninism. The future belongs to communism, comrades.[37]

Capitalism has become so decrepit that it cannot afford to grow. As the saying goes, its problem is that of survival, not of putting on weight.[38]

Capitalism will never break the death grip of its own contradictions.[39]

According to Khrushchev, any attempt to stem the historic tide is doomed to failure:[40]

We proved scientifically why capitalism must perish and be replaced by communism, just as capitalism came to take the place of feudalism. This has been scientifically established. This can be accepted; intelligent people accept it, while fools argue; but history moves not along the line the fools would wish it to take, it goes its own way of development.[41]

Society develops in accordance with its laws, and so the

53

era has come when capitalism has to make way for socialism as a higher social system than capitalism. This does not depend on me, a communist; neither does it depend on you, a capitalist. No, it is an objective historical process.[42]

The decadence and disintegration of the countries of capitalism represent an indisputable proof of the reactionary character of the capitalist order and of the fact that it is doomed; it is proof also of the futility of the reformist and revisionist attempts to improve and to embellish capitalism, to mask its flagrant ills and antagonistic differences.[43]

The imperialists are still trying to impede the progress of history. But all those who have tried to do so in the past have been thrown onto the garbage heap of history.[44]

Until recently every major pronouncement by Khrushchev was, so he claimed, based on Marxism-Leninism, Leninist principles and policy. But Lenin did not paint the same picture as Khrushchev of the transition from "capitalism" to "socialism." Lenin taught that war is inevitable as long as "imperialism" exists.

Lenin predicted that "as soon as we are strong enough to defeat capitalism as a whole, we shall immediately take it by the scruff of the neck." [45]

In Lenin's time, the communists were militarily and economically weak, having barely survived a destructive civil war. They were not strong enough to defeat even so weak a "capitalist" state as Poland by military power.

Today the situation has changed. The Soviet Union has become the second military power in the world, and Khrushchev thinks the balance of military power has already shifted to the "socialist camp." The time has come, he says in substance, to revise Lenin's teachings. Now, Khrushchev feels, he can win without war.

Some of Lenin's theses on imperialism refer to the period when the Soviet Union did not exist yet, when there were no other socialist states. Now, the mighty Soviet Union is growing and strengthening its enormous economic and mili-

54

tary potential, the great socialist camp is growing and strengthening, and it now counts over a billion people; the working class, which even in the capitalist countries is waging an active struggle for peace, has gained in organization and consciousness. . . .

We have every reason to say confidently that under the present circumstances, war is not inevitable. Whoever does not understand this has no faith in the strength and creative possibilities of the working class, underestimates the power of the socialist camp, does not believe in the great power of attraction of socialism, which has, with full clarity, proved its advantages over capitalism.

Is the possibility excluded that the imperialists will start a war in the present circumstances? We have said more than once, and we repeat: No, it is not excluded. But the imperialist countries cannot fail to reckon with the might of the Soviet Union, the might of the entire socialist camp. It is understandable that the imperialists do not want to start a war in order to perish in it themselves. They would like to annihilate the socialist countries. Therefore, even the stupid, even the insane representatives of the imperialistic circles will think, and more than once, about our power before embarking on a military adventure.[46]

This speech was directed against the "doctrinaire" communists, principally the Chinese, who maintained that war with imperialism is not only inevitable, but in fact desirable in order to hasten the world revolution. Khrushchev has, for the past few years, been expounding a different line:

We do not need wars of conquest, or interference in the internal affairs of other states and peoples, or cold war, hatred, and distrust. We need not be scientists or military experts to understand that a future war, if it were unleashed by criminal forces, would cause immeasurable harm to all mankind. We live on the same planet as the capitalist countries. It is better for us not to be engaged in a war. We say this not because we are weak. It is our firm conviction that in the event of an armed conflict, the socialist system would be victorious and the capitalist system would be unable to weather the grave ordeals.[47]

George F. Kennan, former chief of the State Department Planning Staff and former U.S. ambassador to Moscow, points out: "The hostility has been there, certainly; and it has been a deadly hostility, aimed at a destruction of all that we most intimately cherish—a destruction no less sweeping, no less final than that which would be occasioned by an outright war. But the threat has not been one of all-out military attack. It has been a combined political and military threat, but more political than military—a threat intimately associated with the weaknesses of our Western civilization—looking to these weaknesses, in fact, rather than to the strength of Soviet arms, to constitute the main instruments of our undoing." [48]

We shall not foist our socialist system on other countries by force of arms. We are against interference by any country in the domestic affairs of other countries. But we are attacking capitalism from the flanks, from economic positions, from the positions of the advantages of our system. This will make certain the triumph of the working class, the triumph of communism.[49]

We shall never take up arms to force the ideas of communism upon anybody. Our ideas will capture the minds of mankind. The attempts of the imperialists to arrest the spread of the ideas of communism by force of arms are doomed to failure. That is shown by numerous lessons of history.[50]

We shall defeat the capitalist world by using this powerful ideological weapon rather than the hydrogen bomb. We produce the hydrogen bomb with the sole object of cooling the ambitions of some excessively zealous politicians and generals in the capitalist countries. After all, living among wolves one must have the means to let them know how dangerous it is for them to show their fangs. We have no wish to attack anyone. But we do not want to be simpletons who can be

56

taken barehanded. Now we cannot be taken with gloved hands, let alone barehanded.[51]

We proceed from the premise that wars are not necessary for the victory of socialism.[52]

When we say our system will win out, meaning that socialism will triumph, we do not mean we shall try to impose our system on anyone by war. God save us from that! We believe it will win and will capture the minds of the people.[53]

Although we are convinced that the outcome of another war, should the imperialists unleash it, would be the destruction of the system causing it, that is, the capitalist system, and that the socialist system would be victorious, we have no desire to achieve victory in this way.[54]

Communists have no need to impose their ideas by force. Theirs are the most progressive ideas of our epoch; they are found wherever people live. These ideas cannot be destroyed, just as the people cannot be destroyed.[55]

All that is necessary to insure the victory of "socialism," Khrushchev believes, is the stoic acceptance by the "capitalists" of their inevitable defeat:

We are not asking for your approval. We wish one thing: that we should not be impeded. The change of social formations of human society does not represent a process that is taking place simultaneously in all countries. When and in what way the social order is going to change in some country or other—that is a matter that concerns the people of that country. Admit this fact, and peace will be insured. If you do not admit it, then it will be impossible to avoid war.[56]

Soviet spokesmen make it clear how this "change of social formations" will come about:

"The bourgeois state . . . does not wither away, but is destroyed, overthrown. It is pushed into its grave by the victorious proletarian revolution. The liquidation of the bourgeois state is attended by a most acute class struggle embracing all aspects of social relations.

'The replacement of the bourgeois state by the proletarian one,' V. I. Lenin wrote, 'is impossible without a violent revolution.' " [57]

Thus, Khrushchev's challenge to the Western world is plainly stated: Accept revolution or you shall have war. Now that the Soviet Union can bring the United States itself under nuclear attack, the mere threat of it has become an awesome weapon. And Khrushchev uses this weapon freely; nuclear blackmail has become part of his political arsenal.

Khrushchev confronts the West with a combined menace—political and military—and shifts the emphasis sometimes to one, sometimes to the other.

"Like all your countrymen, you are thinking in concrete military terms," Lenin once pointed out to Bruce Lockhart, a British Foreign Office representative. "You ignore the psychological factors. This war [World War I] will be settled in the rear and not in the trenches." [58]

And:

"Dictatorship is the state of acute war. We are precisely in such a state. There is no military invasion at present, but we are isolated. . . . Until the final issue is decided, the state of awful war will continue." [59]

Peace is inevitable. War will not help us reach our goal—it will spoil it. We must rest on the position of coexistence and nonintervention, and eventually Communism will be in force all over the earth.[60]

CHAPTER 4

Peaceful Coexistence

There is hardly an expression more often used and less well defined by Khrushchev than "peaceful coexistence."

A group of American scholars and analysts of Soviet affairs writes:

"Of course in a general sense 'peaceful coexistence' describes what we have been living with for some time, if all that it means is that we inhabit the same planet and are not engaged in a fighting war with each other. But does it mean more than this? Is 'peaceful coexistence' an alternative to the 'cold war'? Or is it a way of describing the continuation of the 'cold war' in some muted form?

"This has been a source of confusion in American thinking, because a dictionary definition does not convey the full implications of the phrase, which is a technical term in Soviet usage." [1]

For Khrushchev, this quite natural confusion smacks of "arrogance":

When during my talk with Dillon [Douglas Dillon, then U.S. Under Secretary of State] I said to him that it was indispensable to create conditions for peaceful coexistence, he asked me a cynical question: What is coexistence? I don't understand what it is.

You see what an arrogant man Mr. Dillon is. Of course he and people of his ilk would prefer to exist alone, without socialist countries. But that no longer depends on them. [2]

Having berated Mr. Dillon, Khrushchev still does not define exactly what he does mean. If one is to take Khrushchev's "definitions" of peaceful coexistence literally, they add nothing to the international

59

lexicon. All the ingredients of peaceful coexistence were written into the United Nations Charter in 1945.

Peaceful coexistence, said Khrushchev in April 1958,

. . . implies complete renunciation of war as the means of settling questions at issue, as well as noninterference in the internal affairs of other countries. This principle also suggests that political and economic relations among states should be built on the basis of full equality of the parties and mutual benefits.[3]

He elaborated:

We stand for noninterference by states in the domestic affairs of other states. That precisely is peaceful coexistence. Every people has the right to the state system that it likes best.[4]

Unless one takes for a definition of policy Khrushchev's analogy with marriage:

It happens that people do not get married for love, but despite that they live their whole lives together. And that is what we want.[5]

Khrushchev adds to the general confusion over what he means by peaceful coexistence when he claims that

From its very inception [the Soviet state] proclaimed peaceful coexistence as the basic principle of its foreign policy.[6]

He compounds his historical distortion by asserting that the principle of coexistence of capitalism and socialism is the very essence of Leninism. As a matter of fact, Lenin thought, wrote, said, taught, and practiced exactly the opposite:

"The existence of the Soviet Republic side by side with the imperialist states for a long time is unthinkable. In the end either one or the other will conquer and until that end comes, a series of the most terrible collisions between the Soviet Republic and the bourgeois states is inevitable." [7]

"The whole history of wars for liberation shows that when these wars embraced large masses, liberation came very quickly. We say: since history marches forward in this way, we will have to abandon peace for war." [8]

"We have just passed from war to peace, but we have not forgotten that war will again return. As long as capitalism and socialism exist, we cannot live in peace: in the end, one or the other will triumph—a funeral dirge will be sung either over the Soviet Republic or over world capitalism. This is a respite from war." [9]

George F. Kennan writes that "literally thousands" of quotations could be adduced to "illustrate the devotion of the Bolsheviki in Lenin's time to socialism as an international cause—the devotion, that is, precisely to the duty of interfering in the internal affairs of other countries with the object of altering their system of government and mode of life." [10]

There can be no question; peaceful coexistence has never been, could never have been, a "Leninist principle." But it was a Leninist tactic. Russia, after a war followed by revolution, needed "breathing space." Was Khrushchev alluding to this when he spoke of Lenin's "flexibility"?

The history of the Soviet state knows no few examples of Lenin's wise and flexible foreign policy aimed at the solution of vital problems of peace. Thus, for example, it was during the period of the Brest peace that Vladimir Ilyich Lenin set the task of concluding peace with Germany in order to insure for the young Soviet state the possibility for peaceful construction of socialism. [11]

Khrushchev, however, has tried to sell the world—East and West —the idea that peaceful coexistence has always been a Soviet policy.

It was not an accident that the very first state act of the

Soviet power was the decree on peace, the decree on the cessation of the bloody war.[12]

The original meaning of peaceful coexistence is made absolutely clear in documentary statements such as:

We cannot forget the saying of Lenin to the effect that a great deal in the matter of our construction depends on whether we succeed in delaying war with capitalist countries, which is inevitable but which may be delayed either until proletarian revolution ripens in Europe, or until the colonial revolutions come fully to a head, or, finally, until the capitalists fight among themselves over division of the colonies. Therefore the maintenance of peaceful relations with capitalist countries is an obligatory task for us.[13]

But Khrushchev, in 1956, rejects any definition that would reduce peaceful coexistence to a tactical move.

The Leninist principle of peaceful coexistence of states with different social systems has always been and remains the general line of our country's foreign policy.

It has been alleged that the Soviet Union puts forward the principle of peaceful coexistence merely out of tactical considerations of expediency. Yet it is common knowledge that we have always, from the very first years of Soviet power, stood with equal firmness for peaceful coexistence. Hence, it is not a tactical move, but a fundamental principle of Soviet foreign policy.

We firmly uphold the Leninist position of peaceful coexistence. That is written into the decisions of the Twentieth CPSU Congress. We wrote those decisions and we shall implement them.[14]

But Stalin's interpretation, too, was unequivocal:
"Some comrades hold that owing to the development of new international conditions since the Second World War, wars between capitalist countries have ceased to be inevitable. They consider that

the contradictions between the socialist camp and the capitalist camp are more acute than the contradictions among capitalist countries; that the United States has brought the other capitalist countries sufficiently under its sway to be able to prevent them from going to war among themselves and weakening one another; that the foremost capitalist ministers have been sufficiently taught by two World Wars and the severe damage they caused to the whole capitalist world not to venture to involve the capitalist countries in war with one another again—and that, because of this, wars between capitalist countries are no longer inevitable. These comrades are wrong." [15]

Khrushchev understands the need for peace if the Soviet Union is to grow in power.

Peace is a prerequisite for the fulfillment and overfulfillment of the majestic tasks set in the new stage of communistic construction.[16]

He confirmed this thought in 1960, during his state visit to France:

To successfully realize our plans, we need peace.[17]

Peace is also required to satisfy the most earnest desire of the Soviet people. All those who know the Soviet Union, whether from recent visits or from lifelong studies, agree that Khrushchev's rejection of war as a means for expansion of Soviet power has the full support of the Soviet people. Boris I. Nicolaevsky writes: "It is not difficult to imagine that this idea [that the Russians do not need war] falls on the most fertile soil [in the Soviet Union]. There is no people in the world who have suffered as much from war and who have a greater yearning for peace than the peoples of the USSR." [18]

In spite of his monolithic power, Khrushchev must also satisfy the demands of Russia's people:

"A good deal of the current Soviet line for pressing for peaceful coexistence, pressing for what sounds like disarmament, is a response to these very great pressures from the Soviet people. The Soviet people have suffered now for . . . almost forty-three years, . . .

63

through Lenin, Stalin, and now Khrushchev. They have built gigantic steel mills, terrific rockets that go to the moon, and so on and so forth. But they still don't have automobiles. They still live jam-packed in one-room-to-a-family kind of conditions. And Mr. Khrushchev is under tremendous pressure from his people to stop wasting the country's resources essentially on things that may look good in the power competition, but don't feed people, don't clothe them, don't house them, don't satisfy human wants." [19]

These pressures certainly exist. But in a totalitarian society they play a much smaller role than in a democratic one. Controlling as he does all media of information, Khrushchev can present his own policies as peaceful and accuse the Western world of warmongering—even when the Soviet Army intervenes in Hungary, or when he sends arms to Cuba, the Congo, or Laos, or when he threatens the West with destruction.

Thus, to a Soviet audience, Khrushchev can state with a straight face:

We declare once again, just as we have declared in the past, that our armed forces will not be used anywhere or at any time for predatory purposes, which are alien to the very nature of our socialist system. We shall never settle controversial problems in relations between states by means of war. We shall endeavor to solve problems of this kind peacefully, by negotiation.[20]

Where are we to seek a way out of the present situation? Shall we settle the matter in a free-for-all? That, indeed, is how disputes were settled in the past. But formerly things were much simpler; people would come to grips and tear out handfuls of each other's hair, beard, and whiskers, and then new beards and new whiskers would grow in their place. But now you know that if a new free-for-all ensued, there would be nothing left to grow; as we say in Russia, "It will be too late to cry over lost hair after your head is cut off." [21]

In the evolution of communist dogma, Baron Karl von Clausewitz played a part only slightly less noteworthy than that of Hegel,

64

Marx, and Engels. Adapting the Clausewitz theme, Lenin laid down the tenet:

"War is simply the continuation of politics by other [i.e., violent] means. This formula belongs to Clausewitz,[22] one of the greatest writers on the history of war, whose ideas were fertilized by Hegel. And this was always the standpoint of Marx and Engels, who regarded every war as the continuation of the politics of the given interested powers—and the various classes within these countries— at a given time." [23]

At home, Leninists of course can quote:

"Socialists, without ceasing to be socialists, cannot oppose any kind of war. . . .

"In the first place, socialists never have and never could oppose revolutionary wars. . . .

"In the second place, civil wars are also wars. He who accepts the class struggle cannot fail to recognize civil wars which under any class society represent the natural, and under certain conditions, inevitable continuation of the development and aggravation of class struggle. . . .

"In the third place, socialism victorious in one country does not exclude forthwith all wars in general. On the contrary, it presupposes them. The development of capitalism proceeds highly unevenly in various countries. This cannot be otherwise under the conditions of commodity production. From this follows the unavoidable conclusion: Socialism cannot win simultaneously in all countries. It will win initially in one or several countries, while the remainder will remain for some time, either bourgeois or prebourgeois. This should result not only in frictions, but also in the direct striving of the bourgeoisie of other countries to smash the victorious proletariat of the socialist state. In such cases a war on our part would be lawful and just. This would be a war for socialism, for the liberation of other peoples from the bourgeoisie. . . . —Only after we overthrow, completely defeat, and expropriate the bourgeoisie in the entire world, and not only in one country, will wars become impossible. And from the scientific point of view, it would be completely incor-

rect and completely unrevolutionary to bypass or tone down the most important, the suppression of the resistance of the bourgeoisie —which is the most difficult, the most struggle-requiring [aspect] of transition to socialism. 'Social priests' and opportunists are always ready to dream of future peaceful socialism, but this is precisely the way they differ from revolutionary social-democrats, because they do not wish to think and ponder the embittered class struggle and class wars which are required in order to bring about this wonderful future.

"Theoretically, it would be absolutely mistaken to forget that every war is merely a continuation of politics by other means; that the present imperialistic war is a continuation of imperialistic policies of two groups of great powers, and this policy has been engendered and is fed by the totality of relations of the imperialistic epoch." [24]

By Lenin's standards, Khrushchev would be the very prototype of the "social priest." Particularly when he says:

Our policy is never governed by expediency, nor does it pursue any selfish goals. We say this from a pure heart. The Soviet government is exerting every effort and will continue to strive to strengthen friendly relations with all peoples and assure world peace.[25]

To noncommunists a debate over the "Leninist" or "non-Leninist" character of a policy may seem academic. But for communists, ideological differences reflect the continuous struggle for power. Each faction tries to cover itself with the mantle of Leninism. Khrushchev has purged Malenkov, Molotov, and others for alleged anti-Party activities said to be based on "anti-Leninist" concepts—Malenkov for advocating more consumer goods; Molotov, the old specialist on foreign affairs, probably for opposing Khrushchev's brand of peaceful coexistence with "capitalism." In 1960 Khrushchev had to face criticism by the Chinese communists, who cited chapter and verse to show that the Soviet leadership "deviated" from Leninism, was not militant enough against the imperialists.

Khrushchev was obliged to admit the obvious: Leninism is being

66

revised. Khrushchev did so in June 1960 in Bucharest. Before the leaders of all European Communist Parties and representatives from Peking, he justified his departure from classic communist dogma:

The frank attitude toward the policy of peaceful coexistence includes a thesis proclaimed at the Twentieth [1956] and Twenty-first [1958–1959] Congresses of our Party, according to which, in our times, war is not inevitable. The theses on imperialism put forward by Lenin remain valid and, as heretofore, serve and will continue to serve as our guiding star in our theory and practice. But it must not be forgotten that Lenin's positions on imperialism were put forward and elaborated by him tens of years ago, when many phenomena, which have now become decisive in the development of the historical process and for the entire international setting, were absent. . . .

We must not mechanically repeat now, on this question, what was said by Vladimir Ilyich Lenin many decades ago on imperialism, and affirm that imperialist wars are unavoidable until socialism has won the world over. . . .

Therefore, what the great Lenin said under completely different historical conditions cannot be repeated without reckoning with the concrete circumstances and the change in the balance of forces in the world.[26]

Khrushchev thus reaffirms what he has held before the world: War is not inevitable.

Because war is now too destructive.

Any new war unleashed by the aggressive forces, involving as it would modern weapons of mass annihilation and destruction, would cause an incalculable sacrifice of human lives and tremendous, unprecedented economic disruption, the destruction of towns, industrial and agricultural centers, and of huge material values created by the efforts of many generations.[27]

Because we want to build.

Comrades, the internal and international situation of our country is good, and stable as never before. The Soviet people are busy with creative labor. We need peace. All can see that the Seven-Year Plan has a peaceful trend, and is imbued with the spirit of peace.[28]

Because our ideas can win the peace.

It is not an army, but peace that is required to propagate communist ideas, disseminate them, and establish them in the minds of men.[29]

Because we can win without war.

What else, then, do we need? We need peace. Representatives of the capitalist countries: If you capitalist gentlemen are certain that your system is firm, that it is unshakable, then let us have peaceful competition. Show in practice the advantages of your capitalist system, and we shall show the advantages of the socialist system. Whichever system provides the best conditions for man's life will win. If you are sure that you will win this "combat," then let us test our strength in peaceful competition. Our socialist regime is young, fresh, vigorous. Socialism moves forward with assurance; the future belongs to it.[30]

Because it is the only way.

In our age of great technical progress, in conditions when there are states with different social systems, international problems cannot be resolved successfully otherwise than on principles of peaceful coexistence. . . . To disregard this is to shut one's eyes, stop one's ears, and bury one's head as the ostrich does when in danger.[31]

Because the camp of peace is strong.

We consider, proceeding from a Marxist-Leninist analysis of the present situation, that war is not inevitable today. And

68

not because the imperialists have become wiser or kinder, but because they have become weaker, because the camp of peace is now strong as never before. The strength of the working class of the world lies in its cohesion, organization, in international proletarian solidarity. Nowadays the international labor movement leans for support on a mighty real force which is growing and gaining in strength—the powerful camp of the socialist countries in which power belongs to the working class, to the working people. The imperialists would like to make short shrift of the socialist camp, to wipe the socialist countries off the face of the earth, but they are powerless to do so. They realize that a war can be started—one need not be too clever for that—but how will it end? We are convinced that should the imperialists touch off such a war it will end in the destruction of capitalism.[32]

The "concrete circumstances" that prevail in the world today are largely dependent on the two superpowers that emerged after World War II. Khrushchev recognizes that "peaceful coexistence" is possible only if there is an understanding between the Soviet Union and the United States.

Tension comes down chiefly to the relations between two Great Powers—the Soviet Union and the United States of America.[33]

We are most anxious to have peace and friendship with the American people. We want friendship not for our two strong Powers to join forces against the weaker. We want it because if we have good friendly relations with the United States, all the other countries will be the gainers. I hardly think that Luxembourg will threaten us. Friendship between our two states would benefit all nations.[34]

The establishment of firm friendly relations between the two biggest powers of the world, the Soviet Union and the United States of America, would be of great significance for the strengthening of world peace.[35]

Khrushchev points out that an agreement with the United States is not only necessary but also possible:

We have repeatedly had to point to the responsibility borne by the two Great Powers—the Soviet Union and the United States—in preserving peace. Our two countries have never had any territorial claims on one another. There are no grounds for clashes between our two peoples.[36]

And adds:
But this does not mean the dilution of the main objective. The struggle continues.

We have never concealed the fact that we have appealed and do appeal for a principled and ideological struggle. In the world today there is a fierce struggle of two ideologies, the socialist and the bourgeois, and in this struggle there can be no neutrals.[37]

We believe that we could have friendly relations, that we could be friends as far as ideological differences allow. That is perfectly feasible. There are many things that unite us, and we would willingly cooperate with the people of the United States.

In the years of World War II, the Soviet Union and the United States of America fought together against the aggressors. One can ask: Why is it that we cannot prevent war now? We can and must do this.[38]

Peaceful coexistence is, for Khrushchev, inseparable from "peaceful competition between the two systems—socialist and capitalist."[39]

We coexist with you on one and the same planet, where there is enough room for all, but where distances, due to modern supersonic aircraft, the development of intercontinental rockets, and other achievements of science and engineering, have become much shorter before the eyes of our generation. For that reason we ought more than ever to show good sense and learn to coexist like good neighbors.[40]

Some people say that when Khrushchev speaks of coexistence he invariably adds that capitalism will perish and that communism will ultimately triumph. To this I can reply that for forty years now messieurs the capitalists have been reiterating that the cause of communism, started by the Soviet Union, will fail and that private ownership will triumph in our country. They say that private ownership is omnipotent. We affirm that the ideas of communism are incomparably stronger, that these ideas will ultimately prevail. Therefore, we repeat again and again: Let us compete, let us coexist peacefully.[41]

Let us prove in practice whose system is better: This is our appeal to the statesmen of capitalist countries. Let us compete without war. Is this really a bad proposal? It is better than saying: Let us compete to see who will manufacture more weapons and who will defeat whom. This is anti-popular competition, competition in the destruction of people. But our proposals are for peaceful competition in raising the living standards of all peoples.[42]

Khrushchev lays particular stress on competition between the Soviet Union and the United States.

To Americans, he says:

In peaceful competition we will work to win out. Here, if I may say so, the Soviet people will be on the offensive. But this will be an offensive in which people will not perish but, quite the contrary, will be improving their life and raising the level of their economy and culture. Challenging the United States to a competition to produce more meat, butter, clothes, footwear, to build more good housing, to manufacture more television and radio sets, vacuum cleaners, and other goods and articles necessary to man, the Soviet people are confident in their victory.[43]

Khrushchev's invitations to coexist and to compete peacefully sound reasonable and would be convincing if his words were not

accompanied by dire threats against the United States and its allies, by the artificially created crises over Berlin, and by warlike acts over the high seas. (See Chapter 5.)

In July 1960, British Prime Minister Harold Macmillan was moved to write to Khrushchev: "I simply do not understand what your purpose is today."

There is also the past record. Although Khrushchev has vigorously denounced Stalin's crimes against the Communist Party of the Soviet Union, he has not dissociated himself in any way from Stalin's conduct of foreign affairs. And this record speaks for itself:

On January 21, 1932, a Treaty of Non-Aggression and Peaceful Settlement of Conflicts between the USSR and Finland was signed in Helsinki. It was renewed April 7, 1934, to expire December 31, 1945. On November 29, 1939, Finland was attacked. A treaty signed March 11, 1940, ceded strategic territory to Russia.

On September 28, 1928, a Treaty of Neutrality and Non-Aggression was concluded between the USSR and Lithuania in Moscow. The treaty was renewed on May 6, 1931, and April 4, 1934. On October 10, 1939, Lithuania granted the USSR the right to garrison troops. In return, Vilna was ceded back to Lithuania and Lithuania's independence reaffirmed. On August 3, 1940, Lithuania was incorporated into the Soviet Union.

On February 5, 1932, a Soviet-Latvian Treaty of Non-Aggression was signed at Riga. On April 4, 1934, it was extended until December 31, 1945. On October 2, 1939, the Latvian Foreign Minister was summoned to Moscow and required to sign a Soviet-Latvian Mutual Assistance Pact. On August 5, 1940, Latvia was incorporated into the Soviet Union.

On May 4, 1932, a Treaty of Non-Aggression and for the Peaceful Settlement of Disputes between the USSR and Estonia was signed in Moscow. On March 28, 1939, the treaty was reaffirmed. On September 28, 1939, under military pressure, a Soviet-Estonian Pact of Mutual Assistance was signed. On August 6, 1940, Estonia was incorporated into the Soviet Union.

Peaceful Coexistence

On July 25, 1932, the Polish-Soviet Non-Aggression Treaty was signed in Moscow. On May 5, 1934, it was renewed for a twenty-year period. On September 17, 1939, Russia, in concert with Hitler's Germany, invaded Poland and annexed the eastern and south-eastern parts of the country.

On August 23, 1939, Joachim von Ribbentrop arrived in Moscow for talks with Stalin. On September 28 a Treaty of Non-Aggression between the USSR and Germany was concluded. A secret additional protocol provided for the partition of Poland, and the annexation of Finland, Latvia, Lithuania, Estonia, and Bessarabia.

On September 17 Soviet troops invaded Poland. On November 29 Soviet troops invaded Finland. On June 15, 1940, the Red Army occupied and annexed Lithuania; on June 16, Estonia. On June 17, 1940, Soviet tanks appeared in Riga, Latvia.

To Khrushchev this record seems only to confirm what one of his marshals says: "Everybody knows that the Soviet Army is an army of peace. . . . During their entire existence, the armed forces of the USSR never attacked anybody. . . ." [44]

And *Pravda* can still write that

"over the span of more than forty years, Soviet foreign policy has been consistent—it has always been, is, and will continue to be Leninist policy of peaceful coexistence." [45]

For noncommunists, the crucial question is, Where does coexistence with Khrushchev lead to? It should at least imply the preservation of the status quo in the world. But here, too, it is a question of definition.

What Khrushchev understands by status quo has been analyzed by Walter Lippmann:

"In his [Khrushchev's] mind the social and economic revolution now in progress in Russia, China, and elsewhere in Asia and Africa is the status quo, and he wants us to recognize it as such. In his mind, opposition to this revolution is an attempt to change the status quo. Whereas we think of the status quo as the situation as it exists at the moment, he thinks of it as the process of revolutionary change

which is in progress. He wants us to recognize the revolution not only as it is but as it is going to be." [46]

Khrushchev makes it abundantly clear that he has no intention of disarming ideologically.

In advocating peaceful coexistence, we of course have no intention of saying that there are no contradictions between socialism and capitalism, that complete "harmony" can be established between them, or that it is possible to reconcile the communist and bourgeois ideologies. Such a viewpoint would be tantamount to retreating from Marxism-Leninism. The ideological differences are irreconcilable and will continue so.[47]

Thus peaceful coexistence must also mean for Khrushchev freedom to expand his empire by "exporting" revolution or by subverting nationalist and social-reform movements.

But in one area Khrushchev insists on the generally accepted definition of status quo: No evolution, revolution, or change whatsoever that is not dictated or accepted by Moscow may take place in the communist empire without endangering "peaceful coexistence."

It is then possible to conclude, as do scholars from Columbia and Harvard:

"So long as Soviet objectives remain unlimited—that is, if they can be realized only by the elimination of our noncommunist forms of government—then a resolution of the conflict is possible only if we are willing to yield to the Soviet Union what it wants. Whatever changes in the climate may take place, or whatever settlements of specific issues may become possible, should not be allowed to obscure the reality of this underlying condition of deadly conflict."[48]

The communists never tire of assuring the rest of the world that "peaceful coexistence" means only that they will realize their unalterable aim of communizing the world without war, and that where they do not succeed in this they will keep in mind the possibility of nonpeaceful means.

Peaceful Coexistence

In his announcement of the results of the November 1959 conclave, published in *Pravda* the following January 17, Khrushchev was frank:

The policies of peaceful coexistence . . . facilitate the victory of the Communist Party and other progressive organizations of the working class in capitalist countries, make it easier for the peoples to combat aggressive war blocs and foreign military bases, and contribute to the national liberation movements.

The Khrushchev brand of coexistence is more than mere "peace." It is the elimination of the cold war by the West. It would see the removal of American bases, the acknowledgment of communist conquests, the scrapping of the nuclear deterrent, the reduction of armed forces, the break-up of NATO and the system of alliances that ties the free world together. It would permit unlimited access by the Soviet Union to American technology, the opening of unlimited trade and scientific exchange, making Western credit available, and amplifying of the communist voice at the conference table. And most important, though, it would acknowledge the dynamism of communism and its "inevitable" triumph.

This is Khrushchev coexistence.

In the meantime, it serves an excellent cold war purpose—distraction, diversion, and the hint at a smile in the somber Soviet foreign policy.

CHAPTER 5

Breaking Through
the Wall

For the first forty years of its existence, the Soviet Union lived in fear of capitalist encirclement. The Bolsheviks never forgot—nor does Khrushchev forget today—that "capitalist" Europe, during the first years of the Soviet regime, threw a *cordon sanitaire* around the country, partly to help force payment on its expropriated $20 billion investment and partly to insulate the rest of the world from the revolutionary ferment.

In the thirties, the situation changed drastically.

In 1934 the Soviet Union joined the League of Nations, which Lenin had earlier called "the lair of imperialist brigands." Soviet foreign policy until the outbreak of World War II consisted in promoting collective security (notably through military alliances with capitalist countries, such as the Franco-Soviet Pact of 1935). But Stalin's spokesmen still propounded the thesis of encirclement:

"It should not be forgotten that as long as capitalist encirclement exists, so long will the danger of intervention, with all the resultant consequences, exist." [1]

In March 1939, while still allied to the Western democracies (but already preparing his friendship pact with Hitler, to be concluded on August 23 of that year), Stalin continued to warn:

"Never . . . forget we are surrounded by a capitalist world." [2]

Two years later, on the very day of Hitler's attack, the "capitalist world" came to the help of the Soviet Union.

When the war ended, so did Stalin's policy of cooperation with

76

the West. Edward Crankshaw, in his *Khrushchev's Russia*, reports that "already in 1946, at the great Victory dinner in the Kremlin he [Stalin] was telling his Marshals that every nerve must be strained to push through recovery of the Soviet economy in preparation for another war."

In 1954, one year after Stalin's death, Khrushchev was again expounding the old doctrine:

The Soviet Union is in a capitalist encirclement and must be ready to deal a crushing blow to any attempt by the aggressors to hinder our peaceful construction.[3]

At present the Soviet leaders seem convinced that they have broken out of "capitalist encirclement" and that it is no longer clear who is encircling whom.

I would like to draw your attention to the fact that at present the concept of "capitalist encirclement" of our country itself seriously needs a more accurate definition. With the formation of the world system of socialism, the situation in the world has altered radically, and it has not altered, as you know, to the advantage of capitalism. At present it is not known who encircles whom. The socialist countries cannot be considered as some kind of island in a rough capitalist sea.[4]

The Western Wall—Germany

Khrushchev now has ambitions beyond "breaking the capitalist encirclement." He wants to rule the whole planet. But he is a realist. He knows that the Soviet Union alone cannot dominate the world as it now stands.

But the situation would be entirely different if the communists, already in control of the enormous land mass of Eurasia, could have at their disposal the industrial power of Western Europe. And in the heart of Western Europe is the country that twice in this century

77

not only unleashed world war, but also, almost alone, withstood for years the combined might of the Allies.

Another German-Soviet pact, like that between Hitler and Stalin, is at least as possible today as it was in 1939. Indeed, Khrushchev insists, it is more probable, since a German attack on the Soviet Union would now be suicidal.

Khrushchev made clear to a German audience that such an alliance is exactly what he is looking for.

Chancellor Bismarck, a farsighted politician of bourgeois Germany, once said:

"It is my belief that, provided no irresponsible parties and individuals gain ascendancy in Germany, there will be no conflicts between Germany and Russia. For us, Russia's friendship is most important of all." Bismarck indignantly rejected the attempts by foreign powers to impose on Germany the role of a hound to be unleashed against Russia.

Another distinguished German personality of a later period, Joseph Wirth, former chancellor of the Weimar Republic, said: "Until Russia and Germany began to quarrel with one another the two peoples lived well in Europe."

These, I think, are very wise words and they should be pondered by those who shape the foreign policy of the Federal Republic.[5]

This echoed the hope of Lenin:

"The principal link in the chain of revolution . . . is the German link . . . and the success of the world revolution depends more on Germany than on any other country. . . ."[6]

"A successful revolution in Germany would immediately and very easily have shattered the shell of imperialism (which, unfortunately, is made of the best steel, and hence cannot be broken by the efforts of any and every . . . chicken). It would have brought about the victory of world socialism for certain, without any difficulty, or with slight difficulty—if, of course, by 'difficulty' we mean difficulty on a world-historical scale and not in the Philistine-circle sense."[7]

After the recall of past wisdom . . . the promise of a bright future:

The German people are a very talented and industrious people. They have given mankind many remarkable discoveries and inventions. The German people do not need aggressive campaigns for *Lebensraum*. . . .

What prospects have the German people, then, with their relatively small territory? They have the broadest and brightest prospects. Today, when one third of mankind is building its life under the banner of Marxism-Leninism, the question of territories has been eliminated.

We do not regard the wealth of the Soviet Union as being solely our own wealth—it is the wealth of all the socialist countries. That, too, is the view of real communists, Marxist-Leninists, of other socialist countries, who look upon their countries' wealth as our common wealth, serving the common interests of the people of all socialist states. And this wealth is so great that it amply provides for the requirements of the peoples of all our countries.[8]

The Soviet people want friendship with the people of the Federal German Republic, the same friendship they have with the people of the German Democratic Republic. Establishment of friendly relations would be a boon to the peoples of the Soviet Union and to the two German states, as well as to all European countries whose interests demand lasting peace in Europe and throughout the world.[9]

We are not competitors. On the contrary, the economies of our two countries complement each other. The Soviet Union possesses inexhaustible raw materials and industrial resources. We have unlimited opportunities for the production of agricultural raw materials and food, and the Germans could cooperate with us. This cooperation would be advantageous to both countries, and the well-being of our peoples would be raised to a new high.[10]

And a not so subtle suggestion:

Some political leaders in countries allied with West Germany in NATO candidly and directly say—behind the scenes, to be sure, and not in public: "Believe and understand us, if the Federal German Republic were not a member of NATO, had no army, and spent nothing on armament, it would have great economic advantages over other Western countries, and would become an even more dangerous trade rival." The West German economy is indeed strong and more highly developed than that of other NATO countries, excluding the United States. Thus, for such Western politicians the development of the West German economy—while West Germany is being dragged into NATO and participating in the arms race —is most beneficial. They are not averse to putting their West German competitor in the heavy chains of armaments and large armed forces in order to weaken the Federal German Republic economically, to create better conditions for competing with it in world markets.[11]

The wounds of the past are far from healed: Germany is still a divided country. Khrushchev does not intend to accept reunification unless a reunified Germany would ally itself with the Soviet Union.

Knowing that Germans desire the reunification of their country, Khrushchev places the blame for the partition on the West.

The Soviet Union, the Soviet people, always were and are for the unity of Germany. It was the rulers of the Western powers who shouted in their time that Germany should be dismembered, and it was precisely their separatist actions that brought about a split of your country. Our government, Stalin, on the other hand, persistently advocated the idea of German unity. And we continue to abide by this decision today. But now, on what foundation should Germany be reunited? We are not for just any reunification. And you, too, will agree, I think, that the question of reunification should be approached primarily from class positions.[12]

It is known to us from reliable sources that the Western states do not want reunification. And their policy is directed toward this. They complicate all questions. For example, the representatives of the Western powers assert that reunification can be carried out only by so-called "free elections." They know that the GDR will not agree to this, and on such conditions there can be no reunification.[13]

This often-repeated assertion of the West's opposition to German reunification has been continuously denied by the White House.

In his *Memoirs*, former President Truman recalls that the Allied occupation zones for Germany were worked out in 1944 by the European Advisory Commission, sitting in London and consisting of representatives of the U.S., Great Britain, and the Soviet Union. Then Mr. Truman adds:

"In November 1944 the European Advisory Commission submitted a final draft agreement on the zones to be occupied by the three major powers. Each power was to have its own zone, and boundaries of each were specifically delineated, although Berlin was made a special joint zone. At Yalta the zones laid down in this draft agreement were accepted by all three powers. Provision was also made there for a fourth zone, for France, the details to be worked out by the Advisory Commission." [14]

Shortly before rewriting history so as to exonerate the Soviet Union of responsibility for the dismemberment of the country, Khrushchev made it clear that a divided Germany was not such a bad thing at all.

Can the world exist without the cardinal solution of the German problem—that is, without the reunification of the two German states? The world can exist; the world exists, and not even badly. Is it possible for the Germans to exist under these circumstances? Yes, they can continue to live like this, and even to live quite well, even very well. This means it is a secondary problem, a partial problem. . . . But it must be solved, because it is a crucial problem, a key point in the solution of the problem of peace and war.[15]

Taking Khrushchev's words at face value, one could almost believe he really wants a unified Germany. He even suggests how it can be achieved:

We are fully aware that at present the unification of Germany is no easy matter. There is a single German people, but there are two Germanies, differing in political and social systems, and poles apart in home and foreign policies. There is no escaping this fact. Those who really desire the unification of Germany cannot but take account of this. It is obvious that in these circumstances any attempt to unite Germany through some formal legal act imposed from without would mean indulging in a dangerous illusion. . . .[16]

If the question of Germany continues to be posed as it is now by some Western leaders—that is, taking into account only the interests of West Germany and with no regard to the interests of East Germany—then no agreement can be reached on this basis. If the status quo is accepted—and the acceptance of the status quo in the German issue means taking into account the existence of two Germanies (the Democratic Republic, a state developing on socialist lines, and the Federal Republic, a capitalist state)—then conditions could be created in which the German problem could be solved. The Germans themselves should negotiate the terms of the peaceful reunification of Germany. At present they cannot agree on unification because the two Germanies have different state systems. But as a first step they could establish, as the GDR government suggests, a confederation and form some all-German state bodies. Then the Germans themselves would take care of further deepening and strengthening the relations between East and West Germany.[17]

And again:

We say: Mr. Adenauer! There is no return to the past. If you indeed wish Germany's reunification, approach this issue not from a position of strength, but from a position of wisdom, taking into account the interests of the German people

82

and the real state of affairs. And the real state of affairs is that there exist two German states, with different social and state systems. You do not want to meet the government of the GDR, but it does not cease to exist because of it. There is but one practicable way to Germany's reunification: talks and agreements between the two German states. The task of re-establishing Germany's unity is first of all a task for the German people itself.[18]

Khrushchev continues to argue for equality between the two German states, ignoring the fact that West Germany has a population of 54.3 million[19] and East Germany 17.8 million.[20]

All sober-thinking people understand that the reunification of Germany by peaceful means cannot be achieved by means of the liquidation of the socialist achievements of the German people in the GDR. The reunification of Germany on the principles proposed by Adenauer would threaten the security of the peoples of Europe, since it would mean the spreading of the domination of militarism, revanchism, and reaction to the whole territory of Germany. Nor is it possible to count on the reunification of Germany by means of the liquidation of the regime existing in the Federal Republic of Germany. It would be wrong to foist on the Germans conditions for the reunification of their country from outside. Let the Germans themselves reach agreement between each other. And it is for this reason that we support the slogan of the democratic circles of Germany: "Germans—to the same table."[21]

But let the people choose . . .

Let us give the people a chance to choose the social system that accords with their interests. Bourgeois leaders often extol the capitalist system. But they back out of peaceful economic competition with the socialist countries. They do not wish to let the people choose their own social system. This shows that they do not trust the people of their country, that they fear the people, that they cannot depend on their people.[22]

83

While repeatedly asserting that "the German question can be solved only by the German people themselves," Khrushchev rejects the Western proposal to ascertain their will through free elections in both parts of Germany. He labels unification by this means an "imposed" solution.

What kind of "referendum" do the imperialist gentlemen now want? . . . Apparently, they want to impose the capitalist system on the peoples of the socialist countries by force.[23]

And with supreme logic:

Some people go as far as suggesting a poll of opinion among the peoples of the socialist countries as to whether they are for socialism or for capitalism. I must tell these gentlemen that they have obviously forgotten history. The peoples of the Soviet Union have already had encounters on these questions with the United States, Germany, France, Britain, Japan, and other states. . . . Who sent troops to our country at that time? At the head of the British Government was Lloyd George, and W. Churchill was Minister of War; Poincaré was the President of France, and Clemenceau was Premier and War Minister; Woodrow Wilson was President of the United States . . . I do not remember who replaced him and with whom the Soviet people finished the "negotiations" he began. In Poland, Pan Pilsudski was in power. Many of these gentlemen who tried to conduct such "negotiations" with the Soviet people are no longer in this world, yet some of them are still alive. Let the present advocates of "opinion polls" consult those who organized the intervention against the Soviet Republic, let them consult these people to find out how such "negotiations" and "opinion polls" end.[24]

And again:

They repeat that an all-German government can be formed only through "free elections" throughout Germany. But this is rank hypocrisy. Can there be free elections in the Federal

Republic when the Communist Party is banned and progressive organizations of the working people and peace supporters suffer police persecution, while war criminals and Nazis play an increasingly important role in political life? The politicians in Bonn want a mechanical union of the Democratic Republic with the Federal Republic, they want to make it a domain of the Junkers and the Rhine and Ruhr magnates.[25]

And now, "interference in the internal affairs":

The essence of the imperialist positions-of-strength policy consists in compelling the Soviet Union to accept the ultimatum demands of the Western powers and in settling political issues on conditions benefiting the imperialists. The Western powers would like, for instance, "to settle" the problem of the people's democracies. But what do they mean by such a "settlement"? They would like, by interference in the internal affairs of these countries, contrary to the will of the people, to liquidate the socialist gains of the working people and to re-establish the rule of capitalists and landowners.[26]

It would be "back to slavery."

So are we supposed to compel the workers of the GDR to go back to the capitalist slavery of West Germany? No! The capitalist gentlemen will have to wait for this till the shrimp whistles, as the saying goes. Anyway, who knows if a shrimp whistles at all?[27]

As for Germany's unity, I am convinced that Germany will be united sooner or later. However, before this moment comes—and no one can foretell when it will come—no attempts should be made to interfere from outside in this internal process, to sustain the state of war which is fraught with many grave dangers and surprises for peace in Europe and throughout the world.[28]

But Hugh S. Cummings, Jr., director of intelligence and research for the State Department, points out: "These are the people of

85

whom it has been said: 'They vote with their feet.' In ten years, 3 million Germans—teachers, physicians, clergymen, engineers, laborers, even state officials—have fled from the Soviet Zone." [29]

To Khrushchev, reunification through free elections means reunification "on a capitalist basis."

The Germans in East Germany do not wish to return to the old way of life. Our attitude to their interests is one of understanding. We have supported and shall continue to support the GDR.[30]

Khrushchev's solution is direct negotiation. Here is a description of a typical meeting:

"German advisers from West and East—from the German Federal Republic and from the so-called German Democratic Republic—are present to assist the four Foreign Ministers. The Soviet Union claims that both sets of Germans should attend the conference as full-fledged participants, representing what the Russians call the 'two German states.'

"As a first step in examining the character of the East German regime, let us have a brief look at the backgrounds of the 'advisers' who have alleged that they represent the national interests of the 17 million Germans who live in the Soviet Zone. Of the four principal 'advisers,' two are Soviet citizens; the third was educated in the Soviet Union and is married to a Soviet citizen. Only the fourth has a reasonably German background, but he is manifestly cast in the role of window dressing and very seldom heard from.

"There are twenty-two Soviet military divisions still in East Germany. While these divisions play their main role in the larger Soviet strategy toward Europe, they have also been an indispensable mainstay to the regime while it built up its own instruments of forcible repression." [31]

Meanwhile, Khrushchev plays a waiting game:

One must say that the general situation now is good with you as to the German issue; the wind is blowing not into your face but into the face of Mr. Adenauer. The time will come when they will come to you, will knock and will say: "We are from Bonn, we have come to you for talks." When they will come, I do not know; that they will come, I am confident. And as to waiting, you can afford it. Every day works in your favor, and at the same time, every day works against Adenauer. Let us, then, wait.[32]

The growing strength of your Republic, the steady rise in output of its industry and agriculture, prove unmistakably that the way it has taken is the sole correct way, one that opens grand constructive prospects for the German people.[33]

Socialism is being consolidated. . . .[34]

After a certain length of time, the need to sign a peace treaty will reach the consciousness of the ruling circles of the Federal German Republic and they will sign it at once. When this time will come, we shall not try to guess. We are not in a hurry. We shall wait, but we shall not relax our efforts to achieve reasonable and mutually acceptable decisions, both in regard to the conclusion of a peace treaty with the two German states and the solution of the West Berlin problem, and other international problems as well.[35]

Despite these soothing words, strikes broke out in East Germany in June 1953 and a genuine popular uprising flared in East Berlin. To quell it, Soviet tanks had to intervene against workers. These were East German workers, those who were said to love the regime.[36] Some 1½ million did vote—with their feet. They escaped through West Berlin.

But to Khrushchev, however, any popular revolt against a communist regime is the work of foreign agents.[37]

We are glad that when a conflict imposed from outside occurred in East Germany, things there did not come to a serious clash. But if it had been required of us, we would not have refused to come to the aid of the working class and of all the working people of the GDR because we are always ready to render timely assistance to a fraternal socialist state.[38]

Therefore we want to warn our enemies—don't trifle with

us, don't feel us out with provocational putsches like the one that was engineered in Hungary. Certain elements in the foreign press are now theorizing about organizing a similar putsch in the German Democratic Republic. Don't miscalculate. We can hit back. Our German friends in the German Democratic Republic, our Polish, Czechoslovak, Hungarian, Albanian, Rumanian, and Bulgarian friends, our Chinese friends, and all our friends can rely on the Soviet Union just as we can rely on our friends. That is what friendship means —all for one and one for all.[39]

Khrushchev explained—in a private conversation—where the interest of the Soviet Union lies.

It is better to have seventeen million Germans in the Soviet bloc than seventy million in a united but neutralized Germany.[40]

There are two Germanies: in the West, the capitalist Germany; in the East, the Germany of people's socialism. It is not our task to help Western capitalists by delivering East Germany to them.[41]

In public, Khrushchev expresses the same idea—in different words:

The Western powers talk a great deal about "settling" the German question. But how do they conceive of this "settlement"? They would like to unify Germany by joining East Germany to West Germany—that is, by abolishing the socialist gains of the German Democratic Republic and adding to the military economic potential of West Germany—and then to bring this unified Germany into the aggressive North Atlantic bloc. As you see, they expect us to agree to the strengthening of German militarism and revanchism.[42]

Khrushchev is thus clear: no reunification—unless the unified Germany is a Soviet satellite. Of course he does not put it that way. But that is what he means when he says:

I want to console Herr Adenauer: We believe that if today

it is only the German Democratic Republic that is socialist, the time will come when all Germany will follow the socialist path, and not just Germany, but the entire world.[43]

. . . the German Democratic Republic is the future, not only the future of the German people. Marx and Engels spoke of that future. We supported the German working people when they began to build their German Democratic Republic on a socialist basis.[44]

Under what circumstances would Khrushchev agree to German unification? a *New York Times* correspondent asked the Soviet Ambassador at Bonn in March 1960. The newspaper reported:

"The Soviet Ambassador has shattered the hopes of some who clung to the belief that terms for Germany's reunification could be negotiated with Moscow short of capitulation to communism. . . .

"One of the group said he wanted to ask the Ambassador a hypothetical question. It was whether the Soviet Union would agree to a united Germany that accepted the Oder-Neisse eastern frontier established after World War II, banned atomic weapons, and was militarily neutral between the North Atlantic Treaty Organization and the Communist Warsaw Pact group.

"The Ambassador, without hesitation, said no. When he was asked what else Germany would need to do, he replied that it would have to be 'peace-loving and democratic,' and he detailed Moscow's meaning of these terms.

"Big industry would have to be nationalized, Ambassador Smirnov said, the power of 'monopoly capital' would have to be broken, and the working class would have to assume political dominance."[45]

Khrushchev is aware of the difficulties of forcing the West to surrender. He first attempts to isolate West Germany from her European allies by frightening Europe with references to Hitler's aggressions [ignoring the Hitler-Stalin pact, which precipitated World War II] and by frightening the West Germans with threats of instant annihilation. The theme of "revanchism" was a major effort to separate Germany from NATO for two years.

Objectives

The peace-loving peoples of Europe are disturbed by the policy of militarizing West Germany, they are disturbed by the fanning of revanchist feelings there. All this should be an even greater cause for anxiety to the French, the British, the Belgians, the Dutch, the Norwegians, the Danes, and others. Even the ruling circles in those countries are pursuing policies fostering the rebirth of German militarism.[46]

I shall mention in passing that our efforts aimed at insuring European security and at reaching a solution of the German question do not contradict in any way the interests of Britain and France. On the contrary, if one were to suppose for a moment that the completely unrealistic dream of militant United States leaders for the inclusion of a United Germany in the aggressive bloc were to be realized, the French and British could hardly live in peace. The hands of the German revanchists would then be freed. They would begin to act in their own sweet way, and France, of course, would be a tempting morsel for them.[47]

He singles out for attack the alliance between West Germany and France.

I should like to call a spade a spade. It is well known how often France has fallen victim to aggression on the part of Germany. Can the French people indeed forget this? Understand me rightly: I do not want to set you at loggerheads with Germany. However, as our saying has it, "You cannot back out now that you have begun." [48]

I do not think we are alone in being displeased by West Germany's wooing of France. Let me tell you frankly what is worrying me. This is a dangerous sort of wooing. The purpose behind it is to lull vigilance. We Soviet people cannot be indifferent in our attitude to German militarism. The Soviet Union sustained tremendous losses in the last war. Millions of lives perished in its flames. There is no family in our country that does not have victims of that war to bemoan. My son, too, lost his life fighting against the Nazis. This is

90

why we have always spoken, are speaking, and will speak about the dangers of militarism and revanchism and shall lay them bare.[49]

It should be borne in mind that if the West Germans use all the economic potential and manpower resources of their country for creating the most powerful army in West Europe, even the strength of that army would not be equal to the power of our army and those of our allies. Even with its allies, the Federal Republic would not be able to equal our strength and power. I am saying this to you, Mr. Chancellor [Adenauer], by no means to intimidate you. Both of us are too far advanced in age to intimidate each other, particularly on such questions. Both of us have seen enough of all sorts of horrors not to resort to such methods.[50]

And:

It is being clamored in France today that the De Gaulle-Adenauer meeting has put an end once and for all to Franco-German conflicts. This is no more than a blind. Only a democratic France and a democratic Germany could really find common language and the way to peaceful cooperation. The friendship of French reactionary circles and the West German revenge-seekers leads to war, not to peace.

It scarcely needs to be emphasized that these plans, carried out to the detriment of French national interests, are contrary also to the interests of the German people and all the nations of Europe.[51]

Says a statement by the East German Ministry of Foreign Affairs, March 21, 1960:

"The continuation of the cold war by the West German Government and its efforts to aggravate the situation and prevent any understanding, particularly in view of the pending summit conference, are a serious warning for all forces of peace. Bonn concentrates all its efforts on continuing nuclear arming and preparing a nuclear war. The Bonn war policy threatens the peace of the German people and of other peoples."

The East Germans echo a refrain Khrushchev sang a few years earlier:

Times have changed. Adenauer will not be able to start things the way Hitler did. One third of Germany is a socialist state. And the people in West Germany have not forgotten the bloody lesson of history either. The Soviet Union, Poland, and Czechoslovakia are also not what they were. A third of humanity is now successfully building a socialist society.[52]

Playing on the world's hope for peace, Khrushchev claims Adenauer's Germany is being used by the United States, Britain, and France to spark a new war.

In this connection the following question must be answered: Is there not a certain analogy between the prewar period and what is presently going on with regard to Western Germany? Are not the very same countries using the very same methods today in their endeavors to push Western Germany onto the path of aggression and new adventures?[53]

They have drawn Western Germany into NATO. They are allotting funds for arming Western Germany and supplying her with weapons. Many leading figures in the Western countries do not even consider it necessary to conceal the fact that they are preparing a West German army against the Soviet Union.[54]

It is not at all impossible, therefore, that West Germany, taking advantage of her position in the North Atlantic Alliance, might provoke a war in order to draw her allies into it and plunge the whole world into the chasm of a devastating war.[55]

The guiding spirit of German militarists is to be found in the imperialist forces of the Western powers. The reunification of Germany on a peaceful, democratic basis runs contrary to their plans. They want to have a united Germany that will be a willing tool for the implementation of their aggressive schemes. In their nightmarish plans for world domination, they clearly assign to the German people the role of cannon fodder. They want to wage war with the hands of the German people.[56]

Such a war, says Khrushchev, would spell the doom of the German people.

In the event that another war is unleashed by the imperialists, it will be precisely here—the places along the dividing line between the countries belonging to the aggressive NATO bloc and the countries of the socialist camp—it will be precisely here that the atomic and hydrogen bombs, constituting a terrible means of destruction, will explode. It is extremely important that the Germans in West Germany should understand that, at least, and prevent such a course of events.[57]

It is high time to realize that the times when imperialists could act from "positions of strength" with impunity have gone, never to return, and try as they may, the imperialists will not be able to change the balance of forces in their favor. Nor should they forget the geographical position of West Germany, which—with means of warfare what they are today—would not survive a single day of modern warfare.[58]

For purposes of pressure, the West German militarists want to make use of such levers as the arming of the Bundeswehr with atomic weapons and the creation on the territory of the Federal German Republic of sites for the launching of rockets. This, however, is utter madness. It must not be forgotten that rocket sites and atomic bases have a boomerang attraction for the rockets of other sites and bases. Only abnormal people can play with the lives of millions of people.[59]

With threats come assurances . . .

The Soviet Union and other socialist countries have never

had, nor do they have now, any hostile intentions with respect to other countries, including West Germany. We are for peace among the nations. The Soviet Union looks on friendship and mutual understanding between the German and Soviet peoples as the paramount guarantee of peace and security in Europe.[60]

. . . and advances.

While strengthening its fraternal friendship with the German Democratic Republic, the Soviet Union builds its relations with the Federal Republic of Germany on a basis of peaceful cooperation and strives to infuse a spirit of mutual confidence and friendship into these relations. In our opinion, this accords with the interests of both the Soviet Union and the Federal Republic of Germany. We would also like to see less attention paid in West Germany to those who still try to raise doubts among the public in Federal Germany about the usefulness of further efforts to develop Soviet-West German relations.[61]

Berlin

If Berlin could be made to fall at a strategic moment, Soviet politicians reason, Germany's alliance with the West might totter and break.

In this connection it is impossible to ignore also the question of West Berlin. It is commonly known that the German revanchists have made West Berlin the base of their constant undermining and subversive activity directed toward the provoking of war. We resolutely reject any attempts to ascribe to the Soviet Union the intention of seizing West Berlin and infringing upon the right of the population in this part of the city to preserve its present way of life. On the contrary, in demanding the normalization of the situation in West Berlin, we have proposed to convert it into a free city and to guarantee jointly with the Western states the preservation there of the way of life and of the social order which suits the West Berlin inhabitants best of all. This shows that the positions of the Government of the Soviet Union and the governments of the Western states, judging by their statements, coincide on this question. We, and so do they, stand for the independence of West Berlin and for the preservation of the existing way of life there.[62]

The "question of Berlin" exists only because Khrushchev has posed it. As he himself has often told his listeners, "one must proceed from the real facts." The facts are that the status of Berlin was agreed on by the Allies at Yalta, confirmed in Potsdam, and reconfirmed in 1949 after the Western powers broke the blockade of the former German capital. It is also a real fact that the Allies paid for their right to maintain forces in West Berlin by evacuating, in the weeks following the end of World War II, large areas of central Germany conquered by their troops.

Another fact is that Khrushchev himself did not question the right of the three Western powers to maintain troops in Berlin. It is noteworthy that Khrushchev reaffirmed this right several months after submitting, on November 27, 1958, his first ultimatum to "get out within six months." [63]

Yes, I believe the United States, Britain, and France have lawful rights for their stay in Berlin. These rights flow from the fact of German surrender as a result of our joint struggle against Nazi Germany. But fourteen years have elapsed since the end of the war, and there is no need for the further occupation of West Berlin. That is why we proposed, at last, the conclusion of a peace treaty with both German states. When a peace treaty is signed with the GDR and the Federal Republic of Germany, the right to occupation becomes invalid.[64]

Some statesmen and politicians of the Western countries say in their statements that somebody intends to hinder the discharging of their functions regarding West Berlin. This is an incorrect interpretation of our attitude. We respect

95

treaties and observe them strictly. This is precisely why we propose the conclusion of a peace treaty.[65]

It is sometimes said that the Berlin question allegedly did not exist a year ago and that the situation in Berlin was not bad. But need we wait until some seemingly insignificant incident in Berlin leads to war? We are in favor of preventing conflicts by measures taken in good time. Neither the Soviet Union nor the German Democratic Republic has any ulterior motives or secret designs with regard to West Berlin. No one has any claim to incorporating West Berlin into the German Democratic Republic or changing the social and economic scheme of things there.[66]

The demand to transform West Berlin into a "free city" was contained in identical notes transmitted to Washington, London, and Paris on November 27, 1958. That same day Khrushchev explained his reasons at a specially summoned press conference. The bargaining leverage comes with the word "abnormal."

There exists a divided Berlin, where the occupation regime is still maintained. The war was ended more than thirteen years ago. I feel that every normal person finds such a situation abnormal.

West Berlin is a convenient place for the Western powers to conduct an aggressive policy against the German Democratic Republic, and against the Soviet Union and other countries of the socialist camp. . . . We wish to establish a normal atmosphere, normal conditions, in which the relations between our countries will become what they were during the war against Hitler Germany. . . .

Certain circles who are in favor of continuing the cold war stand for utilizing West Berlin as a hotbed of discord for kindling a hot war. But we are convinced that such people constitute a minority in the world.[67]

West Berlin lies within the territory of the German Democratic Republic [East Germany], and obviously with the signing of a peace treaty the German Democratic Republic will exercise sovereign rights over her entire state territory.

Therefore, if the Western powers refuse to sign a peace treaty with the German Democratic Republic, this will not reserve them the rights on the preservation of which they insist. They will then obviously lose the right of access to West Berlin by land, water, or air. We have done and will do everything in order that we are correctly understood.

The rights the Western powers obtained as a result of Nazi Germany's surrender, including the right to maintain the occupation regime in West Berlin, would also lose their strength, become invalid with respect to the German Democratic Republic territory.[68]

For some time the existence of free West Berlin has been disturbing the Russians and their East German satellite. West Berlin is a prosperous, new city, almost entirely rebuilt from the ruins of war. The Eastern sector is largely in shambles. Thus the advantages of "capitalism" over "socialism" are clearly visible to the naked eye. They are more than visible. They are attractive, and every month attract thousands of East Germans choosing freedom by taking a one-way trip on the jointly operated subway.

Although West Berlin is a major listening post for the West, it is probably to this mass exodus that Khrushchev is referring when he talks about "subversive activities" allegedly conducted in West Berlin.

It is also well known that the territory of West Berlin is widely utilized for subversive activities against the GDR and other socialist countries. I must say frankly that as a result of the policy of the United States, Britain, and France, as well as of the Federal German Republic, West Berlin has become one of the most painful excrescences of the "cold war." [69]

Here is a typical news report from an American paper:

"East German police entered West Berlin for the second day to try to halt a mass exodus of refugees. West Berlin police over-

97

powered and arrested them. An armed patrol of three Communists crossed the border, ignored a demand by a West Berlin policeman to return, and began searching. They were moving toward the American sector's Wansee station on the elevated railway when ten West Berlin police arrived and overpowered them. East Berlin police had ridden into West Berlin on the elevated yesterday and had questioned passengers and searched their luggage before being chased back into the Soviet sector by West Zone police. Two were arrested. More than 6,000 refugees have entered West Germany in a week in a flight from Communist measures."[70]

Khrushchev does not want to see that the population of East Berlin, and indeed East Germany, is making its way West. He simply states the opposite.

The Germans in East Germany do not wish to return to the old way of life. Our attitude to their interests is one of understanding. We have supported and shall continue to support the GDR. It would be logical to assume that on their part Germans of East Germany regard it as correct in principle to abolish the system existing in West Germany. Such a presentation of the question, however, is not realistic, for social changes are effected by the peoples themselves, and there can be no question of buying and selling in this matter.[71]

Khrushchev's plan:

We propose to set up a free city in West Berlin. This, indeed, will not upset the political order there, will not violate either its social or political principles. We are ready to provide this free city with every guarantee of independence and integrity to which our allies agree; guarantee them by our participation under the aegis of the United Nations or any other acceptable means. We see no other way if we are to be guided by the formula of coexistence and noninterference in the affairs of other states.[72]

We made this proposal a long time ago.

And we return to it and analyze it over and over, trying to see whether it contains anything that would be to the detriment of our partners if this question was solved along the lines we are suggesting.

Frankly speaking, we find nothing of the kind.[73]

What will happen to Berlin? Nothing will happen. The workers will continue to work as they did before. A free city! In West Berlin there are a great number of Social Democrats. If it suits the workers there that the capitalist order exist, well then, let them continue to work in that way! By means of an example of a better living standard, a shorter working day, and satisfying the needs of the working people in a better way, we shall exercise our influence on the brains and the consciousness of the workers in all countries![74]

On the eve of the Paris meeting the aggressive circles wanted to bring strong pressure to bear upon us. We say: Let us conclude a peace treaty with Germany. Some of our former wartime allies are against this.

But why? Plainly speaking, why do the United States of America, France, and the United Kingdom need West Berlin? They need it as a dog needs a fifth leg. West Berlin does not give them anything. By the way, no one encroaches on West Berlin. It is said freedom is at stake, but who encroaches on freedom?

Let the West Berliners continue to live as they do now, and let them have the regime they like. The Soviet Government has long since declared that to select a regime is a matter for each people and that everyone should live as he prefers to.[75]

With this come promises of prosperity . . .

We have stated that the Soviet Union, by the orders it places, will insure that West Berlin's industrial enterprises operate at full capacity. The Soviet Union also undertakes to fully supply West Berlin with food. Naturally, we intend to do both these things on a commercial basis. I think that no one questions the possibilities at the disposal of the Soviet Union. West Berlin workers and employers can engage in activities useful to the Berlin population. Far from resulting in a deterioration of the standard of living, this will insure a higher level of employment and provide the conditions for raising the standard of living.[76]

. . . and promises to keep a demilitarized West Berlin free.

Some people in the West express the fear that someone would threaten the freedom and independence of West Berlin. Such fears are of course devoid of any foundation. We suggested nevertheless that the great powers guarantee the independence and free development of the free city. No state, including the two German states, must interfere in the internal affairs of the free city. We have no objection to the United Nations cooperating in such guarantees.[77]

We are in favor of strict guarantees of the observance of the status of a free city. In this connection we declared in particular that if our Western partners regarded it as desirable to station a token number of troops in the free city, the Soviet Union will be willing to make its contribution by its own troops, with the troops of the United States, Britain, and France. We would also be willing to agree that some forces from neutral states, too, would be in the free city.[78]

After all the sweetness comes the threat.

Should the Western powers refuse to sign a peace treaty with both German states, we shall still sign a peace treaty with the German Democratic Republic. We shall do so whether Herr Adenauer likes it or not. His policy will then be unmasked once and for all as the policy of preparing war. We are convinced the people will not tolerate this, because it knows from personal experience to what disastrous consequences this policy leads. The German people will have the strength and the will. It will proclaim: There must be no war![79]

If we fail to make our old allies understand and if we are forced to sign a peace treaty, that would be undesirable. But not only will we sign, other countries will sign as well.

When the treaty is signed, it must be understood that the German Democratic Republic will have sovereign rights on its territory and all the consequences of the [World War II] capitulation will be lost and all the rights of the occupying powers will lose their validity. I have said that many times.[80]

A few days later, regarding the Allies' stand on Berlin, Khrushchev again holds Adenauer responsible for Western policy.

If, as Khrushchev has said, the right of the Western Allies to stay in Berlin is the result of the "joint" (with the Russians) struggle against Nazi Germany, then such a right cannot be unilaterally abrogated. Nevertheless, Khrushchev claims that it can:

. . . if we sign a peace treaty, the right to occupation flowing from the victory over Germany will be abolished. Peace will be established throughout the German Democratic Republic. Access to Berlin by air, water, and land without permission of the Government of the German Democratic Republic will discontinue. Access will be for those who obtain the consent of the Government of the German Democratic Republic.[81]

There are some in the West who are beginning to console themselves with the illusion that after the conclusion of a peace treaty the rights of the former occupation states to communications between West Berlin and the Federal German Republic through the German Democratic Republic will be preserved. But one may ask what these rights will be based on.[82]

The signing of a peace treaty with the German Democratic Republic will mean the end of all the remains of occupation that still exist on its territory, and it will enjoy all the sovereign rights that every state acquires under a peace settlement.[83]

We should regret it if it were impossible to achieve a

peaceful settlement, but we are aware that it is not in our power to induce the Western powers to sign a German peace treaty. At the same time the Western powers must understand that it is not in their power to hamper the Soviet Union and other states from normalizing their relations with the German Democratic Republic, to close the accounts of the war, and to liquidate all the consequences which derive from the state of war which has not yet ended juridically because there is no German peace treaty.[84]

And promises to defend East Germany.

Should any aggressive forces come out against the GDR, which is an equal partner of the Warsaw Treaty, we will consider it an attack on the Soviet Union, on all the countries which belong to the Warsaw Treaty. We shall rise then for the defense of the GDR, and this will mean the defense of the basic interests of the security of the Soviet Union, of the entire socialist camp, and of the cause of peace all over the world.[85]

And if the access to Berlin were forced:

. . . We will consider any violation of the frontiers of the GDR on the part of the West as a violation of the sovereignty of the republic, as the beginning of war. Therefore, we warn the hotheads in the West who are addressing aggressive statements to the GDR that Soviet and GDR troops stand on the territory of the republic, and let no one dare to violate the GDR's land, sea, or air frontiers.[86]

But this is a very dangerous policy which can bring the world to the brink of war, and our duty is to warn everyone who is interested in the preservation of peace.

We may say that if Adenauer does not give up his policy and if he persists in defending his principles, life itself will throw him over, because you cannot kill everything living.

We can guarantee peace in Europe by a solution of the

disarmament question and by concluding a peace treaty with both German states.

So we say straight to Adenauer and those against the peaceful solution of the question that we will do our best to negotiate on the grounds that can be acceptable to the Western powers.

And we are sure that despite the efforts of Adenauer, the Western countries sooner or later will come to the same conclusion we have.[87]

Coupled with the threat of unilateral action is Khrushchev's claim that all he does is work for peace.

It is difficult to understand this stand of the leaders of the Western powers, hearing their protestations that they desire peace. After all, we propose to solve questions in which the danger of a new military conflict is inherent. The armed forces of the confronting military groupings meet in German territory, especially in Berlin, and the slightest carelessness on any side may produce the spark that starts a blaze over it and explodes the powder keg. We want to separate the contacts so as not to cause the spark and so as not to confront the world with the danger of the greatest disaster: a third world war. Such is the position.[88]

The question of peace, the signing of a peace treaty with Germany—this question must be solved. Honest people who desire peace have no arguments against the signing of the peace treaty with Germany. In Berlin an order is to be created which will be in accordance with peaceful conditions, with the peaceful endeavors of the population of Berlin.[89]

Perhaps I am repeating myself, but this is a question to which we shall have to return again and again until all the interested parties have arrived at an understanding of the seriousness of the situation and until they have weighed up what the further retention of such a situation may lead to, and have come to a correct understanding of the question. The

Soviet Union will not slacken its efforts to reach the goal it has set.[90]

There is a striking parallel between the crisis created by Khrushchev over Berlin and the demands by Hitler, in 1938 and 1939, for an end to the "abnormal" situations resulting from the Versailles Treaty. David Lilienthal has pointed out:

"It was certainly 'abnormal' for three million Germans to live under Czechoslovakian rule. Or so the British and French governments thought in September 1938. The Munich agreements led to the incorporation of the Sudeten Germans into the Reich, and six months later to Hitler's annexation of the whole of Czechoslovakia. A few more months, and Hitler demanded the settlement of another 'abnormal' situation: Danzig, a German city cut off from the Reich and made a free city under Polish administration. The alternative to 'settling' this 'abnormality,' Hitler made it clear, was war. Again there were voices saying, 'Why die for Danzig?'[91]

"This is a test of our resolution. The question is already being asked, 'Why die for West Berlin?' Well, the people who asked in 1939, 'Why die for Danzig?' many of them eventually died for Paris, London, and Moscow. The reason that you have to take the chance of dying for West Berlin is that you, if you don't do it there, then it will be a question of dying for New York. The Russians want to know if we have the guts to stand up to them. And in the last analysis, we have to remember that the Russians want to start a hydrogen bomb war as little as we do, but we've got to make it clear that we are prepared to face the worst. It's a test of our nerve."[92]

And Lilienthal has also noted:

"I'm very troubled by the worship of a number of words by some wonderful people. 'Flexibility' is one. There was one thing that Neville Chamberlain was, and that was flexible. He did not bring peace. He brought on, if any one man can be blamed for it, he brought on by his miscalculations of the importance of making concessions, he brought on war. Now, we want to be flexible in the interests of what appears to move us along toward peace. But let's not make an end of flexibility, or initiative, or any of these other things." [93]

The Eastern Wall—Japan

Berlin is Khrushchev's lever in the West.

Japan's position in the Orient is very similar to the position of West Germany in Europe. Both countries are the industrial giants of their continents. Historically, both have sought to expand, economically and militarily, in the areas now under communist control. Both have, or will have in the foreseeable future, the problems of finding markets and cheaper raw materials. They will have to compete with the other industrialized nations of the Western world. Both have been defeated in war, and to both of them Moscow can offer something: to the Germans, the prospect of reunification, markets, resources; to Japan, the return of some seized territories and perhaps the vast Chinese market.

And finally, if Germany and Japan—or even just one of them— were to leave the Western alliance, the position of the alliance and of the United States would be considerably weakened.

Thus the observation by Maurice Hindus that "Japan is of infinitely greater importance to Moscow than is China or any other Asian country" [94] seems fully justified.

Stalin pointed out Japan's significance to Soviet Russia as long ago as 1925:

"It is true that the Japanese people are the most progressive of the peoples of the East, that they are interested in the success of the movement of liberation against oppressors of the people. A union of the Japanese people with the people of the Soviet Union would mean the beginning of the end of the great colonial empires, the beginning of the end of world imperialism. That union would be invincible." [95]

Thirty-five years later, Douglas MacArthur II, United States Ambassador to Japan, told *Time* magazine correspondent Alexander Campbell in Tokyo:

"Moscow and Peking have made it abundantly clear that neutralization and eventual take-over of Japan is their number-one objective in Asia."

This understanding is a focal point in Soviet policy toward all advanced industrial countries, including Japan, as it is analyzed in an authoritative report submitted to the Committee on Foreign Relations, U.S. Senate, by a Columbia-Harvard Research Group on February 14, 1960:

"The objective of Soviet policy toward the advanced industrial countries now and in the near future appears to be not a social transformation of these countries, but a modification of their national policies. That is to say—and a number of distinguished American observers have gone astray on this point—it is not a question, in any short-range projection, of trying to communize the countries of Western Europe, but rather of seeking to bring about changes in the policies of their 'bourgeois' governments. In the first instance, this means changes that will have the effect of weakening the Western alliance; later, it may be hoped to encourage these governments to orient their policies more favorably toward the Soviet Union to make their industrial output available to the Soviet economic complex. In the short-term situation, the direction of the flow of industrial output of Western Europe is a major factor in the world power balance." [96]

Says Mr. Khrushchev, addressing the Japanese through their largest newspaper:

Our economic interests do not clash with the economic interests of Japan, but with the United States your interests do clash, because you are its rival. But there will be no competition between us. We can sell you coal, ore, timber, oil, and similar raw materials and purchase your industrial products.

Why does Japan not do what is profitable to her? She does not do it because she depends on the United States. By the letter of the law she is regarded as independent, but in reality she is compelled to take into consideration the United States, which has planted its military jackboot in Japan. . . . Japan is in an unequal position. I think that Japan will not tolerate such a position for long. She will press for genuine and not imaginary sovereignty. And we hope that Japan will soon recover genuine, real sovereignty. . . . We have long since offered the Japanese leaders to open a direct air line between our two countries.[97]

For years Khrushchev has been teasing Japan with offers of opportunities in East Asia:

I think it would be beneficial for the Japanese leaders to open a direct air line between our two countries. I think it would be beneficial for both states. But I suppose the Americans do not allow you to do this. . . . You probably cannot agree to the establishment of direct air lines between our two countries because your airports are in the hands of the Americans and you naturally have no place to receive our planes.[98]

The "Asian co-prosperity sphere" can develop without military conquest. But Japan, the most powerful industrial nation in Asia and the Far East—in fact the only modern country in the whole region—cannot stay aloof from the cold war, a conflict that in 1950 erupted into destructive military struggle at Japan's very doorstep, in its former colony Korea. As a result of the Korean aggression, Japan realized it must protect itself against possible attack by the bloc that had already used military force in its attempt to expand the Soviet Union and Communist China. Japan, through its security treaty with the United States concluded at the time of the signing of the Japanese Peace Treaty (September 8, 1951), granted the U.S. the right to maintain forces in Japan in order to protect Japan from foreign attack and to aid in "putting down large-scale internal riots in Japan caused through instigation or intervention by an outside power." The Soviet Union violently denounced these security arrangements and refused to sign the Japanese Treaty. For almost ten years, the main target of the Japanese Communists, Socialists, and neutralists was the U.S.-Japanese pact. The violence that erupted on the occasion of the ratification of a revised security treaty between the U.S. and Japan, and that led to the cancellation of President Eisenhower's visit to Tokyo in June 1960, show how deeply neutralism and pacifism are anchored in Japanese public opinion and how easily a riot could be staged by Communist agitators.

Japan, formerly the most aggressive imperialist power in Asia and rivaled in its drive for conquest only by Hitlerite Germany, is today one of the most pacifist nations in the world. This change is easily explainable: Japan knows from its own experience what an atomic war would be like; its military class has been beaten into submission; the Western empires that once dominated large parts of Asia and had established themselves economically and politically on the Chinese mainland have withdrawn from their possessions; as a result, the immense sources of raw material and the potentially inexhaustible markets of Asia would now be open to Japanese trade if the West allowed it.

Khrushchev's first objective is to foment hostility between Japan and the United States. In this connection, Khrushchev could cite a recommendation by Lenin:

"The practical task of communist policy is to take advantage of this hostility [between U.S. and Japan] and to incite one against the other." [99]

But Lenin's outlook was different; he was intent on creating revolutionary or potential revolutionary situations. In 1920, Soviet imperialism was not yet born, but Khrushchev reads into Lenin's pronouncement what he finds expedient. Soviet propaganda is designed to promote Japanese hostility toward the United States. The atomic bomb is often recalled.

A typical broadcast aimed at Japan reminds:

"Japanese listeners, today is the thirteenth anniversary of American imperialists' cruel atomic bombing of Hiroshima.

"The Stockholm peace conference [organized by the Communist-controlled World Peace Council] decided to make August sixth a day of struggle against nuclear weapons in order to pray for the repose of atomic-bomb victims in Hiroshima, and also to strengthen friendly cooperation in struggling against various preparations for atomic warfare." [100]

The imperialist circles of the Western countries, the United States in the first place, want to establish their world domination. Will the Americans withdraw from Japan voluntarily? No. They will sit there and suck the Japanese people's lifeblood. They will never withdraw from Japan voluntarily. They sit there and frighten you with the Soviet Union, frighten you with A- and H-bombs.[101]

The Soviet Union, on the contrary, is "reasonable and friendly," and ready to give up some of its conquests.

As soon as the peace treaty is signed, the islands of Habomai and Shikotan* will be immediately turned over to Japan.[102]

The policy of the American militarists who established in Japan their military bases directed against the Soviet Union and People's China is one of the main sources of international tension. Fighting against foreign bases on its territory, the Japanese people fight for the lessening of international tension, for the cessation of the "cold war." We wish the Japanese people success in eliminating the unjust treaties and agreements which are imposed upon them. We wish that the Japanese government should be guided by the vital interests of their people and not by the interests of others, imperialist governments. We salute the courageous fight of the Japanese people and we extend them the hand of friendship.[103]

Khrushchev is full of sympathy for the

. . . Japanese people who have experienced the full fury of the first atomic bombs.[104]

*Shikotan is one of the larger islands of the Kurile group, which was given to the Soviet Union in 1945 as one of the spoils of war. In 1947 the Kuriles were incorporated into the USSR, together with the island of Sakhalin. The southern part of Sakhalin has been annexed by the Soviets, also as a result of World War II, as a "region" (oblast.) Thus Khrushchev seems to promise to cede Soviet territory to Japan.

This expression of sympathy closely follows the riots that prevented President Eisenhower from visiting Japan. Khrushchev of course exploits this situation to the full.

With sympathy and good wishes comes the threat. In a note handed to the Japanese Ambassador in Moscow by Foreign Minister Andrei A. Gromyko, the Soviet government states in part: "The criminal actions of the United States military and the attempts of the Japanese government to justify participation in them are again demonstrating the aggressive nature of the Japanese-American military pact." The note points out that "dangerous consequences" may ensue from "basing American planes" on Japanese soil. This danger, the note states, "may arise as a result of the use of the United States of aviation based in Japan for carrying out aggressive acts against the Soviet Union." [105]

All this, in Khrushchev's view, falls within the terms of peaceful coexistence:

> The Japanese people themselves must decide what they are going to have. The political struggle in this or that country is the internal affair of the given country and no outside intervention is permissible.[106]

Although it would be unrealistic to ascribe the fiasco of the anti-U.S. riots in Japan solely to communist agitation, supported (as they were) by Soviet propaganda and funds, a major Japanese crisis at any time would be a great victory in Khrushchev's drive to conquer without war.

Should the mood so violently and effectively demonstrated by Japanese students and workers persist, and should Japan in fact become neutralist, the whole defense system set up by the United States in the Far East would be gravely jeopardized. The Japanese crisis could also set off a chain reaction and thus render precarious the position of U.S. bases in the East. Already a Pentagon official is reported to have warned: "We simply can't depend on all these foreign bases any more."

CHAPTER 6

Neutralizing the Underdeveloped Countries

As the communists see it, the industrial power that dominates the underdeveloped countries will dominate the world. A primary Leninist principle holds:

"Imperialism is capitalism in that stage of development in which the domination of monopolies and finance capital has established itself." [1]

Lenin saw the colonial system disintegrating, depriving the West of raw materials and markets, and leading ultimately to the fall of capitalism. "The outcome of the world struggle," he said, "will be determined by the fact that Russia, India, China, etc., account for the overwhelming majority of the population of the globe." In addition he saw valuable allies in the colonial peoples fighting for independence.

"Great changes have taken place [in the national movement in colonial countries] since the beginning of the twentieth century: millions and hundreds of millions, in fact the overwhelming majority of the population of the globe, are now coming forward as independent, active revolutionary factors. It is perfectly clear that in the impending decisive battles in the world revolution, the movement of the majority of the population of the globe, which at first is directed toward national liberation, will turn against capitalism and imperialism and will, perhaps, play a more revolutionary part than

111

we expect . . . In spite of the fact that the masses of the toilers, of the peasants, in the colonial countries are still backward, they will play a very important part in the coming phases of the world revolution." [2]

Stalin, thinking and speaking in military terms, explained the strategic importance of denying the colonies to the adversary:

"If Europe and America may be called the front, the scene of the main engagements between socialism and imperialism, the non-sovereign nations and the colonies, with their raw materials, fuel, food, and vast store of human material should be regarded as the rear, the reserve of imperialism. In order to win a war, one must not only triumph at the front but also revolutionize the enemy's rear, his reserves." [3]

"Hence the victory of the world proletarian revolution may be regarded as assured only if the proletariat is able to combine its own revolutionary struggle with the movement for emancipation of the toiling masses of the nonsovereign nations and the colonies against the power of the imperialists and for a dictatorship of the proletariat." [4]

Stalin saw the need for a violent emancipation.

"The imperialist war has shown and the revolutionary experience of recent years has again confirmed:

"1. That the national and colonial questions are inseparable from the question of emancipation from the power of capital;

"2. That imperialism [the highest form of capitalism] cannot exist without the political and economic enslavement of nonsovereign nations and colonies;

"3. That the nonsovereign nations and colonies cannot be emancipated without the overthrow of the power of capital; and

"4. That the victory of the proletariat cannot be a lasting one unless the nonsovereign nations and colonies are emancipated from the yoke of imperialism." [5]

In the meantime the Soviet Union grew stronger:

"In the West, in the world of bourgeois democracy, we are witnessing the gradual decline and disintegration of the multinational states into their component parts . . . whereas here, in our federation embracing no less than thirty nationalities, we are on the contrary witnessing a process of consolidation of political ties between the independent republics, a process which is leading to an even closer union of independent nationalities into a single independent state.

"Here you have two types of political union, of which one type, the capitalist type, leads to the disintegration of the state into its component parts, while the second type, the Soviet type, on the contrary, leads to a gradual but stable amalgamation of formerly independent nationalities into a single independent state." [6]

For Khrushchev, the emancipation of China and India was the turning point:

A historic victory has been achieved by the peoples of great China, our mutual friends and brothers.

Great India has achieved political independence.

Other peoples of Asia are freeing themselves from hateful colonial oppression. They are choosing the path of development and noninterference in the internal affairs of other states. We welcome the peoples of these countries in this great cause.[7]

Without communist help, the colonial era died in the years following World War II. After 1945, hundreds of millions of people in Asia and Africa acquired independence. The Middle East shucked off the influence of Britain and France. The British gave up their possessions in Asia, and India, Pakistan, Ceylon, Malaya, Cyprus, Ghana, and Nigeria, joined the Commonwealth.

The Dutch tried to retain their Indonesian colonies by force. They lost after a brief struggle and under the pressure of world public opinion expressed in the United Nations.

France fought for years a losing battle to retain Indochina, Morocco, Tunisia, then tried to surrender gracefully in Guinea, the Sudan, and the Cameroons. In Algeria, the war for independence

113

still rages after six years of continuous fighting. Black Africa is emerging as a free continent.

While this process of national liberation was going on, the Soviet Union was rebuilding its war-torn economy, preparing for a new war, launching a war in Korea, supporting a communist-led independence war in Indochina, and at the same time consolidating its own newly won empire in Europe.

It was only under Khrushchev that the Soviet Union began to fully exploit the new situation that had developed. Khrushchev identified himself as a friend of those who were struggling for national freedom—and warned that imperialists had not given up the fight. In recent years, partly to offset the infiltration of China, it has moved to give a Soviet leaning to newly independent states.

Colonialism is on its last legs now, and millions of people in Asia, Africa, and Latin America are rising to a new life, winning national independence and thereby the right to independent national development. The wave of the national-liberation movement is surging higher and higher, and its mighty blows are undermining and breaking the mainstays of colonialism, even in those countries where the people, if we are to believe the colonialists, recently had no thought of getting rid of their European "benefactors."

Together with all the freedom-loving peoples we rejoice in the success of the great liberation movement of the peoples of Asia, Africa, and Latin America, and express confidence that the day is not far off when the peoples will finally throw off the shameful yoke of colonialism.[8]

Imperialists like to talk of their "friendship" with the colonial peoples. But what they want in this friendship is that the "friend"—for that is the kindly term they use—should in fact be their slave, that he should work humbly for his "friend," the colonialist, and that the latter should enjoy all the fruits of his work.

It is this sort of "friendship" which the imperialist Powers want. What they change occasionally is only the forms of that "friendship," while seeking to perpetuate its essence—the exploitation of one nation by another.[9]

Our disinterested and principled foreign policy . . . is not a contemplative, but an active policy of struggle against evil forces, aggressive, monopolistic and colonialist forces which have not renounced their hopes of perpetuating colonial slavery, of continuing to plunder and exploit the peoples of Asia and Africa.[10]

There are no people more steadfast and devoted to the cause of the struggle against colonialists than communists. More steadfast forces in the struggle against imperialism do not exist than those of communism. It is due to no mere accident that the imperialists are directing the spearhead of their attack against the communist movement.[11]

Our people, like hundreds of millions of people all over the globe, have sympathized with, and still sympathize with peoples engaged in the struggle for freedom, and against the colonizers and grasping imperialists, and wish the oppressed peoples complete success in their struggle for freedom.[12]

The point has been aptly made that while the West has cooperated by liberating thirty-three colonial nations since 1940, the Soviet Union has not only absorbed the contiguous "republics," [13] infiltrated Outer Mongolia,[14] but also added to its own territory all of the Baltic states and virtually annexed the nations of the Soviet bloc.[15]

Khrushchev's attempts to undermine the economic relations between the former colonies and the West reflect an expectation of a cold-war advantage for the Soviet Union by narrowing the market for the West . . .

The problem is becoming all the more acute because the frontiers of the world market are increasingly contracting as a result of the formation of the new and growing socialist world market. Besides, the underdeveloped countries, on casting off the colonial yoke, begin the development of their own industry which inevitably leads to a further narrowing of markets for industrial products. All this means that the struggle for markets and spheres of influence will become still sharper within the imperialist camp.[16]

. . . and denying it raw materials.

Afro-Asian countries play an essential part in limiting aggression in an economic respect. They are important suppliers of raw materials for the Western powers. The supporters of aggression understand that when the majority of Afro-Asian countries follow a peace-loving policy, they are unable to count on the use of the rich resources of Afro-Asian countries in their aggressive plans.[17]

Even more important to Mr. Khrushchev are the political implications of alienating the new countries from Western influence. A major restraint to Khrushchev's expansion has been the United Nations, which acts like an international fire brigade. A major Soviet objective is to dominate or neutralize the United Nations. Probably Khrushchev expected that the thirty-three new African nations[18] would provide the tool for such domination. To this extent he may have been disappointed in the October 1960 session. But the defeat was far from complete. By spurring the African nations to a sense of their new power, he has set in motion pressures for trinary administration in the United Nations as a whole and in each of its committees.[19] Although his success may be limited in this direction, it may well produce stalemates that will prevent effective United Nations action, leading in turn, to compromises more favorable to the communist cause. The Khrushchev antics that met with disgust and disdain served, in a substantial way, to prove to African leaders that even great nations can be bullied. For those who had been humiliated for years by the white man and the northerner, there was a priceless satisfaction in hearing the former masters abused and insulted—even if these were their best friends.

The West is, of course, torn between the indefensible moral position of nineteenth-century colonialism and allegiance to its allies. This provides a major fissure for the entry of Soviet operations.[20]

Neutralizing the Underdeveloped Countries

"In Khrushchev's view, the 'uncommitted' group of states was a sort of infant class or prep school through which the colonial countries pass before graduating as socialist states and joining the socialist camp." [21]

Although they do not belong to the socialist world system, these countries can nevertheless draw on its achievement to build independent national economies and raise the living standards of their peoples. Today they need not go begging to their former oppressors for modern equipment; they can get it in the socialist countries, free of any political or military obligations.[22]

Says one student of Soviet affairs:

"At present, the positive encouragement of Asian and African neutralism is clearly established as a cardinal guideline of Soviet diplomacy; and the reason is clearly discernible. Given the present realities of the world situation, the Soviet Union cannot but prefer this course to a more blatantly aggressive form of attempted southward expansion, which would risk provoking a major armed conflict." [23]

There are countries that are not socialist but which cannot be regarded as belonging to the imperialist system. Having won their national independence as a result of a liberation struggle, these countries want to follow a path of their own, by-passing the capitalist stage of development so that, having done away with colonial oppression, they can start building a society on different principles.

Many of the leaders of these countries say that they want to build socialism. True, they pronounce the word "communism" with difficulty and it is not always clear what they mean by socialism. However, there is no doubt that they are well-disposed to the socialist countries, do not consider them as antagonists, do not regard the socialist countries as opponents of their striving to build a new life without the imperialists, without colonial oppression. For that reason good, friend-

ly relations have been established between the socialist countries and these states, and normal economic relations are developing between them. We are coming forward together in
the struggle for the peace and security of the peoples for
banning the atomic and hydrogen weapons, against the colonialist policy of the imperialists.

And so if we take the countries forming the world socialist
system and the countries waging a courageous struggle
against imperialism and colonialism, for their freedom and
national independence, we shall find that the scale is already
now tipping in favor of these peace-loving countries and not
in favor of the imperialist states. These peace-loving countries
eclipse the imperialist states in territory, population, and natural wealth.[24]

To the world he points out the advantages of neutralism:

History teaches us that certain states which conducted a
neutral policy during war or a policy of nonparticipation in
military blocs have for this very reason helped to secure the
safety of their peoples, and have on the whole played a positive, pacific role. Such a policy corresponds to the national
interests of these states, increases their security, and does
not divert them into any unnecessary and unprofitable waste
of their productive forces in military expenditure.

For many decades now the benefits of neutrality have been
enjoyed by such countries as Switzerland and Sweden. An
important role in the struggle for peace and security is being
played by such states as India, Indonesia, Burma, the United
Arab Republic, Cambodia, and other countries that pursue a
policy of nonparticipation in military blocs. Their position
earns understanding and sympathy.[25]

**Some observers hold that true neutralism, if it can be attained, is
not itself to be feared by the West.**

**". . . 'neutralism' is a perfectly satisfactory, even desirable, policy
for most newly independent countries, from the point of view of our
interests as well as theirs. The key to neutralism is not pro-Commu-**

nism but pro-independence. It is a combination of 'a plague on both your houses' and 'I'll take help where I can get it.' " [26]

Communists, however, do not all believe in neutralism. Their version is known as a "lean-to-one-side" policy, noted by Mao Tse-tung:

"To lean to one side is a lesson taught us by the forty years of experience of Sun Yat-sen and the twenty-eight years of experience of the Communist Party. We firmly believe that, in order to attain and consolidate victory, we must lean to one side. . . . Not only in China, but in the whole world, one leans without exception either to the side of imperialism or to the side of socialism. Neutrality is a hoax." [27]

It is the ties with communism, the beachholds the communists can take, that offer problems.

The commonwealth of socialist countries is not reserved and isolated from nonsocialist nations and their peoples. Our country has consolidated friendly ties with India, Indonesia, and Burma, the United Arab Republic, and other states of Asia and Africa whose peoples have cast off the yoke of colonialism and are at present struggling to consolidate the independence of their young states.[28]

"Because the immediate Soviet objective is to change the power configuration of the world, it is often more important for them to strengthen a nationalistic bourgeois society than to convert it to socialism. In Soviet ideology, this is still described as the period of the first stage of collaboration with 'bourgeois nationalism,' but it must be understood that general Soviet strategy, rather than the revolutionary transformation of these particular areas, is governing, in the present and immediate future period of Soviet policy. It should be understood, however, that the takeover stage is deferred, not abandoned." [29]

One of the cardinal elements of the Soviet outlook is the belief that the revolutionary wave now sweeping across Asia, Africa, and Latin America is an important factor favorable to Soviet interests, perhaps decisively so.

119

The solidarity of the peoples of Asia is a mortal blow for the world colonial system.[30]

The Soviets see the West losing colonial power, markets, sources of raw materials, and substantial investments in the underdeveloped countries.

Analyzing the world situation at the end of the colonial era, Khrushchev decries the persistent influence of the Western nations. [31]

The sharpening of the general crisis of capitalism is making itself felt with particular force in the disintegration of the colonial system. The trend is toward the complete abolition of that infamous system. India, Indonesia, Burma, Egypt, Syria, and a number of other countries have already won their freedom. The Eastern countries that have shaken off colonial tyranny are seeking to build up their economies and regenerate their cultures as speedily as possible. The popular movement for national independence and freedom is expanding in all colonial and dependent countries.

Those countries which until recently were reduced to a colonial or semi-colonial status now want more than political liberation—they also want to get rid of the economic fetters which make them dependent on the capitalist powers. A bitter struggle for influence in the colonial and semi-colonial countries is taking place between the imperialist groups of the United States and Britain. The colonialists have had to withdraw from some of the countries, but they left there helpers recruited among the bourgeoisie and the feudal chiefs, who, while pretending to uphold the interests of their countries, actually implement the policies of the imperialist conquerors.[32]

Every country has its people educated in the colonial systems connected with imperialist circles. History has passed its sentence on colonialism. Its era, cursed by mankind, becomes a thing of the past, but as everything which is old, decrepit, and vile, colonialism does not let go of life without cunning attacks and baseness. The roots of colonialism have been eradicated, but here and there some bits remain. The colonizers attempt in every way to prolong their domination. That is why the peoples who have liberated themselves from the colonial yoke must be vigilant.[33]

Stalin saw the hostility existing between colonial people and imperialist nations as a wedge, one of the contradictions in capitalism to be exploited:

"The practical task of communist policy is to take advantage of this hostility and to incite one against the other."[34]

And Khrushchev denounces the "capitalist" countries and warns the newly independent nations: The United States is a villain, substituting for the old colonial powers.

What is new about the present situation is that although the United States leaders in the past did not openly admit their role as colonialists, they now cannot conceal this fact from the peoples. People can now see more clearly that there is actually no difference at all between the imperialists of Great Britain and those of the U.S.A., since both use armed force against the vital interests of all countries struggling for their national independence, struggling against colonialists.[35]

Again:

It is important for Khrushchev to split the former colonial countries from the West. Most of the newly independent nations were—and are—trying to build a democratic society. Only in exceptional cases —as in Indochina and Cuba—did the communists gain control over the liberation movement.

A first step is to credit Western wealth to exploitation of colonies.

The ruling circles in countries which waxed rich at the expense of the colonies, and go on doing so, do not mind boasting that there is a high standard of living in their countries. However, this high standard was secured at the cost of millions of wasted lives, by the exhaustion of which entire peoples were reduced, and by the fact that millions upon millions of people in the colonies were reduced to death or starvation.

Capitalism cannot exist without plundering the masses of the people, without oppression and exploitation. A small handful of men appropriate the people's enormous wealth. The imperialists waxed rich and do so now by plundering not only the people in their own countries but also the peoples in the colonies. The imperialists plundered and continue to plunder many peoples in Africa and Asia. But the peoples in many countries have thrown off the fetters of colonialism in recent times and have gained their national independence. Now colonialism is cracking along all seams![36]

The exploiting classes seek to enslave and plunder not only their own peoples, but also peoples of colonial and dependent countries. Colonialism is a monstrous outcome of the epoch of capitalism.[37]

Each of the devices conceived as aids to underdeveloped countries, Khrushchev decries as a new imperialism.

An "international gendarmery" . . .

Today the colonial system is disintegrating. The ruling circles of the U.S.A. are trying to stop this process and they are now playing the part of an international gendarmery acting against the peoples who are struggling for freedom and independence. But they do not want to fight with their own hands, for this would be a too obvious interference. That is why the U.S.A. wants to use other countries. And such shameful affairs are concealed under inventions about the "menace of communism." [38]

The imperialists want to build up a kind of international police force which would virtually be under the control of the United States and be used to suppress the peoples who have risen against colonial slavery. This will not succeed! The peace-loving peoples are strong enough to counter intrigues of the imperialists, to frustrate their perfidious designs. There is no force on earth which could halt the movement of the peoples fighting for their independence, for their liberation.[39]

Protective alliances . . .

To maintain their domination, to keep the colonial countries dependent, the imperialists are devising expedients. They are looking for new forms to place the peoples of the economically underdeveloped countries in their bondage. The imperialists are creating aggressive pacts and alliances, such as NATO, the Baghdad Pact, SEATO, and the like. For this purpose the imperialists of the United States and Britain are concluding bilateral treaties and military agreements of all descriptions with a number of countries. But all these pacts, blocs, and treaties are nothing but an artfully disguised aspect of the very same policy of the imperialists: on the pretext of protecting countries from the threat of communism, to keep these countries in complete dependence on the principal imperialist powers and to paralyze the efforts of the peoples in their liberation struggle against the colonialists, those hardened imperialist exploiters.[40]

Especially dangerous to the peoples of Asia, Africa, and Latin America are various forms of collective colonialism. It is impossible not to mention such manifestations of colonialism as military political blocs.[41]

Even foreign aid:

The colonizers give a dollar in "aid" in order to receive ten dollars later in return by exploiting the peoples who have accepted such "aid." After this, they enslave the peoples politically. Such are the "new" forms of colonial domination.[42]

The ideologists of imperialism circulate myths concerning the equality of peoples and countries in the so-called "free world." They make lavish promises of "aid" to small and underdeveloped nations in their efforts to lull the vigilance of the peoples of those countries and make these lands in one way or another subservient to themselves. Pitiless suppression and cruel exploitation of the weak by the strong always was and continues to be the wolf law of capitalism, where the strong devour the weak.[43]

The press in Western states devotes much space to the need for rendering economic aid to underdeveloped countries. We are in favor of such assistance. Let us compete in this field. But such aid must be rendered as to enable the country assisted to really develop its economy and to rid itself of dependence on economically stronger countries, actually ensuring its independence. It is precisely such assistance that the underdeveloped countries need.

If underdeveloped countries are to be helped, this must be done in a way to enable them to increase their economic potential, in order to strengthen these states, and help them stand on their own feet. But the imperialists cannot accept this because it contradicts the essence of imperialism.[44]

The imperialists use their economic relations with the underdeveloped countries as instruments of blackmail and extortion. They saddle these countries with military and political conditions. Our country, on the other hand, bases its relations with all states on complete equality and cooperation, with no military or political strings attached. We do not indulge in charity. The Soviet Union renders help on a fair commercial basis.[45]

It is our belief that the aid which is rendered to the underdeveloped countries should not place them in dependence on the rich and the economically highly developed countries. Many capitalist countries, however, adhere to another policy. They give credits to the underdeveloped countries solely for military purposes. Obviously the receipt of credits does not raise the economic potential of a country which is granted such credit, but on the contrary lowers this potential.[46]

But the Soviet Union finally joined in providing aid on a minimum scale:

The socialist countries help the underdeveloped countries to build up their own industry, whereas the United States are trying to sell them consumers' goods which have no market at home.[47]

Our state renders aid to other countries because we, communists, Marxist-Leninists, do not remain closed up within our frontiers. We consider the cause of building socialism and communism to be a great international affair. It is not accidental that the enemies concentrate their main fire against the Soviet Union. They know that the working people of all countries, the oppressed people, identify the Soviet Union, our Communist Party, with all great transformation which the working class brings to humanity. . . . The imperialists understand that the Soviet Union is a burning torch which is visible to the working people of the whole world and which shows to them the path in the struggle for a bright future.[48]

Another form of relations is that between the socialist countries and the economically underdeveloped countries which need economic aid. As a result of the colonialist policy of many centuries, the economy of many countries of Asia and Africa which recently gained independence is considerably lagging. The Soviet Union and the other countries of the socialist camp deem it their duty to help them, to expand by every means trade with them and other forms of economic relations. One may not, of course, say that in this case our economic relations are based on mutual advantage. Speaking generally from the commercial viewpoint, our economic and technical aid to the underdeveloped countries is even unprofitable for us. But we hold that aid to the underdeveloped countries is necessary from the viewpoint of humanity and of general human solidarity.[49]

The record:

AID FROM THE SOVIET BLOC [50]

Total	3.8 billion*
USSR	2.6 billion*
Bloc countries	1.2 billion

*This represents the amount in credits created, only a small amount of which was actually disbursed; 1.2 billion in materials and advice was also given, of which 800 million was in military aid.

AID FROM THE WESTERN POWERS

Total	18	billion
United States	12	billion[51]
France	3.8	billion
Britain	1	billion
Other Western	1.2	billion

Soviet aid went principally to United Arab Republic ($962 million), Indonesia ($402 million), India ($323 million), Iraq ($257 million), and Afghanistan ($245 million). In 1960 four "trouble spots" were added to the list—Ethiopia, Guinea, Ghana, and Cuba. The political rewards are obvious.[52]

Of the nonmilitary aid, a substantial part is in "technicians"—salaries for well-indoctrinated specialists who serve dual purposes.

The former colonial countries, comprising the underdeveloped areas of the world, need economic and technical assistance. As early as January 1949, in his Inaugural Address, President Harry S. Truman recommended to the United States Congress the launching of a vast program of technical and economic aid designed to bring economic and social stability to these areas, which comprise the majority of mankind.

President Truman's proposal formed the basis for the Expanded Program of Technical Assistance approved that same year by the United Nations.

The Soviet Union denounced the U.N. program as an "imperialist attempt" to dominate economically the underdeveloped areas and refused to take part in it. Only after Stalin's death did the Soviet Union reverse its position and announce that it was willing to assist this program.

Soviet contributions to the U.N. technical-assistance effort are still modest: 4.6 million nonconvertible rubles annually ($1.15 million dollars at the old exchange rate of 25c) versus $40 million from the United States. Use of nonconvertible currency amounts to providing unilateral assistance through international agencies.[53]

Furthermore, from 1949 to 1959 the United States contributed an additional $23.5 million to eight United Nations agencies designed to aid underdeveloped areas; the USSR, $7.5 million, figuring the ruble at the official rate.

Who if not the United Nations should be the first to extend a helping hand to peoples liberating themselves, to insure their inalienable right to be masters of their own destiny and to shape their life without any pressure or encroachments from without? And is it not the duty of the United Nations to contribute to the utmost to the economic advancement of the new states rising from the ruins of the colonial system, to help them speedily to build up their national economies? This can only be achieved by the provision of large-scale economic assistance without any political or other strings attached. And that is the position taken by the Soviet Union on the question of economic aid, which we are rendering and intend to render in future to many countries. This position, we feel, fully accords with the principles of the United Nations Charter.[54]

The principle expounded by Khrushchev, according to which the United Nations is the natural channel for disinterested economic help to needy nations, is hardly reflected in the actions of the Soviet government.

But Khrushchev, with the help of some dialectics and much abuse, can explain why the USSR does not feel obligated to provide more aid to the underdeveloped countries:

The imperialists have reduced those countries to poverty, their peoples are rising in rebellion, and now the imperialists would like us to help them pacify the insurgent peoples for the sake of maintaining the old order and to give our money for this purpose. . . .

The imperialists have been plundering the peoples of Asia and Africa for centuries. They do not mind boasting that high living standards have been attained in their countries. But this is largely due to the exploitation of the Afro-Asian peoples, to the fact that millions of people have died of poverty and starvation.

The imperialists have pumped tremendous wealth out of the colonial and dependent countries. Let them return at least a portion of what they have plundered. They are under obligation to do this.[55]

"The psychological and political effect on the peoples concerned and the propaganda effect in the world at large has been incommensurate with the modest investment of the Soviet bloc—modest if compared with the effort of the Western world, particularly the United States.

"The reasons for this success of the Communists are variously explained.

"A feature of the bloc campaign which has had great appeal to the recipients is the apparent willingness to provide types of projects which an underdeveloped country wants without requiring economic justification for the project or attempting to secure governmental reform of various economic policies. Nor does the bloc appear to require the various accounting checks which are involved in U.S. programs. That bloc aid is not without its political objectives and conditions, however, has been well illustrated by the historic 'postponement' of credits to Yugoslavia when ideological conflict occurred and the pressure on Finland when government policies were offended.

"An important aspect of the Sino-Soviet economic offensive is the employment of bloc technicians in free world countries. At the end of 1959, there were more than 6,500 such technicians, mostly concentrated in seven countries—the United Arab Republic, Yemen, Afghanistan, India, Iraq, Cambodia, and Indonesia. The vigor, skill, and general technical competence with which the Sino-Soviet bloc pursues its expanding economic offensive provides no grounds for complacency."[56]

A recent Congressional study points out:

128

Neutralizing the Underdeveloped Countries

"Western services are usually supplied within a framework of individual projects, many of them small and aimed at very specific training results; this aid is typically supplied free in a setting of mutual cooperation in which the recipient takes care of the local cost. Soviet technical assistance is more frequently part of a larger package, consisting of loans, development goods, and bilateral trade; the services of experts are not free, but are charged against the loan, if not accounted for separately, and these charges are quite high, sometimes higher than the West's." [57]

And:

"There is a second, a psychological factor of equal importance. By accepting local products the bloc not only frees primary producing countries from the periodic worry where to dispose of their surplus but, in fact, undertakes to create a new market for them. More important, it makes these countries feel that they are given the tools for their development and the chance to pay for them with the fruits of their economic growth and the products of their soil, so that the repayment promises to be painless and the loans virtually self-liquidating.

"Finally, the bloc's interest rates are much lower than the West's. This has clearly both an economic and a psychological-political impact. To give an example, the Soviet loan for the Chilai steel plant in India calls for 2½ per cent interest while the World Bank loans for the expansion of the Tata Iron & Steel Company carry interest at 4¾ and 6 per cent: this clearly adds up to sizable sums over a time." [58]

In India, a columnist for *The Hindustan Times* comments:

"The United States is like the older brother who helps to provide food, shelter and clothing for his struggling younger brother but cannot afford to provide spending money. The Soviet Union is like the uncle who gives the boy spending money and wins affection, while the older brother is taken for granted." [59]

"The apparent success of Soviet efforts with foreign assistance has made some wonder whether or not the United States should emulate the Soviet Union in the conduct of its foreign assistance program. It must be remembered, however, that the Soviet program is an imitation of United States aid, particularly as embodied in the Marshall plan and Truman doctrine. Furthermore, the objectives of the two nations must be borne in mind. The Soviet Union hopes to break Western alliances and gain political influence by selective use of small amounts of assistance and a great deal of publicity. The United States is interested in economic development, hoping thereby to create conditions helpful to United States interests in terms of economically and politically stable democratic regimes. If the United States were to try to imitate the Soviet Union, it would do violence to its basic aims and would probably spend its entire time and substance chasing around putting out fires." [60]

Capitalizing on the rising expectations of underdeveloped nations, the Soviet Union holds itself out to underdeveloped countries as a model of the effectiveness of its form of socialism in enabling a nation to pull itself up by its own bootstraps to an industrial stature. (See Chapter 12.)

Obviously the underdeveloped countries are not in the position that the Soviet was in 1913.

But still Khrushchev can say:

Of course the existence and development of the Soviet Union and the other socialist countries play a tremendous role in the growth of the self-awareness of the colonial or formerly colonial and semicolonial countries. Their successful development is there for everyone to see. These countries, such as China, for instance, and some others were also in their time exploited and economically backward countries. Today they have completely changed their faces, have achieved tremendous successes in the development of their economy, culture, and the construction of the new society. Thus the socialist states are manifestly demonstrating the advantages of socialism as a more just, more progressive social system.[61]

The Middle East

It has been noted earlier that the Soviet Union concentrates its economic assistance in certain areas according to the needs, not of the peoples involved, but of the strategic and political interests of Moscow.[62]

The most revealing example is the manner in which the Soviets penetrated the Middle East. Strategically, this area linking Europe, Asia, and Africa, has always been coveted by conquerors, from Alexander the Great through Napoleon, to the empire builders of the nineteenth century, and to the German would-be conquerors of the twentieth.

Not only inescapable logic, but historic documents give the lie to Khrushchev's assertions that Soviet policy in the Middle East is purely altruistic, benevolent, humanitarian.

Thus, while Khrushchev says . . .

Grossly distorting our peace-loving policy, imperialist quarters raise a rumpus about the Soviet Union's "special" interest in this area. We indignantly reject these utterly false assertions. In our disinterested aid to the Middle Eastern nations, we have never pursued any selfish aims.[63]

. . . the secret protocols attached to the German-Soviet Pact of 1939, made public after World War II, clearly state:

"In accordance with the foregoing, the draft of the protocol concerning the delimitation of the spheres of influence as outlined by the Reich Foreign Minister would have to be amended so as to stipulate the focal point of the aspirations of the Soviet Union south of Batum and Baku in the general direction of the Persian Gulf." [64]

And Khrushchev notes:

The Middle East has a great natural wealth and is of key strategic importance. Egypt, for instance, has the Suez Canal. It straddles the way from Europe to Asia.[65]

"Russian ambitions in this part of the world are not new. They go back at least as far as Catherine the Great. In their earlier form, Russian designs on the area were tied up with the urge for warm-water ports on the Mediterranean Sea and the Persian Gulf. Now, of course, they form but a part of the Soviet master plan for world domination.

"In 1913, four years before the revolution, Joseph Stalin wrote a paper entitled 'Nationalism and the Colonial Question,' and this, along with two theses by Lenin presented to Third International meetings in the 1920s, constitutes a sort of handbook of Soviet encroachment on this area. Very simply, the communist plan calls for the Soviet Union to make common cause with the nationalists of the Middle East in their struggles against the colonial powers while establishing and always maintaining a separate communist organization with the tightest internal discipline. When the nationalists have succeeded in expelling colonial forces and neutralizing or destroying Western influence, the communists (by now thoroughly infiltrated into the nationalist organization) turn against the nationalist patriots, seize the levers of power, and set up a communist state linked to the Soviet Union.

"The U.S.S.R. has systematically applied this plan since opposition to Bolshevism was finally suppressed in its own central Asian territories contiguous to the area." [66]

The strategic importance of the Suez Canal hardly needs emphasizing. Added to this is the great dependence of Western Europe on Middle East oil. Former British Foreign Minister Anthony Eden made it clear to Khrushchev just how essential oil is to Great Britain. Khrushchev often refers to it (the essential points are confirmed by Eden in his memoirs). Mr. Khrushchev's version:

In the course of our [Khrushchev and Nicolai Bulganin, then Premier of the Soviet Government] visit to Britain in 1956, for instance, Messieurs Eden and Lloyd said to us: "If anything happens in the Middle East and we stop getting oil from there, we shall not stop at war." We said to them, "It is easy to begin a war, but hard to stop it. Even a fool

132

can start a war, and it is most likely that a war would be started by an unwise man. And it is a hard thing to stop a war, even for a clever man. Please, do not forget this." At the same time we frankly warned Mr. Eden and Mr. Lloyd, "If you start a war in this area, we cannot remain in the role of spectators." [67]

A few months later, Egypt's ruler, Gamal Abdel Nasser, nationalized the Suez Canal, thus precipitating a major world crisis precisely because the oil route was endangered.

By the time Nasser struck, he felt himself assured of Soviet support. In fact, he had already received on credit Soviet-bloc military equipment of an estimated value of $450 million. A new dependence had begun. Egyptian exports to the Soviet-bloc countries had jumped from 12.5 per cent of their total in 1954 to 34.3 per cent in 1956. Khrushchev continued to promise economic aid to Nasser, duly noting that Nasser was supporting Soviet foreign policy.

The Soviet Government is willing to send the necessary number of specialists to the United Arab Republic, to supply the United Arab Republic with the necessary machinery and equipment and with the materials it lacks for the accomplishment of the project [the Aswan Dam], and to grant a loan of up to 400 million rubles to cover the expenses involved.

As in previous discussions between the government leaders of the Soviet Union and the United Arab Republic, we have ascertained that our views coincide on current international problems of decisive importance for the preservation and consolidation of world peace. This identity of views is not a matter of mere coincidence. It follows from the entire course of historical development of our peoples and rests on the principles of sincere friendship and unselfish cooperation, in the name of peace and the prosperity of the peoples of our countries.

At the United Nations, the Soviet Union and the United Arab Republic maintain a common stand on disarmament, the banning of nuclear weapons, the ending of nuclear tests and on other important questions connected with safeguarding international peace and security. [68]

Nasser's United Arab Republic received one-third of all Soviet foreign aid between 1954 and 1959.

Khrushchev makes it abundantly clear that strategic considerations outweigh ideological differences. When Nasser visited Moscow, Khrushchev was lavish in his praise of Egypt's dictator:

I drink to the health of our dear guest, the President of the United Arab Republic, Gamal Abdel Nasser, to the national hero who boldly raised the banner of struggle against the colonialists; who has waged and is waging a struggle for the independence of his Republic and the other Arab nations which have still not thrown off the colonialist yoke.[69]

Later, he commented:

Recently the President of the UAR, Mr. Nasser, was here. Our conversation with him was pleasant and useful. I am a communist and he is the leader of the Arab national liberation movement. He does not share our political views. But when we exchanged opinions on the situation which had arisen in the Middle East there was mutual understanding—I understood him and he understood me.[70]

Nasser is not a communist and politically he is closer to those waging war on him.[71]

And again:

Many Arabs, and I have in mind first and foremost the leaders of the Arab countries, are very remote from communist ideas. In Egypt, for instance, many communists are held in prison. The leaders of the Arab countries are nationalists, they are against colonial slavery and they stand for the consolidation of their political and economic independence.[72]

In this respect as in many others, Khrushchev follows Stalin's line— after all, German communists were crowded in Nazi concentration camps while Stalin concluded a friendship pact with Hitler in 1939.

134

Neutralizing the Underdeveloped Countries

The military action undertaken in October 1956 by the British, French, and Israelis was opposed not only by the Soviet Union but also by the United States, and indeed by the overwhelming majority of the United Nations. Khrushchev, however, takes the credit:

Who has raised his voice in strong protest against these imperialist forces? The Soviet Union has. Not only has it raised its voice in protest, but it issued a stern warning to the aggressors. Today everybody knows that much of the credit for ending the war in Egypt goes to the Soviet Union.[73]

In fact, on the occasion of the Suez crisis, the Soviet Union for the first time used its intimidation-through-rockets technique, later perfected by Khrushchev. The stern warning to which Khrushchev refers above was a threat to subject Britain, France, and Israel to rocket bombardment unless they withdrew from Egypt.

As for the United States position at the time of the Suez crisis, Khrushchev has his own explanation, designed to disturb the Anglo-American friendship.

He [Eisenhower] sees that the decrepit British lion, which once kept many peoples of Asia and Africa in a state of fear by its growling, has now become weak and hoarse and has lost its tail in Egypt.

Now it is American imperialism which is forcing its way into the Near and Middle East to replace this lion, to replace British and French imperialism.[74]

The voice of the Soviet people in Egypt's defense was listened to above all because of the might of the Soviet Union, because all the Soviet people unanimously support the policy of our party and the Soviet government. It was listened to because of the indissoluble friendship between the Soviet Union and all the socialist countries. We must support the Egyptian people in their just struggle for independence and seek the withdrawal of the aggressors' forces from Egypt. The Suez Canal rightfully belongs to the Egyptian state, which has ensured and will ensure freedom of shipping on this canal for all countries concerned after repairs.[75]

The West is continually portrayed as a greedy exploiter.

What are the causes of this dangerous aggravation of the situation in the Near East? The principal cause is the insatiable greed of large oil monopolies and especially of those of the United States, their attempts to assure themselves an unlimited domination in the region of the Near and Middle East.[76]

The people of the Arab world see that it is not the Soviet Union but the British, French, American, and other imperialists who are seizing and plundering their national wealth and are hauling away Near and Middle Eastern oil for next to nothing.

This is something the Soviet Union has never done and will never do. It is rendering disinterested assistance to the Arab countries in their righteous struggle for national independence. These are the facts; this is the truth, obvious to everyone, above all to the people of the Arab countries.[77]

On March 9, 1957, the United States declared its readiness "to use armed force to assist any . . . nation [in the Middle East] or group of . . . nations requesting assistance against armed aggression from any country controlled by international communism."

Mr. Khrushchev erupted:

When the French and British colonialists had discredited themselves, the U.S.A. pretended that it was hastening to their aid, putting forward, among other things, the notorious "Dulles-Eisenhower doctrine." But this "support" on the part of the United States imperialist circles, calculated to retain imperialist influence in the Near and Middle East, is not unlike the support which the rope gives the man on the gallows. Creating the impression of supporting the interests of Britain and France, the U.S.A. is actually doing everything to oust them from the countries of the Near and Middle East, to undermine their influence in the colonial and dependent countries, and take their place. In pursuit of its aims it is conducting a more camouflaged colonialist policy than that of the British and French.[78]

The Eisenhower doctrine and the British-Jordanian treaty were applied in the summer of 1958.[79] At the request of the Lebanese Government, United States troops landed in Lebanon, then threatened by a civil war. Not a shot was fired—a fact admitted by Anastas Mikoyan, then Soviet First Deputy Premier: "There was no killing in Lebanon because the Lebanese decided not to resist when your forces entered the country." [80]

Khrushchev fulminated:

By their actions in Lebanon and Jordan the governments of the United States and Great Britain are dealing a body blow at this international organization. At such a momentous hour in the life of the peoples, the United Nations has actually been pushed out of the way with the bayonets of the American and British forces.[81]

And the Soviet propaganda machine proclaimed: "The Western imperialist powers have barbarously attacked Lebanon. . . ." [82]

"In speaking about the situation in Lebanon, American broadcasts and papers try to conceal the true situation there. Deliberately they fail to mention a single word about the popular resistance which was encountered by the interventionists, although this resistance exists and cannot be concealed." [83]

One means designed by the West and its Middle East allies to stem the Soviet advance toward the Persian Gulf and South Asia was the Baghdad Pact, which united Iraq, Turkey, Iran, Pakistan, Great Britain, and France—with the United States as an associate member.

It is hardly surprising that Khrushchev did not like this defense treaty. This he says in so many words:

We very much dislike the Baghdad Pact. . . . But we have patience and are confident that the Baghdad Pact will burst like a soap bubble, leaving only an unpleasant memory.[84]

This "patience" was not an inactive one. In 1957 Iraq was the center of continuous intrigue and on July 14, 1958, a revolution broke out in that country, overthrowing the monarchy and bringing to power a group of young Army officers. Communists played a leading role in the revolution, which resulted in Iraq's withdrawal from the Baghdad Pact. Khrushchev was exultant:

The imperialists created the aggressive Baghdad Pact. Then the Dulles-Eisenhower doctrine, directed against the national-liberation movement in the countries, was proclaimed. But what came of this? No pacts or doctrines can stay the struggle of the peoples for their liberation. In Iraq the people have overthrown the domination of the imperialists. The U.S.A. sent its troops into Lebanon, and Britain sent its into Jordan. They wanted to strangle the Republic of Iraq. The United States and British intervention aroused the wrath of the peoples of the whole world. The ruling circles of the U.S.A. and Great Britain hemmed and hawed but were compelled to recognize the Republic of Iraq.[85]

And:

We acclaim the Government of the Iraq Republic, we acclaim the Prime Minister of the Iraq Republic, Abdel Karim Kassem, for his courage and determination, for his devotion to his people and fine character—he does not fear the imperialists.[86]

Take the recent revolution in Iraq. Iraq was considered a stanch support for the imperialist countries in the Middle East. Yet the Iraqis managed to break out of the imperialist trap, into which their country had been lured by the reactionaries headed by a traitor king and a corrupt government obedient to the will and directives of foreign monopolists to the detriment of the interests of their country and people.[87]

Now two strong men ruled in the Middle East: Nasser of the United Arab Republic and Kassem of Iraq. But both Khrushchev and

138

Nasser viewed Iraq as their area of influence—Khrushchev, as a potential communist beachhead; Nasser, as part of his greater United Arab Republic.

There are no people more resolute and loyal to the struggle against colonialists than the communists.[88]

Cultivation of friendship with the Arab nations required an anti-Zionist attitude . . .[89]

We understand the aspirations of the peoples of Arab countries who are fighting for complete liberation from foreign dependence. At the same time the actions of Israel, which from the very first days of its existence began to threaten its neighbors and to pursue an unfriendly policy toward them, should be condemned.[90]

It is wrong to accuse the communists of acting counter to the national interests of the Arab peoples. It is likewise naive to place on the same footing communism and Zionism. It is a matter of general knowledge that the communists, including those in Israel, are waging a struggle against Zionism.[91]

. . . and promises of support for the Arabs.

The British statesmen then told us that the correlation of forces in that area was not in favor of the Arabs, and that Israel could defeat the Arab states. We retorted by saying that those who think so were cherishing a futile hope. The population of Israel amounted to approximately 1.5 million, whereas the population of the Arab states was over 70 million. We said that if Israel was to unleash a war against the Arabs, we believed the latter would start a holy war against the invaders, and this war would inevitably end in the defeat of the aggressors. All progressive mankind would back the Arab nations. The moral support of the Arab nations would entail material support in this case, and also participation of volunteers in the Arab struggle against the invaders, we said.[92]

Khrushchev, despite the difficulties he experienced in his relations with the revolutionary Arab leaders, could hope to maintain and increase his influence in important areas of the Middle East; his main objective—destruction of the Western defense positions in the area—remained.

Before the ink had even dried on the joint communiqué on the results of the Geneva conference, some of our partners in the conference had begun to involve new countries in the aggressive Baghdad Pact. They drew in Iran and are dragging in other states. . . . The governments of Iran and Turkey are hardly behaving reasonably when they link their fate to the aggressive Baghdad Pact and refuse to establish good neighborly relations with the Soviet Union.[93]

Ill-disguised threats are directed at Iran, Turkey, Pakistan.

Whom then does the Shah of Iran really fear? He does not fear us, but he fears his own people. He is, it seems, not sure of the stability of his throne. And this is why he keeps his private capital not in Iran but in Britain. He is seriously worried by what happened in Iraq. As is known, the Baghdad Pact was named after the capital of Iraq, Baghdad. And when the people of Iraq rose up against the power of the rotten throne and of the Iraqi Government which had sold itself to the imperialists, then neither the Baghdad Pact nor the Dulles-Eisenhower doctrine helped. The lesson to be learned from this is that neither a bilateral nor even a quinquelateral treaty can save any rotten throne from its own people.[94]

The stand taken by the leaders of Turkey, a neighbor of ours, causes regret. The existence of atomic bases and rocket sites on Turkish territory threatens the peaceful population of the country with catastrophe. Apparently, the bellicose-minded Turkish leaders do not have sufficient information about how hot the things are toward which they are stretching their hands, and forget that they can burn their fingers. This also applies to other countries whose leaders agree to the setting up of military bases.[95]

Pakistan is also a young state. But the policy of the ruling circles of this state alarms us. The facts indicate that their policy is not based on the vital interests of their people, of their state, but is dictated by the monopolist circles of other countries. The present government of Pakistan frankly announces its special closeness to American monopolist circles. It was one of the first participants in, one of the initiators of, the notorious Baghdad Pact, which certainly was not set up in the interests of peace. It allows American military bases to be set up on its territory, very close to the borders of the Soviet Union.[96]

India

In the underdeveloped areas of the world the main objective of Soviet policy—at least the short-range objective—is the denial of their geographical positions, raw materials, and markets to the Western industrialized nations. The Soviet leadership has tried to capitalize on India's policy of neutrality between East and West, which was manifested during the Korean war and since.

The enchanted prestige of the Republic of India and of its leaders, the prestige of Prime Minister Nehru, are due to the policy of neutrality which the Indian Government is pursuing, to its policy of keeping out of the war blocs. Therein lies wisdom and strength. Circumstances have compelled the Soviet Union and the other countries of the socialist camp to launch a military Warsaw Treaty alliance to counterbalance the aggressive military alliances of imperialist powers. But we have declared more than once, and we do declare now, that we would be happy to see all the war blocs abolished because they are heightening international tensions instead of breeding friendship between the peoples. We welcome India's policy of peace and her policy of keeping out of blocs.[97]

We regard our relations with the Republic of India as very good. We have never differed with India on practically any of the issues of the consolidation of peace taken up by the

141

United Nations, or on many other international issues for that matter. The impression I have is that as we know and feel the peace-striving trends of the policy of your Government, headed by Mr. Nehru, whom we respect so much; the relations we have with you today justify great hopes for a further strengthening of cooperation and mutual assistance.[98]

The India of today owes its existence to Gandhi. The same Gandhi who, according to the communists, Russian as well as Indian, "never wanted India to gain full independence: his sole aim was to urge the imperialists to make concessions in favor of the exploited masses of India, to achieve the admission of the bourgeoisie and the land-owning class to the helm of power." [99]

Or:

"Gandhism is . . . a reactionary force directed against the revolution of the popular masses." [100]

"In a demagogical manner, Gandhi . . . preached class peace with landowners and capitalists to Indian workers and peasants. . . . Gandhism has become the avowed national ideology of the Indian capitalists and landowners." [101]

India's present leader, Jawaharlal Nehru, is Gandhi's disciple. To win his friendship and the friendship of India, Khrushchev makes a rare and somewhat abject apology:

In the past, some incorrect pronouncements regarding certain Indian personalities did appear in certain works by Soviet authors. We are trying to rectify this in order to pay tribute to everyone who was truly great in his country and who made a big contribution to the liberation of his native India from the colonialists. We bow in admiration before their outstanding activities and their glowing record, and we do all we can to enable our people to have the correct view about forces which fought for the freedom and independence of India and rallied their people in the fight against foreign colonialists. The Soviet people evince great interest toward the history of India, and we want to know more about this friendly, great, and peace-loving country.[102]

Neutralizing the Underdeveloped Countries

Recalling the past serves to "illustrate" the present and the future.

Your country [India] has great potentialities for the advance of the economy, culture, and living standards of the people. That means that those who retarded and still want to retard, the economic advance of India and of other countries freed from colonialist domination will be disgraced. They cash in on rendering economic "assistance" to those countries, supplying them with consumer goods. But such goods are rapidly expended and those who receive such "assistance" must time and again apply for such goods to the manufacturers, who make fabulous profits on the plea of rendering assistance and keep dependent the people of economically underdeveloped countries.[103]

All this is said in spite of the facts—which Khrushchev knows very well:

Soviet aid to India has consisted of $115 million in credits for Soviet equipment and technicians for a steel mill, granted on February 2, 1958; $10 million in credits for diamond-mining machinery, on June 19, 1956; a contract for a plant for files and rasps, on October 24, 1955; oil exploration resulting in the discovery of two potential oil-bearing areas; credits for the building of two refineries, one by Rumania (capacity: 750,000 tons a year), the other by the Soviet Union (capacity: 2 million tons a year). Total: less than $400 million—in *credits*.

United States assistance to India has included $310 million in direct aid, $1,300 million in agricultural commodities, $120 million from the Asia Development Fund, $225 million from the Export-Import Bank and Development Fund. Total: $1,955 million.

In addition, India received $950 million lent through the International Bank for Reconstruction and Development (the World Bank). The bank, of which the United States is a major subscriber (and to which the Soviet Union does not contribute), also proposed a $400 million loan over a four-year period.

Khrushchev does not explain who makes the "fabulous profits"

143

and indeed how such "profits" can be made through direct aid or development loans. He omits mentioning that the agricultural commodities furnished by the United States (some of the "moldy wheat," as he has called it) to India in emergency situations saved millions from famine.

In the long run, India may become one of the great challenges to the communist regime. China and India have often been compared—considered "laboratories" where the effectiveness of two systems is being tested—total control versus freedom in a subsistence economy. The two giants of Asia cover a combined area of 5 million square miles (greater than all of Europe), and are populated by more than one billion people, 400 million of them Indians. The new regimes came to power almost at the same time, India on August 15, 1947, and China on October 1, 1949. Both countries launched economic-development programs from a small and disrupted industrial base laid on an ancient and primitive agricultural economy. Both have a frighteningly high population density: India, 280 per square mile; China, 123 per square mile in 1951 (compared with 44 in the United States). But even more frightening is the population increase, currently 15 million a year in China, 8 million a year in India. All this adds up to an abysmal poverty. United Nations studies place per-capita annual income for India at $42.61, for China at $23.13 in 1946. By 1949, India had gone up 33.8 per cent to $57, China 16.3 per cent to $27.

Africa

In 1960, black Africa was still freeing itself from the old colonial ties, and new countries were asking for recognition by the international community. The transition to independence was not always peaceful and orderly. United Nations forces had to intervene in the Republic of Congo, aflame with hatred, torn by dissension, and threatened with the secession of its richest province.

Khrushchev had recognized in 1955 that Africa was a fertile ground for "classic" agitation and propaganda:

144

Neutralizing the Underdeveloped Countries

Take Africa, for example, which is completely divided up among European and non-European countries. . . . The peoples of these countries are rising more and more resolutely to fight against colonial regimes. And we sympathize with this struggle and wish success to the peoples who are waging it.[104]

The time has now come when the plundered are beginning to realize who it is that has plundered them, whose fault it is that they are in such a plight. They are already making their voice heard, recalling this. That is why the colonizers are beginning to feel that the hour of reckoning is near and are trying to wriggle out of this situation somehow.[105]

The struggle for national independence forced the colonialists to make concessions. The imperialists, particularly the British imperialists, declare, rather boastfully in fact, that they met the colonial people's wishes halfway granting them independence. But such statements are meant for people not versed in politics. The only reason the imperialists make this or that concession is that they no longer can keep the people down and rule by old colonialist methods. They think it better not to wait until things reach a crisis and then get thrown out by armed uprising.[106]

"During 1959 the Soviet economic offensive achieved its first major successes in Africa; Ethiopia accepted a $100 million Soviet credit, and a $10 million Czechoslovakian credit, while Guinea accepted a $40 million credit from the Soviet Union and Czechoslovakia." [107] The bloc countries took Guinea's cocoa and banana crop, sent in a corps of technicians for charting mineral resources, offered scholarships for African students, formed front organizations, infiltrated the labor unions, and began a propaganda barrage seeking to convince the middle Africans that Russia was their mentor.

By 1960 Khrushchev had assumed the posture of "protector" of the new nations. Congo's Prime Minister Patrice Lumumba appealed to him, and the latent menace of Russian intervention at the same time hastened and hampered the United Nations efforts to bring

145

order into chaos. In the United Nations Security Council, the Soviet delegate acted as if he were the spokesman for the Congolese. In July 1960, *The New York Times* quoted Khrushchev as saying:

The demand of the Soviet Union is simple—hands off the Republic of Congo. The government of the Congo can be assured that the Soviet Government will give the Congo Republic the necessary help which may be required for the victory of your just cause.

Noncommunist spokesmen, noncommunist leaders were denounced by Khrushchev as stooges of the former colonial powers:

While going through the motions of leaving their former colonies, the imperialists are seeking to preserve their influence—through less overt means—so that the peoples of the erstwhile colonies will be governed not by, say a British governor, but by local people in the pay of the imperialists and pursuing a policy desired by the imperialists. Thus the colonialists pretend to entertain the wishes of the peoples, while, in effect, keeping the peoples of some countries in colonial bondage.[108]

By using venal persons who occupy high offices in some countries dependent on them, the imperialists try to draw these countries into the common camp of the imperialists, so that these countries can themselves help the imperialists to bolster up the rotten venal regimes and so that the peoples of the dependent countries will live in bondage to the colonialists. The principal part in this is played by the imperialists of the United States, Britain, and France.[109]

A vital area of propaganda is America's well-known segregation problem:

Capitalism has given birth to the man-hating theory about the superiority of one nation over the other, about the inferiority of the so-called colored peoples. Who doesn't know the attitude in the United States toward the Negroes? Or remember the notorious "theories" of the German fascists about the necessity of establishing the rule of Aryans over all other nations.[110]

Socialism is described as a regime of tolerance, in spite of well-known antagonisms against its own minority peoples:

National barriers disappear only under conditions of a socialist society. Only under socialism is the national question properly solved. In old Czarist Russia, for example, there were frequent Jewish pogroms, Armenian-Tatar massacres and other sanguinary manifestations of national enmity, fomented by capitalism. All this has disappeared under Soviet government. Soviet children and young people learn about these abominable occurrences of the past only from the elder people and literature.[111]

Khrushchev chooses to ignore the long and bitter record of prejudice against Asiatic peoples, Jews, and other minorities, and the dominance of Russians in government, science, and the Party.

Latin America

By mid-1960, Khrushchev had also proclaimed himself protector of Latin America. "Hands off Cuba," headlined the Moscow Party press, and Khrushchev threatened any possible "interventionist" in Fidel Castro's affairs with nuclear destruction. Soviet-Latin America "friendship" meetings were being held in Moscow and Khrushchev proclaimed:

We are happy to hear the pulse of Latin America's struggle for independence against American imperialism. . . . And I cannot but welcome the events in Cuba, where the people proudly and courageously rose up under the banner for the struggle for their independence. I am convinced that other Latin American countries will also rise up in the struggle for their independence. We will sympathize with their struggle and applaud their successes in this fight.

147

I am convinced that the peoples of Latin America are accumulating their forces and that they will play an ever-growing role in international relations. Unfortunately there still exist in Latin America today countries whose governments are taking money from their people but are serving the interests of the American imperialists. But the Latin American peoples are awakening, and we welcome this process and sympathize with it.

It is only when the Latin American peoples have their own governments, governments that will express the will of these peoples, that these nations will be able to truly raise their independent voices in the international arena, including the United Nations, and this will certainly be to the benefit of all the countries of the world, to the benefit of the cause of peace.[112]

In the wake of Khrushchev's statements came promises of technical aid and profitable trade . . .

The USSR supplies a number of countries with the complex equipment [for the peaceful uses of atomic energy] and gives them technological aid in the construction of enterprises and in the training of local personnel for the development of their national industries. Supplies of industrial equipment and technological aid could be arranged on a commercial basis—on the basis of equality without any political strings.[113]

It is not our fault if there are still no broad and mutually profitable relations between the Soviet Union and these countries. This is in particular hampered by some imperialist circles which regard Latin America as their patrimony, which prevent the industrialization of these countries and keep them in the position of raw material appendages.[114]

The Soviet Union at present has trade relations with several Latin American countries. After the war the trade of the Soviet Union with these countries was greatly increased. Nevertheless, the trade volume achieved is still insufficient.

Neutralizing the Underdeveloped Countries

The possibilities of increasing the Soviet Union's trade with the Republics of Latin America remain untapped to a great degree. The Soviet Union could supply to these countries a greater variety of industrial goods and machinery necessary for their industrialization, and also a variety of raw materials in exchange for goods traditionally produced in Latin America.[115]

Soviet economic missions were crisscrossing Latin America, giving more weight to Khrushchev's promises. They were not unsuccessful— a $100 million trade agreement with Brazil, a loan and larger trade pact with Argentina, an oil-for-sugar barter deal with Cuba.

Though all this amounts to less than three per cent of the annual $4 billion United States–Latin America exchange, it is important politically. Trade, aid, "cultural cooperation," are pump-primers for the operations of Soviet agents and local Communist Parties, communist-dominated labor unions, communist-penetrated student organizations.

In Asia, Africa, Latin America, one theme emerges clearly out of the fog of Communist semantics—"Hate America! Western aid is disguised imperialism. Only the socialists are your friends." Tactics vary; success is followed by setbacks and setbacks by success.

The developing countries of the world are kept in constant turmoil, marked by ugly violence or threat of violence. Regimes fall, kings are murdered, dictators flee, new dictators arise.

Not all of this is Khrushchev's doing—far from it. But every instance of chaos presents an opportunity, and Khrushchev takes advantage of every situation that promotes his goal—dumping arms in Cuba, Laos, and Algeria, stirring up civil war in the Congo.

CHAPTER 7

Absorbing the Satellites

Lenin, from the beginning, viewed the socialist aim as a single "commonwealth."

"The socialist movement cannot be victorious within the old framework of the fatherland. It creates new, higher forms of human life under which the best demands and progressive tendencies of the laboring masses of all nationalities will be fully satisfied in an international unity, while the present national partitions are destroyed." [1]

The Soviet breakthrough beyond its borders came as a result of World War II. Under the aegis of conquering armies, the Communist Parties were able to win or take control in Rumania, Bulgaria, Hungary, Poland, East Germany, Czechoslovakia. In Albania, as in Yugoslavia, communist guerrillas had taken over during the war.

For Stalin this was a major objective—primarily as a *cordon sanitaire* to buffer the Soviet Union against possible attack by capitalist nations. But Stalin also had a wider perspective.

"Every base has its corresponding superstructure . . . the capitalist base has its superstructure, the socialist base has its superstructure. If the base changes and is eliminated, then its superstructure changes and is eliminated after it; if a new base is born, then a superstructure corresponding to it is born after it.

"*The superstructure [the Soviet empire] is generated by the base [Moscow] but this by no means signifies that it merely reflects the base, that it is passive, neutral and indifferent to the fate of its base,* to the fate of classes, to the character of the system. On the contrary, having put in an appearance, it then becomes a most active force which contributes vigorously to the formation and consolidation of its base, takes all steps to assist the new order to drive the old base and the former classes into dust and liquidate them." [2]

Mr. Khrushchev echoes:

What do we want? We want unity, closed ranks, and rallied forces. We acknowledge different paths, comrades. But among the different paths, there is the general path, and others are, as you know, like a big river with tributaries. In the same way there are specific peculiarities, but there is only one path, the Marxist-Leninist path. This is the path on which the task of the construction of communist society must be tackled.[3]

While Stalin was alive, he constituted the basic link between the USSR and the satellite nations, the liberator, the symbol, the leader, the builder of socialism. He was deified, feared, and hated, but always a presence in any important discussion. For years all satellite leaders had been personally approved by Stalin. All decisions of the East European governments had been made, not on direct orders from Stalin, but on the principle of "anticipated reaction by attempting to do what Stalin might wish done." [4]

This was the "cult of the personality." For the control of the satellites, Stalin's "being" was enough. The worship of Stalin in school, factory, and government was supplemented by direct consultations between individual communist leaders and Stalin; by instructions issued through the Soviet ambassador; or by his mere presence on the scene. Every Party official knew that periodic assessments of his work and his attitudes were sent to Moscow. Moreover it was, and still is, understood that the Soviet ambassador may go beyond the official government in gathering information, consulting and advising members of the local Party Presidium or its administrators.

Objectives

In the satellites, as in the Soviet Union, the strongest controls operate through the Party apparatus. All important functionaries in East European countries are Party members subject to Party discipline. Many have been trained in the Soviet Union. Many satellite officials are simultaneously members of the Soviet secret police, empowered to arrest officials in their native country. In an era of periodic Party purges, this itself has been a key to total power. The Party line was laid down in Moscow. A pattern of undeviating institutional and ideological uniformity was designed to facilitate decision-making at all levels and in all Communist Parties, and to eliminate divisive tendencies.

The ties between the base and the superstructure are informal and, much like the Soviet political system itself, meaningless unless observed from the special viewpoint of communist dynamism. The formal ties between the USSR and the people's democracies are expressed through bilateral agreements, treaties of mutual aid, friendship, collaboration, and cultural cooperation.[5] The informal, less visible, and more binding ties are expressed through the Party line and made viable through the Party apparatus.

The task lies in developing on an even wider scale the education of the working people in the spirit of proletarian internationalism and Soviet patriotism. The Communist Party considers it its sacred duty to strengthen friendship among the peoples, the basis of the might and invincible strength of the Soviet Union.[6]

The unifying influence of Stalin passed with his death. This was part of the "cult of the personality," which Khrushchev had to destroy and for which he had to find a substitute. The Secret Speech destroyed the Stalin image and consequently its cohesive power. A subtler system of ties with the satellite nations had to be created, with emphasis on economic and military aid.

As an answer to NATO, the Warsaw Pact was signed on May 14, 1955, and the Council for Mutual Economic Aid was strengthened to facilitate exchange of techniques, experience, and knowledge, to foster specializations and division of labor, and to coordinate economic goals. Thereafter, the Soviet Union extended additional credit to the satellites—although this was viewed partially as a sop to restrain restlessness.

Announced Khrushchev, according to the Soviet magazine *Kommunist*, on the signing of the Warsaw Pact:

A new, socialist type of international relations arose with the formation of the commonwealth of socialist states. These are relations of fully equal rights, genuine friendship, fraternal cooperation in the sphere of politics, economics and culture, and mutual assistance in the construction of a new life. These relations are determined by the nature of the social-economic system of the countries of the socialist camp; by the unity of their fundamental interests and ultimate great aim, the building of communism; and by the single Marxist-Leninist world view of the Communist and Workers' Parties. . . .[7]

Mr. Khrushchev declared:

The commonwealth of the socialist nations is the source of the growth of strength and might of the multinational socialist state. Educating the masses in the spirit of proletarian internationalism, our Party has always waged an irreconcilable struggle both against great-power chauvinism and against local nationalism.[8]

The lessons of history show that political cooperation between countries of the socialist camp is a reliable safeguard for their national independence and sovereignty, and that it creates the necessary conditions in each of them for successfully realizing their plans of peaceful socialist construction.

Life also shows that the economic cooperation of these countries, based as it is on principles of complete equality and mutual assistance, enables each of them to utilize, most rationally and fully, its natural resources and to develop its

153

productive forces. On the other hand, it enables them to coordinate and combine their effort in the interests of all and to make the best of the tremendous advantages of the world socialist system in order to consolidate the economic might of the socialist camp as a whole.

The cultural cooperation of the socialist countries reciprocally enriches the spiritual life of the peoples of each of them and helps tremendously in the rapid and all-round advancement of their national culture, science and technology.

All this taken together speaks convincingly of the vast advantages which each socialist country derives from its close cooperation and unity with all the other socialist countries.[9]

The Communist Party of the Soviet Union has always considered, and will continue to consider, that its highest international duty is to develop and strengthen all-round cooperation among all the socialist countries, to strengthen steadily the unity and might of the great socialist camp. In unity lies the strength and invincibility of the growing world socialist system, of the entire international communist movement. And the Communist Parties will continue to strengthen this unity in spite of all the machinations of our class enemies.[10]

The cooperation is essentially bilateral—between the Soviet Union and each satellite.

"One recalls the severe rebuke administered to the Bulgarian Communist leader Georgi Dimitrov for recommending a Federation of Eastern Europe. It is dogma in the Soviet world that no substantial concentration of power may exist in. any part of the world that can be controlled from Moscow."[11]

But Khrushchev makes a point of denying Soviet control over its satellites:

You declare, for instance, that the Soviet Union has imposed its political domination on countries of East Europe.

We are, of course, not surprised by this statement which, nevertheless, has no grounds whatsoever.[12]

The socialist camp is a voluntary union of equal and sovereign states in which no one seeks or strives for any special rights, privileges or advantages for himself. It goes without saying that each socialist country independently decides the question of the forms of its cooperation with the other socialist countries. There is not and cannot be any coercion in this matter.[13]

Why then should such questions of communist domination of East Europe be raised again? We refute them, and not only refute but declare that, in the case of new attempts from the outside to forcibly alter the order in socialist countries, we will not remain just spectators and will not abandon our friends in need. We are true to our obligations and to our international duty, and we would not like anyone to try our patience again. After all, we too can raise similar questions on our part; namely, how long will capitalism exist in West European countries? Is it not time for this regime to give way to the more progressive socialist regime?[14]

Typical is Khrushchev's "noninterference" attitude when he discusses negotiations on German reunification:

We stand on positions of nonintervention in the affairs of other states.

But in the same speech the "we" (presumably Khrushchev and East Germany) is rather dominant.

We did not negotiate with them [leaders of West German Social Democratic Party] but had talks, since they were not authorized to negotiate, inasmuch as they were representatives of the opposition and not the ruling party. From our point of view the Social Democrats hold a more realistic position than the Bonn Government. From my talks with Erich Ollenhauer, Carlo Schmid, and Fritz Ehler, I gained the impression that we could agree on a reasonable solution if they had powers to negotiate and if they sat down with us at a conference table.[15]

It is recalled that similar pronouncements on "noninterference" were made by Vyacheslav Molotov.

"The special character of these mutual assistance pacts in no way implies any interference on the part of the Soviet Union in the affairs of Estonia, Latvia, or Lithuania, as some organs of the foreign press charge. On the contrary all these pacts of mutual assistance strictly stipulate the inviolability of the sovereignty of the signatory states and the principles of noninterference in each other's affairs. . . . We stand for the scrupulous and punctilious observance of the pacts [referring to mutual-assistance pacts with the Baltic states] on the basis of complete reciprocity and we declare that all the nonsensical talk about the Sovietization of the Baltic countries is only to the interests of our common enemies and all anti-Soviet provocateurs." [16]

Less than a year later Estonia, Latvia, and Lithuania were invaded and annexed by the USSR.

Khrushchev acknowledges difficulties between the Soviet Union and its satellites. In speaking to Poles, he admits:

Certain hitches can also arise in the relations between socialist countries because new relations of which there have been no example in history are being built among them. This is not an easy task since in the background there is the great weight of the past and since, furthermore, there are forces which hinder and which will continue to hinder the new relations which have arisen and are developing among socialist countries.[17]

Before a noncommunist audience, Khrushchev glosses over such difficulties.

As regards the socialist countries, there are no antagonistic contradictions, no struggle or hostility between them. This does not mean, of course, that there are no rough edges to their relations. Arguments, lack of harmony and differences on certain questions may occur even between friends. Such arguments can even happen between man and wife. They can have different views on things.[18]

He denies even the existence of tensions.

The farfetched nature of the very talk about the so-called "tensions in Eastern Europe," is also absolutely obvious. The Soviet Union has diplomatic relations with all the countries of Eastern Europe and maintains most lively contacts with them. I must say that we know of no symptoms of any "tensions" in this area.[19]

Only the "enemies of the working class," says Khrushchev, see anything but family differences:

The enemies of the working class calculated to cause "complications" in relations between the fraternal parties, in particular between the parties of the socialist states. With this purpose in view they tried to exaggerate difficulties encountered in socialist construction, to speculate on some individual misunderstandings and irregularities in relations between the socialist states. These misunderstandings can, of course, happen inasmuch as an absolutely new type of relationship is taking shape, relationships which have no precedent in history. As experience has shown, however, all the questions of relations between the socialist states are resolved and can be resolved through friendly discussion on the basis of the strict observance of the principles of proletarian internationalism.[20]

"In most of the world the USSR has an interest in upsetting the status quo. The one area in which change would be damaging to Soviet interests is the communist bloc. It is in this area that United States policy is least likely to score significant victories, and in which ill-considered policies are most likely to erupt in the use of

157

force. And yet it is in those countries, particularly Eastern Europe, that the USSR is potentially most vulnerable. Nationalism is a force in all of Eastern Europe, and in many of the countries cultural and political sovietization has been bitterly resented. While socialization of the economies has enjoyed support among important segments of the population, in certain segments such as agriculture and trade there exist pressures for more freedom of enterprise. As for the political forms of communism, traditions of individual freedom are deep in such countries as Czechoslovakia, Poland, and Hungary, and the Communist Party monopoly is resented by important segments of youth and the intelligentsia." [21]

Khrushchev, who is eager to "examine" any problem affecting the West, resists any attempt to discuss matters affecting the East European countries.[22]

However, we are told that the situation in the East European countries should be discussed. What do they want to discuss? Who has given anyone the right to discuss the question of the internal development of other countries? Nothing doing, my good gentlemen, do not poke your noses into somebody else's garden! The people of East Europe have already solved this problem. They are masters of their own household. They will not allow anyone to interfere in their internal affairs.[23]

Everything emanating from the West is evil.

The imperialists try to cloak their treacherous design to split the unity of the socialist countries by pleading concern for the "independence" of this or that country. In crusading against the unity of the socialist countries, they depict themselves almost as champions of the independence and sovereignty of this or that state. But when they speak of the need to unite the capitalist countries in military blocs, they demand from their partners renunciation of sovereignty in the name of this union, claiming there is no such thing as absolute sovereignty, that it is an anachronism.[24]

No one will ever succeed in taking away from the peoples of the socialist countries their great gains.[25]

And:

The imperialists are animated with deep love for the peoples of the socialist countries, with the desire to "liberate" them from communist "slavery." From what do they want to "liberate" us, comrades?

They want to liberate the workers from the factories and mills in order to take them from the people and hand them over to the capitalists.[26]

The Moscow declaration of November 22, 1957, clearly defines the extent of local autonomy in Eastern Europe—about as far as Poland is going, but not as far as Hungary wanted to go. The Soviet tolerance of disagreement extends to trading prices, allocation of resources, speed of collectivization, and similar questions.

Soviet dominance is maintained principally through the Party apparatus. However, this is strengthened by the presence of Soviet troops in all satellites and the proximity of additional forces. The proximity itself might be sufficient. Khrushchev has offered to remove his troops in exchange for the much-desired removal of U.S. troops and bases from the Continent.

We are not afraid of withdrawing our troops from all countries where they are stationed. Britain, the United States, and France fear this. The governments of Italy and West Germany are also afraid of foreign troops being evacuated from their countries. Adenauer, for instance, asks the foreign troops to remain in West Germany. Why? Simply because the governments of these countries do not know what will happen to them when the American forces leave. They do not know how French, Italians, Germans, Greeks, and others will behave, so this means that they are not sure of themselves. They are not sure of the peoples' adherence to the capitalist system.[27]

The Soviet answer to the Marshall Plan was the Council for
Mutual Economic Assistance, created in January 1949. In essence,
this was a device to stimulate production of military hardware and
to build up the industrial potential of each satellite country through
assistance in capital formation. In the process the ruble was made
the official medium of international exchange and the USSR the
ultimate arbiter of exchange rates. This was later reorganized into
the Communist Organization for Mutual Economic Cooperation. The
"aid" offered was small indeed—less than the drain of Soviet
dominance and reparations. Overshadowed by the dialectical discussion of peaceful coexistence at Bucharest in June 1960 was the
public attack of Polish Representatives on Comecon (Communist
Organization for Mutual Economic Cooperation).

The treaties ending World War II gave the Soviet Union virtual
carte blanche to take reparations in Eastern Europe.

*In the first years following the war, the satellites made substantial
direct contributions to the USSR as reparations. Hungary devoted
26.4 per cent of its 1946 budget and 17.8 per cent of its 1947
budget toward payment of $200 million per year reparations. Ru-
mania's bill was $300 million a year, constituting 37.5 to 46.6 per
cent of the budget. Reparations for Hungary and Rumania were set
in commodities figured at 1938 prices and were to be paid annually
for six to eight years. In 1948 the amounts were reduced slightly.
Poland agreed to sell eight million tons of coal for five years and
thirteen million tons for the next four years at a "special price"
which cost her two billion rubles in 1956. In the 1945–56 period the
Soviet Union received from East Germany $15 billion, from Rumania
$2 billion, from Hungary $1 billion, from Poland $2 billion. Soviet
credits less credit cancellations, given as a form of aid, came to a
total of $3.1 billion.[28]
Relying on an elaborately constructed pattern of unequal trade
relations, as well as the gains realized from the promotion of new
satellite industrial projects—salaries of imported Soviet "technicians"
and advisers, license fees, patent royalties, research and planning
charges—the Soviet Union is able to find much profit in its empire.*

Not the least of the devices used is ruble manipulation. In one spectacular case the Rumanian lei was sharply devalued in February 1954, doubling the value of the ruble from 1.43 to 2.86 billion, just in time for the sale of Soviet rights in Rumanian Sovrom, a jointly owned oil company.[29]

In spite of the record, Khrushchev keeps denying that the Soviet Union has ever even thought of milking the satellites.

In its international relations, since the first days of its existence, our state has categorically refuted all that rests on loot, violence, and occupation. It has resolutely proclaimed the principles of good-neighborly relations and equal economic contracts with all countries of the world. On November 8, 1917, Vladimir Ilyich Lenin stated from the forum of the Second Congress of Soviets, when he substantiated the decree on peace: "We reject all paragraphs on loot and violence; but all paragraphs containing good-neighborly conditions and economic agreements we shall accept heartily; we cannot reject them." [30]

When they withdrew major forces from Hungary, Rumania, Bulgaria, and Poland, the Russians took with them a substantial interest in "joint stock companies" which operated the nations' key industries. In Hungary, for example, the Russians held 50 per cent control of bauxite production, oil and petroleum refining, coal production, power plants, electrical and agricultural machinery, chemical production, air and motor transport development, and agricultural research. These interests were "sold" back to the satellite nations in the 1948–1950 era.

The new Khrushchev policy created a specialization and cooperation within the bloc, a type of community of nations, that would increase the satellites' dependence on the USSR and leave Russia economically independent of the noncommunist world.

The Khrushchev rationalization:

The other socialist countries stand to gain more from specialization and cooperation, because the Soviet Union is so vast that its capacity for production and consumption enables it to specialize and cooperate broadly within its own frontiers. It is the other socialist countries which need cooperation. However, all of them want to cooperate primarily with the Soviet Union. For example, Hungary wants to cooperate with the Soviet Union, and Rumania and Albania also want to cooperate with the Soviet Union alone, and show no particular leaning toward cooperating among themselves.[31]

Today the socialist countries cannot operate their economies in isolation, within the framework of each individual country alone. It is necessary to develop and improve cooperation so as to most rationally utilize the natural wealth and economic resources that are available in the socialist countries.[32]

We have already established fairly good economic relations but they need further expansion in order to attain still better coordination in the work of our industry and agriculture, to bring our economies closer, with the object of making better and fuller use of our technical and economic potentialities and, through coordination, more efficient utilization of factory floor space and the equipment of Soviet and Czechoslovak factories and mills. Coordination is also imperative in order to bring about a further rise in labor productivity through specialization and automation. This will make it possible to further expand the economy of our countries and, in competition with the capitalist world, to secure greater output for labor expended, which will enable us to secure living standards of which the capitalist states cannot even dream.

Socialist economic management, the friendly bonds linking the socialist countries and coordination in solving economic problems enable us to do this, and we, as representatives of our peoples, as representatives of the Communist Parties, must make full use of the possibilities.[33]

The new policy envisioned a "commonwealth of socialist nations,"

its center in Moscow, akin to the nineteenth-century colonial empires, with economic policies coordinated and directed through the Party. Says a recent study:

"Both slavery and division of labor imply dependence, but the latter is more productive of diversity and change." [34]

But Khrushchev does not see it that way.

Looking ahead, I think the future trend of development of the socialist countries will, in all probability, be one of consolidating a single world system of socialist economy. Economic barriers, which divided our countries under capitalism will be pulled down one after another . . .[35]

Similar lowering of economic barriers in the West is "imperialistic."

It is not difficult to see that the imperialist ringleaders and their ideologists, by calling for a limitation of national sovereignty and for a lowering of the customs barriers in other countries are, in fact, pursuing a policy of bringing those countries into submission to the big imperialist monopolies.[36]

Khrushchev finds "new economic laws" . . .

We proceed from the fact that new laws of economic development, hitherto unknown by human society, are in force in the socialist system of economy. For instance, under imperialism, the law of unequal economic and political development of various countries prevails, by which some countries make a leap forward at the expense of others and oppress and exploit them. The countries which have thus advanced protect their privileged position so as to hold the backward countries in subjugation and slavery. In the socialist system of economy the law of planning and proportional development is in force. As a result, hitherto economically backward countries, supported by the experience of other socialist countries, by cooperation and mutual aid, quickly make up the time lost and raise their economy and culture, and thus the general line of the economic and cultural development of all socialist countries is leveled off.[37]

. . . and sees them applied:

Countries which had been undeveloped industrially in the past, have, under the conditions of socialism, caught up with developed capitalist states and are advancing with assurance.[38]

Trade between USSR and each communist-bloc country is designed to equalize in a sort of barter agreement. Prices are set at "world market dollar prices" (until 1961 computed at four rubles per dollar). In practice there were many divergences. By price manipulation, the Soviet Union can take advantage of its satellites by overpricing its exports and/or underpricing its imports.

Here is how Soviet trade with its satellites is analyzed:

"Since the bloc countries are State traders, they can and do practice discrimination. The Soviet Union is, of course, in the best position to discriminate. The only systematic discrimination which has been observed has been against Eastern Europe. According to a careful study of recently released Soviet data, Horst Menderhausen (Review of Economics and Statistics, May 1959) indicates that the Soviet Union charges Eastern Europe more for Soviet exports and pays less for its imports from Eastern Europe than for the same products bought from and sold to Western Europe. Limited evidence also suggests that the Soviet Union, by accident or otherwise, has occasionally taken advantage of its superior bargaining power with primary producers. The bargaining strength of the Soviet Union, however, as well as of Eastern Europe and mainland China, is not sufficiently great to discriminate to achieve price advantages to any significant degree against any of its major trading partners in Western Europe." [39]

Khrushchev, however, pictures Russia as indulging in philanthropy.

For its part, the Soviet Union is doing its best to strengthen the socialist camp. It has always rendered disinterested assist-

164

ance and support to all the socialist countries, and continues to do so.[40]

"Living in an artificial, enforced amicability, it is not possible for the members of the bloc to complain in public about their trade experience with other members of the bloc. On several occasions it has become known that the countries of Eastern Europe and mainland China have been less than fully satisfied with their trade with the Soviet Union. The price disadvantage of Eastern Europe is more apparent to them than it is to the outside and has resulted in forceful representations to the Soviet Union, culminating several years ago in a Soviet agreement that world prices would be the basis of intra-bloc trade. As noted earlier, however, Eastern Europe remains the object of Soviet price discrimination. Mainland China as well as Eastern Europe, has felt that the Soviet Union was not providing enough economic assistance. It is probable that the bloc countries make all of the same complaints about trade with the Soviet Union that free world countries do, and then some, but it is discreetly kept within the family." [41]

A three-year study of Soviet trade made by Dr. Robert Loring for the United States Central Intelligence Agency confirms that (1) Soviet export prices to Eastern European nations were higher than Soviet export prices for the same goods to Western Europe; and (2) Soviet import prices from Eastern Europe were lower than Soviet import prices for the same goods from Western Europe. Although the study was completed in 1958, there is evidence that the situation remains unchanged.

Typically, the Soviet Affairs Analysis Service in Munich reports the price of the Moskva, Soviet's automobile for export: in the Soviet Union, 10,000 rubles; in bloc countries 6500 rubles; in Iceland 4700 rubles; in Sweden 4400 rubles; in Greece 3300 rubles; in Argentina 2500 rubles; in West Germany $1200 (4800 rubles at the official rate).

The "commonwealth" requires a sublimation of nationalism . . .

Unfortunately, there exist some comrades who believe that the love of one's Motherland allegedly contradicts international solidarity of the workers and socialist internationalism. Such an interpretation insults the national feelings of people and certainly does not contribute toward strengthening cooperation between the socialist nations or the development of international solidarity between the workers of all countries.[42]

. . . and elimination of some local influences:

It goes without saying that account must be taken of the fact that remnants of former exploiting classes still exist in Czechoslovakia and that they are not simply living the rest of their days passively, but are trying to offer resistance to the people's democratic system. This resistance is most frequently of a concealed nature and is manifested chiefly in influencing ideologically the politically less stable section of the population, in spreading all kinds of inimical rumors and "theories" of bourgeois propaganda, in agitating against various measures of the Party and the Government.[43]

Eventually, Khrushchev sees one socialist world:

The foundations for communist relationships between peoples have been laid in the Soviet Union and throughout the world socialist camp. Examples of this are numerous. The peoples of the socialist nations are bound together by bonds of fraternal friendship and by their common concern in building socialism and communism. They are constantly giving each other selfless mutual aid and support. Among the sovereign states of the socialist camp, extensive cooperation is developing in all spheres of economic, social, political, and cultural life. Looking ahead, I think the future trend of development of the socialist countries will, in all probability, be one of consolidating a single world system of socialist economy. Economic barriers, which divided our countries under capitalism, will be pulled down one after another and the common economic base of world socialism will be consolidated. It will eventually make frontiers a pointless issue.[44]

The ultimate Soviet aim is, of course, a world of communist nations recognizing the "center" of the CPSU, with national boundaries of only historical importance. This is a sort of imperialism by osmosis.

This is actually what did happen in the integration of the various autonomous republics absorbed in what is now the Soviet Union:

But all the peoples of the union of autonomous republics of our country are united by their common vital interests within a single community and they are advancing together toward one goal, communism. Therefore, the borders between the union and autonomous republics integrated within the Soviet Union are gradually ceasing to mean what they used to mean. As our country moved toward socialism, the borders between its individual republics were, in fact, vanishing, as it were. This process gained momentum as the gap between the development standards of the national republic was narrowed. If you ask any Russian, Ukrainian, or Byelorussian today whether the administrative boundaries of their republics are of any topical interest to them, I think most of them will be puzzled by this question. Why? I think it is because all the nations and nationalities enjoy equal rights within our socialist state; life is based on a single socialist system and the material and spiritual needs of every people and every nationality are met in equal measure.[45]

The objective of one Communist state was cited by the Communist International:

"Thus, the dictatorship of the world proletariat is an essential and vital condition precedent to the transformation of world capitalist economy into socialist economy. This world dictatorship can be established only when the victory of socialism has been achieved in certain countries or groups of countries, when the newly established proletarian republics enter into a federal union with the *already existing proletarian republics, when the number of such federations has grown and extended also to the colonies which have emancipated themselves from the yoke of imperialism and when these federations of republics have grown finally into a World Union of Soviet Socialist Republics uniting the whole of mankind under the hegemony of the international proletariat organized as a state."* [46]

But the time for integration of the satellites is not yet.

The question of frontiers is one of the most acute and complicated questions inherited by us from the old capitalist world. Today, old ideas about frontiers based on bourgeois legal norms still exist in the consciousness of millions of people building socialism, parallel with other remnants of capitalism. Even many communists are not free from these remnants. Therefore, at present, we cannot but take this into consideration and we must lead the masses patiently to the understanding of this question from the position of communism. Communist society which will have at its disposal an abundance of material and spiritual riches will be able to satisfy equally the demands made by every individual as well as by every nation. In these circumstances earlier concepts of frontiers as such will gradually be outdated.[47]

And:

With the victory of communism on a worldwide scale, state frontiers, as Marxism-Leninism teaches, will die off. Probably for the time being only ethnographical frontiers will remain, and even those will apparently only exist conditionally. Obviously, along such frontiers—if they can be called frontiers—there will be no frontier guards, no customs officials, and no incidents whatsoever. These frontiers will only fix the historically established living area of a people or nationality on a given territory. That this will be precisely what will occur is shown by the process which is taking place in the Soviet Union, a multinational state. Every one of the peoples,

168

nationalities and national groups of the Soviet Union has its frontiers established by history, and by its own traditions and culture.[48]

Lenin had foreseen expansion of the USSR and had made a clear distinction between annexation and appropriation.

"Not every appropriation of 'foreign' territory may be described as annexation, for, generally speaking, socialists are in favor of abolishing frontiers between nations and the formation of larger states; nor may every disturbance of the status quo be described as annexation, for this would be extremely reactionary and a mockery of the fundamental concepts of the history of science; nor may every military appropriation of territory be called annexation, for socialists cannot repudiate violence and wars in the interests of the majority of the population. The term annexation must be applied only to the appropriation of territory against the will of the population of that territory; in other words, the concept annexation is inseparably bound up with the concept self-determination of nations." [49]

For Khrushchev, the future is a world without frontiers.

. . . we consider that to us communists the question of frontiers is not of major importance and that there can be no conflicts about it between socialist countries. We Leninists consider the aim of our life to be the construction of a communist society, the bright future of mankind. This society will have no classes, there will be no exploitation of man by man; material and spiritual benefits will belong to all the people; the entire wealth of the earth—no matter where it lies—will serve equally all mankind, freed from the fetters of capitalism. It cannot be otherwise under communism. Matters cannot be presented in such a way that, having built a communist society, we shall spike our frontiers with still more posts, shall maintain frontier troops and officials to issue frontier permits.[50]

169

Yugoslavia

Of the Eastern European nations, only Yugoslavia liberated itself from Hitler's armies. Albanian communists fought the Italian occupation forces with the assistance of the Yugoslavs. Under Tito, Yugoslavia is the only country that had the power to leave the Soviet camp without being crushed by Russia's military might.

The instrument Stalin used to exercise Soviet hegemony over the Eastern European nations was the Cominform (the Communist Information Bureau), founded in September 1947. This was in keeping with the Leninist traditions. (The Cominform replaced the Comintern [Communist International], which was dissolved in 1943 as a "goodwill gesture" toward the Western Allies of the Soviet Union in World War II.)

The Yugoslav Communist Party was one of the mainstays of the Cominform, whose headquarters were established in Belgrade. Tito committed the cardinal sin—he refused to become a simple appendage of Moscow. In June 1948 he was expelled from the Cominform (which moved to Bucharest), and was branded "arch-traitor," "Fascist spy."

For five years, till Stalin's death in 1953, "Titoists," suspected Titoists, and potential Titoists were executed by the thousands in the satellite countries. Among them were well-known Communist leaders, Traicho Kostov in Bulgaria, Rudolf Slansky in Czechoslovakia, Laszlo Rajk in Hungary. Other thousands languished in jail (among them Hungary's future Soviet puppet, Janos Kadar), refusing to "confess" their "criminal" relationship with Tito.

Khrushchev of course participated in the denunciation of Tito.

The Tito-Rankovich band of murderers and spies . . . completed the transition from nationalism to Fascism.

And:

Selling out to the American imperialists, Judas Tito and his clique turned Yugoslavia into a concentration camp. They liquidated the democratic victories of the people of Yugoslavia and established a Fascist regime in the country. Tito and his band are turning Yugoslavia into a colony of the Anglo-American imperialists.

All progressive mankind brands as shameful this band of betrayers. The people of Yugoslavia rise up to struggle against the Fascist clique of Tito. This chained dog of imperialism will not escape the stern judgment of the people of Yugoslavia for all his hideous wrongdoings.[51]

But Tito survived. Supported politically by the Western powers, Tito's Yugoslavia was, in 1949—against violent Soviet opposition—elected a member of the United Nations Security Council. It was made clear to Stalin that an attack on Yugoslavia could provoke a major war, that the West would not remain idle if Stalin tried to solve his so-called ideological differences with Tito by force of arms.

The Yugoslavs received economic help and arms from the West. The rift between the Soviet Union and Communist Yugoslavia widened—till 1953. Then the vilification ceased. But it was not until a year later that so-called Titoists in the satellite countries began to be released from prison.

The post-Stalin era, with the subtler, less than one hundred per cent domination of satellites, made the bitter relationship with Yugoslavia unnecessary and a major handicap. Independence among socialist states was something not to be encouraged. A pact was signed on June 2, 1955, acknowledging "mutual respect for . . . different forms of Socialist development" and providing for "the exchange of Socialist experience."[52]

It was to sign this pact that Khrushchev went to Yugoslavia. On May 27, 1955, alighting from the plane that had brought the Soviet fence-mending mission to Belgrade, Khrushchev accused Lavrenti Beria, Stalin's chief of secret police, of having been responsible for the rift and its consequences.

The Yugoslav leaders knew better. Tito was openly contemptuous of Khrushchev's "explanation." Yugoslav Communists privately remarked that it was an insult to their intelligence.

But Khrushchev considered his mission a success.

The strongest ties are established between the people of both countries which have as their guiding force Parties that base all their activities on the teaching of Marxism-Leninism. The Parties that take the Marxist-Leninist teaching as their guide achieve complete mutual understanding because they have a common aim—struggle for the interests of the working class and the working peasants, for the interests of the working people.[53]

He explained the past unpleasantness in anodyne terms . . .

The Communist Party of Yugoslavia, together with the CPSU and a number of other fraternal parties, was one of the organizers of the Informburo [Cominform] and an active participant in its activity during the first period. This is how matters were up to 1948. Then came a worsening in relations between the Communist Party of Yugoslavia and other fraternal Parties. In 1948, a conference of the Informburo issued a resolution on the state of affairs in the Communist Party of Yugoslavia on a number of questions of principle. This resolution was fundamentally correct and corresponded to the interests of the revolutionary movement. Later on, in 1949 to 1953, conflict arose between the Communist Party of Yugoslavia and other fraternal Parties when, in the course of the struggle, mistakes and stratification which caused damage to our common cause were permitted. Fully conscious of its responsibility in respect to our countries and peoples and the international communist movement, the Communist Party of the Soviet Union took the initiative to liquidate this conflict and achieve normalization of relations between our countries and establish contacts, cooperation, and alliance on Marxist-Leninist principles.[54]

. . . and gave the Yugoslavs a clean bill of ideological health:

As a result of the Yugoslav-Soviet talks an end has been put to the period when the good relations between our countries were disrupted. It is quite obvious that such disruption of relations was of advantage only to the forces of imperialist reaction and aggression which are trying to set the peoples against each other, to sow discord and hostility amongst them in order to make it easier to carry out their cunning anti-popular designs.

Today we can already say that now the road is open for the Soviet Union and all the countries of people's democracy to establish and develop friendly relations with the Federal People's Republic of Yugoslavia.[55]

The relationship that was established during the Khrushchev-Tito talks, as explained in a joint declaration of June 2, 1955, was a relationship between two sovereign states.

Gradually during the rest of the year and under prodding from Moscow, the "people's democracies" also "normalized" their relations with Yugoslavia. By April 1956, as a conciliatory gesture toward Tito, the Cominform, being already obsolete, was disbanded. Khrushchev had a year earlier created new ties between the countries of the Soviet bloc—the Warsaw Pact, ostensibly Moscow's answer to NATO. Yugoslavia did not join the pact and continued to adhere to a position of "positive neutrality" between the two blocs. At that time, such neutrality was acceptable to the Soviets, who were engaged in a "peace" campaign directed against Western defense efforts in Europe.

A few weeks before the dissolution of the Cominform, Khrushchev in his Secret Speech gave a few details on the Yugoslav affair:

The willfulness of Stalin showed itself not only in decisions concerning the internal life of the country but also in the international relations of the Soviet Union.

The July 1955 plenum of the Central Committee studied in detail the reasons for the development of conflict with Yugoslavia. It was a shameful role which Stalin played here. The "Yugoslavia affair" contained no problems which could not have been solved through Party discussions among comrades. There was no significant basis for the development of the "affair"; it was completely possible to have prevented

173

the rupture of relations with that country. This does not mean, however, that the Yugoslavia leaders did not make mistakes or did not have shortcomings. But these mistakes and shortcomings were magnified in a monstrous manner by Stalin, which resulted in a break of relations with a friendly country.[56]

I recall the first days when the conflict between the Soviet Union and Yugoslavia began artificially to be blown up. Once, when I came from Kiev to Moscow, I was invited to visit Stalin who, pointing to the copy of a letter lately sent to Tito, asked me "Have you read this?"

Not waiting for my reply he answered, "I will shake my little finger—and there will be no more Tito. He will fall." . . .

But this did not happen to Tito. No matter how much or how little Stalin shook, not only his little finger but everything else that he could shake, Tito did not fall. Why? The reason was that, in this case of disagreement with the Yugoslav comrades, Tito had behind him a State and a people who had gone through a severe school of fighting for liberty and independence, a people which gave support to its leaders.[57]

Later that year (1956), Hungary revolted. Prime Minister Imre Nagy's stated intention to quit the Warsaw Pact precipitated massive Soviet intervention and the crushing of the revolt by Soviet armor. The Yugoslavs understood the meaning of the revolt as well as of the Soviet intervention. They stuck to their position of neutrality—and even accorded Imre Nagy temporary asylum in their Budapest Embassy. The deposed Hungarian Premier left the Embassy under a safe-conduct issued by his successor, Janos Kadar, only to be kidnaped by Soviet police. He was later executed for "treason."

The Yugoslav position in the Hungarian affair drew sharp criticism from Khrushchev:

Now in this fight which broke out on the Hungarian question, what did we get? We got absolute unity and the rallying of the communist ranks of the whole world. Yugo-

174

slavia remained isolated. Who spoke in its favor, on the questions connected with the Hungarian events? Dulles, Eisenhower, Guy Mollet, and so forth—what a lot!

I am convinced that that company is not to the liking of Comrade Tito—not good company. I used to tell this to Comrade Tito, and he afterward told me: "Listen, do stop repeating!" And I did indeed repeat it many times, for good words should be repeated. I was always greatly impressed by the words of August Bebel, German Socialist leader of the late nineteenth and early twentieth centuries. He said: "If you, revolutionary workers, are praised by the bourgeoisie, think—what nonsense have you committed for which it is praising you?" [58]

Some Yugoslav comrades attempt to find differences in the appraisal of their mistakes by some Communist and workers parties. They attack the CPSU. They want to stress in particular the Chinese Communist Party, asserting that it criticizes their mistakes in a special way. But vain are the attempts to find different shades in the criticism of present-day revisionism on the part of the fraternal parties.[59]

Only Tito is in step.

I recall one conversation which I had with the Yugoslav leaders in 1956 when we exchanged views during friendly talks. Speaking about our differences, I drew Comrade Tito's attention to the need for a deeper analysis of events and our mutual relations, for a more correct appraisal of the situation, so as to arrive more quickly at a unity of views on the basis of principle. I quoted a well-known expression: The whole platoon marches in step and only one soldier is out of step. And I asked: "Who should be corrected, the platoon or the soldier?"

Present at the meeting was Koca Popovic [Yugoslav foreign minister], who asked: "Who is the platoon and who is the soldier?"

175

I replied: "Think for yourself who is the soldier and who is the platoon. In any case," I said, "every soldier knows that a platoon is a platoon, and every soldier is a part of the platoon, and therefore the platoon should not adjust itself to the soldier, but the soldier to the platoon." [60]

Despite their role in the Hungarian question, the Yugoslavs were invited as "fraternal delegates" to attend the ceremonies marking the fortieth anniversary of the Russian October Revolution, and to participate in the conference of the communist world leadership, which culminated in the declaration of November 22, 1957, which acknowledged that the "Socialist camp" was "headed by the Soviet Union." The Yugoslavs refused to sign.

"The struggle against revisionism as an aspect of relations among communist states was rooted in the failure to draw Yugoslavia back into the communist camp. Poland had raised within that camp the problem of Soviet leadership. The November 1957 conference resolved it by re-establishing the general principle of Soviet primacy. Yugoslavia's position as a 'certified' socialist state necessarily raised the question of the unity of the communist camp. In keeping with the established ideological notions as well as internal pressures for unity, the quest for unity had to be resolved either through the forging of close links or by the drawing of a sharp line. If unity was impossible, this in itself signified to the communist leaders that within the pattern of their relations with Yugoslavia there was hidden somewhere an ingredient of heresy which had to be unmasked. That ingredient was revisionism." [61]

"This revisionism became apparent when the Yugoslavs, in preparation of their party congress published on March 13, 1958, a draft program in which they declared themselves to be simultaneously an integral part of both 'the socialist world' and of 'the European and world community.' The Yugoslavs ascribed most of the prevailing international tensions to the existence of 'two blocs' which were fathered by the wartime creation of spheres of influence between the major allied powers. Without differentiating between the two blocs, the declaration flatly asserted that 'the division of the world into blocs impedes the realization of the idea of coexistence, and is at odds with full independence and sovereignty of peoples and states.' The statement, made in the name of Marxism-Leninism, pitted not only capitalism but the communist camp itself directly against the best interests of mankind." [62]

Such a position, labeled "revisionism," was unacceptable to Khrushchev. On May 28, 1958, a Soviet credit of about $285 million for an important aluminum project was unilaterally "suspended" by Moscow.

With economic pressure came verbal attack:

In essence the program of the Yugoslav league [of Communists, the Yugoslav Party] is a debased variant of a number of revisionist theories of right-wing social democrats. Consequently, the Yugoslav leaders were not attracted to the road of revolutionary Marxist-Leninist teaching, but to the road of the revisionists and opportunists of the Second International [the Socialist International group from which the communists withdrew after the 1917 revolution].[63]

In the struggle for peace, we are prepared to pool our efforts with all honest people, whether they are members of the Labor Party, liberals, reformists, or nationalists. On this ground we establish relations of cooperation with all peace-loving forces. When the Yugoslav leaders declare they are Marxist-Leninists and use Marxism-Leninism only as a cover to mislead gullible people and divert them from the path of revolutionary class struggle charted by Marx and Lenin, they want to wrest from the hands of the working class its sharpest class weapon. Whether they wish to or not, they are helping the class enemy of the working people, and in return for this they are given loans; in return for this the imperialists praise their "independent" policy of "no blocs," which the reactionary forces make use of in an attempt to undermine our socialist camp. But we most vigorously and

177

firmly declare: "Nothing will come of it, Messieurs Imperialists—your arms are too short." [64]

Yugoslav leaders even after the normalization of relations
continued to come out with anti-Soviet declarations, making
attacks on the socialist camp and the fraternal communist
parties. Particularly great harm was done to the cause of
socialism by Yugoslav leaders in their public speeches and
actions during the Hungarian events.[65]

The Communist Party guards the unity of its ranks like the
apple of its eye. It wages a decisive struggle against revisionism and dogmatism. In this struggle the principal fire of the
Communist Party is directed toward revisionists, the lackeys
of the imperialist camp. The ancient legend about the Trojan
horse is well-known. When the enemies were unable to
besiege and assault Troy, they presented a wooden horse
to the Trojans, hiding their people inside the horse so that
they could open the city gates during the night. Present-day
revisionism is in its way a Trojan war.[66]

There was not a single Marxist party in the world, not one
group within the party of any consequence, that shared the
anti-Marxist views set out in the program of the League of
Yugoslav Communists and that expressed itself in defense
of the attitude of the Yugoslav leadership. All the revolutionary parties of the working class appraised the Yugoslav
program as revisionist. They sternly condemned the subversive and splitting activity of the leaders of the League
of Yugoslav Communists.[67]

**The fact that Soviet economic pressure on Yugoslavia was offset
by aid from the West is particularly galling to Khrushchev.**

There are reports that the United States is already making
its new "contribution" to the cause of the "building of Yugoslav socialism." But the Yugoslav leaders are ashamedly
keeping quiet about this latest handout because the peoples
know well the price of American generosity. The capitalists

don't give away something for nothing; when they give you something they take your soul in return and their aid is later paid for dearly.[68]

And:

The imperialists aid Yugoslavia, of course, not for the purpose of strengthening the socialist system, not for the purpose of supporting the communist movement, but for the purpose of fattening up, bribing the forces which call themselves "Marxist-Leninist" and are prepared to struggle against the socialist countries, and above all, against the Soviet Union. This "aid" is the tribute for the dissenting policy in the camp of socialism, which the American senators themselves do not conceal.[69]

I don't want to offend anyone, but at the same time I cannot help asking a question which is worrying honest communists everywhere. Why do the imperialist leaders, who seek to wipe the socialist states from the face of the earth and to crush the communist movement, at the same time finance one of the socialist countries, give it credits on easy terms and handouts? No one will believe that there are two socialisms in the world: one that is viciously hated by world reaction, and another acceptable to the imperialists, to which they render assistance and support.

Everyone knows that the imperialists have never given anyone money for nothing, simply because they like his "beautiful eyes." They invest their capital only in enterprises from which they hope to get good profits.

If the imperialists agree to render "aid" to a socialist state they do so, of course, not in order to strengthen it. The monopoly circles of the United States can by no means be suspected of being interested in strengthening socialism and developing Marxist-Leninist theory. Representatives of this particular country allege that we are deviating from Marxism-Leninism, but claim that they themselves are taking a correct stand. We get quite a curious situation—the imperialists want to "develop" Marxism-Leninism through this country. It is appropriate to recall Bebel's apt words: "If the enemy praises you, think what stupid thing you have done." [70]

Yugoslav leaders, including Comrade Tito himself when he made his latest speech, have in vain tried to prove that we are falling into contradiction and give varying assessments of the use of credit from capitalist countries. They claim: Moscow attacks Yugoslavs because they are receiving United States credit, but Moscow itself does not mind getting credit in Western countries; and recently Khrushchev turned to Eisenhower on this matter. You can be sure, Comrade Tito, that Khrushchev did not ask for "alms" with an outstretched hand, but put his request as an equal to an equal and proposed a mutually profitable plan. We do not ask anybody for alms. We do not need them. We do not accept gifts.[71]

The Yugoslavs had to head off the storm.

"In a transparent effort to appear conciliatory once the damage had been done, and possibly in response to Polish pleas for moderation, the Yugoslavs, almost on the very day that a lengthy denunciation of their program was published in the CPSU's *Kommunist*, made certain revisions in their text. Particularly, they rephrased the part pertaining to the two blocs to differentiate between NATO and the 'defensive' Warsaw Pact, omitting the discussion of the ancestry of 'spheres of influence.' " [72]

But to no avail.

The Yugoslav leaders allege that they stand outside the blocs, that they stand above the camps, but actually they belong to the Balkan bloc comprising Yugoslavia, Turkey, and Greece. The latter two countries, as is known, are members of the aggressive NATO bloc, and Turkey is besides a party to the Baghdad Pact [now CENTO]. The leaders of the League of Yugoslav Communists resent it very much when we tell them that they are sitting on two chairs. They give assurances that they are sitting on their own Yugoslav chair. But that Yugoslav chair is for some reason eagerly supported by the American monopolies. And this is why their extra-bloc position and neutrality, which are advertised so much by the leaders of the League of Yugoslav Communists, smell strongly of the American monopolies which are feeding Yugoslav socialism.[73]

The international Communist movement has condemned the outlook and policies of the Yugoslav revisionists. The leaders of the League of Communists of Yugoslavia try to present matters as though the Marxist-Leninist parties had begun an ideological struggle against them because they refused to sign the declaration [the Moscow Declaration of November 1957 stressing the "leading role" of the Soviet Union in the "socialist camp"]. This claim is utterly false. It was the Yugoslav leaders who countered the declaration by coming forth with their revisionist program, in which they attacked the Marxist-Leninist stand of the international Communist movement. One asks: Could Marxists have ignored these facts? Of course not. Therefore all parties that take Marxist-Leninist positions came forth with principled criticism of the program of the League of Communists of Yugoslavia.[74]

And:

Particularly dangerous to the revolutionary movement are all those who call themselves Marxist-Leninists, but in reality, whether they want it or not, carry out the role of agents of the class enemy in the workers' movement. This is why the Communist and workers parties are very touchy about theoretical problems and irreconcilable toward any attempt to revise Marxism-Leninism.[75]

And:

The communists were, are, and will remain irreconcilable in the struggle against the distortion of Marxism-Leninism in order to preserve the purity of the Marxist-Leninist banner. They will not permit revisionists and those who have deserted the principles of Marxism-Leninism to camouflage themselves behind the banner of Marxism-Leninism.[76]

And:

Where contemporary revisionism is leading is seen in the example of Djilas or Imre Nagy, who have arrived at a downright betrayal of the cause of socialism, the basic national interests of their countries.[77]

And:

The attempts of the revisionists to emasculate and distort Marxism, to introduce discord into the fraternal family of the socialist countries, are doomed to failure.[78]

The revisionists want to disarm the working class ideologically, and to sow in its ranks the poisonous seeds of disbelief in its strength. It is not accidental that international imperialist reaction is extolling the revisionists to the skies and supporting them.[79]

Khrushchev tries to drive a wedge between the Yugoslav people and Tito—a tactic reminiscent of the Stalin era.

We have the very friendliest feelings for the fraternal peoples of Yugoslavia, for the Yugoslav Communists, heroes of underground and partisan struggle. On many questions of foreign policy we speak a common language. We shall continue to develop trade with Yugoslavia on a reciprocal basis. We shall seek to cooperate with Yugoslavia on all the questions of the anti-imperialist and peace struggle on which our attitudes shall coincide.

How will matters stand in the Party sphere? Everything will depend on the League of Communists of Yugoslavia. Its leaders have themselves isolated themselves from the international Communist movement. Therefore, it is up to the

Yugoslav League of Communists to make a turn toward *rapprochement* with the Communist Parties on the basis of Marxism-Leninism; this would be also in the interests of the Yugoslav people themselves.[80]

Of course the program of the League of Yugoslav Communists is an internal affair of the Yugoslav communists but, insofar as this draft program contains an insignificant and insulting appraisal of other parties and socialist countries and a revision of the fundamentals of the Marxist-Leninist theory, our party considers it its direct duty to come out with criticism of the anti-Marxist statements in this document.[81]

Yugoslavia remains today a symbol that socialism can exist within a nation not totally dominated by the Soviet Union and of the Soviet attitude toward an undominated socialist state.

Hungary

The almost godlike image of Stalin was a major binding force in the Soviet bloc. The death of the Communist leader was a heavy psychological blow to satellite solidarity.

In October 1956, following disclosures in the famous "cult of the personality" speech, the Hungarian people rose against their communist regime. The revolution was crushed by Soviet tanks.

The whole Soviet propaganda machine went into high gear trying to drown the facts in a tidal wave of accusations against fascists and imperialists. Khrushchev has spoken thousands and thousands of words to justify Soviet intervention in Hungary. He claims, without foundation:

The Hungarian parliament was elected on a democratic basis.[82]

The results of the last free election in Hungary, held on November 4, 1945, when the country was occupied by Soviet troops.

183

SEATS IN PARLIAMENT

	Number	Percentage
Smallholder Party	245	59.9
Communist Party	70	17.11
Social Democratic Party	69	16.9
National Peasant Party	23	5.6
Civic Democratic Party	2	0.49
Total	409	100.00

Despite the fact that it was the Communists who were first to revolt against their leadership, Khrushchev asserts:

Not long ago the imperialist forces attempted to grapple with us by storm, organizing a counterrevolutionary rebellion in Hungary. But there also they did not succeed in accomplishing their black deed. The people of Hungary remained strong. All the brother peoples came to the help of the workers of Hungary. We have said and will say now that we will never leave our friends in the lurch, that we shall always defend the interests of the socialist countries, and if necessary, we shall pull our friends out of difficulty.[83]

And:

The imperialists engineered a plot against people's Hungary. Fascist-like cutthroats, most of whom had been sent in from abroad, began to exterminate progressive people. The Government of Hungary asked the Government of the Soviet Union for help in curbing the counterrevolutionary gangs. And the Soviet Union, true to its commitments, true to the principles of fraternal support to socialist countries, rendered such aid. And today socialist Hungary is steadily growing and developing. The events in Hungary must serve as a lesson for the reactionary forces, so that they, as a Russian proverb puts it, should not plunge into the river without first finding the ford.[84]

The essence of the matter is that in Hungary the [Admiral Miklós] Horthy [World War II leader in the Hitler alliance]

184

elements, the agents of foreign monopoly capital, tried to overthrow the people's democratic order, to restore the hated fascist regime. The handful of fascist conspirators and imperialist agents were followed by a small number of misguided honest people.[85]

Soviet troops regained control of Hungary for the Communists. But according to Khrushchev, this was not intervention at all.

We knew that we might be reproached for having allegedly intervened with our armed forces in the internal affairs of the Hungarian People's Republic. However, we were prompted by our internationalist obligations and came to the decision that a socialist country having the strength and the opportunity to extend fraternal assistance to another fraternal country must definitely do so, since by standing aloof and neutrally watching the bloodshed it could not call itself a socialist country and its representatives could not call themselves communists. In ensuing history no one would have forgiven us if, when workers' blood was being shed in Hungary, we had idly stood aside and looked on. We knew that the imperialists would shout wildly that we interfered in the Hungarian people's internal affairs, but we also knew that within a short time the Hungarian working class, working peasantry, and intelligentsia would realize and understand that there was only one correct road open before our Soviet country: to extend our assistance to our Hungarian class brothers.[86]

Khrushchev has said again and again that the intervention in Hungary was requested by the legitimate government of that country. Following is the last message of the last legitimate Hungarian government, addressed to U.N. Secretary-General Dag Hammarskjöld:

"November 1, 1956, 12:21 p.m. Direct teletype message from Budapest to U.N.:

"*Reliable reports have reached the government of the Hungarian People's Republic that further Soviet units are entering into Hun-*

gary. [*The Prime Minister*] summoned M. Andropov, the Soviet Ambassador, and expressed his strongest protest against the entry of further Soviet troops into Hungary. He demanded the instant and immediate withdrawal of these Soviet forces.

"He informed the Soviet Ambassador that the Hungarian Government immediately repudiates the Warsaw Treaty, and, at the same time, declares Hungary's neutrality, turns to the United Nations, and requests the help of the great powers in defending the country's neutrality. . . .

"Therefore I request your excellency promptly to put on the agenda of the forthcoming General Assembly of the United Nations the question of Hungary's neutrality and the defense of this neutrality by the four great powers. . . ."

It was signed: "Imre Nagy, President of the Council of Ministers of the Hungarian People's Republic, designated Minister of Foreign Affairs."[87]

But Khrushchev continues to accuse fascists:

You recall what howling international reaction raised. Our enemies shouted that the Soviet army had suppressed a popular revolution. What else could they have done? They were compelled to cover up their tracks and to divert the attention from the real organizers of the antipopular putsch. In fact, what kind of popular revolution is it when fascist putsch organizers want to convert the Hungarian workers into their hired slaves and to deprive the peasants of their legitimate right to land, to the fruits of their labor?[88]

The plans of the imperialists, who staked on the forces of counterrevolution in Hungary, failed. The Revolutionary Workers' and Peasants' Government of the Hungarian People's Republic [the group which, with Soviet help, overthrew Nagy], led by Comrade Janos Kadar, mobilized the working class, the working peasantry and the progressive intellectuals of Hungary against the counterrevolutionary forces. It requested the Soviet Union for assistance, and we gave this fraternal assistance. Literally within three days the counterrevolutionary bands were smashed and revolutionary order restored.[89]

As for the part played by Soviet troops in suppressing the counterrevolutionary revolt, the matter is absolutely clear. When the Government and Party of the Hungarian working class approached us, we felt that as communists we were duty-bound to come to the assistance of the workers, the working peasantry, the entire fraternal Hungarian people in their hour of need.[90]

Speaking to Hungarians, who know that it was not a "handful" of fascists followed by "a small number of misguided honest people" who rose against the aggressor, Khrushchev has to explain, and takes into account the fact that once before in Hungarian history Russian troops smashed a popular revolution.

We, leaders of the Communist Party of the Soviet Union and the Soviet Government, had at the time to make a difficult decision. How should we act? Strength was on our side, and so was truth. Our truth is the truth of the working class— the truth of the working people. The difficulty lay in the fact that a certain, least conscious, part of the Hungarian workers had fallen prey to enemy propaganda and participated in the disturbances caused by the counterrevolution. We had to decide what we were to do. Common sense urged us to help the workers and working people of the Hungarian People's Republic. But it is one thing to help economically—to send metal and grain, and to give advice. It is quite another thing to send troops. We never hesitate when it comes to repelling an enemy attack. But we saw that owing to their lack of political consciousness a certain section of Hungarians had become a tool in the hands of their class enemies.[91]

And:

Comrade Hungarians, I think you realize perfectly well that when we sent our soldiers and officers to fight the fascist rebels, we had no other aim than to assist our friends, who were temporarily in trouble.

When bourgeois governments send troops to other countries they do so with the intent to conquer, and seek to establish their exploiter rule over the working people of those countries. We helped you, so that you could defend your interests against a handful of fascist conspirators and safeguard the people's right of building its own life without exploiters. By helping the Hungarian people to smash the counterrevolution we performed our internationalist duty.

What is more, after smashing the fascist uprising we gave Hungary considerable economic assistance, so that you could rectify more speedily the damage done to your country by the counterrevolutionary conspirators. The Soviet Union sent Hungary coal, metal and grain.[92]

Khrushchev goes back to 1848 and nineteenth-century political morality for a precedent:

Comrades, during the Hungarian revolution of 1848, when the Hungarian people were fighting for their national liberation against the troops of the Austrian Emperor Franz Josef, it did not occur to the Russian Czar Nicholas I that he was intervening in the affairs of the Hungarian people. He sent his troops to put down the revolution in Hungary, to come to the rescue of Franz Josef's shaken throne. And the international reactionary bourgeoisie regarded this as right because the actions of Nicholas I accorded with their class interest.

However, in 1956, when the fascist rebels, backed by international reaction, made a bloody attempt to strangle people's power in Hungary, how could we, the working class, the working people of the Soviet Union, who had troops in Hungarian soil by virtue of the Warsaw Treaty, how could we allow our troops to be indifferent onlookers while the counterrevolutionaries were hanging workers, shooting the finest sons of the Hungarian working class, the Hungarian people. Had we not helped you, we would have been called fools, and history would not have forgiven us this stupidity.[93]

The workers of Hungary had fought the Russian tanks. One of the main resistance centers in Budapest was the Csepel plant. This too had to be explained. . . .

We must not ignore the fact, of course, that in the last few years the Hungarian working class has undergone some changes. Its ranks have swelled considerably in view of the rapid development of industry. Thousands of people from the petty-bourgeois sections of the population, and also from among former Horthy officials, gendarmes and officers, have become workers. While wearing workers' clothes, many of these offspring of the exploiting classes have remained hostile to socialism. It was only natural that when they got their chance these so-called "workers" rose against the people's power.

As for the whole Hungarian working class proper, which has had a severe schooling in the class struggle, it could never side with the counterrevolution. It proved its loyalty to socialism and proletarian internationalism by its revolutionary deeds.

Veteran workers in the Csepel and other industries persistently looked for arms to fight the rebels. But owing to the inefficiency of the authorities and the treachery of some of the officials, the workers failed to get arms. By its foul acts the traitorous group of Imre Nagy disorganized the workers' effort at the Csepel Works and in other districts.[94]

In October and November of 1956 the Hungarian people gave proof of their revolutionary maturity and of the fact that, under the leadership of Hungarian Communists, they were capable of defending the great achievements of the people's democratic system. Naturally, we must realize that the mendacious slogans snared certain groups of workers, especially among the intellectuals. They became the victims of bluff and deception.[95]

189

In rather vague terms, Khrushchev refers to "mistakes" made by the former Hungarian leadership as one of the causes of the revolt. These "mistakes" were the terror regime of the Stalin-imported Matyas Rakosi.

At the end of 1956, as a result of mistakes made by the former Hungarian leadership the events took place in Hungary which you all know about. Counterrevolutionary elements, supported by international reaction, made an attempt to overthrow the people's power in Hungary and to restore the capitalist, fascist system. There were certain difficulties in some other People's Democracies as well, primarily in Poland.[96]

The Hungarian Socialist Workers' Party is successfully making good the mistakes made by the former Party leadership. And, as you know, there were quite a few mistakes.[97]

And:

Making the most of the mistakes and distortions of the former leadership in Hungary, the imperialists in October–November 1956 set in motion their criminal machine. The domestic reactionary forces in Hungary, inspired and organized from abroad, staged a fascist uprising. They exploited all possible means to deceive the people.

Naturally, we cannot be blind to the fact that a certain section of the working people, especially among the intellectuals, were taken in by spurious slogans—were deceived and misled. If our enemies were stupid, it would be easier for the people to fight them. But they are crafty and insidious. They do not betray their true intentions at the start. They conceal them. To make their anti-popular handiwork easier, they hide from the people behind high-sounding phrases about "freedom" and "democracy."

But the Hungarian people did not follow the wretched handful of renegades. The conspirators found themselves isolated from the people.[98]

Absorbing the Satellites

Here is what took place in Hungary, according to the Special Committee established by the United Nations General Assembly to investigate the events. The committee studied "copious" documentation, questioned hundreds of witnesses, although the Soviet Union and the Kadar regime in Hungary refused to cooperate with it. The committee, made up of representatives of Ceylon, Denmark, Tunisia, Australia, and Uruguay, drew up a unanimous report:

"What took place in Hungary in October and November 1956 was a spontaneous national uprising, due to long-standing grievances which had caused resentment among the people. One of these grievances was the inferior status of Hungary with regard to the USSR; the system of government was in part maintained by the weapon of terror, wielded by the AVH or political police, whose influence was exercised at least until the end of 1955, through a complex network of agents and informers permeating the whole of Hungarian society. In other respects also, Soviet pressure was resented. From the stifling of free speech to the adoption of a Soviet-style uniform for the Hungarian army, an alien influence existed in all walks of life. Hungarians felt no personal animosity towards the Soviet soldiers on Hungarian soil, but these armed forces were symbols of something which annoyed a proud people and fed the desire to be free;

"The thesis that the uprising was fomented by reactionary circles in Hungary and that it drew its strength from such circles and from Western 'Imperialists' failed to survive the Committee's examination. From start to finish, the uprising was led by students, workers, soldiers and intellectuals, many of whom were Communists or former Communists. The majority of political demands put forward during the revolution included a stipulation that democratic socialism should be the basis of the Hungarian political structure and that such social achievements as the land reform should be safeguarded. At no time was any proposal made for the return to power, or to the Government, of any figure associated with pre-war days. 'Fascists' and 'saboteurs,' heavily armed, could not have succeeded in landing on Hungarian airfields which were under Soviet supervision, or in cross-

ing the Austrian frontier, where a closed zone was shown by the Austrian authorities to the military attachés of France, the United Kingdom, the United States of America and the USSR;

"The uprising was not planned in advance. It was the universal testimony of witnesses examined by the Committee that events took participants by surprise. No single explanation can determine exactly why the outbreak occurred just when it did. Communist spokesmen, including Mr. Kadar and the members of his present Government, have recognized the bitter grievances of the Hungarian people before 23 October.

"Although no evidence exists of advance planning, and although the whole course of the uprising bears the hallmark of continuous improvisation, it would appear that the Soviet authorities had taken steps as early as 20 October to make armed intervention in Hungary possible. Evidence exists of troop movements, or projected troop movements, from that date on. It would appear that plans for action had therefore been laid some time before the students met to discuss their demands. . . .

"The demonstrations on 23 October were at first entirely peaceable. None of the demonstrators appear to have carried arms, and no evidence has been discovered that any of those who voiced the political demands or joined the demonstrators had any intention to resort to force. While disappointment at Mr. [Erno] Gero's speech may have angered the crowds, it would hardly of itself have sufficed to turn the demonstration into an armed uprising. That this happened was due to the action of the AVH in opening fire on the people outside the radio building. Within a few hours, Soviet tanks were in action against the Hungarians. This appearance of Russian soldiers in their midst not as friendly allies, but as enemies in combat, had the effect of still further uniting the people;

"Obscurity surrounds the invitation alleged to have been issued by the Hungarian Government to the Soviet authorities to assist in quelling the uprising by force. Mr. Nagy has denied, with every appearance of truth, that he issued this invitation or was even aware of it. Since Soviet tanks appeared on the streets of Budapest at about 2 a.m. on 24 October, it would have been impossible for him to have addressed any official message to the Soviet authorities, since he held no government post at the time when the tanks must have received their orders. An invitation may have been made privately by Mr. Gero, [then] First Secretary of the Central Committee of the Communist Party [a post assumed by Kadar in 1958], or Mr. Hegedus, the Prime Minister. The Committee, however, has had no opportunity of seeing a text of such an invitation, or of considering the exact circumstances in which it may have been issued. Until further information comes to light, it would be wise to suspend judgment as to whether such an invitation was issued at all.

"Similar considerations apply to the invitation which is alleged to have been addressed to the Soviet authorities before the second intervention on 4 November.

"When Mr. Nagy became Prime Minister, he was not at first able to exercise the full powers of that office. Only when the grip of the AVH was loosened by the victory of the insurgents was he able to take an independent stand. By this time, the real power in Hungary lay with the Revolutionary and Workers' Councils, which had sprung up spontaneously in different parts of the country and had replaced the collapsing structure of the Communist Party. Mr. Nagy, though himself a Communist of long standing who had lived for many years in the USSR, invited non-Communists into his new Government, and listened to the demands of various Revolutionary and Workers' Councils. It would appear that Mr. Nagy himself, like the country at large, was somewhat taken aback by the pace of developments. However, seeing that his countrymen were united in their desire for other forms of government and the departure of Soviet troops, he threw in his lot with the insurgents. By this action, he obliterated the impression which he had created while still under the domination of the AVH, and he became a symbolic figure in the uprising, although he had not instigated it, and was never its actual leader;

"The few days of freedom enjoyed by the Hungarian people provided abundant evidence of the popular nature of the uprising. A free press and radio came to life all over Hungary, and the disbanding of the AVH was the signal for general rejoicing, which revealed the degree of unity achieved by the people, once the burden of fear had been lifted from them;

"There were a number of lynchings and beatings by the crowds. These were, in almost all cases, confined to members of the AVH or those who were believed to have cooperated with them;

"Steps were taken by the Workers' Councils during this period to give the workers real control of nationalized industrial undertakings and to abolish unpopular institutions, such as the production norms. These were widely resented as being unfair to workers and also a reflection of popularly suspected secret trade agreements with the USSR, which were said to make heavy demands on the Hungarian economy for the benefit of the Soviet Union. During the days of freedom while negotiations continued with the Soviet authorities for the withdrawal of Russian troops, attempts were made to clear up the streets of Budapest and life was beginning to return to normal. The insurgents had agreed to amalgamate, while maintaining their identity, in a National Guard, which would have been responsible, with the Army and Police, for maintaining order;

"In contrast to the demands for the establishment of political rights put forward during the uprising, is the fact that basic human rights of the Hungarian people were violated by the Hungarian Governments prior to 23 October, especially up to the autumn of 1955, and that such violations have been resumed since 4 November. The Committee is convinced that the numerous accounts of inhuman treatment and torture by the AVH are to be accepted as true. On the evidence, it is also convinced that numbers of Hungarians, including some women, were deported to the Soviet Union and that some may not have been returned to their homes. These deportations were designed to break the back of the revolution.

"Following the second Soviet intervention on 4 November, there has been no evidence of popular support for Mr. [Janos] Kadar's Government. Mr. Kadar has successively abandoned most of the points from the revolutionary program which he had at first promised to the Hungarian people. On the central question of the withdrawal of Soviet troops, he has moved from complete acceptance of the nation's wishes to a refusal to discuss the subject in present circumstances. Against the workers, he has proceeded step by step to destroy their power and that of the Workers' Councils. Capital punishment is applicable to strike activities. The processes of justice have been distorted by the institution of special police and special courts and by the ignoring of the rights of the accused. The Social Democratic Party has again been forcibly liquidated. General elections have been postponed for two years. Writers and intellectuals are subjected to repressive measures. The Hungarian workers have shown no sign of support for Mr. Kadar's Government or for the prospect of continuous Soviet occupation. Only a small fraction of the 190,000 Hungarians, mostly young people, who fled the country have accepted his invitation to return. The peasants have no reason to be grateful to Mr. Nagy for his attitude towards collectivization of agriculture and forced deliveries of farm produce.

"In the light of the extent of foreign intervention, consideration of the Hungarian question by the United Nations was legally proper and, moreover, it was requested by a legal Government of Hungary. In the matter of human rights, Hungary has accepted specific international obligations in the Treaty of Peace. Accordingly, the Committee does not regard objections based on paragraph 7 or Article 2 of the Charter [barring U.N. intervention in the internal affairs of member nations] as having validity in the present case. A massive armed intervention by one Power on the territory of another, with the avowed intention of interfering with the internal affairs of the country must, by the Soviet's own definition of aggression, be a matter of international concern." [99]

More than two percent of the entire population of Hungary was able to escape guards, barbed wire, and mines to find refuge abroad.

For Khrushchev, the Hungarian intervention is today a "dead rat."

One questioner asks:

"In your speech you pointed out that there should be no intervention in internal affairs of other countries. How do you reconcile these words with the Russian intervention in Hungary?"

195

You see, the so-called Hungarian question has stuck in some people's teeth like a dead rat; they do not like it but they cannot spit it out. If you wish to push our conversation in this direction, I could throw at you more than one dead rat. And it would be fresher than the question of the well-known events in Hungary.

Apparently Khrushchev's interpreter, Oleg Troyanovsky, did not translate the remark about the "dead rat," and the remark did not appear in the American press.[100]

Khrushchev warns:

We do not advise the enemies of the working class to try our patience and organize new provocations. We declare that if another provocation against any socialist country is tolerated, then the provocateurs will have to deal with all the countries of the socialist camp. The Soviet Union is always ready to come to the aid of its friends, and resist the enemies of socialism should they attempt to upset the peaceful labor of the socialist countries.[101]

Even after the brutal suppression of the Hungarian revolution, Khrushchev denies that the communist governments in the satellites are maintained by force.

You think that the communist system in this or that country can be maintained only with the help of our armed forces? I would not fight for such a communist system. The communist system must be based on the will of the people, and if the people do not wish this system let them establish the way of life they prefer best. This is why we will unflinchingly withdraw our troops from all the countries in which they are stationed—from Poland, Hungary, East Germany—and I am sure that the peoples of these countries will defend their system even better then.[102]

PART **3**

METHODS

CHAPTER 8

The Power Front

Industrial Capability

The pathways to power open to the Soviet Union are limited in a modern world. Military action must be restrained in a time when any war may lead to Armageddon. Ideologically, the inroads that communism can make are limited in a world that has a growing appreciation for individual freedom and an increasing hostility toward the totalitarian state. This leaves economic competition as the major open battlefield—a field where ideological implications are minimized. On this battlefield Khrushchev has issued his challenge—not relinquishing, in any sense, the competition in other spheres.

Economics is the main field in which the peaceful competition of socialism and capitalism is taking place, and we are interested in winning this competition in a historically brief period of time.[1]

In this struggle, Khrushchev's chief weapon is his ability to mobilize the productive power of 200 million Russians and the additional millions in Russia's satellites, and to concentrate this productivity on providing the sinews of power—industrial, military, subversive, and ideological.

The principle of limited objectives is basic in Soviet tactics. The major productive effort is concentrated on a dozen essential products, with little regard to popular needs or wants. Among these products are steel, pig iron, petroleum, coal, cement, machine tools.

From this basic industry, the Soviet hopes to derive military capability, trading power, propaganda material—and the ability to produce greater industrial power. The paradox of being a great nation without industrial capacity has plagued Russia throughout its history.

Stalin pointed out:

"One feature of the history of old Russia was the continual beatings she suffered for falling behind, for her backwardness. She was beaten by the Mongol khans. She was beaten by the Turkish beys. She was beaten by the Swedish feudal lords. She was beaten by the Polish and Lithuanian gentry. She was beaten by the Japanese barons. All beat her—for her backwardness; for military backwardness, for cultural backwardness, for political backwardness, for industrial backwardness, for agricultural backwardness. She was beaten because to do so was profitable and could be done with impunity. Do you remember the words of the pre-revolutionary poets: 'You are poor and abundant, mighty and impotent, Mother Russia.' These words of the old poet were well learned by those gentlemen. They beat her, saying: 'You are abundant,' so one can enrich oneself at your expense. They beat her, saying: 'You are poor and impotent,' so you can be beaten and plundered with impunity. Such is the law of the exploiters—to beat the backward and the weak. It is the jungle law of capitalism. You are backward, you are weak—therefore you are wrong; hence, you can be beaten and enslaved. You are mighty—therefore you are right; hence, we must be wary of you."[2]

Communism was designed for a nation with a proletariat—a working class. The Russia of Lenin's time had little big industry and therefore little proletariat, and little of the basis for creating an industrial empire. Lenin noted:

"As long as we live in a small-peasant country, there is a surer economic basis in Russia for capitalism than for communism. . . . We have not eradicated the roots of capitalism and . . . have not undermined the base and support of the internal enemy. (The latter depends on small-scale production.) There is only one way of undermining it, namely large-scale production, and it is only in electricity that we have such a basis. Communism is the Soviet Government plus the electrification of the whole country. Otherwise the country will remain a small-peasant country." [3]

To resolve this paradox, Lenin saw only one way:

"The salvation of Russia lies not only in a good harvest on the peasant farms—that is not enough; and not only in the good condition of light industry, which provides the peasantry with consumers' goods—this, too, is not enough; we also need heavy industry. . . . Unless we save heavy industry, unless we restore it, we shall not be able to build up any industry; and without heavy industry we shall be doomed as an independent country. . . . Heavy industry needs state subsidies. If we cannot provide them, then we are doomed as a civilized state—let alone as a Socialist state." [4]

In 1913, Russia already had a small industrial base, vast resources, water power, and a population ready for technical development. But revolution, war, and, later, collectivization inhibited national progress. In 1928, the over-all productive capacity of the Soviet Union was still lower than in Czarist Russia. Stalin's answer to backwardness was collectivization of the land and industrialization with emphasis on heavy industry:

"What was the main link in the Five-Year Plan? The main link in the Five-Year Plan was heavy industry, with machine building as its core. For only heavy industry is capable of reconstructing industry as a whole, as well as the transport system and agriculture, and of putting them on their feet. It was necessary to start the realization of the Five-Year Plan from heavy industry. Hence, the restoration of heavy industry had to be made the basis of the fulfillment of the Five-Year Plan." [5]

Khrushchev mentions the plans with pride:

The peoples of the Soviet Union have worked hard to industrialize their country. We have had to live through much suffering and great hardships as we built up our national industry. The Soviet people deliberately made all those sacrifices. They stinted themselves of the very necessities of life because they realized only too well that only by developing their own economic and, above all, their national heavy industry, i.e., only by building up their own industry and manufacturing, the means of production, could the Soviet Union survive as an independent nation, develop quickly and steadily, and hit the great targets of our five-year plans. Nor were the Soviet people wrong in their hopes and calculations, for within a historically short period they have created their own large-scale modern industry, surpassed many highly developed capitalist countries, moved up to second place in the world in industrial production, and have now set themselves the aim of surpassing the United States as well.[6]

Khrushchev does not say that five to ten millions died of starvation, that other millions perished in forced-labor camps. Agricultural production declined sharply, but the industrialization went on. The inefficiencies resulting from the relentless pace that Stalin set were ascribed to sabotage. The country lived in an artificially stimulated fear of foreign aggression.

Stalin's successors had to decide the vital question of whether to immediately raise the Soviet people's standard of living by increasing production of consumer goods, or to put the accent on heavy industry. The proponent of the latter solution was Khrushchev. He won over his rival Georgi Malenkov.

In imposing this line, Khrushchev cited Stalin's example (barely a year before denouncing his crimes) and used Stalin's arguments to justify the austerity policy.

But you must know that for all successes of our country we are indebted to the victory of the general line of the Party, the line which was outlined by Lenin, which was undeviatingly carried out by the party under Stalin's leadership and which has been carried out by our entire party. This is the triumph of the line of industrializing the country. Without developing heavy industry, without developing coal mining and the metallurgical and chemical industries, without developing machine building, we could not have developed our national economy, we could not have ensured victory in the hard war years. We live in a capitalist encirclement. Our successes bring joy to our friends and infuriate our enemies. We must constantly strengthen the might of our motherland.[7]

A struggle must be waged against those who consider that we can be satisfied with the level of development of heavy industry so far achieved and can concentrate our main energies on the task of developing the light and food industries. It must be understood that propagation of such anti-Leninist views is particularly unpermissible in present circumstances, when our Party is directing all the efforts of the Soviet people to the solution of the great tasks of Communist construction, when the imperialist states are carrying on feverish preparations for war.[8]

In Khrushchev's Russia, this is the Party line:

The Communist Party of the Soviet Union attaches primary importance to the development of industry, and especially heavy industry, which is the very foundation of the socialist economy, the might of the country and the decisive factor in the development of productive forces and the raising of labor productivity in all branches of the national economy.[9]

As a result, 27 per cent of the Soviet national product is reinvested, compared with 17 per cent of the national product of the United States, whose production is much larger.

But even more important, while the United States places two-thirds of its investment in machinery for producing consumer goods, the USSR invests 65 per cent in capital expenditures for producing more capital goods. Thus the communists pyramid the effect of their investment. One other factor: the Soviet Union discards almost no old machinery. They have little to discard. More than half of America's capital investment is for replacement of old or less efficient models. This high rate of investment in an economy that produces, altogether, 40 to 50 per cent of United States production is made possible by holding down the share of the consumer in the total national product to 27 per cent or less of what they produce. Thirty *years ago this proportion was 60 per cent. In the United States consumers use 67 per cent of the national product.*[10] *The result is an average standard of living in the USSR equivalent to $8 a week in the U.S., about that of pre-Castro Cuba.*

This policy means continuing sacrifices for the Soviet people, but according to Khrushchev, these sacrifices are willingly accepted.

The nationwide discussion has shown that the Soviet people are fully aware that the main task in developing the USSR national economy consists of ensuring continuous technical progress on the basis of the preferential development of heavy industry. Soviet people knowingly accepted a curtailment of their needs in matters of food and clothing, in matters of housing and living conditions, as well as in many other respects. When we are being criticized that we do not always follow the latest Paris fashions of dress, that Soviet people still frequently wear quilted jackets which spoil the figure, we see it and admit it ourselves. We have restricted our requirements in many respects and we had no other way out.[11]

Khrushchev cites examples of the past to stir up enthusiasm and popular support for his policy of unending sacrifices.

During the strained times of the restoration and of the tempestuous construction of industry and agriculture, the Soviet patriots were prepared to wear clothes and footwear which were not of first-grade quality and not particularly attractively designed. They were willing to bear it for a time and to do without the adornments of daily life, though we enjoy—all of us do—the beautiful life and do not renounce the comforts and boons of a prosperous and cultured life.[12]

He promises a better life.

At present, in heavy industry, in machine building, in the development of science and technology, we have reached such a level that, without detriment to the interests of consolidating the defense of the country, without detriment to the further development of heavy industry and machine building we can develop light industry at a considerably higher speed—in particular so we can produce more footwear and textiles for the population so as to meet sufficiently the needs of the population in this type of goods within the next five to seven years.[13]

But the program proved too ambitious. The directives for the sixth Five-Year Plan, adopted in February 1956, provided for a huge capital investment and at the same time for more consumer goods and improvement in housing. It became apparent by the end of the year that the demands of the Plan could not be met. In part, this setback was due to the revolutionary explosions in Poland and Hungary in the fall of 1956. Soviet aid—in the form of short-term loans —was needed to restore stability in Eastern Europe. The emphasis on industry, the extreme constriction of consumption, was continued.

With a better industrial base, consumers can get a little more, but the same policy of reinvestment in production goods persists even in plans made through 1965. Industrial capacity is to be increased by 82–85%, consumer-goods production by 62–65% from the present base. The effect—an even smaller portion of total production will go to consumers.

Comrades, we are implementing a vast program of capital construction, the volume of which is expanding every year. In the two years that have elapsed since the Twentieth Congress of the Communist Party of the Soviet Union, 400,000 million rubles [in prices as of July 1, 1955] have been invested in the national economy. And this is more than the total investments made for the First and Second Five-Year Plans and the three and a half prewar years of the Third Five-Year Plan.[14]

A primary factor in industrial power is labor productivity. On this score the Soviet Union still ranks low among the world's industrial nations. Lenin made the point clearly.

"Labor productivity is in the final analysis the principal and most important factor for the victory of the new social order. Capitalism created a degree of labor productivity unknown under serfdom.

Capitalism can be utterly vanquished and will be utterly vanquished by the fact that socialism creates a new and much higher level of labor productivity." [15]

Khrushchev echoes:

The principal task of the working class in the socialist countries today is to make better, more productive use of our forces, so that more is produced per worker than in the capitalist countries. We do not need to work for this by expending greater physical effort, but by stepping up mechanization, improving production and introducing specialization and automation. We must strive to reduce the working day, rather than to prolong it, and to increase output per worker. It is only by raising the productivity of labor that we shall beat capitalist production, demonstrate the superiority of the socialist system, and thereby create the conditions for building a communist society.[16]

The time has come, comrades, to work on the automation of production processes in earnest. From the automation of separate aggregates and operations one must pass on to the automation of shops, technological processes and complete enterprises. We need all this for one end: for building a communist society. Many processes of heavy exhausting toil have already become obsolete in our country. Labor has become considerably more productive and easier. However, a great deal of manual labor is still used in industry. Manual labor must be replaced by machines while man should manage the machines in production and control the correctness of technological processes.[17]

"Ordinary mechanization has sometimes produced disappointing results in Russia. Down in the Donets coal fields in the Ukraine, the newspaper *Pravda* angrily disclosed not long ago, it takes more workers to produce a ton of coal today than it did twenty years ago, despite costly postwar mechanization. Half the new mining machines are sitting idle, the Communist Party organ declared, either for repairs or in order to free their operators for manual jobs. Sometimes, it said, only one step has been mechanized, throwing the others in utter confusion. In a 'typical case' of a mine which has been hailed as a 'coal enterprise of tomorrow,' the paper said, only surface activity has been mechanized, while underground the miners feverishly try to keep up with these coal processing machines by using hammers and their bare hands." [18]

The complex mechanization and automation of production processes in every branch of the national economy constitute a decisive prerequisite for the creation of a material and technical basis for communism. The theses envisage that in the next seven-year period complex mechanization of production processes will be complete in the main and that a transition from automation of individual aggregates and installations to complex automation, to the creation of fully automatic shops and enterprises, will be in effect.[19]

"At most, it is figured in the West, Russia is devoting less than 5 per cent of its new plant and equipment spending on what even roughly corresponds to automation in the West. In the United States the figure is estimated at 15 per cent to 25 per cent and in some American companies today automation absorbs half the new investment funds. One reason for the Soviet lag is that the Russian program is still somewhat up in the air; it's being held up, among other things, by a lack of agreement on what type of production equipment is to be selected for mass output." [20]

Electrification has special traditional significance in Soviet plans.

If Vladimir Ilyich Lenin could have a look at what the people have done, what miracles they work in transforming their free country, he would take off his cap and make a deep bow. The things Lenin lived for, the things he planned and dreamed of are now being successfully implemented by our people and the party.[21]

Our country has achieved such a high level in the development of our economy, science and technology that we can embark on and implement in the next fifteen to twenty years

207

the task set by the great Lenin: total electrification. This is a great and noble task. It is understandable that all the questions regarding the solution of this task must be well thought out from every angle. To do this, a commission must be set up in which experienced specialists must take part. It is essential to integrate the development of power engineering with the long-term plan for the fifteen-year development of the national economy which is being worked out by the Gosplan [official State Planning Bureau]. This plan will really be a program of communist construction.[22]

In total energy production, the Soviet Union, with an energy output equivalent to 2.45 tons of coal per capita, ranks the lowest on the list of modern nations. The figure compares with the United States, 8.58 tons; United Kingdom, 5.03 tons; and Western Europe, 2.68 tons.[23] In terms of total output the Soviet produces one-third of the United States' electrical energy, hopes to reach 44 per cent by 1965.[24] But almost all of the Soviet production is utilized for industry, little for consumption.[25]

Russia depends principally on coal (for 60.8 per cent of her energy) and oil (23.4 per cent). The Seven-Year Plan envisages by 1965 a shift to 32.2 per cent from coal, 34.4 per cent from oil, and 23.3 per cent from natural gas. Hydroelectricity will provide only 2.4 per cent and atomic energy 3.2 per cent.

The Soviet Union is particularly proud of its progress in pig-iron and steel production. The ferrous metals are a basic factor in Russia's industrial-military potential. The Soviet Union uses little steel for automobiles or household appliances. It requires metals for industrial products, construction and manufactures for which other nations use aluminum, zinc, other metals, and plastics. Mr. Khrushchev boasts:

In the next few years the Soviet Union will occupy first place in the world in the extraction of iron ore.[26]

The Soviet Union, for example, is going to build seven blast furnaces this year and thereby alone increase the output of pig iron by more than four and a half million tons. We shall see by how much the capitalist countries increase their pig-iron output! [27]

The Soviet Union's 1958 output of pig iron was 39.6 million metric tons. Its 1965 plan quota is 65 to 70 million metric tons. The United States 1958 output—53.4 million metric tons.[28]

In the chemical industries the USSR is far behind Western industrial countries. She lacks most synthetic fibers, plastics, basic chemicals, and even fertilizers.

The question therefore arises: Should we not give thought to developing the chemical industry in our countries on the basis of a division of labor? . . .

We have such personnel. But we would gladly enlist the services of German chemical engineers and scientists and other specialists, including experts from West Germany, for work in our chemical industry. West German specialists may say that their political convictions and views differ from ours. But let them set aside questions of political conviction. If a scientist or engineer does not share communist views and communist convictions, let him keep his own convictions and come to us simply as a chemist or scientist. If he really wants to achieve the best results from the application of his labor, we shall offer him every opportunity for doing so. We shall pay him more than the richest concerns and firms are paying. We shall provide such scientists, engineers and technicians with the finest equipment for the tackling of scientific and technical problems.[29]

We have proposed to the government of the United States that an agreement be concluded for the delivery of chemical equipment to our country and that appropriate credits be granted in this connection. But so far we have received no reply from the United States. It is apparently very difficult for the United States Government to reply to our proposals. But we are in no hurry about this—we shall wait. Furthermore, if we do wait, that does not mean we are doing nothing. We are waiting for an answer, but at the same time we ourselves are working on the problem of speeding up the development of our chemical industry with our own resources. . . .

At the same time we are sure that we shall also be dealing with businessmen from capitalist countries, with all who want to earn by taking part in the development of our chemical industry. If they don't want to make money, that is their own affair. The Soviet Union offers them orders, and it is up to them to accept or reject those orders. We do not intend to quarrel with anyone about this.[30]

Khrushchev issues the challenge:

Forty years have now passed. Where was Russia at that time? She held one of the last places. Where is the Soviet Union now, what heights has it reached? As regards the level of economic development it has reached second place in the world, leaving far behind such countries as Britain, France, Germany, and others.[31]

Guided by the teaching of Marxism-Leninism, our Communist Party has brought the Soviet people to a great triumph—to achievements so outstanding that the Soviet Union has now overtaken and outstripped all the capitalist countries, with the exception of the U.S.A., in volume of industrial production.[32]

In 1965 the absolute output of some of the most important types of goods in the Soviet Union will surpass, and the output in other types of goods will approach, the present level of industrial output in the United States. By that time the per capita output of the most important products of agriculture as a whole will surpass the present standard of the United States.[33]

If we calculate on a per capita basis, we will probably need, after the fulfillment of the Seven-Year Plan, about five more years to catch up with and outstrip the United States in industrial output. Thus, by that time, or perhaps even sooner, the Soviet Union will advance to first place in the world both in absolute volume of production and in per capita production. This will be a world-historic victory of socialism in peaceful competition with capitalism in the international arena.[34]

In reporting a recent interview with Khrushchev, W. Averell Harriman, one-time U.S. ambassador to Moscow, quoted the Premier as saying, when describing the "inevitable triumph of communism":

In five to seven years, we will be stronger than you. . . . We developed the hydrogen bomb before you. We have intercontinental missiles, and our rockets carry warheads many times larger than yours.[35]

What do specific figures show?

In the fields in which they concentrate—basic materials and machine tools—the Soviet Union has made and indeed will make substantial progress from a far-behind position.

COMPARISON OF SELECTED COMMODITY OUTPUTS IN THE UNITED STATES AND SOVIET UNION

	Year	Unit of measure	U.S.	USSR	USSR as per-cent of U.S.
Electric power	1957	Billion kilowatt-hours	716.0	209.5	29.3
Coal	1956	Million short tons	529.8	472.1	89.1
Cotton cloth	1957	Million linear yards	9,563.0	6,119.0	64.0
Oil	1956	Million metric tons	364.0	83.8	23.0
Natural Gas	1956	Billion cubic feet	10,082.0	483.0	4.8
Lumber	1957	Million board feet	37,698.0	32,204.0	85.4
Steel	1959	Million tons	77.2	54.9	69.6
Machine tools	1959	Thousand units	32	138	431.0

Khrushchev's big pitch is a planned growth of 80 per cent in gross national output in seven years, 1958–65, and sufficient additional growth during the following five years to surpass the United States in basic industrial products.

Soviet production of industrial equipment in 1959 amounted to approximately 65 per cent of United States industrial-equipment output. However, the Soviet industrial equipment on hand is roughly equal to 40 per cent of the United States installed industrial equipment; thirty years ago it was only 8 per cent. The growth is the result of a highly concentrated effort in Soviet investment.

This concentration has produced an immense armament industry of diversified character, and a capital-goods industry exceeding in some lines, such as machine-tool production, that of the United States.

That the Soviet aims to exploit this industrial power is no secret. However, the use made of the Soviet industrial product rather than its quantity or its quality is a cause for concern. Whereas U.S. steel production goes into automobiles and washing machines, Russia's steel goes into machine tools and armaments. While U.S. oil fuels motor cars on the highways, Soviet oil, sold at 15 to 50 per cent below the world market price, is making friends and influencing people in Argentina, India, Cuba, Sweden, and even Western Europe.

A Party handbook makes the purpose clear:

"We strive to develop the thought that success in diplomacy depends on a country's might, that the international note of the Soviet Union is defined by the greatness of her victory over fascist Germany. Every Soviet citizen, working to increase the economic might of the country is thereby actively assisting the state in its foreign policy. . . . Just as in war each one by his labor made a contribution toward victory, so by unremitting effort now, each one is helping to solve the most vital international problems." [36]

This Mr. Khrushchev echoes:

Many people are interested in the international position. The international position of the socialist countries depends chiefly on their internal position. If our internal position is good it creates for our countries a good international position. The internal position is determined by the results of labor. The higher developed a country's economy the better its position. And the economy depends on the productivity of labor. The higher the level of the economy and labor productivity the higher are wages, the more values man obtains as a result of his labor. That is why questions of organization of labor, its productivity, higher output per worker, are the main things.[37]

Trade

Traditionally the Soviet Union, particularly while under Stalin's leadership, was attempting to build "socialism in one country," and so devoted its resources to attaining self-sufficiency. But looking ahead, Stalin predicted in 1927:

"In the course of further development of international revolution two centers will form on a world scale: a socialist center, binding to itself the countries that gravitate to socialism, and a capitalist center, binding to itself the countries that gravitate to capitalism. The struggle between these two centers for the possession of the world economy will decide the fate of capitalism and communism in the whole world." [38]

The bonds Stalin seemed to envision then were economic. At the time Stalin made his prediction, the Soviet needs were those of a largely peasant economy crippled by the forced collectivization, with a nascent, still-primitive heavy industry—principally geared to defense and agricultural machinery.

Stalin explained a few years later what trade had meant to the Soviet Union during the first Five-Year Plan:

"Of course, out of the one and a half billion rubles in foreign currency that we spent on purchasing equipment for our heavy industry, we could have set apart a half for the purpose of importing raw cotton, hides, wool, rubber, etc. We would then have had more calico, boots and clothes. But then, we would not have had a tractor and an automobile industry, we would not have had anything like a big iron and steel industry, we would not have had metal for the production of machinery—and we would have been unarmed in the midst of a capitalist environment which is armed with modern technique. . . . We would have deprived ourselves of all the modern means of defense without which the political independence of the country is impossible, without which a country is transformed into a field of military operations of foreign enemies.

213

*. . . In a word, in that case, we would have had military interven-
tion, not pacts of non-aggression, but war, dangerous and fatal war,
sanguinary and unequal war; for in that war we would have been
almost unarmed in the face of the enemy, who has all the modern
means of attack at his disposal."* [39]

Khrushchev's Russia is an industrialized nation with considerable
economic potentialities and a strong drive to compete with the most
modern and powerful nations of the world. Khrushchev even feels
strong enough to engage in economic warfare with the United States:

We declare war upon you—excuse me for using such an expression—in the peaceful field of trade. We declare a war. We
will win over the United States. The threat of the United
States is not the ICBM, but in the field of peaceful production. We are relentless in this and it will prove the superiority
of our system.[40]

*However, he does not feel that he can tell this to the Soviet peo-
ple. His remark was omitted from the Soviet versions of his interview with William Randolph Hearst, Jr., editor in chief of the Hearst
newspapers.*

Khrushchev does tell the Supreme Soviet that, according to Lenin,
the general, world-wide economic relations . . . will compel "the hostile governments or classes," to take the path of trade relations with
us. And he adds:

Life has confirmed the correctness of Lenin's words. Despite all the intrigues of diverse enemies, the Soviet Union's
foreign trade is expanding from year to year. Today we trade
with fifty-one foreign countries. In 1953 the volume of our
trade with foreign firms was 11 per cent greater than in the
previous year, and nearly four times the prewar figure.[41]

For the time being, however, trade is not a major item in the
Soviet economy. According to Soviet foreign trade expert and Deputy Prime Minister Anastas Mikoyan, Soviet trade in 1959 amounted
to 40 billion rubles ($10 billion at the official four-to-one exchange

rate), which represents less than 5 per cent of the Soviet national product (and this figure includes trade with countries of the Sino-Soviet bloc). Trade with the rest of the world amounted to about 3 per cent of the national product.

The bourgeois press presents the proposals of the Soviet Government to improve business relations with capitalist sources as "the Soviet Union's economic bomb," as some sort of "communist plot" to conquer the world.[42]

As a political weapon, trade—like aid to underdeveloped countries—can be an important weapon to a regime in a centrally directed economy.

The Soviet Union can shift its trade with deliberate intent and has demonstrated that it can turn it on (e.g., Iceland, Burma, Egypt) or off (e.g., Israel, Yugoslavia, Japan) at the whim of the moment. Moreover, since the bloc's market potential is large, the quantities involved in individual deals are sizable compared with the West's atomistic and impersonal market operations.

It has thus been able to take advantage of difficulties in the free market world—buying fish from Iceland, rice from Burma, cotton from Egypt, rubber from Ceylon, trading oil for sugar in Cuba, oil for coffee in Brazil, offering oil below market price in India and Argentina. Whether these deals (and others) were economically sound or not, they were desirable because of their political impact.

When Iceland's fish was barred in Great Britain in 1952 in a dispute over territorial waters, the Soviet bloc increased its purchases of fish so that its share in Iceland exports rose from 7 per cent in 1952 to 25 per cent in 1954. This dispute between two partners of the Western alliance is continuing, and in 1958 the bloc accounted for no less than 35 per cent of Iceland's exports and 32 per cent of its imports. A few months after the Soviet trade deal the United States, under pressure, began withdrawing some of its troops based in Iceland.

The West is not a large factor in the world's rice markets, though

215

the sale of excess U.S. stocks at the time when Burma's concern over its surplus reached its peak may have been a disturbing element, at least psychologically. In any event, the bloc's timely offer in 1955 to buy up 750,000 tons of rice appeared like a godsend, even though the quantities actually shipped were much smaller. This was not the bloc's fault, but the rice market had turned and rice could again be sold for cash.

An oversupply of cotton gave the bloc an opening in Egypt and Syria.

The bloc has become by far the largest customer of Egypt and Syria, absorbing 44 and 31 per cent, respectively, of their exports and imports in 1958. Reportedly, there was some friction over bloc resales of cotton at lower prices (not surprisingly, since the price of cotton in Alexandria has been driven above the world price as a result of Soviet purchases). In the Sudan, too, where surpluses of long-staple cotton have been increasing, the bloc has made offers to buy on a large scale and pay with development goods and technical assistance. He even offers to buy a nation's entire product.

I am like a merchant who comes to market with a bag full of things. Wrap up all your goods and send them to us. We can buy all of Austria.[43]

The political character of Soviet trade is no secret. When Iceland's Communist cabinet minister was dismissed, Soviet trade was also lost; when a Communist cabinet minister came back, Soviet trade thawed again. When Finland elected a government without Communist representation, the USSR stopped its orders for Finnish goods. Inasmuch as a large part of Finland's industry was created to pay reparations to Russia, there was no other readily available market for these goods. The Finns are substantially dependent on the USSR for economic stability.

Egypt provided the only vulnerable position in the Middle East for Soviet infiltration. Political support, arms, and the Soviet's second-largest aid appropriation were supplemented by trade, which now accounts for 37 per cent of UAR's total. The Soviet Union buys cotton from Egypt, although it produces and is expanding production of cotton itself. Indeed, Egyptian cotton appears on the markets of France and England via bloc countries.

Although the individual circumstances may vary, there is a very real danger that a producer of primary commodities may first seek relief in establishing a relationship with the Soviet bloc and then become so dependent on it that the possibility of losing this market would make it vulnerable to political pressure.

Khrushchev's approach to trade with the industrialized—capitalist—countries is to convince them that such trade with the Soviet Union is commercially profitable and, politically, serves the interests of peace. Urging more exchanges with the United States, he says:

We want to be friends with the United States and to co-operate with it for peace and international security and also in the economic and cultural spheres. We propose this with good intentions, without holding a knife behind our back. We have put forward our proposal not because the Soviet Union cannot live without such a treaty with the United States. The Soviet state existed and developed successfully even when it had no normal diplomatic relations with the United States. We have proposed a treaty to the United States because the conclusion of such a treaty would meet the profoundest aspirations of the peoples of both countries, to live in peace and friendship.[44]

And:

Who can deny the need for doing away with such ugly phenomena in international economic relations as discrimination, all kinds of blacklists and similar artificial obstacles to international trade?[45]

Let us create conditions which would promote greater confidence between our peoples. Let us trade, even if not in strategic goods, as you call them, then in goods in general. If it is unprofitable for you to trade with the Soviet Union, then let us formally eliminate the discrimination which exists in the trade between our countries. This will promote trust.[46]

217

I believe the main thing is to normalize relations between countries and, above all, between the United States and the Soviet Union. I understand normalization as pulling down barriers in trade. . . . So far you have been discriminating, you don't want to trade with us. Your politicians, upon whom this matter depends, believe that thereby they are harming communism. But you see this is doing us very little damage. On the contrary, this compels us to make things we could buy from you, and on which you could profit. Now we ourselves are making these things and are forging ahead. And that is how it will continue to be.[47]

Trade is litmus paper—it shows the state of relations between governments. It shows whether they want to live in peace or not.[48]

In a letter to President Eisenhower suggesting that the United States grant trade credits to the Soviet Union, Khrushchev recalls the past:

Extensive trade between the Soviet Union and the United States would not be something new to our countries, for there have been times when economic relations between us developed most successfully to mutual advantage. In the past ten years, however, the Soviet Union's trade with the United States, far from developing, has dropped to an insignificant level, through no fault of the USSR. The United States is today the only great power which does not have trade agreement with the Soviet Union.

. . . there is no need to speak at length on the usefulness of economic, and primarily trade, relations between countries. The great importance of such relations is obvious and has repeatedly been stressed by statesmen both in the USSR and the United States. We remember, for example, the words of the late Secretary of State, Mr. Cordell Hull, that trade and contracts can be an antidote to war. You will agree, I think, that the world needs this antidote now, perhaps, as never before.[49]

According to United States law, credits can be granted only to countries that have settled previous debts. The Soviet Union still has an outstanding account rising out of the Lend-Lease agreements of World War II. In January 1960, negotiations to settle this debt were renewed in Washington. The United States asked for $800 million for the $11 billion in merchandise shipped; the Soviet Union offered $300 million. These negotiations broke down after a few meetings.

During his visit to the United States in September 1959, Khrushchev sought support for his trade policy from the American business community. Time and again he made the following points:

Economic contacts with us will be profitable, as in the past.

Some thirty years ago, when our country started building a large-scale industry, good economic contacts were established with leading United States firms. Ford helped us build the motor works in Gorky. Cooper, a prominent American specialist, acted as consultant during the building of the hydropower station on the Dnieper, which in those days was the biggest in the world. Your engineers helped us build the tractor works in Stalingrad and Kharkov. Americans, along with the British, were consultants during the construction of the Moscow subway. We were grateful to your specialists for their cooperation and many of them returned home with Soviet decorations and letters of thanks, to say nothing of remuneration in cash.[50]

You are already late—we are trading with some of your allies:

Our trade relations with Britain are shaping out quite well. Trade is expanding with businessmen in West Germany. It should be noted that the government of West Germany also has a correct understanding of the interests of its country in this matter, and cooperates in the development of trade contracts rather than obstructs them. We welcome this. Good economic relations are shaping between us and Italy. Relations with France are not bad. Why then must America stand apart? However, that is up to you. The question of trade is a question of profit. If you find it unprofitable to buy from us, or to sell us some goods, do as you think best.

But bear one thing in mind. It sometimes happens that too choosy a girl lets time slip, stays unmarried too long, and is left empty-handed. Such maidenly indecision is doubly out of place in business, where the rule "First come, first served," perpetuated in an English proverb, operates more than anywhere else. We too have a rather good saying to that effect: "He who comes late gets a picked bone." [51]

Khrushchev makes no secret of his chief aim—to buy American technical know-how. In an interview during his 1959 trip to the U.S., he answered frankly:

Question: Why, in spite of all this, do you adopt a lot of what there is in the capitalist countries?

Because we are not fools! Why should we turn our backs on useful experience? You have set many examples in organizing production. Ford, for instance, started line production. We have adopted that method and are developing it for the better.

Question: We are interested in trading with you. But why are Soviet organizations buying only sample machines?

I'll tell you frankly. If John Deere wants to sell us tractors and agricultural machines, that is not realistic, because we are making our own agricultural machines. We are buying and can buy, say, ten or a hundred tractors and other agricultural machines. That is done to compare them with our machines, to see which are better. But why are you displeased with that? How many tractors or combines do you sell to a farmer? Would Garst buy a thousand tractors from you? I should think that no single farmer would buy even as many as ten machines. He'll buy one or two, but we'll buy ten or a hundred. The argument about samples is unrealistic. I'll tell you frankly that in the sense of purchases we are not interested in tractors, combines, aircraft or rockets. We are interested in chemical equipment, in equipment for engineering works and oil refineries. We can sell you tractors ourselves, gentlemen. If you like we can even sell you one tractor.[52]

And:

We did have considerable trade with many American firms. With Ford, for example. And it was profitable both for Ford and us.

Question: Perhaps it was profitable for Ford but not for America?

But the American business world is made up of Fords! [53]

Result of Soviet borrowing of technology: at least one American manufacturer found himself competing in the world market with his own products, made on his machinery seized after the Communist take-over in Czechoslovakia.[54]

The Soviets do want credits—although Khrushchev says he really does not need them.

We are not asking for credits, but if American manufacturers want to get big orders from us, they will get them provided they give us credits. I have in mind credits from firms, such as the English have given us. As regards government credits these are evidently impossible with the present state of relations between countries. If credits will be forthcoming from firms we shall pay a reasonable interest. But I stress, a reasonable interest. We shall not agree to a high interest. . . .

. . . We are not in a position where we have to ask for credits to help us out.[55]

But when he reported on his trip to Soviet audiences, the question of credits appeared to be quite important:

When I was in the United States a conversation took place there between myself and the Under Secretary of State Mr. Dillon. "Let us develop trade between our countries, improve economic mutual relations," I told him, "for this is profitable for you. Do sell us more goods. We shall buy them, provided you would grant credits to us. For credits are profitable not for the recipients alone but sometimes are more profitable for those who grant them. You need orders for the products of your industry. We shall provide these orders. But give us credit for this purpose. We shall honestly repay the money given us in credit. For should we even borrow from the devil, we would pay that debt to him as well." [56]

All in all, Khrushchev's attempts to promote business with the United States did not yield spectacular results. He commented on his lack of success.

The United States is a very rich country, and some American leaders believe that our economy will not advance if they do not trade with us. But this is an obvious delusion. If they do not want to trade, we shall wait! We can wait, but we believe that in the end the United States will trade with us. Whether this happens in a year or within two or ten years, I do not know, but they will trade with us because they have no other way out. We can wait until this happens. Wait even for a hundred years. Our economy will develop whether or not we have a brisk trade with the United States. This is how we understand this question. [57]

Khrushchev blames the "stagnation of Soviet-American economic relations" on "politicians rather than businessmen." He also maintains that the Soviet Union "derived a certain benefit" from United States trade restrictions:

We have had to develop production of machines that we did not have before and intended to buy from you, and now are not dependent on anyone in this respect. Thus, the artificial dwarfing of trade with the Soviet Union has strengthened rather than weakened us. [58]

These trade limitations were introduced into United States legislation as a result of the Korean war. United States export-control regulations restrict the sale of strategic goods to countries behind the Iron Curtain.

In 1956, while visiting Britain, Khrushchev attacked this legislation:

Certain politicians ask: "Would it not be dangerous to trade in strategic goods if there should suddenly be a war?" But just what are strategic goods? The answer to this question depends on the point of view. Butter, for example, might also be included among strategic goods. In our opinion, this approach must be given up and real trade encouraged. You must sell what people will buy. If you don't want to, don't sell us guns, aircraft and ships, the more so since in the present development of technology, they rapidly become obsolete. What was good yesterday will be old tomorrow. This is clear to everyone.[59]

To U.S. businessmen, Khrushchev emphasized his desire to keep "politics" out of trade, adding that it was the United States that introduced political factors into economic relations.

It is an American institution . . . that invented a special list of embargoes, which you, businessmen, are compelled to observe when trading with the Soviet Union. Let's not argue, however. History will establish who associated trade with politics, and in what way.

I want to emphasize that the Soviet Government has always advocated, and continues to advocate, equitable, mutually beneficial international trade without any discrimination whatsoever—the trade spoken of by Benjamin Franklin, whose words, "Commerce among nations should be fair and equitable," are engraved above the front entrance of the United States Department of Commerce.[60]

The present bad trade relations between our countries are not an economic but a political factor. You did not recognize the Soviet Union for sixteen years, but you traded with us. Now you recognize us, but do not trade. How much longer this will continue, sixteen years or more, I cannot tell. That is your affair, reflect on it and decide for yourself.[61]

In trade as in all other matters, Khrushchev's emphasis is on the United States. But he does not neglect the other industrialized nations of the Western alliance. While in the United States, he mentioned Soviet trade agreements with West Germany, France, Italy, Great Britain.

Abroad, his approach is similar to the one presented in the United States. Thus, through one of Britain's mass-circulation papers, he made the following points:

The most important factor in improving Anglo-Soviet relations is the development of trade. You British are realists. We also regard ourselves to be realists. Britain has reached a high level of development in industry, science and art thanks to her talented and industrious people. Britain to a large extent depends on trade with other countries. She is interested in the further development of trade, including trade with the Soviet Union. We on our side would readily agree to this and we could be very profitable trade partners. Our country could buy from you many industrial products which are made so well by the British. Britain could also buy from us industrial products which she needs. And what is most important, she could buy from us raw materials as her economy depends on imported raw materials. Consequently we could successfully, and with benefit to both sides, develop our relations and consolidate friendship between peoples . . .

The development of Anglo-Soviet trade demands the elimination of discrimination and limitations. When we are told: You can buy this from us but you cannot buy that, then this annoys us so much that we sometimes refuse to buy items which under normal conditions we would have bought. We are a proud people, we do not like to humble ourselves. We do not like to enter a shop where they tell us we can buy one type of goods but not another and that the latter type can only be bought by NATO countries.[62]

To France, he says while visiting that country:

You still do not fully understand the possibilities of the Soviet market . . . Do not let yourselves be outdistanced by your competitors. . . . A commercial agreement for three years has been signed. We could prolong its duration to five years and double the volume of prospective exchanges.[63]

He remains vague, however, on the way in which he will pay. In answer to questions regarding the mode of payment for the increased French exports to the Soviet Union, inasmuch as France does not need the oil and the coal offered in exchange by the Russians, Khrushchev remarks:

We do not have any dollars up our sleeves and are parsimonious with our gold. We have some, but we keep it maybe out of habit or in order, as Lenin said, to pave our bathrooms with gold.[64]

Now the market of the capitalist countries of Europe, already narrowed due to the notorious restrictions in trade with socialist countries, is divided into various zones of insulated associations of states. This by no means promotes the development of normal trade relations between various countries. Restricted economic alignments often lead to political separation and to various complications in relations among states. . . .[65]

Addressing some of his French followers (Lenin would have called them "fellow travelers"), Khrushchev adds a little propaganda.

What does economic cooperation mean? It means trade. It is not we who carry out a policy of discrimination in trade; a policy of discrimination is pursued against us. It is precisely with us that they do not want to trade. And as a pretext they concocted fairy tales about strategic material—but we produced our own rockets. You know full well that there are no more strategic goods than rockets! We do not want to beg Britain or the United States for such "goods." Our goods are better.[66]

When Khrushchev talks about trade he tries to sound like an honest businessman. But an analysis of Soviet practices leads U.S. experts to conclude:

"The Soviet Union is often a difficult competitor, unpredictable and unwilling to enter international agreements. Cutting prices has enabled the Soviet Union to break into markets—such as tin, aluminum, petroleum—in which its activities in the past have been minimal. The other supplying countries complain bitterly, but there is little that can be done. The primary producers—Bolivia, Malaya, and Canada, among others—have received the hardest treatment, but even in the machinery field, Western Europe is beginning to feel some [Soviet] bloc competition. Bloc countries also pursue some other unsavory commercial practices, such as re-exporting commodities in violation of agreements, changing prices of exports, and so forth." [67]

Typical of Soviet trade tactics are its efforts in the petroleum industry.

The output of oil and gas is rising, and we all rejoice in this.[68]

World production of petroleum in 1958 was 791 million metric tons; the U.S. produced 331 million tons, the USSR produced 103 million tons. Because petroleum is sold in a delicately balanced and controlled market and is a major factor in Western trade, it is a logical target for Soviet encroachments.

The Soviets have not only developed their own resources for export—they encourage development of new supplies by furnishing discovery technicians to India, Pakistan, Ethiopia, and Latin American countries.

Oil has been the Soviet's strongest wedge in economic politics. Soviet traders sell to Argentina at 33 per cent below market price, and in 1960 broke the world market price by offering to sell it to India at 15 per cent below current levels. A barter deal with Italy in November 1960, setting the oil price at 69c a barrel, instead of the world market price of $1.59, and made payable in Italian-made pipeline materials, gave the USSR a vital hold on Italy's industrial fuel supply. The price quoted is less than the cost of production of Kuwait oil, the world's cheapest, which formerly supplied Italy. In the Cuba situation, Khrushchev was able to barter sugar at 1 cent above world market prices and supply oil—but here at above market prices.

We will help our Cuban brothers to fight an economic blockade and the blockade will be a failure.

With no stake in a stable market or petroleum conservation, with no Middle East partners to consider, no taxes to pay, Russia has substantial advantages. She will accept coffee, bananas, or sugar in payment. Even the Western Europeans are her good customers. Germany has agreed to take 1.5 million metric tons, France 1.2 million tons, Italy 3.1 million tons, Sweden 1.5 million tons. Finland and Iceland take practically all their requirements. Japan will take 1.5 million metric tons in 1962. Argentina and Cuba, Venezuela's neighbors, are big Soviet customers.

Price is no real object. With a world market price of $21 a ton, Argentina paid 12, Poland 21.50, Italy 14.50, Hungary 22. Any new market can get a bargain, particularly if political considerations may be involved.

"But thus far the battle has been only half joined. Russia, with a productivity rate hardly two-fifths of ours, has concentrated its production in a few fields which can—and which they expect will—help destroy the American economy: petroleum, steel, machine tools and a variety of agricultural products. Their relatively small production of oil, tin, and aluminum has been thrown into world markets to disrupt prices at crucial times. This with no real capability. But in 1961, they plan to make a real bid for a trade war with a hard ruble. Having accumulated $8 billion or more of unmortgaged gold—versus the U.S. $19 billion (against which there is at least an equal amount in short-term dollar claims)—they will undoubtedly use the monolithic force of a government-supported foreign trade monopoly and a captive labor force willing to work for one-fourth American wages—to accumulate power for the communist cause."[69]

It is, of course, not essential for the Soviet objective that sovereignty be placed in communist hands, if fundamental economic control of a country can be obtained. And trade may be not only an entree to a relationship, but a means of creating dependence of increasing dimensions—from the simple economic attachment of Egypt, Iceland, Cuba, and Finland, to a total dependence of Hungary, Rumania, and Bulgaria.

"From the military viewpoint, economic capacity is an essential ingredient of national power, but it is neither direct, nor precise. The use to which economic capability is put is a major factor: A strong economy convertible to the needs of war has been a basic American asset. However, the economic potential for war is limited to capacity in strategic industries, and by the time element of conversion. In a blitzkrieg, with the buffer of the oceans no longer shielding, conversion time must be relatively immediate." [70]

Military Capability

I want to be understood correctly: we do not want to frighten anyone, but we can tell the truth—now we have such a stock of rockets, such an amount of atomic and hydrogen warheads, that if they attack us we could wipe our potential enemies off the face of the earth.[71]

Conquest implies force. Force can be used directly, to crush the enemy. Or it may also be used to threaten, to intimidate, to make the adversary admit defeat before a fight has even started. "Political power," writes Mao Tse-tung, "grows out of the barrel of a gun. Politics is war that sheds no blood, while war is bloodshedding politics." [72]

Countless times, Khrushchev has said that as a communist, a Marxist-Leninist, he is confident of the victory of "socialism." This victory, he maintains, will be achieved by peaceful means, through the interplay of social forces in each country in its own time—without foreign intervention.

Lenin taught that "great historical questions can be solved only by violence." He urged "the building of a revolutionary army" because, he said, "the organization of violence in the modern struggle

228

is a military organization." [73] Lenin emphasized the necessity of calling forth an international revolution, traversing the path from a
strictly national revolution to the world revolution.

Lenin foresaw war—the inevitable war—between the communist
and the capitalist worlds. In Stalin's time, the Communist International
echoed Lenin's belief that war was "inevitable":

"The proletariat in the Soviet Union harbors no illusions as to the
possibility of a durable peace with the imperialists. The proletariat
knows that the imperialist attack against the Soviet Union is inevitable; that in the process of a proletarian world revolution wars
between proletarian and bourgeois States, wars for the emancipation
of the world from capitalism will necessarily and inevitably arise.
Therefore, the primary duty of the proletariat, as the fighter for
socialism, is to make all the necessary political, economic and military
preparations for these wars, to strengthen its Red Army—that mighty
weapon of the proletariat—and to train the masses of the toilers in
the art of war.

"There is a glaring contradiction between the imperialists' policy
of piling up armaments and their hypocritical talk about peace.
There is no such contradiction, however, between the Soviet government's preparations for defense and for revolutionary war and a
consistent peace policy. Revolutionary war of the proletarian dictatorship is but a continuation of revolutionary peace policy 'by
other means.' " [74]

However, in 1941 the main "capitalist" powers rushed to the aid
of the "socialist fatherland" when "imperialist" (therefore also
"capitalist") Germany launched its aggression against the Soviet
Union. The years following the joint victory over Nazi Germany were
years of Soviet expansion. A new empire—socialist in name, totalitarian in form—was being created by Stalin. Khrushchev inherited
Stalin's empire, conquered by force of arms. He also inherited Stalin's
conviction that:

"In our times it is not the custom to give any consideration to the
weak—consideration is given only the strong." [75]

And he proceeded to build up a war machine capable of challenging—if need be—the "capitalist" world or frightening it into surrender.

The cost is high:

Soviet defense outlays in 1955 were about three-fourths of the U.S. level at Soviet prices and almost equal at U.S. prices. However, because of the especially crude nature of the estimate for Soviet defense expenditures and the ruble-dollar ratios for this end use, most economists allow for some understatement of the Soviet level both in rubles and in dollars and consider Soviet defense outlays as approximately equal to those of the United States.

The Soviet Union is thus devoting a much greater proportion of its national income to military expenditures than is the U.S., the Soviet gross national product being even today only about 45 per cent of that of the U.S.

We say to our enemies, to the bourgeoisie of the entire world that there was a time when the capitalists attempted to organize an attack on the Soviet land. This happened during the first years of the Soviet rule. They made an attempt, but nothing came of it. Let the enemies remember this! Now, when the muscles of the Soviet Union became full-blooded, when we are armed with the most modern weapons, we say to our enemies: Do not dare to try us out. If you do—you will find your grave here.[76]

He warns of the power of his nuclear armory:

It will be too late to discuss what peaceful coexistence means when such terrible means of destruction as atomic and hydrogen bombs, and ballistic missiles, which are practically uninterceptible and can carry nuclear weapons to any point on the globe, go into action. Not to reckon with this means to close one's eyes and stop one's ears, to hide one's head in the sand as the ostrich does at the approach of danger. If we humans imitate the ostrich and hide our head in the sand, then, I ask you, what is the use of having a head if it is incapable of averting the danger to life?[77]

The Power Front

By the spring of 1960, Khrushchev could exclaim:

Comrades, at the present time, the Soviet Union is stronger than ever before. Our might is indomitable! [78]

A year earlier, Khrushchev was already sure that the balance of forces was shifting in his favor:

At present the atmosphere is different from what it was before. The USSR and the whole socialist camp are now very powerful. The balance of power no longer favors imperialist countries and, with every year, this balance becomes less in their favor.[79]

In 1957, Khrushchev was already sure that the Soviet Union was leading the U.S. in missiles:

Question: "Do you think that the Soviet Union has outstripped the United States not only in the field of intercontinental missiles, but in the production of missiles generally?"

"Indisputably." [80]

And by 1960, Khrushchev was "watching the United States trying to catch up."

The United States has set itself the task of catching up with the Soviet Union in the production of rockets in five years. They will naturally make every effort to raise their rocketry from the state it is now in and reach a better position. But it would be naïve to think that we are meanwhile going to sit with arms folded.[81]

U.S. experts do not deny that Soviet military power is "awesome":

"[The Soviet Union] has the second largest navy in the world and since World War II has produced more vessels of every type, except aircraft carriers, than the United States. A fleet of well over 400 submarines is already in operation. This number is greatly in excess of the German force which severely menaced Allied surface shipping during the early years of World War II. There is no doubt about the capacity of the USSR to develop naval atomic power plants, or to adapt ships and submarines to launch short and medium-range missiles: in fact, Soviet planners have pointedly discussed the vulnerability of the United States to such attacks. The magnitude of the threat becomes clear when it is realized that 43 of our 50 largest cities and 85 per cent of our industry are located within 500 miles of our coasts. Missile-launching submarines are the Soviet equivalent of our overseas air bases. . . .

"Over the last ten years, the USSR has not only maintained the largest number of planes in the world, but has progressively re-equipped its air force with new and modern aircraft. The Soviet Union now produces many aircraft at least as advanced as our own—and produces them in large numbers. Moreover, the Soviets have demonstrated their ability to manufacture modern electronic equipment and to master the techniques required to guide and direct defensive and offensive aerial operations." [82]

Khrushchev puts it more brutally and succinctly:

We are unassailable and we have with us the peoples of the entire great socialist camp, which has sufficient moral and material strength to break the neck of anyone who makes an attempt against our freedom and independence, against the independence of peoples of socialist countries.[83]

He indicates whose neck he means:

If a war is unleashed now by the aggressive circles of the U.S.A., it will be waged not only in Europe, in Asia or Africa; this war will immediately be carried on to the territory of the United States of America because now the intercontinental ballistic missiles make it possible to hit a target in any area of the globe. In this case, the American people will suffer enormous losses. All means—intercontinental ballistic missiles, submarine missiles and other means which now exist—will be used in case of an armed conflict. You yourself understand that is the logic of war, the logic of struggle.[84]

The London Institute for Strategic Studies and other sources figure the Soviet armed forces currently at 4 million men, down from 5 *million in 1958. There are an equal number of reserves, plus a similar force in China and the satellite countries—a total of some 20 million men. This force is equipped with 20,000 front-line tanks, 15,000 second-line tanks, 240-mm. atomic cannons with a twenty-mile range and 203-mm. cannons with a twelve-mile range. The 100,000-man army air force can drop 10,000 men in a single operation.*

In addition 20,000 air-force craft includes 6,000-mile-range bombers based largely on the Arctic coast. There are 100 operational missile bases on the Baltic coast, in Southern Ukraine and the Carpathians.

The navy is quoted at 37 cruisers, 230 destroyers, and 1400 other craft. Jane's 1960–1961 edition adds 10 nuclear submarines and 425 other undersea craft.

The United States, barring the Civil War and the small campaign against Mexico, still does not know what war means. If war is not averted, the Americans will experience the most devastating war ever known by mankind. It will rage not only in Europe and Asia, but with no lesser fury, in the United States.[85]

This is the difference between our country and the United States. Some exceedingly boastful American generals and admirals say that the United States, if it started a war now, would destroy the USSR in several days. Obviously they are weak in mathematics. Otherwise they might ask themselves the question: And how long would it take to destroy the United States if it unleashed a war? For war is not a one-sided operation, it can turn badly against the side which begins it. It is common knowledge that the other side has no fewer forces and possibilities than those represented by [General] Taylor and [Admiral] Burke.[86]

And again . . .

We know that the United States has atomic and hydrogen bombs; we know that you have an air force and navy. But you are also well aware that the Soviet Union, too, possesses atomic and hydrogen bombs, an air force and navy, plus ballistic missiles of all types, including intercontinental ones.[87]

And more of the same:

One cannot help feeling surprise at the shortsightedness of the American ruling circles which hope to divert a retaliatory blow from themselves toward their allies in case the United States unleashed a nuclear war. Certain people should not forget that now intercontinental ballistic rockets and other modern means of warfare can strike anywhere on the globe.[88]

Despite Khrushchev's complaint about American shortsightedness, there is full realization in the United States of what a modern war could mean to the world and in particular to the United States:

"The largest conventional bomb of World War II had an explosive power of 20 tons of TNT. The first atomic bomb had an explosive power equivalent to 20 thousand tons of TNT. Today, weapons with an explosive equivalent of 20 million tons (20 megatons) have been tested and there is no theoretical upper limit. It is possible to construct weapons of almost any explosive power." [89]

"As the weapons have become more powerful, their speed of delivery has grown ever faster. Missiles are able to travel intercontinental distances and wipe out whole cities in one blow. A blow on 50 of our most important metropolitan areas would bring under attack 55 per cent of the United States population and 75 per cent of American industry. Moreover, the area of 'fall-out' could cover an area of 10,000 square miles, the size of the State of New Jersey. A successful attack on 50 of our most important urban centers would produce at least 10–15 million dead and 15–20 million injured from blast and heat and another 25–35 million casualties from 'fall-out,' or a total of 60–65 million dead and injured." [90]

There is also among responsible U.S. officials full realization of what is needed to withstand a possible Soviet attack. And of what is available:

The American military must have three different types of forces:

1. A first-blow force capable of knocking out enemy launching sites and air bases, and destroying strategic nuclear power.

2. A deterrent second-blow retaliatory force capable of surviving a first attack—by reason of its hardness, dispersion, mobility, and warning system—and designed for mass effect.

3. A deterrent power sufficient to restrain local aggression and suitable for limited war.

The United States defense posture is evaluated in many ways, depending on the background of those who are commenting. It is apparent that the intercontinental ballistic missile became available in 1960, and it may be assumed that it will be generally available by 1962. Operational Atlas missiles are ready for launching from the West Coast. But these are stationary and are considered vulnerable to a near-miss nuclear attack. Moreover, it is assumed they would never be sent until a nuclear attack was made.

Thus the United States places heavy reliance on manned bombers of the B-52 class, which can deliver many times the explosive potential of the Atlas with greater accuracy, selectivity, and flexibility, easier maintenance, and the ability to return and report. Although the bomber is vulnerable, it is equipped with Hound Dog missiles, which permit it to reach a target several hundred miles away.

In 1960, the United States had at least 2,000 long-range strategic bombers, some on fifteen-minute ground alert and a few always airborne. By the end of 1960, Polaris-equipped submarines were operational, ready to provide a fleet of mobile, virtually invisible nuclear launching pads surrounding the Iron Curtain.

In a recent exchange of letters between Pentagon officials and a Congressional committee, the question was raised:

"Could a sneak attack of 300 Soviet missiles wipe out our ability to counterattack?"

The answer: "This refers to a hypothetical mathematical exercise developed as part of the argument in support of an airborne alert.

"The validity of this hypothesis, which assumes the Soviet ca-

pability to launch 300 long-range missiles against the United States targets of today, depends on a number of 'ifs,' such as:

"—if the Soviets have not only the missiles but also the required numbers of launching complexes from which 300 missiles could be launched at close to the same time.

"—if these missiles have such reliability—could be launched on such a perfect count-down schedule and would perform so perfectly thereafter—that they would land on their targets in the required numbers at the precise planned moment. (If a carrier in the Mediterranean is struck before a base in Alabama, we can put much of our retaliatory power on its way.)

"—if the massive national effort required for such a gigantic operation could go undetected by our intelligence.

"—if all of our long range strategic bombers were on the ground at their bases, and the locations of our aircraft carriers known.

"—if the Soviets are willing to take the gamble that every detail would work perfectly, as it would have to work for such an attack to succeed—knowing that any miscalculation or slip-up would wreak havoc on their country.

"The improbability that all of these conditions would obtain is obvious." [91]

Left largely unsaid is the basic military advantage of a closed society. Every U.S. target is plainly marked; every vital Soviet military target must be discovered and mapped.

Officials in the United States of America have repeatedly stated that they have patrolling atom and hydrogen bombers which at the approach of a foreign aircraft are to take off and to head for targets set for each of these bombers. And that would mean the beginning of war.

I should like to ask these American officials, if they are thinking of taking such measures unilaterally in the event of a hypothetical aggression against your country, why don't you consider that we, too, can reply with the same kind of measures if a foreign plane endangering the security of our homeland appears over our country? Can one deny that we have the same rights on the basis of which you intend to act in such cases? [92]

The Congressional correspondence referred to further indicates that early in 1960 the United States had two wings of tactical bombers with nuclear capability on 110 overseas bases; fourteen aircraft carriers considered "virtually invulnerable to ballistic missile attack because of their shifting position."

These carry more fighter planes than there are bombers in the Soviet Union; fourteen wings of nuclear-capable tactical fighters; an operational squadron equipped with 5,500-mile-range SNARK; two cruisers and five submarines equipped with surface-to-surface missiles; four operational squadrons equipped with shorter-range missiles holding more explosive power than was expended on all Axis military targets in Europe during World War II; intermediate-range THOR, with atomic warheads, stationed in the United Kingdom.[93] To offset the Soviet lead in explosive thrust, military men offer lighter warheads with more punch to the pound.

We can stop the bombers, says Khrushchev, but missiles can't be stopped.

Unquestionably, bombers could in their time be stopped by anti-aircraft fire, artillery, or rockets, but there is no stopping the intercontinental ballistic missile.

You will say: But will not the Soviet Union suffer too? Of course, we too will suffer great losses. But look at the vast spaces on our map and look at Germany, France, and Britain. One does not have to be a strategist, a military man, to see the difference.[94]

The United States deterrent capability is being continuously developed with new generations of Atlases, Titans, submarines equipped with operational Polaris missiles, railroad-car Minutemen, B-58 supersonic bombers, thirteen squadrons of Atlas ICBM forces, additional B-52s with Hound Dog missiles, surface-to-surface and surface-to-air missile battalions, nuclear-propulsion carriers, and a Ballistic Missile Early Warning system. By 1965 or earlier, the United States will have four strategic intercontinental missiles operational, Atlas, Titan, Minuteman, and Polaris.

For limited wars, the United States capability has also been strengthened. It has fourteen Army divisions (seven in Europe and Korea, one in Hawaii); four fleets of Naval alert forces, including fourteen attack carriers, thirteen cruisers, 237 destroyers, 115 submarines, 32 mine craft, and 7000 operating aircraft; 34 tactical Air Force wings, and 200 additional allied divisions with air and naval support. Before 1962 man-carried nuclear-capable rockets will be available for front-line troops. They will have other lightweight surface, and surface-to-air missiles, M-60 tanks equipped with long-range diesel engines and 105-mm. high-velocity guns, surveillance drones, and new modern small arms.

This "melancholy paradox," as Winston Churchill puts it, of "mutual terror" provides some reassurance against a planned, rationally calculated "total war."

However, by definition, it provides no reassurance against irrationality, miscalculation, or "less than total" war.

In addition, the tremendous advantage of striking a first blow, the rapid changes in technology, the extension of nuclear capability to China, with its own problems of demography, create a huge question mark for civilization. And to all this must be added the biggest question of all—What other weapons lie in the labyrinths of research and development?

Military power is only a means to an end. The end Khrushchev seems to seek is not "mutual annihilation," but conquest of a world still intact. However, in the view of U.S. analysts of Soviet affairs, there are situations in which the Soviet leadership could resort to the use of force:

"The main weight of Soviet policy is being articulated to the Russian peoples and to the world in terms of a nonmilitary struggle, which is, indeed, being energetically and frankly pursued. But there is no evidence whatsoever that the Soviet military effort is being reduced; and there are no grounds for building American policy on the assumption that if the Soviet Government believed that it

enjoyed a sufficient advantage in nuclear weapons to take out American retaliatory power at a blow, it would not do so." [95]

"Although the Soviet leaders may be genuinely concerned about the risks of war, the possibilities of the destruction of cities in the Soviet Union, the setback to their hard-won achievements; and although they may prefer to achieve their objectives in the world by peaceful means, and are now confident they will do so—the question remains what they would do if it appeared to them that their confidence was mistaken, that the tide of history was flowing (even though temporarily, in their view) adversely for the Soviet position in the world. Mr. Khrushchev has left no doubt that he would fight rather than relinquish a foot of territory now under communist control. If this adverse trend were to come at a time when the Soviet leaders were convinced of their own military superiority, could the rest of the world afford to put its faith in the restraint of the Soviet leadership?" [96]

There is no lack of verbal assurances of Soviet peaceful intentions. In statements so numerous that it would be tedious to quote even a fraction of them, Khrushchev has said:

We do not intend to attack anyone.[97]

The arguments he puts forth to support this assertion are based on the "peaceful nature" of socialism. Thus, while on the one hand . . .

It is *"an indisputable fact"* that the United States and her allies are planning aggression against the Soviet Union because:

A country which does not want war would not stockpile weapons but would seek agreement with the other side.[98]

. . . on the other hand:

The fact that the Soviet Union is ahead of the Western powers in nuclear and rocket weapons is of great importance for the preservation of peace.[99]

Only madmen, says Khrushchev, can want war.

But, of course, no one can say categorically that there will be no war. It is a matter of common knowledge that there

239

are statesmen in some capitalist countries, statesmen holding important government posts, who advocate war. Can anyone vouch for madmen? [100]

Madmen have always existed and, apparently, will not disappear in the future. But one must not forget that if in the past the accession of such madmen to power led to bloody wars it would now be an entirely unprecedented disaster. Like those of us who on leaving home make sure that no inflammable material, matches or certain electric appliances fall into the hands of a silly child and unwittingly provoke a terrible disaster for the home and the whole town, thus, nations ought to take care that the government, parliament, and responsible posts for insuring peace are not penetrated by people who have mad and criminal aims. Great vigilance is required of people to prevent madmen from using rocket and nuclear weapons against mankind until a solution is found for the question of full and universal disarmament and, consequently, the destruction of all means of warfare.[101]

Since "madmen" seem to exist in the "socialist camp," Khrushchev has some difficulty in persuading communists (the most vociferous adherents of Lenin's thesis on the inevitability of war are the Chinese) that war would be a universal catastrophe.

Communists, men who think in terms of facts, realize that under the present conditions, when there are two world systems, it is indispensable to build up mutual relationships between them in order to exclude the possibility of a war among states. Only madmen and maniacs can come out today with appeals to a new world war. As to men with a sane mentality and they are still in the majority, even among the most overt foes of communism—they cannot fail to recognize the fatal consequences of a new war.[102]

On this, the Chinese Communist Party organ, the People's Daily, comments: "The working class and its political party absolutely cannot base all their work solely on the possibility of a peaceful transition [from capitalism to socialism]" but must prepare for the "possibility" of a "nonpeaceful transition."

Whatever Khrushchev's verbal assurances that he will not resort to force, that he does not want to intimidate anybody, the recent years are full of rocket-rattling emanating from the Kremlin. In 1956, the Soviet Government intimated to France, Britain, and Israel that unless they put an end to their action against Egypt, Soviet missiles might fall on Paris, London, and Tel-Aviv. (Meanwhile, Soviet tanks were fighting Hungarian workers in the streets of Budapest.) Many times (see Chapter 9) Khrushchev has threatened West Germany with extinction through nuclear weapons. Rockets have rattled over the issues of Cuba and the Congo.

For the past several years, Khrushchev has warned countries allied to the United States that if they permit U.S. military bases, they subject themselves to the danger of Soviet rocket bombardment. The U-2 incident of May 1960 provided Khrushchev with an excuse to make his threats more precise:

We shall administer shattering blows at the bases whence they come and at those who have set up these bases and actually dispose of them.[103]

The Soviet Union is in a capitalist encirclement and must be ready to deal a crushing blow to any attempt by the aggressors to hinder our peaceful construction.[104]

At the U-2 press conference, Khrushchev indulges in a characteristic touch—some vivid language that his own interpreters had to tone down:

Someone tried to poke his snout into our affairs and we clobbered his snout—so that he now certainly knows where the [Soviet] border is. If he comes again, we shall clobber him again—and we shall clobber the bases from which he takes off and where he intends to land. [The interpreter spoke of "punching the nose."] [105]

By June 1960 Khrushchev was threatening neutral Austria and all other neutral countries. He said that neutrality would be violated if the air space of the neutrals was used by planes or missiles hostile to the Soviet Union.

In July 1960 the Russians shot down a U.S. patrol aircraft over the high seas. Khrushchev declared the plane was over Soviet territorial waters. Again he threatened—the British, the Norwegians, the U.S. On July 23, 1960, Italian communist leader Palmiro Togliatti, whom Moscow recognizes as one of the best communist theoreticians, summed up present communist policy: "Brandish the right fist—hold up an olive branch in the left hand."

The power of military capability is thus important even if it is never used. But, in his present posture of constructing socialism, Khrushchev professes that he wants very much to avoid an arms race.

Messieurs Imperialists, you once cherished the thought that you might win the "cold war" without a shooting war, that is, compel the socialist countries to squander material resources for nonproductive ends by heating up the international situation and following the policy of "brinkmanship." As you can see now, gentlemen, this policy has already failed.[106]

James R. Schlesinger has aptly pointed out:

"An armament race . . . is far less a burden on the more affluent contestant than it is on the contestant attempting to make do with less. . . . The armaments race since the Korean War has, however, damaged the Soviet Union in innumerable ways. . . . The drastic upheaval in East Europe in 1956 . . . was not unrelated to the heavy armaments burden that the Russians had imposed upon the satellite economies after the outbreak of the Korean War." [107]

The present balance of terror makes surprise a permanently operating factor. For who is to judge when a pre-emptive blow is to be struck against an enemy whose preparations for immediate attack seem clear? Who is to judge where brinkmanship ends and disaster begins?

The Soviets with the relative security of a closed economy have a major opportunity to achieve this advantage, if and when they can create the industrial potential that would prove a real threat to a world already highly industrialized and already mightily armed.

Education

"Like every other form of state-directed activity in the Soviet Union, education is conceived as a weapon serving the interests of the Communist Party and dedicated to a single objective—the victory of the Soviet system." [108]

The basic capital investment a nation can make is in the education of its human resources for greater productivity. This the Soviet Union proceeds to do with particular vigor. Soviet education is aimed primarily at production and scientific progress, designed in turn to produce economic, literary, and political weapons. The Soviet Union spends a sizable portion of its gross national product (6.5 per cent), on education, compared with the United States' 3.7 per cent.[109]

All our children are enjoying not only high school but college education as well. It's free in the Soviet Union. The students receive scholarships from the state. In general we are giving a great deal of attention to bringing up the children—the young generation. The nursery, kindergarten, schools with full board and then a start in life—such is the prospect for the rising generation.

The merits of the Soviet system of education are well known. It is the graduates of Soviet schools—scientists, engineers, technicians and workers—who astonished the world with the first earth satellite. We are proud that the Russian words "sputnik" and "lunik" are understood all over the world without translation.[110]

But in 1960 most Soviet children ended full-time education at fifteen or sixteen, after eight years of schooling.

Khrushchev insists on presenting all achievements of the Soviet Union as "victories" over the United States. Statistics are not entirely convincing, particularly in such a complex field as education.

In 1959 the United States graduated 365,748 from undergraduate colleges; the USSR graduated about the same number. But in Russia some 25 per cent—about 80,000—were specialists in science, compared with 10 per cent with engineering degrees, approximately 34,000 in the United States.* Obviously, the definition of engineer varies radically in the two countries. Many of the Soviet engineers have the training equivalent of technicians in the United States.

The United States had 46,102,000 enrolled in school in 1959, compared with 36,442,000 in the USSR.

	USSR	U.S.
Elementary-school graduates	100	100
High-school graduates	30	60
College entrants	10	30
College graduates	7	15

Other comparative figures:

	USSR	U.S.
Population	212,000,000	175,000,000
Total school enrollment	36,442,000	46,102,000
College enrollment	2,179,000	3,402,000
Number of colleges	726	1680
	of which 22 are correspondence schools only	for full-time resident students

The Soviet college enrollment in 1958 included 127,500 part-time and 756,000 correspondence students; full-time students numbered approximately 1,178,000. Recent legislation for part-time work reduces the percentage of full-time students today.[III] In 1960, 37.1 per cent of eligible Americans enrolled in college; in the Soviet Union, the comparable figure was 17.5 per cent, and half of these were in correspondence schools.

Let anyone try to name any other country, apart from the Soviet Union, where the higher schools graduate so many specialists as we do in the Soviet Union. Today the U.S.A. is setting the task of overtaking the Soviet Union in science and in the training of specialists. . . .

---

*Including those from correspondence schools.

However, we are absolutely convinced that the U.S.A. will not overtake us in this field.[112]

The Americans are now studying our system of education in secondary and higher educational establishments and value it highly. Meanwhile, we Soviet leaders consider that in this system there are still some weak links and are at present making efforts to improve still further the training of specialists with a secondary and higher education, to raise the standard of education. That will be our next "sputnik" and we shall launch it without any doubt.[113]

Some American educators have noted that Soviet education:
1. Produces more technicians than the United States;
2. Provides a free college education;
3. Maintains appreciably more stringent curricula.

There is much to be said beyond the raw statistics. Soviet Russia has a right to be proud of its progress. But the Soviets need more engineers for an economy that must build its whole industry with no reserves of mechanics and other trade technicians. (Many Soviet "engineers" would be considered technicians in the Western nations.) Moreover, engineers are widely used for other jobs—in government service and business administration.

In old Russia 76 of every 100 people over nine years of age were illiterate. Nearly 80 per cent of the children and teen-agers had no opportunity of going to school. Whereas today all our children go to school and there are practically no illiterate people in the country. We now have forty times more specialists with a higher or special secondary education than there were in pre-Revolutionary Russia, and our higher schools train almost three times as many engineers as American universities and colleges. Last year [1958], for example, we trained 94,000 engineers while you trained 35,000.[114]

But even today success is far from complete:

In the course of the census, lists of illiterate persons between the ages of nine and forty-nine were compiled. They include 1,929,000 persons.[115]

"The rewards in income and prestige in the United States and Soviet economies are such that a larger proportion of the best young people in the USSR turn to careers in heavy industry, science, and higher education, whereas in the United States a larger proportion of the best talent flows into such fields as heavy or light [consumer-goods] industry, finance, commerce and trade, law, medicine, etc. Higher education, particularly technical, is more of a prerequisite for the attainment of a top business career in the Soviet Union than in the United States." [116]

Two million teachers and almost 400,000 doctors are serving the welfare of Soviet people.[117]

To a Soviet audience, Khrushchev explains that much remains to be done:

We must not forget the fact that at present, despite the compulsory seven-year education a considerable number of young people not only do not get full secondary education, but do not even finish the seven-year education. According to the figures of the Central Statistical Board of the USSR, in recent years only about 80 per cent of the children who attended schools have finished the seven-year education, even taking into consideration those who remain two years in the same grade. That means that we are still far from having realized the principle of compulsory seven-year education.[118]

A study by the U.S. Department of Health, Education, and Welfare reports:

"The Soviets are, roughly speaking, producing two or three times as many engineers as the United States. Yet this does not tell the whole story. In the first place, the Soviet level of development—across the board—is about where we were at the turn of the century. They need many more engineers in order to industrialize than we—already a highly industrialized nation—need to sustain and develop further our economy. Also, the Soviet population is approximately 19 per cent greater than ours. And finally, the key figure may not be the number of engineers produced, but the numbers of *skilled and semi-skilled workers that are being turned out. In this category the Soviets are deficient, but they recognize the need and are expanding their program."* [119]

Moreover, another study finds, managers of industry are almost all technical men (which creates other problems), and are at the head of almost all Soviet industries, while the United States trains all types of business specialists. A management analysis of Soviet industry points out:

"1. There is a considerably higher proportion of college graduates among Soviet than among American managers.

"2. Of the college graduates, a much larger percentage of the Russians have engineering degrees.

"3. Soviet college education provides a firmer factual base than does American, but a weaker analytic training.

"4. At the same time, the total Russian tradition is more theoretic. The Soviet manager, after his school years, is more prone to do general reading than is the American manager.

"5. The Soviet manager is much less likely than is the American to have received any formal training in human relations. On the other hand, because of his Young Communist League activities he will probably have had a good deal more practical experience in this during his years in school.

"6. The Russian's first major practical experience in business is during his last college year, and thus it occurs while he is still under academic tutelage. This year serves as a strong bridge between college and the 'real world.' Such a bridge is generally missing in the American manager's experience.

"7. Russian managers have an early, heavy dose of work directly in production. By and large, this is not true of American managers.

"8. Early jobs held by Russian managers are most often those of minor executives. American managers are much more likely to begin with staff or other technical roles." [120]

There are now 1,750,000 scientists and engineers in the Soviet Union, compared with 1,540,000 in the United States. This gives

247

the Soviet Union a particular advantage in providing personnel for underdeveloped countries, including bloc partners which require greater industrialization.

Whereas in 1928 the engineers and technicians in our country numbered only 98,000, this year [1954] we have nearly 1,800,000. However . . . part of the engineering and technical personnel are employed in the ministries and departments and do not work directly on production. . . . It should be said that the engineers and technicians are now being released from the ministries and departments.[121]

The Seven-Year Plan provides for a further considerable expansion and improvement in training specialists with a higher or secondary education. In 1959–1965 universities and institutes will graduate 2,300,000 specialists, as compared with 1,700,000 people graduated in the preceding seven-year period. In 1965 the total number of specialists with a higher education will exceed 4,500,000, i.e., will be 50 per cent greater than in 1958. Particularly rapid will be the growth in the number of specialists engaged in the sphere of material production.

The main thing in reorganizing the system of higher education is to link it closer with life, to improve markedly the practical, scientific-theoretical training of specialists, bringing them up to be active builders of communism.

The reorganization of the secondary and higher education systems will require time and effort. The Supreme Soviets of the Union Republics will adopt laws on the educational system conforming to their national traditions and features.[122]

But in 1954, Khrushchev noted a problem:

Unfortunately there are men calling themselves scientific workers who have no relation to science. It is essential to devote more attention to scientific establishments to help scientific workers, and to get rid of people who manage to get into scientific establishments but who are of no use.[123]

The aim of Soviet education is productive capability, or, as Stalin put it: "Universal obligatory polytechnical education so that a member of society may find it possible to make a free choice of occupation and not be shackled for life to any one task." [124]
Says Mr. Khrushchev:

It is essential to start preparing people at school for production, for useful work in society, give them the maximum possible education and later to send them to work. While working in production and at the same time studying at a school, a young person will more easily find his or her place in society, will ascertain his or her inclinations and wishes. He or she may specialize in some field and, after having worked on production, proceed to the corresponding educational establishment. But it is essential first of all to test him or her at evening study without interruption of work. I repeat that there must be no exceptions in this matter, whatever the position of the parents in society and the posts which they may hold.[125]

The mission of the school is to train people with all-round education, with a good basic knowledge of sciences and at the same time capable of systematic manual labor, to instill in youth the striving to be useful to society, and to take an active part in the production of material values necessary for society.[126]

But, Khrushchev points out, secondary-school graduates are not properly trained for vocations.

During the period from 1954 to 1957, out of the number of people completing secondary school studies, over 2.5 million did not go to higher educational establishments or technical colleges. In 1957 alone, over 800,000 persons who had graduated from secondary schools did not go on to higher educational establishments or technical colleges. Owing to the separation between the program of secondary education and life, these youths and girls are quite unfamiliar with production, while society does not know how to make the best use of these people, who are young and full of vitality. It therefore appears that a considerable part of youth and parents are dissatisfied with this situation, and as time goes on this process does not diminish but grows stronger. I think that this state of affairs should cause us great anxiety.[127]

College education is free in the Soviet Union. But it has only half as many college graduates as the United States, including correspondence-school graduates.

With a population 19 per cent larger than that of the United States, the Soviet Union has only 42 per cent as many resident college students.

Although few American students receive living stipends, 1,687,000 students attend publicly subsidized colleges and universities. In New York State alone, 100,000 attend tuition-free city and state colleges. In addition, at least 300,000 students receive scholarships in one form or another, and long-term Federal loans are available to virtually everyone who asks.

It is because of the subsistence economy of the Soviets that students receive allotments for board, but almost all students must work part time.[128] And even these are recruited largely from the privileged classes. Says Khrushchev:

We cannot overlook the fact that we still have few children of workers and collective farmers attending universities. In Moscow higher education establishments, for instance, only 30 or 40 per cent of the students are children of workers and collective farmers. The other students are children of employees, or intelligentsia. Of course, this is an obviously abnormal situation.[129]

The existing system of admittance to higher schools is also to be criticized. There are cases when it is not those who are well prepared who get into the university, but those who have an influential father or mother who can help to push their children into universities. Such a situation is in contradiction with the very essence of our socialist system; for often it is not the most worthy ones that get into higher schools, but those who have easy access to persons at universities who make decisions as to who can be admitted and who cannot.[130]

Those must be admitted to higher schools who reveal the greatest ability and wish to continue their studies. Not only the wishes of those who enter the universities must be taken into consideration, but also the reports on the candidate's work by social organization, the trade union and the Komsomol. In this way the solution will be made according to the standard of training, the inclinations, and the certitude that the person will justify the expense involved in his or her training, and can become a really useful executive in production work.[131]

One should say that the practice existing hitherto of creating privileged conditions for entering higher educational establishments for persons graduating from secondary schools with gold and silver medals had complicated the situation still more. The fact was that teachers used to be influenced by some parents who wished their children to get medals. There are also many mistakes in the practice of selection of young people and their admission to higher educational institutions. Although there are competitive entrance examinations for those entering higher educational institutions, it must be admitted that often it is not enough to pass the exam well in order to get into a university. Here too the great influence of parents is felt. That is why one can often hear young people trying to enter universities say that if they pass their competitive examinations, their parents will have to pass their competition, which will often decide everything. That creates inequality of opportunity to enter higher and secondary specialized schools.[132]

"Education and particularly higher education, is more important in the USSR than in the United States as the gateway to a prestigeful and highly remunerative career. Competition is keener for higher education, the cost of education to the individual is less, and the standards of admission and performance are higher in the USSR. Both nations lose part of the potential pool of managerial talent, the USSR because of its large rural population, the United States because of financial burdens and racial and sex discrimination." [133]

There is also a marked discrimination against minority nationalities in the Soviet Union.

Soviet education has its problems, many reminiscent of those in Western nations.

The state of people's education in the republic as a whole is still substandard. In some rayons [districts] the plan for compulsory general education is not being carried out. Some pupils leave schools before they have completed the appropriate course of education. At some schools, especially village schools, teaching and general education are on a low level and the children make slow progress in their studies.[134]

We cannot be satisfied with the state of affairs and with the system of higher and secondary education itself. There are great shortcomings in the work of our schools and higher educational institutions. . . . The main and fundamental fault of our secondary and higher schools lies in the fact of their being divorced from life. For that shortcoming, workers in people's education and higher schools have often been subjected to criticism, but the situation is practically unchanged.[135]

Says one Soviet educator:

"We have universities in which there are no leading scientists in the field of mathematics, engineering or physics. Because of this, the level of instruction in leading disciplines of the exact sciences is too low. The result is that frequently young specialists are graduated who are poorly acquainted with modern scientific discoveries and techniques." [136]

In spite of emphasis on education for production, there are still problems. Khrushchev holds up capitalist education as an example:

Let us consider the branches of agriculture. In many capitalist countries students of agricultural universities must work in agriculture during the period of their university course. But we often give incorrect training to our students. Take, for example, the Timiryazev Agricultural Academy. They do not study in the fields, but mainly at small experimental gardens. They do not study the cow and other farm animals at farms, as happens in real life, but mainly from plaster models. On an average there is more than one assistant per student to help him. And that is called a Soviet higher school! I think this is wrong.[137]

The countryside—state and collective farms and experimental research stations—has wonderful youngsters who were trained in secondary schools and know collective and state farm production. And yet we now have students—even in the Timiryazev Academy—who in their younger years will not be able to distinguish hemp from nettles unless stung by them. Some of our agricultural higher education establishments have training farms. But workers look after the animals the student is supposed to study. What is this lordly state of affairs? With this system the student, when he comes to a farm, is scared stiff when a cow shakes her head.[138]

And:

Our ten-year school trains youngsters only for entry into higher educational establishments. Life showed long ago that this attitude to secondary schools is wrong. See for yourselves what happens in fact. The country's higher educational establishments have to admit about 450,000 people a year. Of these, about half are admitted to daytime sections. Yet the majority of young people who went to school for ten years fail the finals for entry into higher educational establishments and turn out to be untrained for practical life.[139]

Those young men and girls who went to work on the collective farms or plants and factories when they finished the tenth year of school, acted correctly. This is a better thing to do than to sit in an office and file papers. Working in production, they create material values for the people. It is pleasant to note that youth correctly understands the tasks set by the Party. More and more young men and girls are going to work on the collective farms, state farms, plants, and factories, when they finish school. While doing production work they study through correspondence courses at higher educational establishments and technical colleges.[140]

Khrushchev also has to react to the class differences being created by differences in education.

There still exists in our country a substantial difference between physical and mental work. We have inherited from old times a situation in which preference seems to be given to that part of youth who must unquestionably enter higher educational establishments, instead of going to factory and collective farms. It is felt that the remainder who have not made good and have not shown any abilities are the ones who should go into production. This view is fundamentally wrong and runs counter to our ideas and aspirations.[141]

Incorrect views about labor in our Soviet society have recently begun to appear within a certain section of youth. The following instances are examples: Some young men and women say, when they have finished the ten-year course, "It isn't suitable for us, now that we are educated, to work in a factory, at a construction site, at a state farm or a collective farm." These educated people do not stop to think that it was workers who built the house they live in, that their fathers work in factories and mills, that the bread they eat was grown on state farms and collective farms by our Soviet people, indefatigable toilers.

It is apparently not only the young people who think this way; some members of the older generation are also to blame. It is no secret, after all, that some parents reason thus:

"But my daughter has completed the ten-year course— she cannot milk cows!" [142]

This lordly, supercilious, incorrect attitude to physical labor is also being shown in the family circle. If a boy or a girl is not good at his or her studies, the parents and relatives hold out the bogey that if he does not get a gold or silver medal, he or she will be unable to enter a higher educational establishment and will be an ordinary worker in a factory. Physical work is, therefore, becoming some kind of scarecrow for children.[143]

If some people believe that second-rate people should go to work in production, they err in principle and contradict the spirit of socialist society. We must see to it that every young boy and girl, irrespective of the position held by their parents, should train for labor activities on a basis general for all. Son and daughter must know that Daddy is Daddy, while they themselves must use their own labor to win people's respect and not live at the expense of their parents' merits.[144]

Khrushchev's rhetorical outbursts against privileges and against the low place accorded to manual labor in Soviet society may not be entirely motivated by his ideological zeal. One of the big problems facing the Soviet Union now—and for several years to come—is shortage of manpower, due to the lower birth rate during the war. The need for more manpower was probably the reason for the 1958 school law, under which fifteen- and sixteen-year-olds, in the eighth and ninth years of schooling, must work twenty-five hours a week and may complete their secondary education at night or through correspondence courses. Khrushchev puts it this way:

In my opinion, after they have finished seven or eight years at school, all school children without exception should take part in socially useful labor at enterprises, collective farms, and other places of work. Both in town and in the countryside, as well as at workers' settlements, all children finishing schools should go to work in production. No one must evade this stage. First, this will be democratic because equal conditions will be created for all citizens. Neither the position of the parents nor their influence will free anyone from productive work. Second, this will be an excellent way to inculcate in all young people the heroic traditions of the working class and working peasantry. Thus the only possible and essential method to overcome the shortcomings in our schools is for all boys and girls during their school years to be prepared to take part in physical labor at plants, factories, collective and state farms, in any labor which is useful for society.[145]

He denies it is a labor problem.

When we raised the question of reorganizing the school system, some "prophets" abroad shouted: "They are short of labor, that is why they want to make juveniles work." Let such augurers crow. They will never understand us in any case. We are reorganizing the school system not because we are short of labor, but because we want further to improve the educational system, because we want to link the school still closer with life.

The reorganization of the educational system fully conforms to the spirit of the Marxist-Leninist teaching on education and upbringing and opens the way to effective polytechnization of the school system. As far back as the end of the last century, Lenin, thinking of the ways of molding the new man, the builder of the new society, of combining education with productive work, wrote:

"It is impossible to conceive of the ideal future society without the younger generation combining schooling with productive work: neither schooling and upbringing without productive work, nor productive work without parallel schooling and upbringing could be raised to the heights demanded by the present state of technology and scientific knowledge."

The close link of schooling with life, with production, with communist construction must become the leading principle in learning the fundamentals of science in school, the basis

256

for educating the growing generation in the spirit of communist ethics.[146]

The best way to a higher education lies through enterprises and construction projects, through work on collective farms, M.T.S.* and state farms. We could not do this before, since an insufficient number of people were qualified to enter higher educational institutions. Now tens and hundreds of thousands of young men and women who have completed their ten-year education are joining factory workshops and construction projects, or are going to work on collective and state farm fields. The number of workers—fitters, metal-workers, builders, chemists and textile workers—with secondary education is growing constantly. By working in production they gain a better understanding of life, they know what attracts them, they test their powers—and when they come to decide where to go for further study, they choose their profession in a more mature fashion. More concern must be shown for higher and secondary evening and home-study training institutions, so that working and collective-farm youth may be given a higher or secondary education without leaving production work. There can be no doubt but that a specialist who receives a higher or secondary education this way will progress more rapidly than one who goes straight from school to a higher educational institution or a technicum. This is natural, for a man may graduate from an institute and then be frightened by a grinding gear when he goes to the factory. But if he goes to the higher school from production work, he won't be afraid of machines; he will deal with them boldly, for they are his element. I say all this so that you will not think that by going off to the construction projects you will lose the opportunity for a higher education. If you have a desire to study, each of you will find a way to continue to study.[147]

------

*Machine Tractor Stations, centralized machinery depots which undertook work for collective farms until the 1959 reorganization.

The Seven-Year Plan appears to take into account the need for more workers. Thus it calls for developing general secondary education, higher and specialized secondary education through evening and correspondence courses, and for extending the network of evening schools.

By 1965, the number of students in elementary (seven-year) and secondary schools will have increased to 38 or 40 million, as against 30 million in 1958. The number of students in boarding schools is to grow from 180,000 in 1958 to 2,500,000 in 1965 (thus freeing more mothers for work).

CHAPTER 9

The Diplomatic Front

Psychological Warfare

Not the least of the tactics employed by the Soviets in their struggle for world power is the creation of a climate of capitulation at the conference table. The world situation provides ample opportunity for maneuver. And the universal communications system outside the Iron Curtain provides ample opportunity for Soviet verbal barrages to condition the world population and its leaders to accept the Soviet will.

Even before the days of Joshua, strategists used men's emotions to help defeat them. Fear, hope, anger at their leaders, division among allies, diversions and distractions from objectives—these have been basic Soviet tactics. With modern mass communications, these devices have evolved to an almost exact science.

In a shooting war the psychological-warfare unit has a comparatively simple problem: What will make the opposing unit surrender? What will lessen its will to resist? In the cold war the objectives are the same, but the complexity and multiplicity of forces requires diversified technique.

In general, Mr. Khrushchev uses the same approaches as any other field commander: "It is useless to resist. . . . We are winning. . . . Surrender will not be so bad. . . . If you resist, we will give no quarter. . . . Our cause is just. . . . You were the aggressors. . . . Your leaders are incompetent. . . . The whole world is with us. . . ." [1]

259

Because steady pressure loses its effectiveness,[2] Khrushchev's methods involve alternate threat and blandishment. These may be motivated by other political reasons. Nevertheless, many psychologists see the zigs and zags of Soviet attitudes as an adaptation of Pavlov's "behaviorist" techniques.[3]

And in the meantime Khrushchev recommends:

"Make the imperialists dance like fish in the frying pan."[4]

The zigzag technique commonly used has a variety of purposes: it confuses; it creates a setting in which the next threat has more potency; it rationalizes the more unethical postures.

"If the conditioned inhibition points become fatigued under the influence of such strong new stimuli, they lose their inhibitory action and are transformed into positively acting points (or disinhibition). . . .

"Upon what depends the persistent and marked deviation from the normal brought about by our procedures? We have the right to answer, I believe, that it is a difficult collision, an unusual confronting of two opposing processes of excitation and inhibition (be it in time or intensity relations or even both together) which leads to more or less permanent destruction of the normal balance existing between the two processes."[5]

Or perhaps again Lenin set the pattern:

"The strictest loyalty to the ideas of communism must be combined with the ability to make all the necessary practical compromises, to 'tack,' to make agreements, zigzags, retreats, and so on, in order to accelerate the coming into power . . . and subsequent loss of political power of the Hendersons [the heroes of the Second International] if we are not to mention the names of individuals; the representatives of petty-bourgeois democracy who call themselves socialists" . . .[6]

Technique of the Threat

Fear is the basic weapon of psychological warfare. "Since the early months of 1956 down through the Berlin crisis, the Soviet

Union has on a number of occasions used the threat of the missile capabilities to strengthen the hand of its diplomacy. It comes, in the end, to a simple test of nerve and will." [7]

Khrushchev uses the threat in almost every situation. Suez, Iran, Iraq, Norway, Greece, Austria, Britain, Italy, Germany, each NATO nation, Cuba, Congo, have all figured in recent rocket-waving (see pages 268-270).

We have already developed an intercontinental ballistic missile with a hydrogen warhead. However, the tests were conducted with blanks. We would like never to have to launch rockets with hydrogen warheads . . .[8]

I hope you would not say that I am trying to frighten you if I remind you that the Soviet Union has rockets in a quantity and of a quality unequaled by any other country in the world. This can be confirmed by the launching of our sputniks and cosmic rockets. Under these conditions to settle disputable questions in the way the militarist-revanchist quarters of West Germany apparently want—by war—is tantamount to suicide, to destruction of one's country.[9]

The threat of a devastating attack or of war itself provides a climate in which untenable positions and unacceptable compromises may find acceptance. This is not because people are cowards. But public opinion and the representatives of public opinion find it easier to believe that a concession will bring lasting peace when the alternative is the obliteration of cities and nations. Munich was only one example.

The Americans thought we were incapable of producing an intercontinental rocket and they lost in this matter. . . . The fact remains that the Soviet Union was the first to produce an intercontinental rocket. This means we are ahead and gives us the possibility to improve the production of rockets, to lead the U.S.A. in this matter and to accumulate the necessary stocks of rockets if we do not come to terms on disarmament.[10]

I think I will not be revealing any military secrets if I tell you that we now have all the rockets we need: long-range rockets, intermediate rockets, and close-range rockets. Of course, these are not the limits of what can be achieved, for engineering is not marking time, but these means fully insure our defense. . . .[11]

We now possess the absolute weapon, perfect in every respect and created in a short period of time.[12]

In 1958:

Now it suffices to press but one button and not only airfields and the means of communications of various headquarters, but whole cities will be blown sky-high, whole countries can be destroyed. Such is the enormous destructive power of modern weapons created by man.[13]

In 1959:

Wars between states have always brought grievous distress to the people. But a future war, if the aggressors should succeed in unleashing it, threatens to become the most devastating war in the history of mankind, because there is no guarantee that it would not become a nuclear war, with all its catastrophic consequences. In the conflagration of such a war millions of people would perish, great cities and industrial centers would be razed from the face of the earth; unique cultural monuments created by mankind throughout the ages would be irrevocably destroyed, and vast territories would be poisoned with radioactive fall-out.[14]

And in 1959 mass production of ICBMs:

In point of fact, the Soviet Union today has the means to deliver a crushing blow to the aggressor at any point of the globe. After all, it is not a mere figure of speech when we say that we have organized serial production of intercontinental ballistic rockets. Nor do we say it to threaten anyone, but rather to bring clarity into the existing state of affairs.[15]

262

We are not among the faint-hearted, and we are ready to give the due rebuff to any attempt to use force against us or our friends. Gentlemen, you should therefore be a little more careful with the use of all these "ifs" and "buts" and of threats. You hint at the use of military means, but do not forget that we also have such means. They have been created for the very purpose of preventing the hotheads from losing their heads. They should not lose their heads and be more careful with words, particularly with deeds.[16]

But communism would survive.

Herbert Cutler, Columbia Broadcasting System: "Mr. Khrushchev, you have just said a future war would destroy capitalism. Don't you think that a future war would destroy communism, too?"

KHRUSHCHEV: No, it wouldn't. War would be a calamity for mankind, would take a heavy toll of human life and values. But man, nevertheless, would not perish. And since man will survive, the ideas with which he lives will likewise endure, and the ideas of Marxism-Leninism are immortal. Humanity would rid itself of capitalism. But the price would be such that there should be no resort to war. Both the socialist and capitalist countries would suffer. So we shall just have to live side by side on one planet.[17]

In saying that a new world war could end only in capitalism's crash, we do not mean to say at all that the socialist countries would not have any losses in that war. With modern weapons of destruction such as they are, the losses would, of course, be colossal. But we are convinced that socialism will live on, while capitalism will not survive.[18]

The threat is unmistakable and omnipresent—although more often than not, Khrushchev introduces his rocket-rattling with phrases such as: "We do not wish to intimidate anybody, but . . ." or "We do not threaten, but . . ." Sometimes there are no "buts," and German Chancellor Adenauer is a frequent target.

Hitler opened his mouth and wanted to swallow everybody. Adenauer licks his lips, he gets angry, but he cannot move from the spot. Should he attempt to touch the socialist countries, he will be smashed immediately on the spot. Immediately.

There were no "buts" in Khrushchev's threats following the U-2 incident.

Those countries that have bases on their territories should note most carefully the following: If they allow others to fly from their bases to our territory we shall hit at those bases . . . planes, intruding into our air space, enemy planes, will be shot down and crushing blows by rocket forces will be struck at the bases from which they took off. The [Soviet] Government issued instructions to this effect to the Minister of Defense and the minister issued an order to the commander of the rocket forces.[19]

Technique of the Thaw

To avoid the monotony [of a constant threat], Pavlov suggests, there are alternating intervals of *détente*. Khrushchev applies the Chinese proverb enunciated by Mao Tse-tung:

"Enemy advances, we retreat; enemy halts, we harass; enemy tires, we attack; enemy retreats, we pursue."[20]

In 1955:

We do not intend to attack anyone, we do not think of intimidating anyone. We want everyone to realize the meaning of war and to rise decisively to fight for averting war, for the prohibition of atomic and hydrogen weapons.[21]

In 1958:

We will work hard to remove the obstacles hindering a rapprochement between peoples and to put out the sparks that may set off the flames of war. Those sparks must be stamped out by all means, and pressing issues must be settled, so that peace can be assured for all nations.

You and we are living in a rather complicated world situation, although, at times, there are bright patches in the overcast sky. Are these present days not one of them? It is not for nothing that the state of world affairs in recent years has been given the name of "cold war." Under conditions of tension the "cold war" can easily turn into a hot one, into a very hot one indeed, a nuclear war, that will not only scorch but will burn to ashes.[22]

In 1959:

We want to reach an understanding on improving our relations. Our countries are very strong. They must not quarrel with each other. If small countries quarrel, they can do little more, to put it figuratively, than scratch each other. And in a day or two cosmetics will efface the traces of that quarrel. But if strong countries were to quarrel, such as the United States and the Soviet Union, it would not be our countries alone that would suffer enormous damage, but other countries as well would inevitably be drawn into a world-wide fray.

We are confident that our two states and our peoples can live in friendship and work in common for an enduring peace. You have mentioned the fact that it will soon be a hundred and fifty years since diplomatic relations were established between the United States and Russia. I should also like to say a few words in this regard. I think that when the United States ambassador presented his credentials to Emperor Alexander I, the emperor did not trust him much, because the United States ambassador represented a republic, while Alexander I was an absolute monarch. Yet, in spite of this, diplomatic relations were established between our countries. There was mutual understanding between the United States and Russia, and contacts between them grew stronger.

Our countries have never waged war against each other;

indeed, they have never had any major quarrels, with the exception of the well-known events in the early years of Soviet rule. Of course, I don't lay claim to a profound knowledge of history, but I feel sure that this is precisely how matters stand.[23]

Much is made of the elementary technique of building the image of a winning team, creating a band-wagon psychology.[24]

The ways of international public relations are as varied as the techniques every American press agent knows. For the Soviets, the weapon is seen as sufficiently important to employ their chief executive most of his time. As a result Mr. Khrushchev appears in the American press[25] and throughout the world at least as often as the American president, making his points more bluntly and with some effectiveness.[26]

The Great Divide

"Divide et impera," said the Romans, divide to conquer. Lenin put it this way:

"As long as we have not conquered the whole world, as long as, from the economic and military standpoint, we are weaker than the capitalist world, we must adhere to the rule that we must know how to take advantage of the antagonisms and contradictions existing among the imperialists. Had we not adhered to this rule, every one of us would have long ago been hanging from an aspen tree, to the satisfaction of the capitalists." [27]

At his last appearance before the Congress of the Soviet Communist Party, in 1952, Stalin foresaw the sharpening of the contradictions between capitalist states that might even develop into war. Khrushchev also insists on such inevitable contradictions.

Of course they [contradictions between capitalist countries] exist, and cannot but exist. For such is the nature of capitalism. Not only is it impossible to deny the contradictions between the capitalist countries, but it can also be as-

266

sumed that they will become sharper. I won't say anything about the contradictions between the United States, Britain, and France, for instance, in their struggle for "dominant influence" in various regions of Asia and Africa. The West German and Japanese economies are expanding rapidly at the moment, a development which cannot but alarm the British monopolies. West Germany's emergence to a leading position can hardly be to the liking of the United States monopolies since the former need markets, and the markets, for the most part, are now in the grip of the American monopolies. This means that the West German monopolists will have to wrest positions from the American competitors. And sweet words won't be of much help in this matter. I could list "knots of contradictions" without end. And it's only fear of communism, of the popular movement for freedom and independence that, to a degree, tones down and smooths the contradictions between the imperialists, explains why they have not yet found expression in the form of armed clashes.[28]

Khrushchev thus ignores the fact that is was U.S. aid which was largely responsible for the rehabilitation of West Germany and Western Europe.

It is not so much fear of "communism" as a revolutionary movement but the determination to stem Soviet expansion—Soviet imperialism—that is responsible for the alliances formed in the postwar period.

These alliances—and most important NATO—have brought United States forces into areas living under the direct threat of the Soviet Army. United States military bases in Europe, Asia, and Africa guarantee swift intervention and/or retaliation by the only power Khrushchev respects. Khrushchev puts it the other way:

United States leaders responsible for American foreign policy obviously bank on the existence of American bases in Europe to assure the automatic involvement of these countries in a war which might be unleashed by the United States.[29]

A major aim of Soviet policy has been and continues to be the disruption of NATO, which would result in withdrawal of United States forces from Europe. A United States study points out what the breakup of NATO would mean:

"In order to appreciate the military importance of NATO we need only to contemplate our situation were Western Europe in Soviet hands. The Communist Bloc would then have an industrial potential at least equal to our own. It would lie astride the world's main communication lines. It would flank and engulf the Middle East. It would be able to manipulate the manpower, factories and cultural prestige of Europe to dominate Africa and infiltrate South America. . . .

"Nevertheless, whatever the disagreements within NATO, the USSR has demonstrated the significance it attaches to NATO by its incessant efforts to disrupt it." [30]

To this end, Khrushchev does not rely on the "internal contradictions of capitalism" alone. He resorts to the oldest and crudest methods of threat and intimidation.

The United States bases are not in deserts; they are located in densely populated areas. What are bases? They are the territories of Britain, France, West Germany, Norway, Denmark, Italy, Spain, Turkey, and a number of other countries. These bases are close enough to us for a blow against the Soviet Union and the other socialist countries, but they are just as close to us for a counterblow. It can be assumed that realization will come ultimately to the Germans in West Germany, to the French, Italians, Britons, Turks, Spaniards, Danes, and others, that should the American imperialists use the territories of their countries for attack against the Soviet Union and the other peace-loving countries, retaliatory counterblows will come from the Soviet Union. The peoples will understand that and, no doubt, raise their voices.[31]

We tell the Governments of those countries, if you leased your territory to others, then you are not the masters of your land, of your country; hence we shall have to understand it in

268

our way. Those who lease your territory, operate against us from your territory. Their lands are far from us while your land is near. That is why as a warning to remote targets, we shall find the range to the near ones. Let them draw the appropriate conclusions.[32]

The bases, says Khrushchev, can be destroyed in minutes.

These bellicose militarists should ponder about their country and its follies. If such a country as ours, which occupies one-sixth of the globe, can, as they assert, be destroyed in a brief period, how much time is needed to destroy other smaller countries, the allies of the United States, by resorting to the same means with which we are threatened? If the American generals and admirals ignore their allies and write them off, it is their own affair.[33]

Modern military bases inevitably threaten the peaceful population of entire countries with annihilation.[34]

In case a war is unleashed, devastating retaliatory blows will be struck both at those countries on whose territories NATO bases are located, and at those countries which are creating these military bases for aggressive purposes. Nowadays there is no place where an aggressor could escape just punishment.[35]

Each nation is threatened in turn.

Imagine what it would mean to explode rockets over the British Isles. How many rockets with hydrogen warheads would be needed to destroy almost every living thing? Well-informed people say only a few. And even those not killed would be doomed to a slow death as a result of the contamination of the soil and atmosphere by radioactive fallout. Who can be indifferent to such a terrifying prospect? [36]

If war is launched with present-day weapons, it threatens literally catastrophic consequences for the people. While this policy is dangerous for all countries it is even more hazardous for countries like Britain, France and West Germany, with high population densities and relatively small areas. The governments of these countries are risking the complete annihilation of every living thing on their territory.[37]

The most tangible force is the West Germans. But not even they have any desire to fight, they've had enough, they still haven't got over the last war. The lesson they learned has not been forgotten, neither the young nor the old want to fight, apart from the militarist circles tagging in the wake of United States policy. The German militarists realize that if they were to unleash war, then a few hours would suffice to put all the bases of military significance in West Germany out of commission.[38]

Threats are directed at the countries of NATO's northern flank . . .

If we are to mention other members of NATO, it should be noted that Norway, for example, evidently is in that organization by mistake. Most Norwegians are thinking of how Norway could leave the North Atlantic bloc. The same applies to Denmark, which could do little even if she became angry with the Soviet Union. That also concerns the Netherlands. We regard Canada as another peace-loving power which found herself in NATO by mistake as a result of conditions that took shape in the recent past. In addition to the United States of America, the only power that might threaten the Soviet Union is Luxembourg.[39]

. . . and the south . . .

The Italian Government acted unwisely in putting its territory at the disposal of the United States for establishing rocket bases directed against you and the Soviet Union. By doing this the Italian Government is exposing its country to incredible danger.[40]

. . . Greece . . .

We would like to warn the Greek Government once more that it should not be unreasonable and permit the establishment of rocket bases on its territory.[41]

. . . even neutral Austria . . .

You should understand that the presence of these foreign rocket installations in northern Italy, if they should be used against the socialist countries, would constitute a violation of Austrian neutrality.[42]

. . . and Africa and Asia.

As for the military bases in Europe, Africa, and Asia, rockets have long since been available which could reach any point in these continents. It is no secret, of course, that these rockets are now provided with atomic and hydrogen warheads.[43]

The fault of such nations as Turkey and Pakistan is that they have joined aggressive blocs. The people's saying on this score is "One sells one's soul to the devil; before one has done so, one can be one's own master, but after it is the devil that is the master." That is how matters are at present with Turkey, Pakistan and Norway.[44]

With the threats of annihilation comes the verbal barrage of propaganda directed at splitting the Western alliance. Says one United States study:

"It is clear that Soviet policy is immensely alert to the possibility of exploiting schisms as among the Western European nations and as between Western Europe and the United States." [45]

In a similar situation Lenin recommended:

"We are at present between two foes. If we are unable to defeat them both, we must know how to dispose our forces in such a way that they fall out among themselves; because, as is always the case when thieves fall out, honest men come into their own." [46]

The United States is ruining her allies, says Khrushchev.

Under the present "position of strength" policy, the powers participating in NATO have spent a total of more than $400,000 million for military purposes in the period from 1950 to 1957. However, these vast military expenditures have

271

not helped them to evade the mounting difficulties in the economy which is clearly evident in the United States, now undergoing an economic crisis, as the Americans themselves admit.

Nor has this policy of the United States benefited the countries which support the cold-war policy and the arms drive. Quite the contrary, by fettering themselves with the "position of strength" policy, these countries are forced to shoulder unbearable military expenditures. Their economy is being undermined and civilian production is being curtailed— a fact which allows the American monopolies to reduce these countries to a position of ever greater dependence, in the economic as well as the political sense.[47]

The contradictions and rivalry between the colonial powers for spheres of influence, sources of raw materials, and markets are growing. The United States is out to grab the colonial possessions of the European Powers. South Viet-Nam is passing from France to the United States. The American monopolies are waging an offensive against the French, Belgian and Portuguese possessions in Africa. Once Iran's oil riches were fully controlled by the British, but now the British have been compelled to share them with the Americans; moreover, the American monopolists are fighting to oust the British entirely. American influence in Pakistan and Iran is increasing under the guise of "free enterprise." [48]

The United States and West Germany, says Khrushchev, are the real threat to the other members of the alliance.

The United States has emerged to the forefront of the imperialist states, and West Germany is now out to do the same by elbowing and jostling Britain, France and other capitalist countries out of its way. Such is the law of capitalism—the strong beats the weak and the cash nexus holds sway.[49]

Khrushchev flatters Great Britain and warns the British to watch the United States.

British policy is in general more refined and flexible, because the British are more skilled in diplomacy than the Americans and do not behave so rudely as their American colleagues.[50]

As before, the main conflict is that between the United States and Great Britain; Anglo-American antagonism embraces a wide range of questions. Under the "Atlantic cooperation" slogan the transatlantic competitors are taking possession of the principal strategic and economic positions of the British Empire, they are working to obtain a grip on the imperial lines of communication, break up the system of preferential tariffs, and get control of the sterling area.[51]

France, says Khrushchev, had better realize that the United States is out to grab Algeria.

The United States is following the same policy with regard to Algeria, taking active steps to elbow the French out and to take their place. Unless the French Government heeds the voice of reason and resolves the Algerian problem in a way that would take into account the interests of the Algerian people as well as the interests of France, the United States imperialist circles might pocket Algeria, too.[52]

But in France, it is easier to sell Germany as the hereditary foe. Khrushchev plays on memories of the past to make his point.

I should like to call a spade a spade. It is well known how often France has fallen victim to aggression on the part of Germany. Can the French people indeed forget this?[53]

We would like to hope that France and the French will understand us. The German revenge-seekers are again dreaming about marching along their former routes.[54]

And again:

I was told that you often compare Stalingrad with Verdun. This comparison is not without reason. Both Stalingrad and

Verdun are heroic cities symbolizing the spirit of fortitude and courage in the struggle against German invaders.[55]

And again:

I believe that German revanchists will threaten France more than any other country.[56]

He also knows how to butter the French . . .

Today, at the tomb of [your] Unknown Soldier and at Mont Valérien [the French Resistance memorial], we have paid homage to the heroic sons of France who have given their lives in the struggle against the German aggressors for the freedom and independence of their motherland.

Is it only to you that they are dear? No, they are dear to us, too. At the decisive moments our peoples have fought together against their common enemy.

We know that in France you are aware of the presence of the threat of a revenge. Certainly, the leaders of France want to prevent the growth of this threat by different methods from ours. We are aware of this difference in the way of facing the problem, but we also see possibilities of reaching an understanding on the fashion in which a solution should be sought.[57]

. . . and their chief of state . . .

What do I like in General de Gaulle? I like his resolute determination to serve France as a patriot of his country. . . . The persistence with which he expresses his will on French national policy also appeals to me. We highly respect and esteem General de Gaulle for this.[58]

. . . whom eighteen months earlier, he had likened to Hitler.

The same strategic line of reaction manifests itself now in France. The project for the establishment of a personal dictatorship, which is at the basis of the new constitution, is aimed at nullifying the role of parliament, at establishing a

regime of severe police reprisals, and at some places, for example in Algeria, the terror inspired by the Hitlerite model, at
surrendering command posts in the state to the military
clique, and gradually suppressing the liberties conceded by
bourgeois democracy, and of depriving the working class of
its social achievements, and levying attacks against its democratic organizations. All this naturally evokes the memory of
the events in Germany of 1933.[59]

According to the Great Soviet Encyclopedia, De Gaulle is a
fascist who even cooperated with Hitler and Vichy France:

"Created by De Gaulle [during World War II], the 'Central Bureau of Intelligence and Action' [BCRA], a sort of Gestapo, operated
in close contact with the Hitlerites and Vichyites. . . . De Gaulle and
his clique are to blame for the annihilation by the Hitlerites of a
huge number of French patriots. The De Gaullist clique stubbornly
propagandized the criminal policy of *attentisme* [waiting out]—a
policy of betrayal and aiding the enemy." [60]

A *History of the Great Patriotic War of the Soviets*, published in
August 1960, treats De Gaulle better than any of the other wartime
leaders of the West.

Khrushchev wants something from France now and he does not
hide what it is:

If in the past republican France could enter into alliance
with Czarist Russia there are all the more reasons for friendly
relations between France and the Union of Soviet Socialist
Republics, whose banner from the first days of Soviet power
bore the words "peace and friendship among nations." The
alliance between our countries is dictated by common interests, the geographical positions of our countries, and the
necessity of defending peace in Europe. French-Soviet alliance has invariably contributed to consolidating the security
of both countries, and the absence of such an alliance has on
many occasions in the past harmed the national interests of
both the Soviet Union and France.[61]

Conveniently, Khrushchev omits mentioning that the French-Soviet alliance concluded in 1935 was broken by Stalin four years later when he signed an agreement with Hitler—the pact that made World War II possible.

Problems, difficulties, divergences of interest, exist and will continue to exist among the European allies and between these allies and the United States. But for the time being there seems to be little chance that Soviet cajolery or threats will disrupt the alliances between North America and Western Europe. These are deeply rooted in geography, history, religion, and culture, tested in war and peace over two centuries. However, American leadership will certainly be questioned as the Western European nations regain some of the strength and influence lost during World War II.

Harnessing the Hopes For Peace

"From time immemorial the idea of disarmament has been one of the most favored forms of diplomatic dissimulation of the true motives and plans of those governments which have been seized by a sudden 'love of peace.' This phenomenon is very understandable. Any proposal for the reduction of armaments could invariably count upon broad popularity and support from public opinion." [62]

Thus a Soviet historian explains the true meaning of disarmament proposals: first, they are a cover-up; second, propaganda.

Khrushchev, educated by Soviet history books, knows this very well. He also claims to be a Leninist—he must not only know but agree with Lenin's approach to "peace programs":

"Every 'peace program' is a deception of the people and a piece of hypocrisy unless its principal object is to explain to the masses the need for a revolution, and to support, aid and develop the revolutionary struggle of the masses that is starting everywhere (ferment among the masses, protests, fraternization in the trenches, strikes, demonstrations . . .)." [63]

In Stalin's time, Soviet disarmament policy was explained in the following way:

"The disarmament policy of the Soviet government must be utilized for purposes of agitation. . . . However, they must not be utilized as a pretext for advancing similar demands in capitalist countries but as a means: (1) for recruiting sympathizers for the Soviet Union —the champion of peace and socialism, (2) for utilizing the results of the Soviet disarmament policy and its exposure of the imperialists in the effort to eradicate all pacifist illusions and to carry on propaganda among the masses in support of the only way toward disarmament and abolition of war, viz., arming of the proletariat, overthrowing the bourgeoisie and establishing the proletarian dictatorship." [64]

"The proposals for general and complete disarmament submitted by the Soviet Government . . . differ radically in aim, sincerity and objective significance from the phrases and schemes submitted by the imperialists and their Social-Democratic flunkeys.

"The aim of the Soviet proposals is not to spread pacifist illusions, but to destroy them; not to support capitalism by ignoring or toning down its shady sides, but to propagate the fundamental Marxian postulate that disarmament and the abolition of war are possible only with the fall of capitalism." [65]

But, of course, times have changed. War today is infinitely more destructive than in the pre-atomic age. Khrushchev is well aware of it when he argues before the United Nations . . .

I shall not be disclosing any great secret when I say that the explosion of one—only one—big hydrogen bomb releases a tremendous energy of destruction. Recently I read some remarks by the American nuclear physicist, William C. Davidson, stating that the explosion of one hydrogen bomb releases more energy than all the explosions effected by all countries in all the wars in the history of mankind. And, by all the indications, he is right. Can one disregard the fact that the destructive power of the weapons of war has reached such colossal proportions? And can one forget that there is not a spot on the globe today that nuclear and rocket weapons cannot reach?

It is hard to imagine the consequences for mankind of a war with the use of these monstrous instruments of destruction and annihilation. If it were allowed to break out, its toll would run not into millions but into tens and even hundreds of millions of human lives. It would be a war that would know no distinction between front and rear, between combatants and children. Many large cities and industrial centers would be reduced to ruins, and great monuments of culture, created by the efforts of man's genius over centuries, would be lost irretrievably. Nor would this war spare future generations. Its poisonous trail in the form of radioactive contamination would long continue to cripple people and claim many lives.[66]

. . . or before a communist forum, saying that for this reason

. . . the Marxist-Leninist parties always and in all their activities are the consistent partisans of a sensible peace-loving policy, for the prevention of another world war.[67]

It is because he recognizes today that a world war could be all-destructive that Khrushchev is moving toward conquest without war. His "love for peace" serves as a cover-up for his real designs, and his disarmament proposals do receive support in many countries of the noncommunist world. Says David Lilienthal, coauthor of the United States proposal for control of nuclear weapons, submitted to the United Nations in 1946—and rejected by the Soviet Union:

"The various forms of disarmament that have been proposed, have actually diverted our attention. They have done what the Russians set out to do. They have brainwashed us, they have diverted our attention from things that are possible, to things that are not now possible. And this is a major victory on their part, we better get over it real fast, even at the risk of being called warmongers."[68]

Khrushchev's disarmament proposals must be viewed in the light of the avowed objective of the "peace offensive":

In its peace policy, as well as in all its other activity, the Soviet Government, under the leadership of the Communist

Party, carries out an offensive against the bourgeois world; struggles for influence on the widest multimillion masses; endeavors to imbue them with ideas which have inspired the workers and the peasants who have accomplished the greatest revolution and calls upon them to actively check the resistance of the bourgeois world and to defeat it. . . .

The working people of the Soviet Union are firmly aware of the fact that the final triumph of their peace aspirations is possible only when imperialism will be disarmed and defeated by the international proletariat.[69]

Khrushchev dismisses the dangers of war in a speech to the Soviet military.

The fatalist conclusion of the ideologists of imperialism about the "annihilation of world civilization" in the course of a new war is unfounded and aimed at deceiving and frightening the popular masses.[70]

Khrushchev himself claims that his policy is consistent with communist heritage.

The Soviet Union, together with other socialist countries, is carrying out an indefatigable struggle for the defense of peace and against the threat of a new devastating war. . . . The policy of peace and peaceful coexistence, which is pursued by socialist countries, is not a haphazard phenomenon but it is organically inherent in socialist society. The policy of peace is inseparable from socialism in the same way as aggression and war are inseparable from imperialism.[71]

Khrushchev makes a case out of the announced reduction of armed forces carried out by the Soviet Union.

The Council of Ministers puts before you for consideration and confirmation the proposal to reduce our armed forces by another 1.2 million men. If such a proposal is accepted by the Supreme Soviet, our army and navy will have a complement of 2,423,000 men. Thus the complement of our armed forces will be below the level proposed by the United States, Britain, and France during the discussion of the disarmament problem in 1956. These proposals envisaged for the Soviet Union and the United States armed forces at a level of 2.5 million men each.[72]

In submitting this proposal to the Supreme Soviet, Khrushchev made it clear that:

, The proposed reduction will in no way weaken the firepower of our armed forces, and this is the main point. In fact, the state maintains its army for the very purpose of having the firepower necessary to withstand the likely enemy and prevent him from attack or give him a proper rebuff should he attempt to attack our country. The Soviet Army now has combat means and firepower never before possessed by any army.

In our time the defense potential of the country is not determined by the number of our soldiers under arms, by the number of persons in naval uniform.[73]

Under present conditions wars would not be carried out as before and there would be little to resemble previous wars. Formerly states tried to keep armies as near as possible to their frontiers in order to have available, as it were, a live barrier of soldiers and guns at the right moment. If a state wanted to invade the territory of another, it had to attack these border troops. That is how a war usually began. The first days of fighting occurred on the frontiers of the fighting countries where the armies were concentrated. Now if war begins, military operations would proceed differently, since states will have the means to deliver weapons over thousands of kilometers. War would begin in the heart of the warring countries; moreover there would not be a single capital, not a single major industrial or administrative center, not a single strategic area which would not be subjected to attack, not only during the first days, but during the first minutes of the war.[74]

The following question arises, however: If the possibility is not excluded that some capitalist countries will draw even with us in the field of modern armaments, will they not, possibly, act perfidiously and attack us first in order to make use of the factor of surprise attack with such a formidable weapon as the rocket-atomic weapon and thus have an advantage for achieving victory? No, modern means of waging war is to not give any country such advantages. One can be the first to attack; for this one does not need to be particularly clever, one must rather be reckless to do this. We, of course, are aware of the fact that some of our possible adversaries are inclined this way. . . . Let us, however, assume that some state, or group of states, succeeds in preparing and carrying out a surprise attack on a power with nuclear and rocket weapons. But could the attacking side, even if one supposes for a moment that it succeeded in inflicting a surprise attack, be able to put out of order immediately all the stocks of nuclear weapons, all the rocket installations on the territory of the power attacked? Certainly not. The state subjected to a sudden attack, if, of course, the state in question is a sufficiently big one, will always be able to give a powerful rebuff to the aggressor. We take into account the fact that foreign military bases are located around our country. That is why we site our rocket facilities in such a way as to insure duplication and triplication. The territory of our country is immense. We have the possibility of dispersing our rocket facilities, of camouflaging them well. We are creating such a system that if some means earmarked for a retaliatory blow were put out of commission one could always send into action the means duplicating them and hit the targets from reserve positions.[75]

Khrushchev recognizes that his motives for demobilization are self-evident.

In Western countries it is often written that the striving of the Soviet Union for disarmament is dictated by the fact that we allegedly encounter some difficulties in the implementation of the Seven-Year Plan, in the development of our country's national economy. The argument goes so far as to suggest that the Soviet Union submitted its disarmament proposals only in order to find means to carry out the Seven-Year Plan. Naturally, this is nothing but fabrications of the ill-wishers toward the Soviet Union. If anybody in the West imagines that the situation in the Soviet economy does not permit the maintenance of the necessary army which would insure the defense potential of our country, then so much the worse for those who think so.[76]

But Khrushchev does not deny the economic implications of this reduction—which comes at a time when the growth of the labor force is reduced by the lower birth rate during the war.

And as for the development of our peaceful economy, such a unilateral initiative in the field of disarmament will do us much good. It will save us 16 to 17 billion rubles annually. Besides, more than a million young, energetic, capable workers will go to work in the fields, factories, power plants, and construction projects. All this will of course be beneficial for a further rise in the living standards of the people.[77]

Having explained at home that cuts in the armed forces are meaningless in modern warfare and that the saving in manpower is important, Khrushchev makes a great virtue of necessity.

The Soviet Union is proposing a radical approach to the solution of the key international problem—the disarmament problem. As you know, we have proposed to deprive war of its material potential. We were the first to take a concrete step, unilaterally reducing our armed forces by one-third. Our proposals cannot just be brushed off or called "propaganda." Let others also embark on such "propaganda" and unilaterally reduce their armed forces substantially.[78]

By virtue of the socialist nature of its system, the Soviet Union has not and cannot have any vested interest in main-

taining an atmosphere of cold war and suspicion. In fact, we
have been doing our best to restore trust and eliminate tension. To those who voiced their suspicions we held out a
friendly hand and repeatedly took specific unilateral action
of the kind you suggest in the sphere of disarmament, expecting others to follow suit. During the last two or three
years we have reduced our armed forces by nearly two million. But no one has followed our example.[79]

**Rewriting history is a specialty with Khrushchev, as it was with his
predecessors.**

The Soviet Union in 1945 embarked on a considerable
reduction of its armed forces in the hope that the Western
powers would also be guided by the ideas of maintaining
peace and friendship and strengthening the relations which
developed among the countries of the anti-Hitlerite coalition.
Our hopes, however, were not justified. As a result of the
formation of the aggressive NATO bloc in the West and the
atom-bomb blackmail at the time when we had none, the
Soviet Union was compelled, in the interests of strengthening
its defense in the case of a provocation, to increase the number of its troops, which by 1955 reached 5,763,000. In the
next period 1955–1958, as I have already reported, the armed
forces were reduced by 2,140,000 and now total 3,623,000.
Such are the figures on the state of armed forces of the
Soviet Union during the past ten years.[80]

**The record of the relative announced armed forces of the United
States and the USSR is illuminating:**

	USSR[81]	U.S.[82]
1945	11,364,000	14,529,449
1947	2,874,000	1,794,152
1948	3,800,000	1,359,131
1949	3,000,000	1,527,616
1950	Not available	1,384,302
1951 (Korean War)	3,300,000	3,054,785

1952	4,500,000	3,392,432
1953	4,500,000	3,304,166
1954	4,750,000	3,076,649
1955	5,763,000	2,728,247
1956	3,623,000	2,594,958
1957	2,300,000	2,593,186
1958	2,300,000	2,409,385
1959	3,623,000*	2,326,926
1960	3,623,000*	2,086,635

*On January 14, 1960, Khrushchev announced that 1,200,000 would be cut from the armed forces of 3,623,000 because of rocket superiority.

This record omits a few—not insignificant—facts. Robert Lovett, former Secretary of Defense, points out:

"Between 1945 and 1949, the full defense expenditures of the United States and Great Britain were cut by 85 per cent, while Soviet defense expenditures, including only those admitted on their published budget were reduced only 48 per cent."

In 1948 Stalin, by taking over Czechoslovakia and by blockading Berlin, showed that he was intent on moving west. The Czechoslovak coup and the Berlin blockade alerted the West to the necessity of taking defensive measures. The NATO treaty was signed in 1949. In 1950 Stalin struck in the East; Korea became a battlefield. The free world united its forces, the defense treaties in Asia followed the communist aggression in Korea.

Khrushchev, emulating Stalin, accuses the West of warmongering.

The ruling circles in the imperialist countries are pursuing a policy of further strengthening military blocs, are trying to unite all the aggressive blocs, such as NATO, the Baghdad Pact [now CENTO], and SEATO, into a single military aggressive bloc led by the United States. Does such a policy of the present claimants to world domination not remind one of the policy pursued by Hitler and Mussolini, when they were also building their policy on the basis of force and created the notorious anti-Comintern pact and the Berlin-Rome-Tokyo axis?[83]

And:

The Western countries are afraid of disarmament. They fear disarmament because their governments (above all in the United States of America) are dependent upon monopoly groups who do not want to reorganize their economy in order to manufacture the civilian goods because they are deriving immense profits from the manufacture of armaments. In order to insure the continuance of such profits in the future, they use every means to keep the cold war at a certain height, increase international tension and intimidate people with the "communist menace." The monopolists hope in this way to continue to extract large sums from the population in the form of high taxation and maintain a favorable economic situation enabling them to obtain high profits.[84]

Again:

A handful of millionaires and billionaires are reaping huge profits from the suffering and plight of the people, while the million-strong masses of working people are compelled to make lengthy, futile attempts to find work, having no means to feed their children and their aged fathers and mothers. At the same time the United States Government spends billions of rubles in constructing military bases. The monopolists see an advantage in the arms race. They are not worried by the urgent needs of the people. Such is the nature, such is the essence of capitalism—gains, enrichment, and the reaping of maximum profits. This is the goal to which the people in power in the capitalist countries aspire. Such is the motive power of the capitalist society. This is what the capitalist prosperity looks like in practice. This is what is meant by the capitalist freedom! [85]

Meanwhile Khrushchev carries on diplomatic moves and proposals for pacts and agreements.

Agreement between our two countries [the United States and the USSR] and between all the great powers on the problem of disarmament would be welcomed with great satisfaction by ordinary people in all corners of the world and would open the door for broad cooperation between states and for a stable peaceful coexistence of all countries and peoples.[86]

We believe such a question as the conclusion of a nonaggression pact between the members of the Warsaw Treaty organization and the NATO countries has long been ripe for solution. . . . It is superfluous to say that the danger of war would decrease immediately because it is absolutely obvious that a new war conflagration in Europe, and not only in Europe, can in present conditions result only from conflict between the two basic groups of powers.[87]

The alleviation of tension in Europe would, in our opinion, be greatly promoted by a nonaggression pact between the two alignments of states. The conclusion of such a pact would constitute the first concrete step along the road toward eliminating existing military alignments. This would at the same time prepare the ground for a future effective system of security in Europe. We think that the problem of concluding such a pact has long been ripe.[88]

But commentators recall the history of nonaggression pacts and the official Soviet documents on foreign policy that say:

"As a matter of fact, bilateral nonaggression pacts do not always serve to promote the cause of peace. The most avowedly aggressive State may conclude pacts of nonaggression with some States in order to free its hands and secure its rear or flanks for an attack on other States." [89]

Periodically Khrushchev pours out "peace" plans which the West could not accept without seriously upsetting the balance of forces.

Disengagement—withdrawal of troops from foreign countries— would leave the two-million-man Russian Army a few hundred miles from Central Europe, United States forces 3,000 miles away.

The suggestions for disengagement have three major failings:
1. Any withdrawal of Soviet troops from bloc countries would

certainly be succeeded by other forms of control on the local military and civilian government.

2. Political, economic, and military changes following U.S. withdrawal would create a power vacuum and make the evacuated areas an easy prey for subversion in line with the Soviet's admitted commitment for expansion.

3. The ambiguity and uncertainty which would follow withdrawal would create an instability and consequent danger even greater than the present opposing forces.

This is Khrushchev's approach:

One must not forget for a moment the danger of another military explosion.[90]

After all, as long as your military bases are around the frontiers of the Soviet Union, friction between ourselves and the United States is inevitable. The danger is always present that the friction might produce a fire. When two soldiers from different countries face each other accidents can always happen, accidents which can lead to catastrophic consequences. Then why allow this to happen? It is better to conduct affairs in a way which will avoid a situation. It is better to liquidate foreign military bases on foreign territories and to withdraw troops within the limits of one's national frontiers. Then there will be no points of contact between our armed forces, and no reaction which might produce the spark capable of starting a fire.[91]

In view of the mounting military threat from the German Federal Republic, the Soviet Union has recently made a number of new proposals on the German problem. We suggested a gradual reduction of foreign armed forces in Germany, or, better still, their complete withdrawal. We stand for a "zone of disengagement" of the armed forces. The farther apart they will be, the less the danger of clashes and conflicts. The Soviet Union is prepared to withdraw its forces not only from Germany, but from Poland and Hungary, where they are stationed under the Warsaw Treaty, if all the NATO countries will withdraw their troops to within their national boundaries and abolish their military bases in other countries.[92]

What steps should be taken to prevent war? Why does not the United States, and the others, withdraw their troops from West Germany, from the Western countries—France, Italy, Turkey, Greece, and I don't know where else. We could then move our troops out of East Germany, Poland, Hungary, and Rumania. We have no troops anywhere else. This, besides being very useful, would be the first step in testing good relations and in establishing a good atmosphere that would not reek of war. It would facilitate good peaceful relations which could develop between our countries. We have said this before, we repeat it now, and we are prepared to do everything necessary.[93]

United States military bases—an essential element of United States defense strategy as long as ICBMs are not operational in sufficient numbers to maintain the "balance of terror"—remain Khrushchev's principal target.

If the Western powers had really wanted to solve the disarmament problem and to achieve a relaxation of international tension, they should have wound up their military bases abroad and withdrawn their armed forces. It would also be logical to reduce armed forces by an amount at least equivalent to the number of troops at present manning these bases. The whole world is aware that the overwhelming majority of the military bases are to be found close to the frontiers of the Soviet Union, the people's democracies and the peace-loving countries of Europe, Asia and Africa. If the United States of America and the other Western countries were to wind up their bases, then the Soviet Union and the other peace-loving countries would immediately carry out measures for further disarmament.[94]

Knowing that the West could not dismantle its bases now without endangering the whole defense structure, Khrushchev throws down the challenge, "You're afraid to leave for political reasons."

We are not afraid to withdraw our troops from all the countries where they are stationed now, but Britain, the United States, and France are afraid. The governments of Italy and West Germany are afraid of the withdrawal of foreign troops from their countries.[95]

Khrushchev says there are no rockets in East Germany.

The leaders of the North Atlantic bloc are spreading fabrications of all kinds in order to somehow justify in the eyes of the peoples the establishment of rocket bases on the territories of West European states. An example of these fabrications can be found in the false reports alleging that the Soviet Union has bases for intermediate-range rockets on the territories of the German Democratic Republic, Poland, and Czechoslovakia. It can easily be seen that such reports are aimed at aggravating international tension for the purpose of continuing the arms race.[96]

An East German newspaper puts it another way:

"In future we will continue to prove our readiness for negotiations. . . . Nor will our defensive measures, including the stationing of rockets, if that should be necessary, change our attitude toward this question.

"Rockets and rockets are not the same thing. In the hands of socialist states and governments, which persistently fight for negotiations, rockets serve peace and the principal methods to safeguard peace, namely to solve all issues through negotiation." [97]

This is like the parable of the mote and the beam. Khrushchev does not recall that Soviet tanks suppressed the workers' uprising in East Germany in 1953, or that in 1956 Russian armor crushed the Hungarian revolution a few days after his promise to withdraw Soviet forces from Hungarian soil.

Nuclear disarmament is a favorite Khrushchev proposal.

What would have happened if in 1945 the United States had not developed the atomic bomb? Here is an authoritative answer:

"Since World War II it has been primarily the U.S. nuclear stockpile and delivery capability which has stood in the way of Soviet domination of the world. That the Soviet Union is well aware of this is shown by its persistent 'ban-the-bomb' propaganda. Even a U.S.-Soviet equality in nuclear weapons will not change the fact that nuclear weapons complicate the tasks of an aggressor and reduce the significance of Soviet numerical superiority in conventional forces. The argument for not renouncing the use of nuclear weapons is that it represents our best chance to maintain the peace and to eliminate the Soviet advantage in conventional forces. The willingness to engage in nuclear war, when necessary, is part of the price of our freedom." [98]

So Khrushchev suggests:

Common sense suggests to people the only way out of the impasse in which the disarmament problem has found itself. This way out lies in the complete prohibition of nuclear weapons. We are, apparently, approaching the moment in which the governments, if they want to preserve their links with the peoples, will no longer be able to turn a deaf ear to this universal demand of the present day, and even failing to achieve agreement among themselves, will be forced unilaterally to discontinue manufacture of atomic and hydrogen weapons. [99]

A little more rewriting of history is helpful:

After the Second World War, reactionary circles wanted to frighten us with atomic bombs, to keep us in submission. But, as is known, nothing came of this. Soviet scientists have discovered the secret of atomic energy. In order to paralyze the aggressive intentions of certain belligerent foreign figures, we were compelled to begin producing atomic and hydrogen bombs. But, after producing these weapons, we immediately stated that we hoped that they would never be used. The Soviet Union, for the first time in the world, placed atomic energy at the service of peaceful development. We have submitted proposals on banning the use and production of atomic and hydrogen weapons, proposals that governments solemnly promise not to use these weapons. But up to now, the Western powers have not agreed to these proposals.[100]

At present, when the advantage of rocket technology is on our side, we once again propose to the United States, Britain, and France: Let us ban forever the testing, manu-facture, and use of atomic, hydrogen, and rocket weapons.[101]

Khrushchev's record as a man of "honor," a "gentleman," is of course well known. The case of Hungary has been mentioned before. And the entire biography of Khrushchev, as well as the history of the Soviet Union's pledges and promises, suggest that reliance on his word, even his "word of honor," is hardly a policy any responsible statesman can adopt, particularly when Khrushchev balks at any meaningful measures of supervision and control of disarmament.

A United States commentator notes:

"The common interest does not depend on trust and good faith. In fact, it seems likely that unless thoroughgoing distrust can be acknowledged on both sides, it must be hard to reach any real understanding on the subject." [102]

This is how Khrushchev presents his case to a United States publisher . . .

Prominent personalities in your country publicly say that, using military bases around the Soviet Union, they can wipe our country off the face of the earth any time they see fit to do so.

You yourself know how much and how unreasonably certain noted United States personalities, and more especially some of your generals, boast. And yet they say in the same breath: Give us the right of inspection of the territory of the Soviet Union. Do they need this for peaceful purposes? Of course not. . . . The way you raise the question is, first inspection, then the establishment of confidence. But we believe that first confidence between countries should be achieved and then inspection established. The solution of this complicated problem can be reached gradually by bringing about mutually acceptable solutions. And then if the mutual desire exists it will be possible to arrive at adequate inspection which is conceivable only in conditions of mutual trust.[103]

. . . and to a communist audience:

We are in favor of control. But they want the kind of control that would be tantamount to interference in the domestic affairs of our state, infringement of our sovereignty. In short, give them an inch and they'll take a mile. We are in favor of establishing control, but we say: Don't fly where you shouldn't. The holy grave of Gandhi is in India. If you want to visit this grave you must, in deference to the country's traditions, remove your shoes and approach it barefoot.

We were there and respected this tradition. So you, gentlemen, ought to respect not only your own moneybags. Respect the traditions of other peoples and remember that they, too, have their own pride, their own interests, and wish to insure their own security.[104]

The "open skies" proposal submitted in 1958 by President Eisenhower was met with derision by Khrushchev:

It is obvious to all that this kind of control is unacceptable, since it does not solve the problem. Imagine American planes flying over the Soviet Union and Soviet planes over the United States of America. What would be the use of this? The plane flies, and the pilot sees that there is a city here and a village there. Here there are troops and there are some sort of factories. Suppose we see that the Americans have a large number of airfields. We would then have to conclude that we would have to be more active in order not to lag behind and would have to build several more airfields.

The Americans would in turn see what we have and would also say that they needed still more airfields, planes, and, perhaps something else besides.[105]

Judge for yourselves. Here is what they want: They want all the control posts to be created for the detection of explosions to be manned only by foreign personnel and for the foreign inspectors to travel unhindered all over the territory of the signatory states. They also want to create a situation in which the control commission to which these posts and inspectors are subordinated could by a mechanical majority and the votes of Western representatives impose decisions that affect the interests of the security of the Soviet Union.[106]

For Khrushchev, Russia is sometimes like a bedroom . . .

Do not force your way into another's bedroom when the door is locked. It is indecorous. What sort of a taste is it to look through keyholes? You want the lifting of restrictions on travel in the Soviet Union. Let us then agree on the liquidation of war bases in foreign territories, and let us withdraw troops from other countries to within our national boundaries.[107]

. . . sometimes like a church . . .

What does control mean? To allow one state to exercise thorough control within the boundaries of another state means to open all the doors to the other country, to admit its inspectors and control officials to places which are forbidden even to the people of the country in question. Each church, in any case, each orthodox church, has a place in the altar where only the priests are allowed to enter. Other people, even religious believers, are not supposed to go there. In the same way, every country has its own altar and its own sacred places, where not even all friends are admitted; and if they are, they are the closest friends who have merited such trust.[108]

. . . and sometimes like account books.

As far as I know, you do not let your competitors look into your account books. Don't look into our accounts, then, for we have our own communist system of bookkeeping. Let's better live in peace. There are cases with you too, aren't there—though they may be rare—when competing corporations come to an agreement not to attack each other. Why then, to use your language, should not we, representatives of the communist corporation, and you, representatives of the capitalist corporation, agree on peaceful coexistence? Let each abide by his own views.[109]

It has been a long-standing communist claim that the West does not want disarmament.

We cannot, nor shall we, agree to disarmament's being replaced by control. On our part, we shall do everything to bring about disarmament, combined with the most comprehensive and far-reaching control.

Our objective is to get all means of annihilation, including nuclear weapons and missiles, scrapped and the armies disbanded. And we also want disarmament to be under most strict and reliable control, so that no nation could carry out aggressive designs on its neighbors or other countries, stockpile the means of warfare and raise armies.

We are in favor of strict control over actual disarmament, but we are against control without disarmament. The Soviet Union sticks to this position, and will never retreat from it.[110]

In 1959, from the rostrum of the United Nations General Assembly, Khrushchev proposed "total disarmament" to the world.

Unless Khrushchev has ceased to be a communist, which he himself says he has not, one must consider his proposal as consistent with a resolution of the Seventh World Congress of the Communist International in 1928:

"The workers in the Soviet Union . . . may adopt a new method

294

in their fight against pacifism—that venomous tool of imperialism
—namely, to propose general disarmament to the imperialists." [111]

Khrushchev proposes:

The Soviet Government, having comprehensively considered
the situation, has come to the firm conviction that the way
out of the deadlock should be sought along the lines of
general and complete disarmament. With such an approach,
the possibility of any military advantages being created for
any states is completely ruled out. It is general and complete
disarmament that will remove all barriers raised during the
discussions on partial disarmament and clear the way for the
establishment of comprehensive, complete control.

What does the Soviet Government propose?

The essence of our proposals is that over a period of four
years all states should effect complete disarmament and
thereafter no longer possess any means of waging war.

This signifies that land armies, navies, and air forces would
cease to exist, general staffs and war ministries would be
abolished, military-training establishments would be closed.
Tens of millions of men would return to peaceful constructive labors.

Military bases on foreign territory would be dismantled.

All atomic and hydrogen bombs in the possession of states
would be destroyed and their further production discontinued.
The energy of fissionable materials would be used exclusively
for peaceful economic and scientific purposes.

Military rockets of all ranges would be eliminated and
rockets would remain only as a means of transportation and
of the conquest of outer space for the good of all mankind.

The states would retain only strictly limited contingents
of police [militia] agreed for each country, equipped with
small arms and designed exclusively to maintain internal
order and protect the personal security of citizens.[112]

Khrushchev's plan, as well as Western proposals for disarmament,
was discussed for weeks in Geneva by the ten-power—five com-

munist and five noncommunist countries—Disarmament Commission in the spring of 1960.

The group adjourned early in May, leaving disarmament on the agenda of the summit meeting scheduled for May sixteenth. There was no summit, but on June second Khrushchev called a press conference in Moscow to announce that he had forwarded to the West revised proposals for "general and complete" disarmament. This is the gist of Khrushchev's presentation:

We propose that the implementation of the program of general and complete disarmament should begin with the prohibition and destruction under international control of military rockets, war planes, surface naval vessels and submarines, artillery capable of firing nuclear shells, and other means of delivering to the target weapons of mass destruction and also with the liquidation of all military bases on foreign territories.[113]

The ten-power commission reconvened in Geneva on June seventh. The new Khrushchev plan was thoroughly examined; Soviet delegate Valerian Zorin remaining vague about the control procedure.

Here is one U.S. analysis of Khrushchev's proposal:

"Moscow's plan . . . would create this military picture at the end of its first stage:

"The United States would be withdrawn from Europe and from bases in other continents. The West's means of replying to an attack —missiles, long-range planes and rocket-carrying submarines—would be destroyed.

"Western European armies would be cut off from quick United States support. But the Soviet Union would have large ground forces still in existence and would be able to move them and supply them overland."[114]

In addition:

"Effective control has been complicated by the increasingly rapid advance of technology. Scientific research and development can decide the armament race. Hence no reduction in standing forces, however scrupulously carried out, can protect a nation against a technological development which drastically changes the strategic balance. The fact that so much of the armaments race occurs in laboratories makes control and inspection more and more complex. It is difficult to find something when one does not know what it is one is looking for." [115]

Western delegates sought instructions from their governments. By June twenty-fourth the United States announced that in a few days it would be ready to submit a detailed proposal to the conference. But on June twenty-seventh the five communist delegates—Russian, Bulgarian, Czechoslovak, Rumanian, and Pole—walked out of the conference, denouncing the West for "sabotaging disarmament." The Soviet government demanded that Khrushchev's plan be discussed in September 1960 by the full General Assembly of the United Nations—a larger forum than the business meetings in Geneva. What Khrushchev has shown is that he wants propaganda —not negotiations.

Khrushchev thus demonstrates again that he is faithful to communist doctrine. For communists (see beginning of this chapter), disarmament proposals are "one of the most favored forms of diplomatic dissimulation" and can "invariably count upon broad popularity and support from public opinion."

Today this is truer than ever. Wars are more dangerous and armament more costly. Khrushchev hammers on the two themes:

The position in the world today is a dangerous one. Various military alliances are in existence and the arms race never stops for a moment. So much inflammable material has accumulated that a single spark could touch off a catastrophe. The world has reached a point where war could become a fact owing to some stupid accident, such as a technical fault in a plane carrying a hydrogen bomb or a mental aberration in the pilot behind the controls. [116]

Khrushchev offers many carrots.

Although the opportunities offered by disarmament can be used better and more fully by a socialist economy, general and complete disarmament creates great economic opportunities for other countries as well. Therefore, not only the Soviet Union, but all countries, big and small, all people on earth, are bound to benefit economically from disarmament.[117]

Economic assistance:

And if a program of universal and complete disarmament is adopted, then the peoples of countries needing economic assistance would be able to receive it in considerably larger amounts. Thus the cause of progress would advance more rapidly, and if universal and complete disarmament triumphs on earth it will mean that all the achievements of science and technology of the great twentieth century will in full measure serve the people and their material and spiritual development.[118]

And reduced taxes:

Surely there are grounds to expect that a switch of production capacities to the production of peacetime goods would make it possible sharply to reduce taxes imposed on the population, to increase the capacity of the domestic market, and at the same time spend more on education, health services, and social security?[119]

There is no doubt that, with disarmament, opportunities for disposal of peacetime products on foreign markets would increase immeasurably and that the widest prospects for development of world trade would be opened. Disarmament does not solely benefit one given state or group of states, but paves the way for stable peace and economic development for all countries and all people.[119]

And more business.

All the artificial obstacles in the way of the developing of international trade which today exist in the shape of discriminatory restrictions, prohibition lists, etc., would vanish.

The industries of such countries as the United States, Britain, France, West Germany, and other highly developed countries could at last receive large orders from other states. The utilization of the money, the resources released as the result of disarmament would create the broadest possible opportunities for the employment of the population. Consequently, assertions to the effect that disarmament would lead to a crisis or economic depression in the industrially highly developed countries of the capitalist world are erroneous.[120]

Closely connected with disarmament is suspension of nuclear tests.

The first three atomic powers—the United States, Great Britain, and the Soviet Union—have been meeting in Geneva since 1958 to draft an agreement that would, under adequate supervision, put an end to testing of atomic weapons.

This question has two sides: it is highly technical and it is highly effective in the "peace offensive."

Khrushchev is all in favor of ending tests:

The Soviet Government stands firmly for the complete and unconditional cessation of atomic and nuclear weapon tests.[121]

The need immediately to suspend the tests of various types of atomic and hydrogen weapons is one of the most urgent questions of current international relations, a question deeply agitating the minds of millions in all countries. It is easy to realize the anxiety which continuing experimental nuclear-weapon blasts arouse among all people, from political leaders and scientists to common folk, the working people of town and countryside, and mothers of families.[122]

But as to inspection, Khrushchev is more reluctant.

As for the international inspection, should the need of such inspection be recognized, the Soviet Union is ready to agree to it, although even without inspection it is impossible to conceal a single test of A- and H-bombs. Any atomic explosion becomes known even without inspection thanks to contemporary science and technology. Nevertheless, the

Soviet Union, wishing to facilitate the solution of this problem, agrees to the setting up of control posts on the territory of the USSR, as well as in America, Britain, Canada, in different parts of the world, wherever necessary.

We will agree to this in order that no one should be able to test atomic and hydrogen weapons covertly or overtly.[123]

Controls? Khrushchev thinks they are not necessary at all:

In your letter you mentioned the question of control. Opponents of banning nuclear-weapon tests, who, unfortunately, are also to be found in influential circles in your country, attempt to assert that it is impossible to end such tests until a preliminary system of supervision has been established for the ending of these tests. They claim that nuclear-weapon tests can be carried on secretly. However, there are no grounds at all for such fear in this respect. Present-day science already possesses the necessary apparatus and methods for detection, which completely excludes such a possibility.[124]

He prefers a sort of "honor system."

Let us concede that sometimes modern technical equipment cannot provide absolute certainty that all underground explosions of nuclear weapons can be detected. Let us concede that sometimes it is not easy to distinguish underground explosions of nuclear weapons from earthquakes and explosions of a volcanic nature, but if an appropriate agreement is signed, it must, of course, be honestly observed by all parties. This will be of great advantage to all the peoples of the world. All nuclear explosions, underground, underwater, and in the air, will be discontinued. People will feel confident that the atmosphere is not to be contaminated with radioactive fallout. Meanwhile, the further development of science will provide the possibility of discovering and establishing all nuclear explosions with absolute accuracy. But even if there is no guarantee today that all explosions are being fully established with absolute accuracy, the conclusion of an agreement on the discontinuation of tests will place great obligations on the participants of this agreement, and it is understood that all will have to adhere strictly to such an agreement. Should any side violate the obligations to which it has committed itself, the instigators of such violations will cover themselves with shame, and they will be condemned by the peoples of the world.[125]

While Khrushchev talks in generalities, Western scientists deal in realities:

"Unfortunately a nuclear test is easily recorded or monitored only if no serious attempt is made to keep it secret. If a nation wants to hide its tests, observation will become very complicated and uncertain. To be sure, secret tests require considerable effort. But the Soviet Union has never spared resources in order to secure a military advantage. On the other hand, our history and our free society make it certain that we will respect the international obligations which we undertake." [126]

In March 1960, Khrushchev assured his French friends that in Geneva there was progress.

Now there are differences only on the most insignificant range of problems: underground explosions which cannot be recorded by any instruments. What is our attitude to such explosions? We accepted the proposal of the United Kingdom and the United States and said: Let us work together to identify such explosions, but as long as there is no method of distinguishing these explosions from natural volcanic tremors, let us act in this way: Each side undertakes not to stage such small explosions. We never staged underground explosions, and we are not preparing for them. If this solution is adopted, all issues will be settled, and a protocol can be signed. We have already agreed on all other questions.[127]

But in June 1960, there was a zig and a zag.

"In a much publicized 'concession,' the Russians announced that they would agree to a series of United States nuclear tests as part of the program of research. But in Geneva they have objected to seven of the twelve tests the United States proposed to hold.

"The Soviet Union said it would not hold nuclear tests of its own but Soviet scientists in Geneva outlined a program of chemical explosions that were to take place in the Soviet Union.

"The United States made it clear it expected to have observers at those tests, just as the Soviet Union would have observers at the tests in the United States. Mr. Semyon Tsarapkin, Soviet delegate, suddenly disavowed his own scientists and said there would be no such explosions in the Soviet Union." [128]

Negotiation

The harvest of Soviet psychological warfare is designed to be reaped at the conference table. Here the objectives of Soviet policy, small or large, are to be moved forward. Here the effects of threats and blandishments, of distractions and diversions, of divisions and promises, are consolidated and a new forum is made available for more of the same.

Moreover, negotiation is a necessary corollary to the slogan of peaceful coexistence:

"Negotiation is merely one technique, albeit a highly effective one, prescribed by the doctrine of protracted conflict."[129]

Here again it becomes necessary to define what is meant by "negotiations"—for which Khrushchev has called increasingly over the past few years. Stalin had his own definition—and at least it was clear:

"Words must have no relations to actions—otherwise what kind of diplomacy is it? Words are one thing, actions another. Good words are a mask for concealment of bad deeds. Sincere diplomacy is no more possible than dry water or wooden iron." [130]

Chapter 3 contains a few examples of how Stalin applied this definition in practice—how the "words" of the nonaggression pacts "had no relations to actions"—the absorption of the partners to the agreements. While Khrushchev is not Stalin and may have his own ethics, he seems to endorse the actions of his predecessor when he states:

We have lived up to our obligations and will continue to carry them out conscientiously.[131]

Not infrequently our opponents attempt to accuse the Soviet Union of not observing international treaties. This is not true. This can only be stated by people who consciously distort facts. The Soviet Union has always fulfilled and will continue sacredly to fulfill all its international obligations.[132]

Despite the past performances of the Soviet government, Khrushchev is quite indignant when anyone casts doubt on his good intentions and his good faith:

We are being told that it is useless to meet the Soviet Union because it is irreconcilable and it adheres to a tough position and that should one succeed in agreeing on any questions, the Soviet Union allegedly does not carry out its obligations, and does not keep its word. Such assertions are quite groundless.[133]

He insists that all problems can be solved by negotiation . . .

It is now clear that it is possible to solve the problems confronting the world only if one acts not from a position of strength but from a position of reason. These questions must be solved with the aid of the only sensible method, the method of negotiation.

. . . during which, he says,

It is essential . . . to seek agreement on a mutually acceptable basis. . . .[134]

This should imply mutual concessions. But Khrushchev does not think so.

. . . When we worked out our proposals we did not approach the question like merchants who triple the fair price and then haggle and sell their goods at a much cheaper price than the one quoted at the beginning of the deal. We do not negotiate on the basis of the principle "concession for concession." We do not have to make any concessions because our proposals have not been made for bartering.[135]

Khrushchev qualifies the concessions he will not make . . .

One must not confuse mutual concessions in the interest of peaceful coexistence with concessions of principle, in matters that concern the actual nature of our socialist system, our ideology.[136]

. . . and fails to mention that there has never been in past negotiations between the USSR and the West any demand or even any suggestion that the Soviets "concede" in matters of ideology.

Having thus set the framework for future negotiations and expressed his readiness to "seek mutually acceptable agreements on the most acute international problems," Khrushchev outlines the form these negotiations should take:

We have said more than once that the most complicated international questions can be solved only by heads of governments who are vested with greater powers. Only they are in the position to remove the conglomerations of abnormalities of international relations which have developed in many years of the cold war.[137]

The "summit diplomacy" of which Khrushchev has become the most active promoter—before and after blowing up the Paris summit meeting in May 1960—"may have several explanations, but one likely reason is that this kind of negotiation has the maximum 'atmospheric' effect, and puts the Western negotiators under maximum public pressure to reach agreement. It adds to the

Soviet advantage if Western governments fall into debate about the holding of a summit meeting as an end in itself, rather than as a channel of negotiation about particular issues. It also reinforces the Soviet purposes if the public impression of the discussion is allowed to remain at the general level: for or against disarmament, for or against a relaxation of international tensions, for or against peace." [138]

Khrushchev's attempt to force a summit meeting during the 1960 meeting of the U.N. General Assembly gives considerable weight to this explanation.

A summit meeting may have another attraction for Khrushchev. Negotiations through normal diplomatic channels, and even negotiations at the level of foreign ministers, are not likely to produce major concessions. These can only come from the highest authority.

Khrushchev does not refer to major "concessions"; he speaks of the "solution of major questions." But inasmuch as Khrushchev does not intend to make "concessions," the "solution" must depend on concessions made by the other side.

Some statesmen in the West are now expressing the view that a meeting of the heads of government should be held after major controversial questions have been decided beforehand. They claim that it is only in this case that a meeting of the heads of governments would be effective. But only those who do not take the real situation into consideration or who wish to lead astray people innocent of politics can speak like this. If the major questions were solved before the meeting of the heads of governments, it would be a meeting not for the solution of urgent questions but for joint fishing. However, I am not a fisherman.[139]

The chain of events leading to the 1960 summit fiasco started with a demand by Khrushchev, in November 1958, for a major concession: evacuation of West Berlin by the forces of the United States, Britain, and France. Khrushchev felt encouraged when, during his talks with Eisenhower at Camp David, the President called the situation in Berlin "abnormal."

But a few weeks before the summit, the United States put Khrushchev on notice that no major concessions would be forthcoming. Khrushchev reacted:

Take a recent speech by the United States Under Secretary of State, Douglas Dillon, which is presented as a statement of the United States policy on the eve of the summit conference. That speech just reeks of the "cold war" spirit. Dillon's statement is more like a collection of trite inventions about the Soviet Union and the socialist countries than a responsible policy declaration. He held forth about a constant communist threat of peaceful coexistence to be cast overboard, grossly misrepresented the Soviet proposals for disarmament and also [those] for the conclusion of a German peace treaty and the conversion of West Berlin into a free city.[140]

The United States position remained firm. The statements from Washington could leave no doubt in Khrushchev's mind—there would be no surrender on Berlin. And so there was no summit. (Khrushchev found a handy pretext in the U-2 flight.) The smile disappeared from Khrushchev's face. The Camp David Eisenhower was described by Khrushchev as "my fishy friend" (according to the official translation into English; what Khrushchev said in Russian during his press conference following the collapse of the Paris summit meeting was ruder) and insults were followed by threats, and threats by insults.

Khrushchev wanted and still wants "negotiations"—but on his terms. He has made it abundantly clear that he wants to negotiate mainly with the United States. Such bilateral talks between the two superpowers would no doubt arouse suspicion of a "deal" that others would have to pay for. These suspicions could in particular be justified if one is to read Lenin:

"It is possible to conquer the more powerful enemy only by exerting the utmost effort, and by necessarily, thoroughly, carefully, attentively, and skillfully taking advantage of every, even the smallest

'fissure' among the enemies, of every antagonism of interest among the bourgeoisie of the various countries, the smallest opportunity of gaining a mass ally, even though this ally be temporary, vacillating, unstable, unreliable, and conditional. Those who do not understand this fail to understand even a grain of Marxism and of scientific modern socialism in general." [141]

But Khrushchev is emphatic in his denials.

We have, of course, no intention or wish whatsoever to reach agreement with the United States at the expense of the interests of any other state, of West or East, large or small, or at the cost of a deterioration in the United States' relations with any other country. On the contrary, we consider that an improvement in Soviet-American relations could only be of use, and that no one would lose by it.[142]

As far as the Soviet Government is concerned, it has never had and does not have any intention of negotiating behind the backs of other states about matters having a direct bearing on their interests. We think that any attempts to gain unilateral advantages at the expense of other states would contradict all the aims of the conference which is to be convened, the results of which must benefit the cause of general peace and, consequently, all states—large and small.[143]

Khrushchev cannot escape the alternatives: either he is a Leninist as he claims to be, or he is sincere in his present profession of good intentions.

CHAPTER 10

Subversion

The Communist Party

"Perhaps Lenin's most conspicuous contribution to twentieth-century politics," one commentator has observed, "is his conception of the Communist Party as a creative history-making force and as the general staff of world revolution. In the Bolshevik movement, he created the model on which many other modern totalitarian parties have been built." [1]

This international Communist Party, with 36 million members in eighty-six nations outside the Soviet Union, is the hard-core army whose goal is the dictatorship of the Party.

Khrushchev has made plain that the communist objective is to transform the world by revolution.

We, the communists, are people of positive revolutionary activity. We see our goal as that of transforming the world, of building the communist society. The strength of our theory is that it is firmly tied with life, it combines the creative experiences of millions, it stands in defense of the basic interests of the toilers which make up the majority of the world's population. The strength of Marxism-Leninism is that in essence it is revolutionary, it does not suffer from stagnation, custom, or inertia, it lights the way to the communist future, it leads the masses forward, helping them to overcome the difficulties and roadblocks on the path to that goal. [2]

We have always declared and continue to declare that we do not want war, but we do not renounce class warfare. Class warfare will last as long as capitalism lasts.[3]

For us reconciliation between classes is impossible![4]

This struggle goes on notwithstanding the policy of peaceful coexistence.

We cannot pass by the fact that some people are trying to apply the absolutely correct thesis of the possibility of peaceful coexistence of countries with different social and political systems to the ideological sphere. This is a harmful mistake. It does not at all follow from the fact that we stand for peaceful coexistence and economic competition with capitalism, that the struggle against bourgeois ideology, against the survivals of capitalism in the minds of men, can be relaxed. Our task is tirelessly to expose bourgeois ideology, reveal how inimical it is to the people, show up its reactionary nature.[5]

The struggle is of long standing. It is noted in a 1917 decree[6] signed by Lenin, as President of the Council of People's Commissars, and Trotsky, as Commissar for Foreign Affairs:

"Taking into consideration that the Soviet regime stands on the platform of the principles of international solidarity of the proletariat and of the brotherhood of the workers of all countries, that struggle against war and imperialism can lead to complete victory only on an international scale, the Council of People's Commissars considers it necessary to come to the aid of the Left, Internationalist wing of the working-class movement of all countries with all possible resources, including money, quite irrespective of whether these countries are at war or in alliance with Russia or whether they occupy a neutral position.

"For this purpose the Council of People's Commissars decides to place at the disposal of the foreign representatives of the Commissariat for Foreign Affairs two million rubles for the needs of the revolutionary Internationalist movement."[7]

Violence is necessary only if capitalists resist.

Leninism teaches us that the ruling classes will not surrender their power voluntarily. And the greater or lesser degree of intensity which the struggle may assume, the use or the nonuse of violence in the transition to socialism, depends on the resistance of the exploiters, on whether the exploiting class itself resorts to violence, rather than on the proletariat.[8]

Marxism-Leninism teaches that this transition from capitalism to communism will take place not by way of evolution but through fierce struggle between labor and capital, through a revolutionary struggle of the proletarians against the class of the capitalists. Precisely from this follows the need for the working class to have a militant political organization of its own—the revolutionary Marxist party which is called upon to head the proletariat, to safeguard its unity and solidarity, to develop international ties, and to consolidate the international solidarity of the proletarians of all countries.[9]

The victory of socialism in one country is only a first step, as both Lenin and Stalin have made clear. It is a base for the world movement.[10]

Said Lenin: "The victorious proletariat of that country, having expropriated the capitalists and organized its own socialist production, would rise against the rest of the capitalist world, attract to itself the oppressed classes of other countries, raise revolts among them against the capitalists, and in the event of necessity come out even with armed forces against the exploiting classes and their states." [11]

If anyone thinks we shall forget about Marx, Engels, and Lenin, he is mistaken. This will happen when shrimps learn to whistle.[12]

And Stalin quotes Lenin: "Lenin never regarded the Republic of the Soviets as an end in itself. To him it was always a link needed to strengthen the chain of the revolutionary movement in the countries of the West and East, a link needed to facilitate the victory of the working people of the whole world over capitalism. Lenin knew *that this was the only right conception both from the international standpoint and the standpoint of preserving the Soviet Republic itself. Lenin knew that this alone could fire the working people of the world to fight the decisive battles for their emancipation. That is why on the very morrow of the establishment of the dictatorship of the proletariat, this most brilliant of all leaders of the proletariat laid the foundations of the Workers International. This is why he never tired of extending and strengthening the union of the working peoples of the whole world, the Communist International."* [13]

"The victory of socialism in one country is not a self-sufficient task. The revolution which has been victorious in one country must regard itself not as a self-sufficient task, but as an aid, a means for hastening the victory of the proletariat in all countries. For the victory of the revolution in one country, in the present case, Russia, is not only the product of the uneven development and progressive decay of imperialism; it is at the same time the beginning of and the groundwork for the world revolution." [14]

The Comintern is even more specific: "The USSR inevitably becomes the base of the world movement of all oppressed classes, the center of international revolution, the greatest factor in world history. In the USSR, the world proletariat for the first time acquires a country that is really its own, and for the colonial movements the USSR becomes a powerful center of attraction." [15]

Stalin asserts: "The very development of world revolution . . . will be more rapid and more thorough, the more socialism fortifies itself in the first victorious country, the faster this country is transformed into a base for the further unfolding of world revolution, into a lever for the further disintegration of imperialism.

"While it is true that the final victory of socialism in the first country to emancipate itself is impossible without the combined efforts of the proletarians of several countries, it is equally true that the development of world revolution will be the more rapid and thorough, the more effective the aid rendered by the first socialist country to the workers . . . of all other countries.

"In what should this aid be expressed?

"It should be expressed, first, in the victorious country 'carrying out the maximum realizable in one country for the development, support, awakening of revolution in all countries . . .'

"It should be expressed, second, in that the 'victorious proletariat' of one country . . . 'after organizing its own socialist production,' should stand up . . . *against* the remaining capitalist world, attracting to itself the oppressed classes of other countries, raising revolts in those countries against the capitalists, in the event of necessity coming out even with armed force against the exploiting classes and their governments." [16]

"The goal is to consolidate the dictatorship of the proletariat in one country, using it as a base for the overthrow of imperialism in all countries." [17]

The means by which this base was established was unlawful only by bourgeois law, which Khrushchev does not recognize.

It should be said that many workers' organizations and workers' parties in the capitalist countries got a wrong idea of the essence of the great gains of the working class and of the working people of Russia. Eminent Social Democratic leaders, who called themselves Marxists, asserted that the birth of the Soviet state was unlawful, that the socialist revolution in Russia was an illegitimate revolution. Why? Simply because that great revolution did not fit into their concept of things. But bourgeois laws, dear friends, are the laws of a society of exploiters. Naturally, the exploiters never will recognize as legal the act of the overthrow of their rule. And there are in general many such "laws" in bourgeois morality and law. They have, for instance, the concept of illegitimate children. The birth of the new is a natural and a normal process. The new is born, asserts itself, and develops in a hard struggle against the old, the moribund. The question of how this new birth should be regarded—whether it should be considered legitimate or illegitimate—is the province of the social, the legal superstructure. If the bourgeois world says that this or that phenomenon is not legitimate, it only states its own attitude to this phenomenon. The laws of life, the laws of the development of society are much broader and richer than the dogmas of bourgeois law. The life of society develops according to its own objective laws which demolish and brush aside the formulas of bourgeois science when they come into conflict with them.[18]

Vladimir Ilyich Lenin taught us that a revolutionary party of the working class must be a party of a special type, militant, closely connected with the masses, united organizationally, irreconcilable toward its class enemies, irreconcilable toward revisionism, opportunism. At the same time it must be flexible, must be able to find a correct solution of any problem, must not yield its class positions on anything, must always keep pure its ideological weapon in the struggle against the capitalist system which is outliving its age, the struggle for the new, the progressive, for communism.[19]

The main question of revolution is power.

The main and fundamental question of any revolution is the question of power. There have been many revolutions in the history of mankind, but not one of them in the past has led to a victory of the toiling people over the exploiting class and consolidated the power of the workers. Only the October Revolution, for the first time in history, solved the question finally in favor of the workers and the people, and thus opened up a new era, the era of the triumph of socialism and communism.[20]

Marx called revolutions the locomotives of history. These words have been clearly proved by the experience of our proletarian revolution, which speeded up in an unprecedented way the forward development of history and which laid the foundation for the great world socialist camp.[21]

Our great teacher, Vladimir Ilyich Lenin, attached tremendous importance to the revolutionary creative endeavor of the masses in producing, developing and perfecting concrete forms and methods of struggle for the triumph of the socialist revolution and the new social system. "Marxism," wrote Lenin, "differs from all other socialist theories in the remarkable way it combines complete scientific sobriety in the analysis of the objective state of affairs and the objective course of evolution with the most definite recognition of the importance of the revolutionary energy, the revolutionary creative genius and the revolutionary initiative of the masses. . . ."[22]

Lenin saw armies of the working class leading to the victory of world revolution.

"Everywhere we have proletarian armies, although poorly organized and requiring organization. We are able to organize these into a single detachment, a single force. If you will help us to accomplish this, then no mental exercises or guesses with respect to what cannot be known and what no one can know will prevent us from accomplishing our task, and this task will be that of leading on to the victory of the world revolution and the establishment of an international proletarian Soviet Republic." [23]

The "socialist state" cannot exist without a Communist Party, says Mr. Khrushchev.

Modern conditions have given rise to various forms of the socialist state. At the same time it should be stressed that without a Marxist-Leninist Party a socialist state cannot exist, the working class cannot be organized as the leading force of society, the indestructible alliance of the working class and the peasantry cannot be ensured, and the tasks of socialist construction cannot be successfully carried out.[24]

But Khrushchev denies that this Communist Party must be Soviet-controlled . . .

In the same speech he [Richard M. Nixon] said that the U.S. Communist Party, like all Communist Parties in the world, is directed and controlled by Moscow. As in the past [he said], it will in the future occupy itself with espionage and subversive activity to serve the interests of communist governments wherever they are in conflict with the interests of the United States or other free countries. These are old and stale inventions, calculated to frighten inexperienced people and to incite them against the Soviet Union. What data does Mr. Nixon possess on this point? Precisely none at all because it does not and cannot exist. It would of course be better not to repeat such assertions. They are only needed to keep up the cold war and to retain international tension.[25]

. . . although the CPSU stands at the head, the relationship is "fraternal."

Some say that the "dependence" of the Communist and Workers' Parties on Moscow is corroborated by statements to the effect that the CPSU stands at the head of the international communist movement. In doing so they refer to the well-known clause in the Declaration of the Moscow Meeting, which says that "the camp of socialist states is headed by the Soviet Union."

The Communists of the Soviet Union and of all the other countries think that thereby tribute was paid to our country and to our working class, which has, under the leadership of the Communist Party headed by the great Lenin, been the first to carry out the socialist revolution, the first to take power. In these forty-odd years we have traveled a long way along a difficult road of struggle and victory and have built up a powerful state, the bulwark of all the socialist countries and of the world communist movement.

It must be emphasized, however, that there has always been complete equality and independence for all the Communist and Workers' Parties and the socialist countries in the communist movement and in the socialist camp. The Communist Party of the Soviet Union does not control any of the other parties, the Soviet Union does not control any other country. There are no "superior" and "subordinate" parties in the communist movement. All the Communist and Workers' Parties are equal and independent.[26]

Stalin said it in a different way:

"A revolutionary is he who without arguments, unconditionally, openly and honestly . . . is ready to defend and strengthen the USSR, since the USSR is the first proletarian, revolutionary state in the world. . . . An internationalist is he who, unreservedly, without hesitation, without conditions, is ready to defend the USSR because the USSR is the base of the world revolutionary movement, and to defend, to advance this revolutionary movement is impossible without defending the USSR." [27]

In Stalin's lifetime, Khrushchev echoed without hesitation: loyalty to communism is determined by the attitude toward the Soviet Union.

Loyalty to the great cause of Lenin and Stalin, to the cause of internationalism is determined and verified by the attitude toward the Soviet Union, which stands at the head of all forces of democracy and socialism. Treachery toward the Soviet Union and treachery toward proletarian internationalism inevitably lead into the camp of nationalism, fascism and imperialist reaction.[28]

Ten years later he expressed the same idea in different words.

Solicitude for the unity and strength of our ranks is the highest international duty of every Communist and Workers' Party. The success of the international cause of the working class is unthinkable without international solidarity of all its detachments.[29]

Stalin's mouthpieces were even more specific. Says Comrade A. Vyshinsky:

"At present the only determining criterion of revolutionary proletarian internationalism is: Are you for or against the USSR, the motherland of the world proletariat? An internationalist is not one who verbally recognizes international solidarity or sympathizes with it. A real internationalist is one who brings his sympathy and recog-

nition up to the point of practical and maximal help to the USSR in support and defense of the USSR by every means and in every possible form. Actual cooperation with the USSR, the readiness of the workers of any country to subject all their aims to the basic problem of strengthening the USSR in its struggle—this is the manifestation of revolutionary proletarian internationalism on the part of workers in foreign countries. . . . The defense of the USSR, as the socialist motherland of the world proletariat, is the holy duty of every honest man everywhere and not only of the citizens of the USSR." [30]

Khrushchev reiterates the thesis that the revolution is international in scope.

Of course, we are for the union of our forces. We adhere to Marxism-Leninism, and the slogan proclaimed by Marx and Engels: "Workers of the world, unite!" is a sacred motto for us. Only through the working class of all countries pooling and coordinating its efforts will it speed up its emancipation. And this has been understood by the workers.[31]

And:

We are internationalists and therefore we must strengthen by every means the ideological ties between the Workers' and Communist Parties and strengthen and develop proletarian solidarity.[32]

And again:

Marxists understand the final victory of socialism to mean its triumph on an international scale.[33]

And again:

We have always held the view, and still do so, that none must retire to their national "domains" and withdraw into their own shells. We think that the might of the socialist camp must be reinforced in all ways and that the unity of the international communist movement must be further cemented

317

in accordance with the principles adopted by all the fraternal parties in the Moscow Declaration.[34]

Western scholars have written volumes, and could write many more, to show how "proletarian internationalism" works out in practice. In the United States, the Communist Party was opposed to Roosevelt's policy of helping the anti-Hitler coalition as long as the Soviet-German pact was in force. Communists were picketing the White House to protest Lend-Lease when news came of the Nazi attack on Russia. They discreetly withdrew and changed their slogans overnight—in the name of "proletarian internationalism"—to vociferous demands for more Lend-Lease, accusing the United States of lagging behind in her duty to defend the democracies.

In France, Communist Party leader Maurice Thorez deserted in September 1939, a few weeks after being drafted into the French Army, and went to Moscow.

Until Hitler attacked Russia, the Communists held that the "have-not capitalists" (Germany) had been attacked by the rich imperialists (Britain and France).

Polish Communists hailed the Soviet invading army as "liberators," as did Finnish Communists. Today, according to Khrushchev himself, Israeli Communists fight Zionism (which means the Jewish state itself), and coincidentally Moscow supports the Arab nations against Israel.

The Yugoslav Communists, who have had some experience with the international Communist movement, do not agree with Khrushchev that talk about dependence on Moscow is an "old, stupid fable." Khrushchev reserves particular abuse for them. Having accused them of taking "their cue" from "imperialist ideologists," Khrushchev adds:

The Yugoslav revisionists, who allege that our Party seeks "hegemonism" in regard to the other parties, show particular zeal. They went so far as to include a thesis on "hegemonism" in their program. They contend that our Party interferes in the internal affairs of other countries and wants to control the other Communist Parties. And the reactionaries are very grateful to the Yugoslav revisionists for this slander.[35]

Khrushchev rationalizes:

The interests of the working people of the USSR coincide completely with the fundamental interests of the working people of the whole world. The working class and all progressive mankind see their own future in the construction of communism in the USSR and in all the socialist countries. The world socialist system is the greatest achievement and pride of the working people of all lands. The working people perform their internationalist duty by actively supporting the building of the new society in the Soviet Union, in the Chinese People's Republic, in all the socialist countries, and by guarding this construction against the intrigues of imperialist reaction.

The development and flourishing of the USSR and of the world socialist system facilitate the struggle of the working class and of all the working people of the capitalist countries for their vital interests, for peace, democracy, and socialism.[36]

The Soviet Union is the acknowledged vanguard . . . the center.

Whatever the form of transition to socialism, the decisive and indispensable factor is the political leadership of the working class, headed by its vanguard. Without this, there can be no transition to socialism.[37]

Stalin put it even more bluntly:

"There is also no doubt that the revolution in the USSR not only has obligations with respect to the proletarians of all lands, and is fulfilling them, but that the proletarians of all lands have some sufficiently serious obligations with respect to the proletarian dictatorship of the USSR. These obligations consist in supporting the proletariat of the USSR in its struggle with internal and external foes, in a war against war, directed toward the strangulation of the proletarian dictatorship of the USSR, in preaching that the armies of im-

*perialism should go over directly to the side of the proletarian dic-
tatorship of the USSR, in case of an attack on the USSR. Does it not
follow from this that the revolution in the USSR is inseparable from
the revolutionary movement in other countries, that the triumph of
the revolution in the USSR is the triumph of the revolution in the
entire world?"* [38]

Every Communist Party is responsible to the entire movement,
but must be linked with the working class of its own country.

Every Communist and Workers' Party is responsible to the
working class, the working people of its country, and the entire international workers' and communist movement. Communist Parties, in the struggle for the interests of the working
class and for socialism, combine the universal truths of Marxism-Leninism with the concrete historical and national conditions of their countries. Only a Marxist-Leninist Party linked
with the working class, with the people of its country, can
know the concrete conditions of the struggle. Such a party
alone can evolve a political line which corresponds to these
conditions and takes into account the traditions of the workers' movement in that particular country. Such is also the
case in practice. On the foundation of full independence and
the principles of proletarian internationalism, on the foundation of voluntary collaboration and mutual aid, all Communist
and Workers' Parties live and fight. This is the way our Party
understands the nature of relations among fraternal parties.[39]

The means to the end are not limited: violent revolution is the accepted form.

Our enemies like to depict us Leninists as advocates of violence always and everywhere. True, we recognize the need
for the revolutionary transformation of capitalist society into
socialist society. It is this that distinguishes the revolutionary
Marxist from the reformists, the opportunists. There is no
doubt that in a number of capitalist countries the violent
overthrow of the dictatorship of the bourgeoisie and the sharp

aggravation of class struggle connected with this are inevitable. But the forms of social revolution vary. It is not true that we regard violence and civil war as the only way to remake society.[40]

We do not have to teach Englishmen, for example, to make a revolution and establish the socialist system in their country. They will do it themselves when they come to realize that the system which we have here in the Soviet Union and in socialist countries presents greater advantages to the people than the capitalist system and that under the socialist system unlimited possibilities are opened up for people to develop all their abilities.[41]

Communist ethics are clearly laid down by Lenin:
"We repudiate all morality that is taken outside of human, class concepts. We say that this is deception, a fraud, which clogs the brains of the workers and peasants in the interests of the landlords and capitalists. We say that our morality is entirely subordinated to the interests of the class struggle of the proletariat. Our morality is deduced from the class struggle of the proletariat." [42]

"Inexperienced revolutionaries often think that legal methods of struggle are opportunist because in this field the bourgeoisie most frequently (especially in 'peaceful,' nonrevolutionary times) deceived and fooled the workers, and they think that illegal methods of struggle are revolutionary. But this is not true. What is true is that the opportunists and the traitors to the working class are those parties and leaders who are not able or who do not want (don't say you cannot, say you won't) to apply illegal methods of struggle in conditions such as those which prevailed, for example, during the imperialist war of 1914–18, when the bourgeoisie of the freest democratic countries deceived the workers in the most impudent and brutal manner and prohibited everyone from speaking the truth about the predatory character of the war. But revolutionaries who are unable to combine illegal forms of struggle with every form of legal struggle are very poor revolutionaries." [43]

321

And again:

"Referring to the network of agents and correspondents of the Party's newspapers in the early days of the Party. This network of agents will form the skeleton of the organization we need, namely, one that is sufficiently large to embrace the whole country; sufficiently tried and tempered unswervingly to carry out its own work under all circumstances, at all 'turns' and in unexpected contingencies; sufficiently flexible to be able to avoid open battle against the overwhelming and concentrated forces of the enemy, and yet able to take advantage of the clumsiness of the enemy and attack him at a time and place where he least expects attack." [44]

Strange conclusions are drawn by capitalists, says Khrushchev.

Certain personalities in the United States, repeating the well-worn anti-Soviet fables, try to accuse the Soviet Union of interfering in the internal affairs of other countries. They assert that the Communist Party of the United States allegedly acts at our behest. In saying this, they want to blame us for all their sins and ills, including the mass strikes of workers taking place in their country. "No!" I said to these gentlemen. "You are to blame for the fact that workers go on strike in your country, and it is for you to suffer the consequences. You will not manage to foist upon the communists the responsibility for all the difficulties and conflicts of capitalism." An unending struggle has been going on between labor and capital ever since the emergence of the private ownership of the means of production, and for as long as classes have existed. It will continue until it ends with the victory of those who create all the material wealth in life. The working class will prove victorious, the toiling people will be victorious. They will win their rights and will eventually possess everything that is created by their labor.[45]

There have been times in the history of the communist movement when the revolutionary slogans were temporarily discarded, put in mothballs, so to speak. Stalin's policy, particularly in Germany in the early thirties, and of course the policy of the German Communist Party, consisted in continuous attacks on the Socialists, who were labeled "Social Fascists"; Communists predicted that they would "march to socialism over the corpse of Social-Democracy." These attacks, by weakening the Socialists, helped Hitler considerably in his rise to power. Nevertheless, all those who appealed to the communists to join forces with the opponents of fascism were promptly denounced as "traitors," "reformists," "collaborators with the class enemy."

In 1935, the switch came. All over the world, the communists "stretched out a fraternal hand" to Socialists, to "bourgeois" republicans, to Catholics, to "all anti-fascists." This was the period of the "Popular Front," which lasted till August 23, 1939, when Stalin decided to ally himself with Hitler.

Today the "Unified Front for Peace" has replaced the "Popular Front Against Fascism." Again communists propose to all to "cooperate":

Even some conservatives, religious ministers, and different kinds of bourgeois public and political leaders are struggling for peace. Naturally we are uniting our efforts in our struggle for peace. Thus in the struggle for peace, forces and organizations of various views and political opinions can be united. It is another question when we speak of the struggle for the victory of socialism. Here one cannot rely on uniting the efforts of the working class with the capitalists, of the Communist with the bourgeois parties.[46]

Khrushchev is explicit enough: he wants help to secure "peace"— his brand of "peace"—Pax Moscovita. And then he will deal with the "capitalists," distinguishing not between those who helped him and those who did not. It is surprising that in view of past, but by no means ancient, history, and of the disdainful way Khrushchev treats these "fellow travelers," he still finds a sympathetic audience among his "class enemies." Psychiatrists may be able to explain this strange phenomenon.

But in the softening-up period that must precede conquest without war, this chiming in with Khrushchev's call for total disarmament (without adequate controls) and with his repetitious propaganda for "peaceful coexistence" (at any price) is an important political factor.

Proxy Wars

Communist theory envisages the world's turning toward socialism by a revolution of the proletariat of each nation, led by the organized vanguard, the Communist Party. But those nations that have a proletariat are, by and large, industrialized nations where the standard of living and the understanding of freedom are comparatively high. Communism's appeal to these people is limited. The expansion of communism seems most promising in areas where earning power, living standards, literacy, and understanding are lowest.

The expansion of Soviet influence must proceed, therefore, through a sociological war on a different level: the exploitation of discontent wherever it can be found and the creation of factions where none exist. Military adventure is made impractical by fear of nuclear destruction, and so a new technique has been developed: the proxy war. This is not pure "aggression" in the old legal sense; the hand that pulls the trigger is far behind the scenes. Because of the legalistic concepts of the West, the true aggressor is protected by sacrosanct boundaries; yet communist arms are permitted to move abroad.

Lenin laid down the principle:

"We are not pacifists. We are opposed to imperialist wars for the division of spoils among the capitalists, but we have always declared it to be absurd for the revolutionary proletariat to renounce revolutionary wars that may prove necessary in the interest of socialism." [47]

And this is incorporated into communist dogma:

"The Bolsheviks hold that there are two kinds of wars: (a) just wars, wars that are not wars of conquest but wars of liberation, waged to defend the people from foreign attack and from attempts to enslave them, or to liberate the people from capitalist slavery, or lastly to liberate colonial and dependent countries from the yoke of imperialism and (b) unjust wars, wars of conquest waged to conquer and enslave foreign countries and foreign nations." [48]

Sending "volunteers" is a new method of warfare designed to avoid national responsibility. This technique grew out of the Spanish Civil War, in which planes, tanks, and men from Germany and the Soviet Union "enlisted." Some 500,000 Chinese "volunteers" fought with Ho Chi-minh in Vietnam.

The technique developed by Khrushchev is somewhat different from Stalin's approach. In Stalin's time proxy wars were real wars fought by satellites or obedient communist movements, as in Korea and Indochina. Khrushchev uses the technique of supplying arms and giving diplomatic as well as economic support to governments that are nationalistic in their outlook but that can be used, even without their knowledge, to foster Russian aims. The arms deal with Egypt was arranged by Dmitri Shepilov when he was not even foreign minister of the Soviet Union, but "only" editor of *Pravda*. On September 27, 1955, Nasser announced that he had concluded an agreement whereby Czechoslovakia would supply Egypt with arms. He gave no details, but Anthony Eden, then British prime minister, speaks (on the basis of British reports) of "considerable quantities of MIG fighters, Ilyushin jet bombers, Joseph Stalin Mark III tanks, Czech T. 34 tanks and heavy equipment." During the Israeli conquest of the Sinai peninsula in 1956, it was reliably reported that the Israelis had captured military equipment made in Iron Curtain countries and valued at $450,000,000. They also captured about two hundred Russian technicians who had come with the matériel. (In order not to complicate matters, this fact was not announced by Israel and the Russians were quietly released.) Egypt had to pay for these weapons. Eden says that through these payments Nasser was "mortgaging the country's economy."

It is of course because of the encouragement and equipment he received from the Russians that Nasser struck against the Suez Canal when the United States withdrew its offer to help finance the Aswan Dam. Said Mr. Khrushchev:

The participation of volunteers from other countries in events in the Middle East would mean a real war! It would be better if there were no such war, if in that country there were neither volunteers nor soldiers sent in on the order of certain governments. I believe it would be far better for the Lebanese to be in Lebanon, for the Jordanians to be in Jordan, and for the peoples of these countries to live without uninvited outsiders.[49]

Guerrilla wars and revolts were sparked, supplied and often led by Soviet agents in Malaya, the Philippines, Burma, Iraq, Korea, Vietnam, Laos, Cambodia. Ho Chi-minh went to Singapore as a Comintern representative in 1930 and served there before he organized the "revolution" in Vietnam. Agents stir trouble in Algeria, Morocco, Tunisia, Guatemala, the Cameroons—wherever there is discontent (and where is there none?). In a typical projection, Khrushchev accuses the West of inventing the device of the proxy war . . .

The theory of so-called local or minor wars with the use of mass-destruction weapons has now sprung up in the West. With such wars the imperialists want to suppress the national liberation movement and do away with governments which do not suit them. Yet we must not think that under present conditions minor wars would be localized. Should such wars break out, they could soon grow into a world war.[50]

. . . and of setting up strong-arm governments:

The reactionaries are using an old anti-popular weapon— they are doing away with the democratic system and setting up "strong-arm" governments. But just as in the period when fascist dictatorships were established in Italy and Germany, the tendency toward the open dictatorship of the monopoly bourgeoisie is not a sign of strength, but a sign of weakness. Yet it should be borne in mind that under an unlimited dictatorship reaction has a better chance of starting a reign of terror and repression, of suppressing all opposition, of indoctrinating the masses to suit its ends, of infecting them with the poison of chauvinism, and of freeing its hands for military gambles. For this reason, the people must be vigilant. They must be ever ready to repel the reactionary offensive and the threat of resurgent fascism.[51]

With a new philosophy—"We are winning peacefully, let's avoid war"—Khrushchev backed away from overt action in Suez, Iraq, Lebanon, and Jordan.

Nasser's victory in Suez paved the way for the Iraqi revolution. There is considerable evidence that communists, and indeed Soviet agents, participated in the Iraqi revolution of July 14, 1958. For the Soviet Union, Iraq had acquired an added importance because the Baghdad Pact had its headquarters in the Iraqi capital. Soon after the revolution Iraq quit the pact, creating a tense situation in Iran, which became the next country under direct Soviet and also possible proxy (Iraqi) threat.

Having fed a seemingly successful revolt, Khrushchev saw in the landing of American troops in Lebanon a new proxy war.

The people of Iraq have successfully carried out a revolution. Complete order has been established in the Republic of Iraq. The people are supporting the new Government and the republican system that has been established in the country.[52]

The imminent arrival of American troops stopped the Iranian takeover.

The question of subversive activities is a question of struggle against an internal enemy. If we go back to the question of the Iranian-American military treaty, who is the so-called "internal enemy"? Evidently, the phrase refers to the Iranian people. But no outside forces can protect anyone from his own people! [53]

Arming of militant minorities is a simple device for causing trouble. Of this Khrushchev says:

The system under which some states sell arms to others is not our invention. France, Britain, and the United States have long since been supplying arms to very many countries, and particularly to the countries whose governments take the most hostile attitude toward the Soviet Union. Therefore we have nothing else to do but to act in the same way. We sell arms to countries which ask us to do so and want to be friendly with us. Apparently they buy arms because they fear the countries which you supply with arms. Thus we are doing only the same thing which you have been doing for a long time. If the Western powers want to come to agreement on this score, we are willing to do so. We said this as far back as 1955 in London and made a statement to this effect. The Soviet Union is prepared to reach agreement that no country should sell its arms to any other country. If the countries of NATO, CENTO, and SEATO, affiliated to the Western bloc, are prepared to conclude such an agreement, we shall welcome it.[54]

The Algerian war has been maintained, through the "sale" of arms by Czechoslovakia and aid from China, as a constant drain on the West.

The Soviet Union has not concealed and does not conceal that its sympathies are on the side of those people who are struggling against colonialism, for their independence and national liberty. It is not hard to see that a peaceful settlement of the Algerian question would help enhance the international prestige of France and her role as a great power.[55]

Khrushchev reminds France of Indochina.

The conscience of mankind cannot reconcile itself with the situation which has arisen in Algeria. A bloody war is going on there; the Arab population is being exterminated. And, although the Algerian question was discussed in the United Nations, the complaints of the imperialist states turned away from the fears of millions of Algerians and the terrible tragedy through which they are living. It is time to stop this bloodshed and to contribute to reaching agreements on the

328

Algerian question in accordance with the interests of the Algerian population, while taking into account the interests of France.

Cannot French ruling circles really understand that if they do not seek, if they refuse to seek, a peaceful settlement of the Algerian question, they risk involving the country in an even greater failure than was the case of Indochina? It is time for the colonizers to realize that every people can and must be the master with full rights over their destiny.[56]

Aid is offered to all African nations.

Take Africa, for example, which is completely divided up among European and non-European countries . . . The peoples of these countries are rising more and more resolutely to fight against colonial regimes. And we sympathize with this struggle and wish success to the peoples who are waging it.[57]

And Khrushchev offers help to the Congo.

Nor is the American continent immune.

On May 17, 1954, a bloc shipment of 2,000 tons of weapons arrived at Puerto Barrias, Guatemala, consigned to Lieutenant Colonel Jacobo Guzman Abenz. It came from the Skoda Works, via the Sevendish ship *Afhem,* which cleared from Dakar.

On June seventeenth, Guatemala was invaded from Honduras by about two hundred volunteers under Colonel Castillo Armas, an exiled Guatemalan officer.

Similarly, in Nicaragua and the Dominican Republic bloc arms flow to prospective areas of revolution. Cuba is prepared for a proxy war against Haiti and the Dominican Republic. Impoverished herself, Cuba offers aid to British Guiana and other revolutionists.

Under the guise of nationalism, each country is encouraged to extend its contacts with the USSR. The Party works subtly so that the case of aggression is never quite clear. Czech arms go to Guinea for the Cameroons; to Cuba for Guatemala; to Egypt or to Morocco for Algeria; to China for Laos; etc.

The Soviet pattern, however, is quite clear—a proxy on every continent.

CHAPTER 11

The Propaganda Front (I)

Selling the Socialist System

A major technique of Soviet expansion is creating the image of socialism as a progressive, enlightened, and effective system; and from this, it reasonably follows, the tide of the future. A world-wide propaganda machine is employed on this project, but Khrushchev is easily its loudest and most present voice.

In this struggle for men's minds, truth has its own meaning for communists. Mikhail Kalinin, an old Bolshevik and onetime chairman of the Presidium (1938–1946), recited the official dogma for Party affairs at the Congress of the Victors:

"The idea that the truth remains the truth is admissible in a philosophical club, but in the Party, the decisions of the congress are obligatory also upon those who doubt the correctness of a decision. . . . Our Party is strong through the fact that the decisions of the majority are obligatory upon all not only in form, but in substance."[1]

And George Kennan, a longtime student of the Soviet Union, has pointed out:

"From the time of their seizure of power, forty years ago, the Russian Communists have always been characterized by their extraordinary ability to cultivate falsehood as a deliberate weapon of policy."

The New York Times reports a November 8, 1960 speech:

We shall win only through the minds of men. We must rest

on the position of coexistence and nonintervention. It is not necessary to whip people along this road . . . but communism eventually will be in force all over the world.[2]

Mr. Khrushchev, as general of an army of propagandists, endeavors to spread the concept of a battle between two systems—one good and ascendant, the other simply bad and decadent. In essence, this is a distraction from the prime movement—Soviet imperialism. In this campaign, details are of less importance than selling the idea that the Communist Party is creating the inevitable system that will replace capitalism, that its strength and its ranks are growing. All this adds up to the creation of a band-wagon psychology. This Mr. Khrushchev pushes with diligence and order.

The simultaneous existence of the two opposite world economic systems—the capitalist and the socialist—developing according to different laws and in opposite directions—has become an indisputable fact. The socialist economy is developing toward an increasingly greater satisfaction of material and cultural requirements of all members of society, continuous expansion and perfection of production on the basis of higher techniques, the strengthening of cooperation and mutual aid between socialist states. The capitalist economy is developing in the direction of a still greater enrichment of monopolies, further intensification of exploitation, and the lowering of the living standards of the multimillion masses of the working people, particularly in colonial and dependent countries, in the direction of an increasing militarization of the economy, a sharpening of the competitive struggle between capitalist states, a ripening of new economic crises and upheavals.[3]

People who are well grounded in history know that when human society was completing the transition from feudalism to capitalism there also was a struggle between the old and the new. Like other nations, the American people also fought for a transition to the more perfect social form of that day. You fought against slavery and feudalism, you fought for

331

progress, against the old system which impeded the development of the productive forces, and in the end you were victorious. But at the time when the American people established a republic, Czarist Russia was still a semi-feudal country where serfdom obtained. Your economy progressed rapidly, while the economy of Czarist Russia lagged considerably behind the American economy in its development. And that was only natural, because the social system which triumphed in your country was more progressive than the system that preceded it.[4]

I am a communist, a firm supporter of the theory of Marxism-Leninism which has proved scientifically that communism is the most advanced, the most progressive system. Our conviction is that mankind's dream of building a communist society will inevitably be realized. We wish all people, black and white, red and yellow, to take their place under the communist banner. There will be enough room for everybody under this banner. And the sooner it happens the better for all peoples, for the whole world.[5]

Lenin says that uneven economic and political development is an absolute law of capitalism. Proportional economic development is impossible under capitalism with its anarchy of production, crises, bitter competition between the monopolies and the capitalist states. Force is the dominant principle of capitalism. Hence the tendency to deal with contradiction by means of threats, diktat, war and the seizure of foreign territory, sources of raw materials and markets. The fact that some of the capitalist countries have outstripped the others is due solely to the plundering of millions of toilers by a handful of capitalist monopolies and to ruthless exploitation of the dependent and semi-dependent countries.[6]

The system appeals to workmen even if they don't quite know what it is all about, he says:

It is well known that socialism appeals to the working people even if they do not have a complete grasp of the theory of scientific socialism. The working people want to get rid of capitalism and of its incurable evils and vices. They are looking for a way out of the hopelessness of capitalism, and only when a revolutionary party, armed with the scientific theory of communism, organizes the workers, peasants and intelligentsia in the right way and leads them to fight for the building of a new life—only then does Marxist-Leninist theory become comprehensible and accessible to the broadest mass of the working people.[7]

The world of capitalism that Khrushchev paints is out of a communist textbook, a world of eighteenth- and early-nineteenth-century England, Germany, and Russia. In this world wages were at subsistence levels, children of six labored sixteen hours a day, uncontrolled monopolists owned and used the resources and power of nations for their personal aggrandizement. The Party presents this picture of venal capitalism.

The basic contradiction of capitalism is the struggle between the classes which must, Khrushchev holds, lead to the overthrow of capitalism.

The ideologists of the bourgeoisie say that economic progress is possible only under capitalism. The capitalists represent their greed, their desire to get rich by exploiting millions of the working people, as a moving source of progress. They call this the "free world." They include the capitalist countries in the "free world," because it provides for conditions for the free exploitation by the capitalists of the working class, the working people. And now the bourgeoisie begins to tremble because its so-called free world begins to shake under the blows of the working class, as a result of the successes in the development of the socialist countries. And it does not shake under the blows of our armed forces, not under the blows of our rockets, but under the blows of the growing consciousness of the working class, the millions upon millions of the working people, the conscious attitude of the working class, of the working people to their duty.[8]

If we reject all kinds of cunning formulas by the defenders of capitalism with which attempts are made to muddle people and lead them astray, then the substance of the question becomes perfectly clear; the capitalists say that only an order in which conditions are created for free enterprise—but one should read free exploitation of the people—that only such an order is capable of progress.

The capitalists assert that the mainspring of economics, culture, science, and art is business; is profits. They endeavor to prove, by citing America, that only by means of free enterprise—that is today free exploitation of millions of workers—can the progress of mankind be insured.

We communists, on the other hand, basing ourselves on the great Marxist-Leninist teaching and on the experience of building socialism, say: No, Messrs. Capitalists, a real progress of society is insured under a system which liberates the people from capitalist enslavement, when the working people become the masters of their products, when the means of production belong to his majesty the working class, the working people, and not to a handful of exploiters.

It is under such a system that the abilities of each man in particular and of society in general are really unfolded. The free workers of this free socialist society are capable of accomplishing wonders and blazing a trail to the bright future of mankind, communism.[9]

And he derides "people's capitalism":

Things are different in the capitalist states, where the people who create the wealth essentially have no rights.

To mask the antipopular, exploitational essence of capitalism, its defenders have of late created many legends about "people's capitalism." They praise this "people's capitalism," which supposedly exists today in the United States and several other capitalist countries, to the skies. These people even call themselves socialists, although they are actually the yes-men and lackeys of the capitalists.

The Propaganda Front (I)

"People's capitalism is the true road to socialism," these "socialists" shout, like hired barkers for a cheap show at the fair. "Look," they say, "the workers and employees in the capitalist states are now becoming capitalists like the millionaires and billionaires. They are buying stock and now have the right to call themselves the owners of factories, mills and other stock company enterprises."

But what actually happens to the workers and employees who fall for this bait, buy a few shares of stock with their hard-earned savings and thus become stockholders, "owners" of capitalist enterprises? When crisis phenomena appear, the real owners take these stockholding "owners" by the neck and throw them out of the enterprises in which they hold stock. The stockholder is out of a job and joins the army of the unemployed, which numbers in the millions. And so this "owner" takes his place in line to wait for fortune to smile on him once more so that he and his family will not die from hunger. Many of these "owners" take part in strikes against the real owners of plants and factories, against the exploiting classes and the governments of the so-called "people's capitalist" states.

However beautifully the ideologists of imperialism may dress up the capitalist system, it still remains a system by which millions upon millions of people are enslaved by a comparatively small handful of exploiters. It remains a system in which poverty and mass unemployment reign.[10]

Members of the governing, industry-controlling party in the Soviet Union number 8 million, less than 4 per cent of the population. Owners of shares in large American corporations number 13 million. In addition, practically every American participates in capitalism through bank deposits, insurance, pension funds, or ownership in one of the 2½ million small enterprises.

. . . the state's intervention in economic activity does not eliminate the fundamental defects of the capitalist system. The state is powerless to do away with the objective laws

335

of the capitalist economy which lead to anarchy of production and economic crises. Crises are inherent in the very nature of capitalism; they are inevitable.[11]

Khrushchev neglects to note that although the business cycle has not been completely conquered—and possibly cannot be under capitalism—at its lowest ebb in the business cycle, the modern capitalist system offers substantially more good and less hardship to all the people than the constant "war economy" of the Soviet system. On the international scene he notes:

The United States of America is losing the monopoly position it held during the first postwar years. As a result of competition from other countries, the United States' share in world exports, after reaching a peak in 1947 (32.5 per cent), later dropped sharply (to 19 per cent). In 1947–48 the United States accounted for nearly three-fifths of the industrial output of the capitalist world, but today it accounts for only half. The United States has already made the most of its postwar economic opportunities; no new markets are in sight. There is therefore no prospect of a further substantial increase in production.[12]

Khrushchev, of course, ignores the fact that U.S. aid helped to re-create the industry of Western Europe. He points to the rising share of the world's production contributed by Marshall Plan countries as a sign of America's decadence.

But there are no contradictions in socialism, Khrushchev claims:

The peculiarity of the economic development of the socialist countries consists in the fact that as they progress their mutual relations grow stronger and the world socialist system gains in solidarity. A quite opposite tendency reigns in the capitalist world. There, any increase in production in this or that country leads to a deepening of contradictions between the capitalist countries, to a strengthening of the competitive struggle, and to mutual clashes.

Marx and Engels saw the basic contradictions underlying

the capitalist system. They pointed out that the principal social contradiction of capitalist society was that between the antagonistic classes of the capitalists and proletarians —that is, between the class which is in possession of all means of production and the class of the poor, which can only sell its labor. The capitalists want to establish as low as possible a remuneration for labor and to gain even more profits through intensification of the exploitation of the working people. The working class, on the contrary, is concerned with the improvement of its living standard and wants to get more for its labor and to shake off, by means of class struggle, the very cruel yoke of exploitation, the yoke of capitalist slavery.[13]

He sees capitalist people impoverished.

. . . the invincible law of capitalism is the law of the impoverishment of the proletariat and the ruin of the peasants.[14]

On the other hand, this is hard to sell in Moscow.

There is no need to go to America to see if she is strong or not. Only a fool can fail to see that America is strong and rich.[15]

In Moscow, Khrushchev describes capitalist peasants as ruined.

Capitalism is developing according to its own laws. Under capitalism the landlords and kulaks ruin the small peasants, buy up their lands, and even throw them out of the village. Then the peasants move to the towns to reinforce the army of unemployed, or else remain as farmhands of the big land-owners. The well-off peasants do not buy machines; they exploit their fellow peasants who sold them their land.

This is the capitalist way of production. The United States, among others, is following this road. Countless thousands of farmers are being ruined in the United States every year. They sell their land and remain landless. Of course, this road is a painful one; it is the road of ruin of the toiling peasantry.[16]

On the other hand, in the United States:

We have a very high opinion of American farming, American industry, the hard-working and gifted American workers, farmers, engineers, and scientists. We have learned much from them and are ready to learn from them now, and to teach them a few things ourselves. It will thus be a good, businesslike exchange of experience.[17]

Of course Khrushchev knows, and has often noted, that American farmers are three times as productive as Soviet farmers. Actually, the average farmer's income in the U.S. is four to ten times that of his Soviet counterpart. More than 40 per cent of the population on the farm does not produce enough food for the Russian people adequately, while 9 per cent of the American population provides surpluses.

The average Soviet collective farmer receives approximately 1,000 rubles a year in cash plus 300 to 400 kilograms of produce. This is the equivalent of $140 a year.

Says Khrushchev:

After the liquidation of classes, we have a monolithic society.[18]

On the other hand, the Soviet press has noted:
"Nevertheless, there is a certain discrimination because of ancestry in the life of the developing socialist society. . . .

"In the period of the struggle for the completion of socialist construction, discrimination because of ancestry is necessary in filling functions in public life and certain spheres of work and it is temporarily necessary also in the registration of students at courses and high schools. Apart from justified exceptions, class-alien persons must be excluded and suitable workers must be given preference in filling certain spheres of work and public functions. This class policy aimed at the political strengthening of the workers' class is necessary. . . .

"The purpose of discrimination because of ancestry is first of all to insure the political leading role of the workers' class on the one hand and to insure the correct enforcement of its alliance policy on the other hand. At the same time, apart from exceptions, an exclusion from public functions of class-alien elements is enforced, as well as the policy of restriction when filling certain positions. . . ." [19]

Capitalist workers are "enslaved," Khrushchev says.

We regard the capitalist system as a system of slavery for the working people, for the overwhelming majority of the people. Many years ago, Karl Marx convincingly showed that the capitalist system is a system under which the majority of the people are mercilessly oppressed.[20]

We regard the people under capitalism as living in capitalist bondage.[21]

The reason why Roman civilization, as well as Greek civilization, declined was that it was a civilization built on slave labor, which shackled man's energy, will and freedom. Science and the arts can attain full bloom only if there is the fullest freedom of the individual and of society.

You and we have different ideas of this matter. You say that profit, or business as you call it, is the prime mover of people's energy, of their intellect and initiative. We say a different thing: The prime mover is man's consciousness, his awareness of the fact that he is free and working for himself, for his kin, for the society in which he lives, that the means of production belong to society and not to some individual who grows rich by exploiting other people's labor.[22]

But Khrushchev admits:

I have come here to see how the slaves of capitalism live. And I must say that you don't live too badly. But neither do we, we live well and we are going to live still better. We shall stand up for ourselves and for our country, and are sure that we want to catch up with you and outstrip you.[23]

Capitalist workers are exploited, Khrushchev says:

Under capitalism the actual distribution takes place not

339

according to work but, first of all, according to capital. It is regulated by the laws of value, profit, and land rent. Therefore it is not those who work more who receive a greater income there, but those who have more capital.[24]

Marxism-Leninism teaches that while classes of exploiters and exploited exist there is and can be no true equality. The great significance of the October Revolution consists precisely in the fact that it led to the triumph of socialism, to the establishment of a society in which the exploiting classes have been liquidated and the exploitation of man by man has been abolished.[25]

Under the Soviet system the worker gets 27 per cent of what he produces, under the American system, 67 per cent. And Americans produce twice as much.

In the United States, the capitalist classes appropriate more than half of the national income, while making up only about one-tenth of the country's population. In the USSR the working people receive about three-fourths of the national income for the satisfaction of their material and cultural requirements.[26]

Actually, the distribution of national products is more egalitarian in the U.S. than in the USSR. Of $383.3 billion personal income in the U.S. in 1959, $258.2 billion (67 per cent) came from wages, $10 billion (2½ per cent) from other labor, $46.5 billion (12 per cent) from proprietors' income, $12.4 billion (3 per cent) from rentals, $13.3 billion (3½ per cent) from dividends, $23.5 billion (6 per cent) from interest, $7 billion (5 per cent) from net social-insurance benefits.[27]

In the Soviet Union, egalitarianism is taboo.

In the Soviet Union the socialist principle of distribution by labor is in action, in accordance with its quantity and quality, and this creates the personal material interest of every worker in the results of his labor and is an important stimulus in raising labor productivity and the growth of production. Vladimir Ilyich Lenin has taught that without material incentive it is impossible to lead tens and tens of millions of people to communism. The founders of Marxism-Leninism underlined the importance of the principle of the material interest of all toilers in the growth of communal production, for the creation of an abundance of products which would insure the transition to communism, and in their time, they criticized the principle of equalization in distribution.[28]

"In the Soviet Union, the highest basic wage rate for skilled workers in each of these industries was approximately 3.6 times that of the lowest for unskilled workers, while in the United States, it was found that the ratio was approximately 2.2 in each industry."[29]

As we see, there is a radical difference in the distribution of the values produced under capitalism and socialism. The socialist principles of distribution according to work is based on the admission of the impossibility of an equalizing distribution in the period of socialism. This is the only sensible and just principle of distribution in the given conditions. One cannot fail to see that equalization would lead to unjust distribution. Both the good and bad workers would receive the same. This is advantageous only for idlers. Thus, the material incentive of people to work better, to increase labor productivity, to produce more, would be undermined. Equalization would mean not a transition to communism but the discrediting of communism.[30]

USSR mimimum wage (scheduled for 1961): 300 rubles a month. Salary of high-ranking Party officials: 20,000 rubles a month. This, of course, was not Lenin's idea: "Pay for all civil servants, who are to be elected or recalled at any time, no higher than the average pay of a good workman."[31]

Nor Stalin's: "Difference between skilled and unskilled labor breaks with Marxism, breaks with Leninism."[32]

But under Stalin the differences in pay became enormous. The Stakhanovist heroes became "Soviet millionaires."

341

In the USSR, no selfishness.

Socialism affirms a socialist morality—a morality of collaboration and collectivism, friendship and mutual help. Here solicitude for the general welfare of the people, for the all-sided development of the individual under collectivist conditions where man is not enemy to man but a friend and brother, is put in the foreground.[33]

While capitalism is a "selfish" system.

In the capitalist world the rich, wealthy people strive to live well and do not care about others. In America at present a sharp reduction of output is taking place and unemployment is steadily rising. There, a small handful of millionaires and billionaires have accumulated vast wealth and many millions of people are at present unemployed. They can die from need and privation and lead a dismal existence and no millionaire or billionaire is stirred by this. This is the law of capitalism where private ownership of the means of production reigns. And most of these millionaires consider themselves to be people who believe in God. What is such a faith in God worth? We communists are against this.[34]

In the capitalist world this law prevails: If you do not oppress someone, you will be oppressed. If a country is weak, it will be kept in a dependent position. We resolutely oppose this idea.[35]

The spirit of individualism, self-interest, the thirst for profit, hostility and competition—these make up the essence of the ethics of bourgeois society. Exploitation of man by man, upon which bourgeois society rests, tramples ethics underfoot. It is not accidental that the ethics of the exploiting classes is typified by the brutal formula: "Man eat man." [36]

Khrushchev would like to forget 5 to 10 million Russians killed and 10 million sent to forced-labor camps during collectivization, and the additional millions "purged" under communism.

But in his Secret Speech, Khrushchev admits:

The Propaganda Front (I)

All the more monstrous are the acts whose initiator was Stalin and which are rude violations of the basic Leninist principles of the nationality policy of the Soviet state. We refer to the mass deportations from their native places of whole nations, together with all communists and Komsomols without any exception; this deportation was not dictated by any military considerations.

Thus, already at the end of 1943, when there occurred a permanent breakthrough at the fronts of the Great Patriotic War [World War II], a decision was taken and executed concerning the deportation of all Karachai from the lands on which they lived.

In the same period, at the end of December 1943, the same lot befell the whole population of the Kalmyk Autonomous Republic. In March 1944, all the Chechen and Ingush peoples were deported and the Chechen-Ingush Autonomous Republic was liquidated. In April 1944, all Balkars were deported to faraway places from the territory of the Kabardino-Balkarian Autonomous Republic and the Republic itself was renamed Autonomous Kabardian Republic.

To this Boris I. Nicolaevsky adds a footnote:

"Khrushchev does not mention two Soviet republics liquidated during the war on Stalin's orders, whose populations were deported to Siberia and Kazakhstan—the Autonomous Volga German Republic and the Crimean Republic." [37]

It is well known that the capitalist system makes a man reserved and solitary, makes him rely only on his own forces—because there is nobody else on whom he can rely. He knows that if he is without work, he is deprived of the means of existence, and is doomed to poverty and hunger. Things are quite different under socialism! Here, every man feels the solicitude of society and of the state toward him.[38]

In the U.S. contributions to charitable, educational, civic, and other nonprofit social organizations amounted, in 1959, to $7.8 billion in cash and billions more in time and effort.[39]

343

In the USSR there are practically no voluntary, nongovernmental organizations outside the trade unions and the Communist Party.

During the fifteen postwar years, U.S. aid to other nations totaled $60 billion; Soviet aid $2.7 billion.[40]

Unemployment is painted as the great disaster of capitalism:

Unemployment is the inevitable companion of capitalism, whose sores were profoundly revealed by Marx and Lenin. They pointed out to the working class and working people the way to get rid of the chains of capitalism, the way to win power for themselves and the way to socialism. If the question arises as to which world—the world of socialism or the world of capitalism—has the genuine right to be called "free," then there cannot be two opinions. Only socialism brings a real and not fictitious freedom to mankind. And it is precisely to this world that the future belongs.[41]

The unemployed in the United States receive in benefits almost twice as much as the Soviet worker is paid when he is employed.

In the USSR there is no unemployment, says Mr. Khrushchev.

Unemployment, so terrible a scourge to working people, has forever been done away with in our country.[42]
. . . the economic life of the Soviet Union, like that of all socialist countries, is free from crisis and mass unemployment, the inevitable corollaries of capitalism.[43]

Unemployment in the Soviet Union is more theoretical than real. While there is a "labor shortage," technological unemployment is now reported as a major problem. The difficulty of assimilating young workers is occasionally noted by Khrushchev. Unemployment due to job changing and job seeking still exists in spite of the pressure of a "job assignment" that will send the unemployed to the frontier. And down on the farm there are unemployed, which the Soviet Union euphemistically calls "surplus."

Victor V. Grishin, head of the Soviet Union Federation of Trade Unions, noted at the May 1960 meeting of the Central Committee of the Soviet Communist Party:

344

The Propaganda Front (I)

"It is known that as a result of the introduction of new technology, mechanization and automation of production, part of the labor force is freed. Already there are surplus workers at many factories. In our view this problem requires an organized solution." [44]

The dean of Soviet economists, Academician Stanislav Strumilin, writing about farm employment in *Voprosy Ekonomiki*, forecasts 12 million surplus farm workers by 1965 and 20 million to 30 million by 1970 or 1975 because of increased productivity. He points out that if the dependents of these surplus workers were taken into account, some 60 million to 90 million people would be affected in the next ten or fifteen years.[45]

The New York Times notes:

"The problem has reached such a stage that the head of the Soviet trade-union movement—a movement not usually noted in Russia for its zeal in behalf of its members—has called for an organized solution to the problem. Such an organized solution would obviously have to include the setting up of unemployment insurance, the creation of labor exchanges to help displaced workers find new jobs, the setting up of a large-scale system of retaining workers, and the like.

"But any such comprehensive system of measures would require explicit admission that technological unemployment exists in the Soviet Union. Once this form of unemployment has been recognized, pressure will arise for recognizing other types of unemployment as well. It will be interesting to see how Soviet leaders handle this problem of reconciling the reality of their society with one of the hoariest propaganda myths at their command." [46]

Mr. Khrushchev admits:

The task of providing employment for such a great number of young people is not simple, primarily because at present economic executives are very much against employing adolescents and young people under eighteen.* But the task is

---

*The 1958 law took fifteen- and sixteen-year-olds into the factory on a part-time basis.

of first and foremost significance to the Party and state. It will be necessary to break bureaucratic red tape which prevents the employment of adolescents in the national economy, and to instruct the USSR Gosplan to draw up a long-term plan for the employment of adolescents who will leave the eight-year school. Such a plan must be based on every administrative economic area, taking into account the employment of adolescents residing in that area.[47]

Another Soviet commentator remarks:

"There were those who wrongly understood the right to work to mean the right to choose their own places of employment in disregard of the interests and needs of the state."[48]

Paul Barton, a student of Soviet labor conditions, has pointed out:

"The freedom to choose and change employment has not, in fact, been restored at all. A worker who leaves his job against the wish of the director runs the risk of being entangled in a whole network of constraint and administrative chicanery, which may finally prevent him from being hired where he wished. The police, from whom, on the presentation of his internal passport, he must obtain permission before every change of residence, can forbid him to leave his home. Even if he manages to find work where he lives, he may be threatened by 'organized recruitment,' a process by which the authorities obtain labor for the sweating industries."[49]

The complaint is a carryover from Czarist times, regarding which Lenin demanded of the officials of his time:

"What does this mean, this freedom to move from place to place? It means that the peasant must be free to go where he pleases, to move wherever he wants to, to choose for himself the village or the town he prefers, without having to ask for permission.

"It means that passports must be abolished in Russia too (in foreign countries passports were abolished long ago), that no police officer, no Zemsky Nachalnik must be allowed to stop any peasant from settling down or working wherever he pleases. The Russian peasant is still the serf of the officials to such an extent that he is not free to move to a town, or free to settle in a new district. The Minister issues orders that the governors should not allow unauthorized settlement! The governors know better than the peasant what is good for the peasant! The peasant is a child who dares not move without authority! Is this not serfdom, I ask you?" [50]

Mr. Khrushchev warns those who do not work.

Any work—be it at a factory, a collective farm, an industrial enterprise, a state farm or an office—any honest work useful for the society is sacred labor which is essential for every person who lives and enjoys the benefits of society. An able-bodied person who does not work steals from those who work, that is, lives at the expense of those who create material or spiritual values. An atmosphere must be created in which those who despise work are not tolerated Every person who lives in a communist society must make a contribution by his or her labor toward the building and further development of that society.[51]

And now about the loafers. When I spoke of this matter at the conference in Gorky I had in mind a bill which should grant the right to collective farmers, workers, employees, the whole population, to decide the question of what to do with the loafers, good-for-nothings, people who live without specific occupations, at who knows what standard. The workers have the right to check up on them, and if it is established that they do indeed live at the expense of others and have no wish to mend their ways, remove them from their midst. This is what I call an end to the loafers. It is you who must expose the loafers and good-for-nothings and take the steps.[52]

In the USSR women are "emancipated":

The Soviet state has delivered the woman from the humiliating semi-slavery in which she languished under Czarism and is still kept in many capitalist countries. Soviet women are an active force in all spheres of governmental, political, economic, and cultural life; on a par with men they enjoy all

347

the rights of a citizen of socialist society. But many women are engaged in housework and taken up with care of their children, which makes it harder for them to participate actively in public life.[53]

One of the most remarkable achievements of the socialist revolution is the emancipation of women, their introduction into active social work. With their creative labor in all sections of economic and cultural construction Soviet women are making enormous contributions to the all-national struggle for the victory of communism, to the rearming of the growing generation.[54]

In the USSR there are only 82 men for each 100 women. In the 15-to-59 age group, the figure is even lower—77 men for each 100 women. In the USSR 53 to 67 per cent of the women over sixteen work; in the United States 32 per cent do.

Women make up 45 per cent of Soviet factory workers, 31 per cent of construction workers, 59 per cent of farm workers, 32 per cent of transportation workers, 65 per cent of trade workers, and 51 per cent of government employees. Except for token or ceremonial positions, practically no important jobs in industry or government are held by women. Khrushchev continues:

Merciless oppression, cruel exploitation of the weak by the strong, have always been and still remain the law of the jungle of capitalism, where the strong swallow the weak.[55]

Let them name a bourgeois state where the shortening of the working day would be envisaged while wages were maintained or even raised.[56]

The answer: The United States.

The weighted average work week for the entire private labor force is roughly 37.5 hours in 1960, compared with 40 hours in 1950. This represents a drop of 2.5 hours during the fifties, compared with a decline of 4 hours in the forties and an average decline of 4 hours in each decade since 1900.[57]

Average weekly earnings in United States manufacturing industries rose from $48.30 in 1939 to $87.60 by June 30, 1960 (in terms of 1957 prices). On July 1, 1960, average weekly earnings were $98.98 before adjustment for price changes.[58]

Lenin promised a shorter work week. Stalin promised it in 1952. But by mid-1960 most Soviet workers were still on a basic 46-hour schedule—five days of eight hours, one day of six hours.

In 1956, at the Twentieth Congress:

A seven-hour working day is being introduced in all branches of the national economy with a six-hour day in the coal and ore mining industries.

In 1957:

The time is not far off when, after introduction of the seven-hour working day we will effect the transition to the six-hour working day.

In 1959, at the Twenty-first Congress, Khrushchev repeated:

Starting from 1964 workers engaged in underground work, and in work involving harmful labor conditions will gradually go over to a thirty-hour week, and the rest of the workers to a thirty-five-hour week. That means that if there is one full day off a week the working day will be five or six hours, depending on the nature of the job. Since the majority of factory and office workers prefer to have two full days off each week, it is intended to introduce a five-day working week with a six- or seven-hour working day.

A shorter working day and working week will be introduced in our country without reduction in wage; rather wages will rise substantially. The USSR will have the shortest working day and the shortest working week in the world, with a simultaneous rise in the living standard.

In May 1960, for most Soviet workers, the shorter work week was still a dream, and those who had received working-hour reductions also got proportionate wage cuts. Said Mr. Khrushchev, to the Supreme Soviet:

349

As of April 1, 1960, about 16 million people have been transferred to a shorter seven- and six-hour working day. The changeover of all factory workers to a seven- or six-hour working day will be completed in 1960.

That September Komsomalskaya Pravda, organ of the Young Communist League, complained that workers in the Karelian engine-repair shop had suffered salary cuts of 200 to 250 rubles from their base of 1,200 to 1,400 rubles a month after their hours were reduced. The article, quoted in the Paris edition of the New York Herald Tribune, *noted that many similar complaints had been received. Inasmuch as most Soviet workers are on a piecework basis, hours reduction was usually at the employee's expense.*

No hard work some day is the promise:

Communism means an abundance of products and consumer commodities. Yet, communism is not only that; communism is the most progressive and best-organized society of all those that have existed on earth, a society with the highest standards of production, without exhausting physical labor. Under communism work will be fully mechanized and man's effort will be reduced to skillful control of machines.

This will mean the elimination of the difference between intellectual and physical effort under communism. Machines will be designed and operated by people on an equally high level of technical training and intellectual development. Under communism man will be able to fully reveal his great creative possibilities. It will indeed be man with a capital "M" as Gorky said.[59]

But today:

You probably have seen more than once how men and women clean ice from the pavements with crowbars. This is unproductive labor. When one sees this one is simply ill at ease. What a great deal has been accomplished by us in mechanizing complicated production processes, what a large number of labor-saving machines have been designed! The first artificial earth satellites have been designed, but we have not reached the stage of replacing crowbars and spades by machines. What do we lack? I think the main reason is that we pay very little attention to such problems, considering them trifling. But are they trifling? No, the work of many people consists of such "trifles." Many foreign visitors to the Soviet Union say that when you walk along Moscow streets in winter you see many women with little crowbars and picks in their hands. On this basis they assert that women are not held in esteem with us.[60]

The workers' medical bills:

In the capitalist countries nobody has concern for the working man, for his health and life. All medical services, big and small, are paid for by the individual. . . .

The *U.S. News & World Report* says that medical costs in the United States become "a great burden upon an average family." The magazine reports that the cost of surgical treatment for stomach ulcers runs up to $1,264.50, of which $325.50 is the charge for staying in hospital for 21 days, $500 is paid for the operation, $75 for the use of the operating room, $3 for staying in the convalescence ward, $78.60 for treatment, $21.50 for oxygen, $56.30 for bandages, $99 for laboratory services, $50 for anesthesia, $55 for X-ray examinations.[61]

The workers of the capitalist countries know well enough what it means to fall ill and have no money for treatment, for the doctor, for medicines sold at exorbitant prices; what it means to have no possibility of sending one's child to school. And when the people in the capitalist countries compare the conditions of their life with the conditions of life in the countries of socialism, they hear that all this misery has been eliminated there. It is not difficult to guess at what conclusions they arrive when they compare the slow pace of development in the capitalist countries. When they compare the imperialist policy of the cold war and arms race with the peaceable for-

351

eign policy of the countries of socialism and its struggle for disarmament—it then becomes clear what social regime is the more progressive and fair.[62]

At the end of 1958, 71 per cent of the United States population (123 million people) were covered by some form of health insurance.[63] Workmen's compensation and disability insurance covers those employed in industry. For those in need, free medical care is available at municipal and voluntary institutions.

"The Soviet Union boasts that it has one physician to each 631 persons compared to one per 756 in the United States. The Russians also claim their medical schools graduate 16,000 physicians a year. [USSR figures include dentists. The 1960 *Statistical Abstract* gives the U.S. figures as 191,947 physicians and 74,855 dentists in practice, one to each 675 persons.] The U.S. Public Health Service figure for the U.S. is 6,800 graduates annually. Russian doctors, however, receive only six years of training, while their American counterparts get eight to ten.

"Under socialized medicine, Soviet citizens pay nothing for doctors, hospitals, [most] drugs or ambulance service. But like factory workers, most doctors have norms. They can devote only a few minutes to each patient—and paper work pre-empts much of even that brief period. . . . The physician's starting salary of 800 rubles a month equals that of the average factory worker. . . . Three-fourths of Russia's doctors are women." [64] Soviet specialists may charge a fee, as do doctors who make home calls. Because of its predominantly rural population and bad roads, the Soviet Union actually requires more physicians than a more developed nation.

A team of American physicians sent to study Soviet medicine reported that physicians there were "trade-school graduates" left to learn much "on the job," that laboratory techniques were little used, that although top men were the equal of those in the West, the average doctor was much inferior in training and skills. Public sanitation was seen a half a century behind that in the United States.[65]

We are taking care of the health of our people; the sick rate has sharply declined in our country and the death rate is the lowest in the world. Every factory and office worker is granted paid leave every year. The working people have the best sanatoriums, health resorts and holiday homes at their disposal. Medical treatment is free for all in our country, and neither a minor operation nor the most complicated one entails any expense for the patient. Sometimes you don't understand certain aspects of our way of life. And Soviet people find it hard to understand how it can be that when you are in trouble because someone in your family is seriously ill and has to be operated on or sent to the hospital, you have to pay money for it. And what if you have no money? What happens then—must the sick man die?

When somebody is ill in our country and cannot work, he gets his pay just the same. And when old age comes along he does not feel abandoned, for he gets a state pension. Peasants are pensioned out of the funds of their collective farms.

You may ask: Is everything really so good and smooth in your country? I am afraid not, because we also have our difficulties, shortcomings and unsolved problems. I can assure you that we Soviet people are the most scathing and uncompromising critics of our own shortcomings.[66]

For this health insurance, Soviet citizens pay in their 45.8 per cent "turnover" tax. But the type of monopoly medical service is the subject of constant complaint.[67]

"The Supreme Soviet noted that there are serious shortcomings in the work of the public-health organs and in many local Soviets of Workers' Deputies of the republic in the field of organization of medical services in the rural areas. More qualified medical assistance is not provided for the entire rural population in some rayons [districts] of the republic. The medical and preventive treatment establishments in some oblasts [regions] of the republic are not sufficiently provided with the required equipment, furniture, medicines, and items needed in nursing patients.

"The organization of special medical assistance, especially psychiatric, traumatological, urological, stomatological, and other services is at a low level in the rural areas.

"Very slow progress is being made in the elimination of the shortcomings allowed by some medical workers in the diagnosis and treatment of patients, in refusals to hospitalize patients, and in delays in the treatment of patients in their homes.

"The construction and commissioning of medical establishments is being conducted in a most unsatisfactory manner by the Ministry of Agriculture. In five months in 1959 the above-mentioned ministry fulfilled the plan for the construction of hospitals only 10 per cent." [68]

"The death rate of 7.5 per thousand which was reported along with the census results is not the lowest in the world as claimed, but is nevertheless an impressively low rate. It represents real gains in Soviet science, medicine, and sanitation, and also reflects a favorable age and sex structure of the population.

"If the United States death rates for individual age-sex groups are assumed for the population of the USSR, a death rate of 6.4 per thousand is obtained. This strongly suggests lower mortality for specific age and sex groups in the United States than in the Soviet Union.

"Additional evidence that mortality in the USSR has not reached the level of the United States comes from a comparison of infant mortality rates, one of the most sensitive indicators of the general level of health in a population. The Soviet infant mortality rate as reported for 1957 (45 per thousand live births) exceeds that of the United States (26) by 73 per cent. It is about the level of the prewar United States rate and very close to the present rates for Italy and Japan. Nevertheless, a rate of 45 per thousand for the USSR represents a striking decline from its prewar level of 184 per thousand, which is higher than the rates currently reported for any of the underdeveloped countries of the world." [69]

354

The Propaganda Front (I)

The pride of the Soviet Union is its super-welfare-state philosophy, its progressive labor legislation. Here, somewhat simplified, is the comparative picture of Soviet and American practice in key areas of labor legislation. Not covered are the 40 per cent of the population on collective farms.

	USSR	U.S.
Work week	6 days, 46 hours	5 days, 37.5 hours (a)
Scheduled to go to	41 hours	
Wages		
Average (per month)	796 rubles (b)	
Minimum (per hour)	1⅓ rubles	$1.00
Average (per hour)	5 rubles	$1.98 (a)
Pensions		
Minimum (per month)	270–300 (b)	$143–$229
Average (per month)	487 rubles (c)	$229–$460
Union members	50% of wages	55%–90% of wages
Nonunion members	25% of wages	50% of wages
Paid Holidays	4 days	7-11 days
Disability		
Minimum	50% of wages after 3 years, to 90% of wages after 12 years	50% of wages
Nonunion members	Half	

Sources: (a) Bureau of Labor Statistics, U.S. Department of Commerce.
(b) Various speeches by Khrushchev quoted elsewhere in this volume.
(c) Prudenski.
*For valuation of a ruble see pages 356-7. These old rubles had a purchasing power of 6 to 1.

No inflation:

There cannot be any inflation in our country for in preparing the budget and production plans we take into account the sum of money to be paid in the form of wages and the necessary quantity of goods to be manufactured in order to maintain the balance between the stock of money and the stock of manufactured goods, etc. Thus, in our socialist economy inflation can only be a result of erroneous calculations while working out the plans, in other words, it is impossible.[70]

The Soviet price index, figured at 1 in 1913, rose to 21 by 1918, to 164 by 1919, to 2,420 by 1920, to 16,800 by 1921, to 288,000 by 1922, to 21,242,000 by 1923, to 5,457,000,000 by January 1924, and to 61,920,000,000 by March 1924. At that time the ruble was revalued at 1.943 to the dollar. When the dollar was revalued in 1932, the ruble ratio was changed to 1.15. On April 1, 1936, the ratio was changed to 5.06 rubles to the dollar; in 1937 the ratio was 5.3 rubles to the dollar, but embassy employees were allowed a special rate of 12 to the dollar. In 1947 10 old rubles were converted into one new one, and bank deposits adjusted. (Balances over 3,000 rubles were reduced 3 for 1 up to 10,000 rubles, 2 for 1 for amounts over that.) In 1950 the value was again changed to 4 rubles to the dollar, with a tourist rate of 10 to the dollar, but the gold sales price was fixed so that a ruble could buy only 1¼ cents worth.

INDEX OF STATE RETAIL PRICES IN THE SOVIET UNION [71]
1940 Average = 100

	All Commodities	Food
1950	186	203
1951	170	181
1952	161	166
1953	146	146
1954	138	141
1955	138	141

In January 1961 a new ruble was created, priced at $1.11 in American money, with prices adjusted at one new ruble for ten old. This had no internal effect but made prices of imported goods 10 per cent higher. In February an announcement indicated that tourists would be compensated by special lower prices to offset the change from 10 rubles to the dollar to 9 rubles to the dollar. The change-over from an official 25-cent ruble recognized the disparity between the nominal rate and real purchasing power. In effect, the ruble was devalued 56 per cent, from 25 cents to 11 cents.

On April 10, 1957, the Soviet government decreed repudiation of the 253-billion-ruble bond issue "purchased" by compulsory with-holding of workers' wages for from two weeks to two months of their annual salaries. Interest payments were stopped and repayment was postponed for twenty to twenty-five years. Excluded were 3 per cent bonds issued in 1938 which had already been reduced to one-third of their original value.[72]

The Khrushchev version:

Let us take, for example, the measure carried out on the initiative of the people with regard to the state loans. Millions of Soviet men and women expressed themselves in favor of deferring the redemption of old state loans for twenty to twenty-five years. This fact reveals to us such new traits of character, such moral qualities of our people, as are unthinkable under an exploiting system.[73]

Absolute government control of the economy allows all prices in government stores to be fixed. But shelves are often empty, and a black market exists in most goods—including food.

The capitalist, that mercenary who would buy up his own father for one-half of one per cent interest, will never understand the soul of our Soviet man. He will never believe that you support this voluntarily. He will read about it in the newspapers and will say, "The workers and peasants were cowed into agreeing." [74]

The great majority of Soviet citizens live to accumulate

more funds for the common cause, for the state; to raise the level of production, economy and science so that even more machines will be made and more grain produced . . . No capitalist will ever understand this. As a pig cannot look up in the sky, so the capitalist cannot understand our psychology, the psychology of our Soviet man.[75]

No depressions . . .

Socialist economy progresses along a path of steady up-surge, knowing no recessions and crises such as are characteristic of capitalist economy.[76]

But in 1959, the Soviet worker had to work longer to pay for the basic necessities than in 1940.

No income tax, Khrushchev has promised.

. . . to discontinue as of October 1, 1960, the levying of income tax and tax on bachelors, single persons . . . receiving wages of 500 rubles per month. At the same time, taxes on earnings from 500 to 600 rubles will be reduced 40 per cent. This will increase the annual cash earning of this population group by 3.6 billion rubles.

Effective October 1, 1961, taxes levied on earnings up to 600 rubles will be abolished and taxes on earnings of 601 to 700 rubles [a month] will be reduced an average of 40 per cent. This will increase the earnings of this group of workers by 4 billion rubles.[77]

It will not be long before we abolish—I repeat, abolish—all taxation of the population. I believe you fully appreciate the significance of this measure.[78]

Khrushchev ignores the fact that Soviet taxes are primarily sales, not income, taxes. Of course, on comparable income levels—$600 to $840 a year (figuring a 10-cent ruble)—there have been no income taxes in the United States for many years.[79]

The Soviet Union takes a total of 53 to 56 per cent of all national income for its budget—compared with 30 to 33½ per cent paid in

all taxes by an average American. The chief source of income for the Soviet government is a turnover, or sales, tax, which is the most regressive known, placing the greatest burden on the poorest classes.

The turnover tax ranges from zero to 88 per cent, depending on the items purchased, averaging 45.8 per cent. It makes up almost half the government income. "Profits" make up another 20 per cent.

In May 1960 Khrushchev told the Supreme Soviet, of what he termed a "contrast":

By bourgeois economists' estimates, direct and indirect taxes take away 30 per cent of the income of the average American family.

In the USSR there is religious freedom.

To blacken the communists in the eyes of those people who are not well versed in political questions many bourgeois representatives call communists godless. Communists, though atheists, are guided by the most humane considerations in relations between human beings.[80]

But the Soviet press reports:

"The state security organs have unmasked a group of organizers and leaders of the illegal religious sect of Pentecosts or Flagellants. . . .

"Recently the case was heard by the investigations board for criminal cases of the Crimean Oblast Court. The accused were charged in accordance with the criminal-responsibility law for treason. The Pentecosts belong to a secret sect which hinders the education of Soviet people in communist ideology. The materials of the preliminary investigations, the statements of the accused, and the evidence of the witnesses constitute conclusive proof of the reactionary attitude of the Pentecost sect and have fully exposed the accused in their harmful anti-Soviet activities."[81]

The question as to who believes in God and who does not

is not a question for conflicts. It is the private affair of every person.[82]

"Freedom of conscience for parents who are believers must not be turned into a denial of the freedom of the public and the state to intervene positively in questions of family training. . . . Our public and legal organs must enter into the defense of children subjected to spiritual and moral mutilation on the part of parents." [83]

Khrushchev's big promise is ultimate communism:

Our country's enemies are now guessing about whether a communist society will be built in our country. We do not wish to frighten them, but it should be said that the victory of communism is historically inevitable, whether they like it or not. We are confidently going along our direct road, which was pointed out by Marx, Engels, and Lenin—forward, to a communist society! [84]

Communism is no longer a remote dream but our near tomorrow. It grows out of the stubborn labor and creative activity of the Soviet people. Generations to come will be proud of the people who, after having achieved socialism, went further, and by their self-denying labor, realized the cherished dream of mankind. Now, it is the people of our time who are called upon to fulfill the task of constructing the best and the most just society on earth—a communist society.[85]

But:

The advent of communism is not fixed by any calendar date. There will be no particular moment when we shall shut one door and say, "The construction of socialism is finished," and then open another door and say, "We have reached communism." The transition from socialism to communism proceeds continuously. We are already opening the door to a communist society.[86]

We must look into the future. It is essential to prepare material and cultural conditions for the transition from socialism to communism. This problem is not solved by magic; one cannot go to sleep under socialism and wake up under communism. Only naive people can have such an idea of the process of transition to communism. In reality it is a gradual process. As production forces develop, man ascends from one step to another and creates conditions in order that, on the basis of an unprecedented growth of labor productivity, there will be an abundance of material and spiritual wealth and there will be a transition from socialist to communist principles of distribution.[87]

Eventually, to each according to his needs.

In the communist society, everyone will work according to his abilities and receive according to his needs.

The meaning of this classic formula is that no one will be just a bystander or a well-wisher of communism. Having rolled up his sleeves, he will work like a genuine toiler for the new society. Communism will mean not a lordly life in which idleness reigns supreme, but a working, cultured, and interesting life.[88]

But:

One must bear in mind that at the present level of development of production, there is not yet sufficient wealth to satisfy everyone's needs fully. Such egalitarian communism would lead to the eating away of accumulated means and would make further successful development of economy and expanded production impossible. We must move forward step by step, creating the material and spiritual prerequisites for a logical transition to communism.[89]

No more want!

Communism is something which never occurred in the world before, and you know very well that everyone clings to his old shoes, particularly old people. They are now buying new shoes, but they continue wearing the old ones because they fit better, because they are accustomed to them and find them more comfortable. The same applies to communism and the people are behaving toward communism as they do toward new shoes; they are afraid that they might pinch them. But, comrades, just as all clouds dissolve before the sun and things become clear and all colors become radiant in their true hues, so will communism—no matter how it may be slandered—shine.[90]

But that is after Russia produces more than the most advanced capitalist countries.

The basic practical task for our country at present is the creation of a material-technical base of a communist society, a new and powerful upsurge of socialist productive forces. Why does this task at present constitute our basic task in the development of the economy of the country? At the present level of socialist production we are not yet in a position to insure fully the abundance of material and cultural wealth that is essential to meet the growing needs of the people and their comprehensive development. Yet, without this, communism is impossible. Hence, above all, it is essential to develop productive forces still further, to raise the production of material wealth. Communism can be brought about only if we surpass the level of production of advanced capitalist countries and insure new and much higher labor productivity than under capitalism.[91]

In essence: When Russia produces enough there will be plenty.

The necessity of regulating the distribution of products among members of society will disappear only under communism, when productive forces will be developed so far that there will be plenty of all necessary consumer goods, and when everybody will, voluntarily and independently of the amount of material value received, work to his full capability, realizing that this is necessary for society.[92]

But of course people will still have to work a little.

Naturally in a communist society there will be planned and organized distribution of work according to various branches of production, and social regulation of working time, with special reference to the specific characteristic of production processes. Machine production has a definite rhythm which is impossible to maintain without corresponding planning of human work. Some people have a vulgar concept of communist society as a formless and unorganized, anarchistic mass of people. No, this will be a highly organized and harmonious fraternity of working people. In order to control machinery, everybody will have to fulfill within a definite time and in a definite order his function of work and his social duty. The highly mechanized and automated production of the future will not demand many hours of work by an individual. There will be much free time to be occupied by sciences, art, literature, sports, and so forth.[93]

On the other hand:

"The struggle for absolute implementation of the principle 'He who does not work does not eat' against persons evading participation in socially useful work . . . must hold a leading place in all ideological work. . . .

"There must be less political blather and more concrete struggle for an acceleration of the pace of communist construction work in propaganda. Oral and printed propaganda must serve the mobilization of the masses for the successful implementation of the Seven-Year Plan." [94]

A great hope of the Russian people, accustomed to ever-present police, is that the time will come when the police state will be no more.

Henry Shapiro of U.P. queries: I would like to ask you about the theory of the withering away of the state.

This process, properly speaking, is already under way. The functions of government are changing as the Soviet state develops and changes are taking place in some organs of compulsion. As for our army, it has the function of protecting the Soviet state against an attack from without. Take our judicial organs. Crime has decreased considerably in the USSR. Our militia and judicial organs usually have to deal with hooliganism and petty crimes while political crime has become a rare phenomenon in our country. Of the people justly punished for anti-Soviet activity in recent years, a majority are agents sent into the Soviet Union from abroad. Our organs are vigilantly guarding the interests of the people, the interests of the Soviet state, and they expose such agents. A great, and one may say, decisive, role in this is played by the population itself, by our Soviet people.[95]

We are guided by the Marxist-Leninist teaching on the state by the splendid ideas expounded by Lenin in his classic work, *The State and Revolution.* We have said, and we say now, that the state organs of compulsion will gradually wither away and ultimately die out, as will the state itself. But this, of course, will not take place abruptly, but gradually, when communist society arrives at a certain stage of development. It would be a gross error, a leftist blunder, if at the moment we permitted any weakening of our state organs of administration, or abolished the organs of compulsion which, as I have already said, are now primarily organs for defense against machinations by external enemies.[96]

When the conditions for the transition to a communist society are created in our country, many organs of state administration will gradually wither away. Thus the army, the court, the prosecutor's office, and other organs will wither away. The court is evidently destined to outlive the army and other administrative organs. The court evidently will exist, naturally in a different form because there still will be conflicts of different kinds between people and there must be some kind of an arbiter to settle these conflicts. I do not intend to make longer term forecasts of changes in our society, but even now social life here is developing exactly along the lines following from the theoretical principles of Marxism-Leninism.[97]

The citizens will then manage the nation.

But one must not represent the dying-away process of the organs of the state too simply, as though it were leaves dropping in autumn, when as a result of this dropping of leaves, the tree remains only with bare branches. The question of the dying off of the state, if it is to be understood dialectically, is a question of the development of a socialist state system into communist public self-government. Under communism certain public functions will remain, analogous to present state functions. But the nature and means of implementing them will be different than at the present stage of development. The remaining orientation of the socialist state is the all-out development of democracy, the inclusion of the widest strata of the population in the management of all the affairs of the country, the inclusion of all citizens in the management of economic and cultural construction.[98]

We say that under conditions of communism the state will wither away. What organs will be retained? The public organs. Whether they will be called the Komsomol or trade unions or something else they will be public [voluntary] organizations through which the society will adjust its relations. We must clear the way for this, to teach the people to acquire the habits of such life.[99]

Q.E.D., says Mr. Khrushchev:

Speaking thus, I do not in the least want to offend all Americans; they are mostly good people, but their system is a bad one—it is capitalistic—but they are not yet able to understand this. But sometimes it happens that unless a person comes a cropper and gets a few bumps, he does not know what is good or bad for him. Why is it that the United States, whose wealth and scientific and technical development have been a cause of universal amazement—why is it that that country is now repeatedly trying to launch a rocket to the moon, but instead of going to its target, it sinks to the bottom of the sea? It is not a case of their having insufficient dollars;

they have plenty of dollars; they are richer. It is not a case of their having no materials; they have materials. It is not a case of their having no scientists; they also have scientists. What then do they lack? They do not have the kind of system we have.[100]

The super-welfare state that is the Soviet Union still hopes for a work week of 42 hours versus U.S. capitalism's 37.5; a minimum wage of 13 to 15 cents an hour versus Puerto Rico's 64 cents; an average wage of 37½ cents versus $1.98 in the U.S.; socialized medicine on the scale of America's free clinics; education that stops at fifteen for most of the people; no unemployment insurance—all this only for the 40 per cent of the people in state factories. The rest, including 24 million collective-farm workers, have none or few of the "social benefits."

To each his own.

We Russians have a proverb which says that every snipe praises its own bog. You extol the capitalist bog; as for us, I shall not, naturally, say that socialism is a bog, but you can, of course, speak of our system much as I speak of yours. But, as a matter of fact, the proponents of capitalism are now beginning to be ashamed of praising it. They are saying that it is no longer the capitalism that Marx wrote about, but people's capitalism.

God knows, I see no difference between the capitalism Marx wrote about and the capitalism Lodge spoke of today.[101]

Herbert Woodman put the question bluntly when Mr. Khrushchev spoke at the Economic Club of New York:

"Tell us, if we show that it will be better in our country than in yours, will you go on fighting capitalism just the same? I should like to assure you that the members of our Economic Club are willing to compete with the Soviet people in peaceful pursuits."

Ladies and gentlemen, everybody will be winners in the peaceful competition that we are offering you. If the cause, the system which you represent, gives people more blessings and creates better living conditions for them, if it gives more scope to the productive forces of society than socialism, I shall come to you and ask you for a job. But at the moment, gentlemen, do not offer me "causes," because the cause I serve, the great cause of communism, is the best and noblest cause of all! Why then should I change it for something else! [102]

"But what happens," Senator Fulbright, chairman of the Senate Foreign Relations Committee, once asked Khrushchev, "if it suddenly develops that the capitalist system is better and that more and more people prefer capitalism to socialism? Will you put up with that, or will you use force to hold your positions?"

Let us not read the tea leaves, but if history were to confirm that the capitalist system really offers the best opportunities of developing the productive forces of society and of providing a better life for man—and we don't believe that a kopek's worth—I would be the first to vote against communism. If I really satisfied myself of the superiority of capitalism over communism, then I would consider which way to turn and whether I should join the Republicans or the Democrats, though there is hardly any difference between them. It would be a difficult choice to make.[103]

The Battle of Semantics

In many areas, the Soviet rationale is impossible to defend on the basis of plain facts. To overcome this forensic problem, the communists have devised a simple technique: they make the "good" words mean what they want them to mean. Thus *peace, freedom, democracy, status quo*—all words suggestive of progressive, reasonable government—are adapted to the Soviet purpose.

Language is a weapon; Stalin defined it as "an instrument of struggle." Says a British writer:

"The language of communism . . . is not so much a means of explaining to an unbeliever what communism means, but an armory

367

of weapons and tools intended to produce support or dissolve op-position to communist policies on the part of people either hostile or indifferent to them. The meaning of a communist word is not what you think it says, but what effect it is intended to produce." [104]

Thus communist officials can present the Soviet Union as a peace-loving nation where freedom, democracy, and justice for all reign supreme. Thus, too, if the world wants peace, the communists offer it "peaceful coexistence," loosely defined or not defined at all.[105] For a world that wants freedom, the Soviet Union has it, its own variation. Even *God, sin,* and *motherhood* acquire special meaning when used by the Party propaganda.

Freedom in "capitalist countries" is the freedom to starve to death. *Status quo* involves change. Peace is the acceptance of Soviet will. Work under "capitalism" is exploitation; under "social-ism" freedom. A protective Western force requested by a threatened nation is an invading army, while a Soviet invasion is "liberation." Inspection of disarmament becomes spying, and so on.

Khrushchev insists:

Peace partisans in your country [France] and in other countries are frequently called communists. As a communist I am proud of this. If reactionary forces are to consider every man who fights for peace a communist, by this very act they will be helping to make people aware that the part played by communism is most progressive. All peoples, you see, want peace, and only madmen are capable of wanting war. But it is not madmen who should determine the policy of states! Consequently, if reactionaries identify the word "peace" with the word "communism," then that is a compliment to communists.[106]

We firmly uphold the Leninist position of peaceful co-existence.[107]

The Leninist position of peaceful coexistence was simply, War between the communist center and the capitalist center is inevitable, but a period of peaceful coexistence may be necessary for socialist construction. "Socialists, without ceasing to be socialists, cannot oppose any kind of war."[108]

This every trained communist knows. And it was this distortion of communist ideology that created opposition for Khrushchev at home until the matter was laid to rest (rather than resolved) in Bucharest in June 1960 and in Moscow in November 1960.

Stalin had declared: "We cannot forget the saying of Lenin to the effect that a great deal in the matter of our construction depends on whether we succeed in delaying war with the capitalist countries, which is inevitable but which may be delayed either until the proletarian revolution ripens in Europe or until colonial revolutions come fully to a head, or finally, until the capitalists fight among themselves over the division of the colonies. Therefore the maintenance of peaceful relations with capitalist countries is an obligatory task for us. The basis of our relations with capitalist countries consists of admitting the coexistence of two opposed systems." [109]

One of the boldest moves of the communists in the years following World War II was to appropriate the word *peace*. In 1947 they created the "World Peace Council" to fight for the "unconditional prohibition of the atomic bomb" (which only the United States then possessed). The "peace partisans," as members of the "Peace Council" call themselves, are in fact communist-controlled—whether they are card-carrying members of the Party or not. The "peace partisans" denounced "the United States aggression in Korea," vituperated against the "germ warfare" invented by Chinese propaganda, but kept silent on Hungary. The word *peace* is attractive to everybody, and Khrushchev's major theme is to show he is for "peace."

However, we are told that this is propaganda! Yes, it is propaganda, but not for war but for peace, because in the Soviet Union, as distinct from the United States, for instance, propaganda for war is considered a grave crime and is punished by law. What is wrong with propaganda which calls for peace? We are ready to listen to the same sort of propaganda from the Western states daily, hourly. Instead of this, day after day, from official representatives, generals, and admirals of the Western countries we hear calls for war, and threatening statements are made—statements that with the aid of the newest means of warfare it is possible "to annihilate the USSR" and "to wipe off the face of the earth" whole towns and industrial centers of our country. When they want to say something injurious and unpleasant in relation to the peace-loving steps of the USSR they turn to the word "propaganda." [110]

To his question, "What is wrong with propaganda which calls for peace," Khrushchev provides his own answer:

The ruling circles of certain states have been compelled to disguise their real aims. Fostering their aggressive schemes, they often resort to peaceable phrases in order to lull the vigilance of the peoples.[111]

Inasmuch as Khrushchev does not specify which ruling circles and of what states, we may draw our own conclusions.

If we show persistence—the people are now beginning to press increasingly on their governments—with every year and with every month, the champions of the cold war will find it harder and harder.[112]

What Khrushchev wants (see Chapter 4) is to maintain the geographical status quo . . .

The experience of history reminds us that the state frontiers have never been changed without war.[113]

. . . and at the same time to promote social upheavals that will bring new countries into the Soviet bloc.

We have always declared and continue to declare that we do not want war, but we do not renounce class warfare. Class warfare will last as long as capitalism exists.[114]

We have never renounced and will never renounce our ideas, the struggle for the victory of communism. They will have to wait forever for us to disarm ideologically.[115]

This should imply interference by Soviet-directed Communist Party apparatus (see Chapter 10) in the "internal affairs" of "capitalist" countries. But in Khrushchev's lexicon, "interference in internal affairs," too, has a special meaning.

The intention of regaining their islands of Chinmentao [Quemoy] and Matsu and liberating Taiwan and Penhuletao [the Pescadores] is an internal affair of the Chinese people. It is common knowledge that these lands belonged to China long before Columbus discovered America. And the United States government's attempts to prevent the Chinese people from completing their struggle against the Chiang Kai-shek clique expelled from the mainland, and from liberating the age-old Chinese territory constitutes gross and open interference by the United States in the civil war in China.[116]

The United States is itself carrying out not only indirect but also direct aggression in the Far East by occupying the Chinese island of Taiwan and propping up the anti-national clique of traitors to the Chinese people who have entrenched themselves on the island under the protection of American arms and are using it as a base for piratical attacks against China.[117]

I can say that he [Japanese Premier Kishi] also interferes in our affairs because the treaty Kishi signed in Washington—the treaty with the United States—leaves American forces in the Japanese islands. . . . What is the purpose of leaving American troops in Japan, I may ask. I think not to fight the typhoons, which sometimes rage in this area, but to threaten People's China and the Soviet Union first and foremost. Consequently, this is interference in our affairs. If our affairs are meddled with in this manner, then let us pay back in the same coin.[118]

Democracy is a particularly important word in communist semantics. Communist nations are "people's democratic republics." The party is proud that 99 per cent of the eligible population votes and that it unanimously endorses the communist government. The fact that there is only one candidate, approved by one party, or that failure to vote is considered disloyal is not a deterrent in communist rationale. The fact that elected officials have no real power is inconsequential.

Webster defines democracy as "a form of government in which the supreme power is lodged in the people collectively."

Stalin's version is somewhat different:

"There have been times in the history of our Party when the opinion of the majority or the momentary interests of the Party conflicted with the fundamental interests of the proletariat. On such occasions Lenin would never hesitate and resolutely took his stand on principle as against the majority of the Party. . . . 'A policy of principle is the only correct policy.' " [119]

Lenin was even more clear:

"Soviet socialist democracy is in no way contradictory to one-man rule and dictatorship, . . . a dictator sometimes fulfills the will of a class." [120]

Having ignored the Nazi precedent, Khrushchev—defining democracy and freedom as he does—can assert:

The freest elections are held precisely in the socialist countries. Here everything belongs to the people. But in the United States everything is in the hands of the capitalists. They own the newspapers, radio, cinema, etc. In the United States freedom exists in the sense that everyone can apply for work, but also can find no work, can die from starvation. This is freedom to die. We do not recognize such freedom. [121]

Bourgeois democracy is the democracy of the rich. Under it the popular masses are pushed aside from administration; the popular masses cannot take part in the discussion and decision of social and political questions concerning the people as a whole. Thousands of obstacles are raised before the working class of the capitalist countries in order to prevent any of the workers from getting into Parliament or Congress. . . . In the people's democracies power is completely in the people's hands. The workers in those countries are free from exploitation; they are not threatened by destitution and un-employment.[122]

The working people of our country are deeply interested in electing as deputies the best and worthiest representatives of the people. It is for this reason that our people regard the elections to the Supreme Soviet as their vital concern. Almost the entire electorate takes part in the voting.[123]

Khrushchev does not say that the Supreme Soviet is elected only from candidates approved by the Party and when elected has no power except to "approve" Party decisions.

Khrushchev adheres to his own definition of democracy when he draws a parallel between bourgeois democracy and "people's democracy."

There is a great difference between governments in social-ist countries and governments in capitalist countries. Whereas in socialist countries the people send their most worthy representatives—who are the faithful servants of the people, workers, peasants, intellectuals—to become members of gov-ernment, things are altogether different in capitalist countries. For instance, take the United States. There, representatives of monopolist consortiums, lawyers or bankers, members of the boards of leading corporations and firms are cabinet mem-bers. Whom do they serve? Of course they serve those very monopolies and banks whose servants they are. After some time, when such a person leaves the government, he again goes back to his bank or the board of a corporation; or back to the firm which had put him up for a government post, which made propaganda on his behalf, and which spent con-siderable sums to secure his election. There are no such cabinet members in governments of socialist countries. There-in lies the enormous difference between the governments and parliaments of capitalist countries and governments and parlia-ments of socialist countries.[124]

"The West and the Soviet Union mean entirely different things by the term free elections. At the end of World War II, statesmen in

*the West were highly gratified when Stalin, by signing the joint
declaration on liberated Europe, agreed to set up democratic institutions and to hold free elections in Central and Eastern Europe.
They were very much surprised at the form those free elections took
under Soviet management. So, wherever the Soviet Union holds
military preponderance and can consequently play her two-sided
game of political pressuring accompanied by the threat of force,
there are no longer any elections involving a genuine choice."* [125]

The communists, of course, see nothing wrong with a one-party
system.

It is known that certain statesmen in capitalist states regard
the socialist regime set up by the peoples of a whole number
of countries in Europe and Asia as an abnormal phenomenon.
The fact that there is only one party in our country, the Communist Party, does not suit them either. What do they care
about the fact that for a long time there have been no
mutually hostile antagonistic classes in the Soviet Union and
that, for this reason, there are no different parties? A party
expresses the interests of a given class. Workers, peasants,
and intellectuals in our country form a single, united family,
a monolithic society of workers having equal rights, and
whose interests are expressed and defended by the Communist Party, the leading portion and fighting vanguard of
the Soviet people. The CPSU is at the head of the Soviet
people's struggle for the construction of a communist society.
In our country the party and the people form one entity.
Why, then, should the Soviet people have other parties? One
can hardly expect us to invent them for the sake of personalities in capitalist countries who are dissatisfied with the socialist regime! [126]

In a more truculent tone:

The lackeys of imperialism babble allegations to the effect
that the communists keep themselves in power by force, that
the peoples of the Soviet Union and of the socialist countries

374

are only waiting to free themselves from the "yoke" of the communists. But everybody knows what these fabrications are worth! The recent claimants to world domination—the Nazis—babbled about the same things when they launched their predatory attack upon our country. By their own experience, however, they learned that the Soviet people and the Communist Party are a united and truly invincible force.

The Communist Party, which is the vanguard, the advanced section of the people, is of the flesh and blood of the people.

In these elections to the USSR Supreme Soviet, as in previous election campaigns, our Party is in close alliance with non-Party people. This means that the Communists will cast their votes both for Party and non-Party candidates. There is no doubt that the entire electorate will cast their votes unanimously for the candidates of the bloc of Communists and non-Party people and thereby again demonstrate their unbreakable unity and solidarity with the Communist Party and the Soviet Government.[127]

After the liquidation of classes we have a monolithic society. Therefore, why find another party? That would be like voluntarily letting someone put a flea in your shirt.[128]

Only in undemocratic countries do several parties exist:

Why are there several parties in bourgeois society? This is because that society is divided into a variety of classes. Some of them possess the means of production, while others have nothing except their own working hands. This is why the capitalist class has a party of its own, and so have the landowners. The working class forms its own political party, and so does the working peasantry, which, oppressed as it is by the landowners, also has to organize and find a way of carrying on the fight. The petit bourgeoisie has to create its own political organizations to defend itself against monopoly capital, and so do the intellectuals who seek to have political organizations of their own to protect their interests. This is

375

an inherent feature of the evolution of a society in which there are different classes and social gradations. This is the explanation of the multiparty system.[129]

Freedom—now there's a word with a ring, a word that stirs men's souls. The party has put the word to work on many fronts. Stalin made it clear:

"During the epoch of the dictatorship of the proletariat there can be no policy of universal freedom in our country, i.e., no freedom of speech, press, etc., for our bourgeoisie. Our domestic policy reduces itself to granting a maximum of freedom to the proletarian strata in town and country, and to denying even a minimum of freedom to the remnants of the bourgeoisie. That is the essence of our policy, based on the dictatorship of the proletariat." [130]

Lenin was even stronger:

"The state belongs to the sphere of coercion. It would be madness to renounce coercion, particularly in the epoch of the dictatorship of the proletariat. Here 'administering' and the administrator's approach are essential." [131]

On America's freedom, Khrushchev has this to say:

In organizing its onslaught on the workers' and communist movement, international reaction resorts to social demagogy, to deception of the masses by using false fables about the so-called "free world." The ideologists of imperialism are trying to embellish the antipopular capitalist order. Prominent bourgeois leaders in almost every speech assert that the capitalist countries of the West are "free" countries, and that the capitalist world is a "free world." Indeed, there is freedom in the capitalist countries, but for whom? Of course not for the working people, who are forced to hire themselves out to the capitalists on any conditions just to avoid finding themselves in the ranks of the huge army of people who are "free from work." Neither is there freedom for the peasants who are being constantly threatened by "liberation" from their holdings as a result of bankruptcy. Nor is there freedom for the intelligentsia, whose creative activity is in the grip of material dependence on the moneybag and the spiritual management of various commissions set up to check on loyalty. "Freedom" in capitalist countries exists only for those who possess money and who consequently hold power.[132]

And again in an election speech:

It was precisely socialist democracy that enabled the Soviet people to get rid of such "freedoms" as the right to choose one's exploiter or to be unemployed, the right to starve or to be a hired slave of capital. No, it is not in that way that our people conceive freedom! We see in freedom the right of people to a dignified life, without exploiters and exploitation; the right to a genuine political equality; the right to use all the achievements of science and culture. We understand freedom as the liberation of the people from the horrors of unemployment and misery, from racial, national, and social oppression.[133]

What is the dictatorship of the proletariat? It is working-class leadership in the struggle to overthrow the power of capital, to win and consolidate people's government and build a communist society.[134]

Freedom in the West is a big lie, Mr. Khrushchev holds:

In Western countries they are still spreading various inventions and fabrications about the Soviet Union, claiming that there is no democracy in our country, no freedom of the individual. Some even make utterly absurd statements about the existence of something like slave labor in the Soviet Union. But can a country which has no freedom for its people, which has no democracy, and where personality is oppressed, develop its economy and culture so successfully?

We believe that man's supreme right, which assures his freedom, is the right to work, to be provided for today and tomorrow, and to be spared the dreadful threat of unemploy-

377

ment and poverty. The supreme expression of personal freedom and a guarantee of the exercise of man's rights is his
deliverance from exploitation by those who hold in their
hands all the means of production—plants, factories, banks,
houses, land and minerals—and are using all this for personal
enrichment. The opportunity to work for oneself and for the
community, and not for the exploiters, is, in our view, the expression of genuine social justice, the achievement of mankind's long-cherished dream and a manifestation of human-
ism.[135]

Mr. Nixon [former Vice President Richard M. Nixon] expresses readiness to compete in assuring better conditions in
order to liquidate tyranny. We differ with Mr. Nixon with
regard to our concepts of tyranny. What he regards as freedom
for the rich to exploit the poor, we regard as tyranny. We forbid exploitation and he regards our measures against exploiters
as tyranny. These are different concepts.[136]

The free press was one of the basic tenets of the communist
revolution—while it was trying to win power. Lenin was emphatic:

"We demand immediate and unconditional recognition by the
authorities of freedom of assembly, freedom of press and an amnesty
for all 'political' prisoners and dissenters. Until this is done, all
words about tolerance, about religious liberty, will remain a
miserable game and an indecent lie. Until freedom of assembly, of
speech and of the press is declared, there will not disappear the
shameful Russian inquisition which persecutes profession of unofficial faith, unofficial opinions, unofficial doctrines." [137]

Khrushchev has what he calls an "objective" press:

When I read articles which are objective, I often ask that
they be published in the Soviet press. . . . Our press is
objective, and truthful. You probably do not like it when
it gives a rebuff to those who slander us.[138]

Indeed, the Soviet has a "free press" of sorts, but not the sort
that the West considers free.

378

The Propaganda Front (I)

Asked Turner Catledge of *The New York Times:* "As a representative of a big American newspaper, I stand for free exchange of information. In this connection I should like to ask you if you do not think that the censorship in the Soviet Union for foreign correspondents defeats its purpose and creates bigger problems than it settles. In the U.S.A. and other Western countries the reports of foreign correspondents are not censored."

In the Soviet Union a check on the flow of news, or, as you put it, censorship, is applied only in the case of slanderous reports. Soviet people cannot be impartial to slanderers who distort reality in their reports, who write all sorts of fabrications.

We in the Soviet Union cannot remain impartial also to people who call for the disruption of the normal life of society or for murder. If the utterances of such people are restricted it does not mean that freedom of the press is curtailed. In cases where a correspondent wants to send abroad a report that distorts the real life of our country, our institutions take measures to prevent such distortions and slander from appearing. I think that is right.

I would not call this censorship but only a more rational use of the material means at the disposal of society in order not to waste money on telegraph communication, paper and so on. We want to use everything to benefit and not to harm society. Therefore, when an authorized person holds up wrong, false reports, does not publish them, that benefits society. That is how we understand this question.[139]

In fact "freedom of the press" is guaranteed by the constitution of the USSR:

"Article Seven—Anti-Soviet agitation and propaganda.

Agitation or propaganda, conducted with the aim of undermining or weakening the Soviet power or committing individual, particularly dangerous crimes against the state, the spreading of slanderous fabrications with the same aim, defaming the Soviet state

379

and social order, and equally the spreading or printing or storing of literature of this nature with the same aim will be punishable by imprisonment for a period ranging from six months to seven years or banishment for a period ranging from two to five years." [140]

Every nation has its traditions, and every country has its constitution. In your country, the newspapers see fit to print every possible slanderous fabrication and every possible comment, often provocative and nothing short of an outright appeal to war. But in the Soviet Union, anyone who took it into his head to write an article of that kind would be prosecuted, because we have a law prohibiting war propaganda. Your correspondents send any information or article from the Soviet Union quite freely, unless it distorts the facts, unless it is grossly slanderous and insulting to the Soviet people, and unless it calls to war.

Many of your correspondents send fairly sensible articles and our press even reprints some of them. But there are also correspondents who abuse the freedom of the press.[141]

If any Soviet correspondent working in the United States sent a false report, he would be immediately dismissed by his office. Soviet journalists honestly fulfill their mission. But some Western correspondents in Moscow sometimes permit themselves to write such things that if his dispatch were given to a teletypist for transmission, she would be so indignant about it that she would refuse to send this rubbish abroad. We have no censorship, only control to prevent misuse of the freedom of the press.[142]

In the USSR, ideological work is paramount:
"To all oblast [region] newspapers published in Kazakh and Russian. By instructions of higher authority, it is obligatory to publish in all papers the *Kazakhstanskaya Pravda* editorial of November 18, entitled 'Speed Up Tractor Overhauling.' " [143]

James Reston of *The New York Times:* "But I would like to say that we fail to understand, especially considering your implicit faith in the future, why after forty years of Soviet power, when people in your country have reached such a degree of material progress, you will not allow a greater degree of freedom in your country. Why, for instance, must your poets, writers, and musicians follow a narrow line in their work? We do not understand why, for example, I can buy *Pravda* in New York, but my colleagues here cannot buy *The New York Times.* I repeat that this is all the more incomprehensible, considering your absolute faith in the future."

Firstly, things in the U.S.A. are far from what you say. The progressive press in the U.S.A. is subject to various forms of repression. Secondly, if we speak of why Soviet people do not buy your papers, you know that people buy what they need. Our people feel no need to read American newspapers. I'm told that the number of subscribers to your papers in the Soviet Union is literally only a few score. This is understandable. Soviet people want to know the truth, they want to have good spiritual food, which helps them better to arrange their lives and understand world events more clearly. As for your papers, they print a lot of untruths and misinformation. Why should we force that on our readers?

We want our people to have good-quality products, including newspapers and magazines, so that these newspapers and magazines should help people to understand the internal and international situation more clearly, and not mislead them.

As for Soviet writers and poets, evidently you understand their literary work quite incorrectly.[144]

Many bourgeois newspapers and journals have sent their correspondents who are traveling with us, accompanying us on this tour. These correspondents write in different ways, in the ways they understand things. But the secret is that not everyone rightly assesses what he sees, just as not everyone can gaze at the heavens and see the sun as it really is.[145]

Although the press is "objective," being "objectivist" is objectionable:

"The press is a powerful force in the ideological indoctrination of young persons. However, at one time certain newspapers and journals of Latvia were somewhat drawn to objectivist reporting of various aspects of life in capitalist countries. Weak and ideologically depraved literary works were also printed. Party agencies were forced to take serious measures for improving the ideological content of printed matter." [146]

I drew the attention of bourgeois correspondents to the fact that they distort our statements. Let them not take offense, but most of them serve the one who pays the money, and if you don't write the way the boss wishes, he won't pay you for it. That is how things stand in the capitalist world.[147]

The editor of the newspaper *Evening Moscow* has been fired for a major journalistic oversight—he did not get around to printing the news of the launching of the Soviet rocket that hit the moon last September.

" 'This serious political mistake was not accidental,' said the monthly magazine *Soviet Press* in reporting the incident. 'The editorial board of the newspaper has not displayed the necessary operativeness and sharpness in reflecting events of domestic and international life.' " [148]

Question: "In the framework of the rapprochement of the Soviet Union and France, do you think that the censorship which does not exist in Paris for any correspondent could be eliminated in Moscow where it exists for noncommunist correspondents?"

Sir, our conceptions of this problem are different. You say that there is no censorship in your countries. I see here a representative of the Hearst trust whom I know. Let him try to write something with which Hearst would not agree. Not only would it not be published, but he would be fired. This is a censorship which is much stronger than any other

382

censorship. In Moscow there is no censorship. Every correspondent can write what he wants except lies.[149]

William Randolph Hearst, Jr.: "Mr. Khrushchev is quite right when he said our papers and the free American press in general have different conceptions of censorship from his.

"If I fired everybody who wrote opinions with which I disagree at times, I'm afraid we would not have many people left in the editorial department." [150]

Freedom to listen is the other side of freedom to tell. This is the Soviet version:

Now you have asked me about the "Voice of America." Our country is very musical. You know that very many fine singers have come from Russia. Even today we cut a good figure in this field. Therefore, if we hear a good voice, far from jamming it, we try to amplify it, so that it could be heard throughout the length and breadth of the country. But should a strange voice jar the ear, anybody will switch off the radio if he can, and if he can't he jams it, because this voice acts badly on his hearing. Therefore we shall not jam the "Voice of America" if it is really the voice of America—we respect the American people. But when it is not the voice of America, but some sort of malicious howling which is called the "Voice of America," we do not want the Soviet people to have a wrong picture of the American people and their voice.[151]

By reciprocal arrangement 50,000 copies of *Soviet Russia Today* are sold in the U.S. by the Russian government and the same number of copies of *Amerika,* published by the U.S. State Department, are to be offered to Soviet citizens. Most copies of *Amerika* are hard to find in Moscow, and hundreds are returned as unsalable. When two American students attempted to distribute *Amerika* in Moscow, they were promptly arrested and asked to leave the country. Reported twenty-one-year-old George B. Merlis, "There is a fantastic demand for *Amerika*. The Soviet authorities don't sell it; they don't even put it on the newsstands." [152]

Khrushchev is keenly aware that knowledge of the Western world stimulates consumer wants in the Soviet Union.

At the Economic Club of New York, Khrushchev was asked:

"You have said more than once that you would like to see the Soviet people and the American people know more about each other and receive more information about each other. Why, then, do you not allow your people to listen to the American radio whenever they want to? Why, then, do you not allow the free distribution within the Soviet Union of American newspapers and magazines? Why, despite the fact that Soviet correspondents in America may send from here any news at any time without any control on the part of the government or on anybody's part— why, then, do you insist that it is indispensable to apply censorship to American correspondents in the Soviet Union?" [153]

In *Pravda*, the same question is presented thus:

"Why do our broadcasts beamed to the Soviet Union not reach the listeners? Further, the representative of a tobacco firm speaks in favor of the distribution within the Soviet Union of all sorts of bourgeois publications, in favor also that within the USSR there would be organized as large a radio audience as possible for the 'Voice of America' and similar radio stations."

Gentlemen, please, understand me correctly. I came here on the invitation of the President. We have invited your President to come into our country. We have agreed that our discussion will not concern other countries and also that it will not be an intervention into each other's internal affairs.[154]

According to *Pravda:* "From the balcony one can hear exclamations of a clearly provocative character. But also some people on the floor associate themselves with the voices from the balcony." Khrushchev continued:

Gentlemen, I am an old bird, and you will not frighten me

away with your shouts. If you want, you may not listen to me, but it would be good to show me your hospitality and not interrupt me. If you do not want to listen to what I want to say, *I can go away.* (According to *Pravda,* "I can stop speaking.")

The question of how and what our people should hear is the affair of our people, the affair of Soviet people. These questions are decided, and will always be decided by the Soviet people themselves and their Government, without foreign interference.[155]

I should like to say a few words about my talks in America. In the course of these talks certain American representatives repeatedly spoke about the so-called free dissemination of ideas. They tried to convince me of the need of wider dissemination in our country of books and films especially selected by them, and of the need for free broadcasting. They want to foist upon us all kinds of trash that would poison the minds of Soviet people. Can we agree to this? Of course not! Our people do not want to consume food poisoned with the venom of bourgeois ideas.[156]

In the Western world the words *trade union* arouse varied emotions. But by and large the trade union is accepted as a voice of labor, a means through which employees can bargain collectively, can refuse to work, can present their grievances to the public or to judicial tribunals. In the Soviet Union the words are the same but the meaning quite different.

The eleventh Conference of the Communist Party in December 1921 describes the policy toward trade unions—subvert them:

"Taking into consideration the enormous significance of the trade-union movement and the danger of opportunist deviations therein without the constant and firm leadership of the party, the conference resolves to direct to trade-union positions of responsibility only experienced party members of long standing, who in the past have not belonged to any other political party. The replacement *of leading trade unionists must be carried out with the necessary gradualness and caution. The minimum length of party membership required for an appointment is: pre-October 1917 membership for chairmen and secretaries of union central committees; three years' membership for secretaries of provincial trade-union councils."*

The Soviet trade unions have a big role to play in educating the millions of workers and employees, in mobilizing their creative energies for advancing and improving production, in raising the working people's living standards and cultural-technical level.[157]

The role of the trade unions has grown considerably—they are devoting more attention to production, are more energetically working to raise productivity and improve labor and living conditions, are doing more to bring the masses to share in the administration of the economy.

Guided by Lenin's injunctions, the trade unions must encourage and foster the activities of the working class and all working people, directing their efforts toward fulfillment and overfulfillment of the state plan in every single enterprise, and toward technical progress. The trade unions must give even greater scope to the socialist emulation movement, supporting and encouraging production innovators, inventors, front-rank workers, and popularizing their methods.[158]

It is easy for Khrushchev to dismiss the question of union rights.

I know that in the capitalist countries some newspapers allege that our trade unions have no freedom, and in doing this they refer to the fact that the workers in our country do not strike. This is correct—the workers do not strike in our country. Why don't the workers strike? Because ours is the worker-peasant state. Against whom are they to strike? Everything is owned by the people. Against themselves?[159]

The term *enslaved nations* is particularly galling to Nikita Khrushchev.

386

The Propaganda Front (1)

Now about the term *liberation of the enslaved countries.* The imperialists give this term a meaning which is exactly the opposite of the essence of genuine liberation. Enslaved peoples liberate themselves from the chains of slavery when they gain their social and national freedom, when they become the real masters of their countries, without exploiters. This is the real liberation of peoples!

Imperialists understand liberation in another sense. They consider only those countries to be free where monopolists can rob the people unpunished and where the exploiters are in no way responsible to the people for their anti-popular actions. With regard to your wish—you monopolists—to help the suffering peoples, would it not be better for you to raise your voice against the shameful system of colonialism, in which many peoples languish in the fetters of colonial slavery and suffer from the oppression of alien exploiters![160]

You like to call our socialist system a slave system. We, on the other hand, regard the capitalist system as a system of slavery for the working people, for the overwhelming majority of the people. Many years ago, Karl Marx convincingly showed that the capitalist system is a system under which the majority of the people are mercilessly oppressed. I think that at the moment we had better not argue this point.[161]

CHAPTER 12

The Propaganda Front (II)

The Battle of Statistics

To prove to the Russian people, and to the whole world, the superiority of the Soviet socialist system, Khrushchev has created a statistical myth based on half-truths, distortions, pure fantasy, and delusions that make Bulfinch appear as factual as a telephone directory.

The plain truth is that the Soviet Union has rebuilt and expanded its industrial capacity and has improved the standard of living of its people from the sub-subsistence levels that existed under Stalin to a level approximating the prewar level. But Soviet progress is impressive only when compared with the fantastically low levels that preceded the Khrushchev "thaw," and its claim to industrial power is accomplished by concentrating on a small fragment of the industrial economy.

Essentially, the image of a high standard of living and a high industrial capacity was developed with three objectives: to bid for a place among world powers; to convince underdeveloped countries that the socialist system could be effective as a means of improving their economies; and to distract the world's attention from the direction of industrial growth, political capability.

We are now in a phase of struggle between labor and capital, between socialism and capitalism, when the balance of strength between them is decided in a field of peaceful co-

388

existence and peaceful competition. In the course of such a competition, it becomes clear which system can develop productive forces better and increase the productivity of labor, and which system can better secure and satisfy the material and spiritual demands of the peoples.[1]

We are firmly convinced that socialism will win the peaceful competition of the two systems. And win it will by dint of its great advantages, by dint of its inspiring example. The only right road to victory is through the utmost development of the productive forces. The socialist countries must have the highest productivity of labor to produce a maximum of output at a minimum outlay of labor. That is the mighty source which enables us to steadily raise the living and cultural standards of the peoples of the socialist countries.[2]

It is toward the underdeveloped countries of Asia, Africa, and Latin America that this example of progress is primarily directed.

In our time many countries have freed themselves from colonial dependence. Having inherited a backward economy, the peoples of these countries are seeking ways to pull their countries out of their backwardness and onto the wide road of independent development and promotion of their economy and culture. Two roads lie before them—the road of capitalist development and the road of socialist development. . . .

The experience of socialist construction in the Soviet Union is an obvious example, an open book that tells how our people, during forty-two years of which almost twenty were taken up by wars imposed upon us and by postwar economic rehabilitation, changed their country into the world's second-strongest . . . power.[3]

As has already been noted, the analogy between the Soviet Union in 1913 and present-day underdeveloped countries is, of course, specious. In 1913 Russia was already emerging as an industrial nation, producing seven times as much steel as India in 1956, eight times as many locomotives, six times as many sewing machines, four times as much paper. India's population is 2.6 times as great as Russia's in 1913. In 1913, Russian industry, accounting for one-fifth of national income, was growing at the rate of five per cent per year.

Basic to the problem in all nations is the ratio of resources to population. Pre-Revolutionary Russia had tremendous untapped resources, vast undeveloped land areas, and many skilled workers. Her economy was saving ten per cent of the national income.

"Moreover, the long process followed by Russia, of seizing power, eliminating all opposition, dissolving religious, social and cultural values, and mobilizing manpower and resources, is a long, trying evolution costly in national dignity and human life. It never had—or could have—spontaneous support from an informed majority."4

It is rather obvious—even from the Soviet experience—that as an aid to growth, no backward country can possibly learn as much from Russia as from the United States.

Like words, statistics have a special meaning in the Soviet Union. Never averse to distortion, Soviet officials find that statistics require special treatment in a planned economy, where management must know how much it can produce and how much it is producing in each sector.

But production must be the Soviet Union's prize exhibit. When it does not measure up to standards, it must be rationalized or magnified. And the audience here is not only the underdeveloped world, which the Soviets hope is watching with bated breath, but also the more sophisticated world and the home management, which is expected to believe most of what comes out of Moscow.

What results is a special semantics of statistics, a system of index numbers with bases in 1913, 1928, and 1940—very low years in Russia's production—and a series of blank spaces for statistics that are better left unmentioned.

Moreover the definitions of various key titles are purposely left vague for foreign identification, are made invalid from year to year, or are "adapted" to the changing values of the ruble. The gathering of statistics is left to those who have a basic interest in the size of the figures.

The Propaganda Front (II)

But most distorting of all is the selection of areas for "peaceful competition"—statistically. As long ago as 1924, Stalin complained of the same trouble:

"At a recent conference Rykov said that during the period of War Communism he had a statistician who gave him a certain figure in answer to a question one day and the next day another figure for the same question. Unfortunately we still have such statisticians with us. . . . In bourgeois states a statistician has a certain minimum amount of professional honor. He cannot lie. He can be of any political conviction and inclination but wherever facts and figures are concerned he will submit to torture but will not tell an untruth. If only we had more such bourgeois statisticians, people who respect themselves and possess a certain minimum of professional honor." [5]

Mr. Khrushchev does not agree:

In our country statistical data on the industrial development have been very extensively published, particularly after the Twentieth Congress of the CPSU held at the beginning of 1956. In the Soviet socialist state, the national economy is developing according to plan. You certainly realize that without statistics it is impossible to draw up a plan, to check its fulfillment, to find reserves for its overfulfillment, etc. In our country, therefore, great importance is attached to statistics.[6]

Soviet statistics fail to give a true picture of production, even for their own purposes, for a number of fundamental reasons:

1. Definitions of terms are unspecific, coverage is unexplained, presentation is designed to be misleading for propaganda purposes, and substantial portions are withheld.

Explanations in the Soviet handbook take up seven pages; the United States counterpart several hundred pages.

It is probable that in most cases the management of Soviet industry does not itself have a realistic appreciation of the significance of statistics until years after they have been published. A classic example is the "biological crop yield capacity," noted by Mr. Khrushchev.

391

Malenkov acted dishonestly, juggling with the data of the so-called "biological crop yield capacity," since nobody fails to know that the "biological crop yield" is far from being the same as real grain in corn bins, for one cannot bake bread out of the concepts of "biological crop yielding capacity" but it is baked out of grain which has been garnered.[7]

But five years earlier Malenkov had made the same point: "It is time to end the incorrect practice of judging crops on the basis of biological, not barn, yield."[8]

"The propaganda uses of Soviet economic statistics also mean that definitions are sometimes changed to mask failure or exaggerate gains. The most infamous example of such a change is the shift from the 'barn yield' concept to the 'biological yield' concept of grain output in the thirties, adopted to make grain output appear larger than it actually was. Even though it was possible to find out from Soviet sources that this change in definition had been made, the appropriate correction to achieve comparability with a barn-yield concept remained unknown. Not until Khrushchev's speech to the plenary session of the Central Committee in December 1958, was it revealed precisely how great the difference was. The figures he cited for 1952, i.e., barn yield as 30 per cent less than the biological yield, involved a bigger difference than had commonly been estimated. A more recent example of the subversion of intertemperal and international comparability to propaganda objectives is the change in the definitions of meat and milk output. Khrushchev has made catching up with the United States in meat and milk production one of the important goals of his agricultural program, and to make the fulfillment of this goal easier, the scope of the definitions of meat and milk output has been broadened beyond past definitions and beyond the American concepts."[9]

2. Almost all published data is based on index numbers with a base year of 1913, 1928, or 1940. Changes in product make the evaluation of production almost entirely subjective under this circumstance. The official index shows industrial output 27 times greater in 1955 than in 1913; indexes presented by Western observers,

based on official Soviet data on physical output, indicate the output multiplying five to six times.

3. Statistics are unreliable.

One official statistician is realistic: "After publication of the results of the All-Union census of 1926 the Central Statistical Administration over a period of several years prepared for the third general census. This census was carried out on the sixth of January, 1937. The census should have reflected the historical achievement of our fatherland in the period of the first two Five-Year Plans, which was written into the Constitution of the USSR and should have given material for planning the further development of the people's economy. However, since the enemies of the people infiltrated the control and implementation of the census, it was carried out with the deepest violations of the elementary basis of statistical science and the approved instruction. After studying the procedure of the census and its results the government recognized the organization of the census to be unsatisfactory and its results defective. A new census was decreed for January 1939." [10]

Stanislav G. Strumilin, the Soviet's leading statistician, notes that growth rates and production figures are much exaggerated by multiple counting. Thus the automobile manufacturer gives a figure for annual production that includes the figures previously given by parts makers, steel producers, pig-iron processors, and mines. The total gross national product thus overstates the total product, in some cases by as much as two or three hundred per cent. Strumilin cites the 1956 gross national product, after his adjustments, as 147.7 billion rubles, compared with the 492.4 billion rubles previously reported—and upon which Khrushchev based most of his claims.[11]

4. All production on all levels is keyed to statistics, not demand. Production planning is concentrated on the ten basic industries that make up the price index. Plant managers concentrate on meeting and overfulfilling quotas in statistical terms, regardless of what they produce. Workers concentrate on meeting their quotas, regardless of quality or considerations of long-term conservation.

How does the manager meet his quota? If his quotas are measured by weight, he orders production curtailed on lightweight products. His pipes become thicker, his sheeting of higher gauge, his machinery heavier. Sometimes normal rejects are passed through or the quality of the product is depreciated. The equipment runs continuously, without change of design or pattern. Difficult orders are refused.

Mr. Khrushchev is well aware of the problem.

Some officials, as is shown by the facts uncovered by the Central Committee and the government, try to be cunning with the Party and state, take the path of deceit, of concealing from the state material resources at their disposal. . . .

Some officials try to sweeten the state of affairs, engage in window dressing, in padding reports on plan fulfillment.

One encounters officials who violate or circumvent Soviet laws and produce unfinished products or low-quality goods and pass them off for first grade. . . .[12]

The factories strive to produce the machines, but certain managers of works are little interested in whether the machines correspond to modern standards, or whether they will be economically profitable for the collective farm and the state.[13]

And . . .

This frequently led to the fact that MTS workers, in order to register large figures for tractor work, carried out unnecessary work with no thought of increasing fertility. For instance, unnecessary cultivation or plowing was carried out. Thus, labor and material resources were frequently spent, not to increase the production of agricultural produce, but to achieve a formal fulfillment of the plan for tractor work.[14]

And . . .

Some workers' main consideration is that all collective farmers be given the opportunity to earn as many work-days as possible; not to produce as much as possible, but precisely to earn as many work-days as possible. There are collective-farm chairmen who consider that the more work-days a collective farmer earns on the average, the higher is discipline and labor productivity. But that is not always the case. Level of production is governed not by the number of workdays, but by the amount of products produced per unit of expended labor. Wise management is where the utmost production is obtained from the least expenditure of resources and labor.[15]

"Deception and simulation take the form of statistical manipulations by both workers and management in Soviet enterprises, who, because of the rigorous structure of incentives and penalties under which they operate, are pulled in the direction of write-ups of output and simulation of plan fulfillment. 'Borrowing' output from succeeding periods, the inclusion of spoilage and sub-standard goods in reports of finished output and the devaluation of the product assortment produced, all tend to impair the numerical accuracy of the data reported to the Soviet authorities by their subordinates. But while there is much evidence of data distortion and even falsification of this sort, there are also definite limits placed on such opportunities for misreporting and, by and large, it may be reasonable to assume that the relative magnitude of distortion from this source is not fatal for our purposes." [16]

Says Mr. Khrushchev:

It became the tradition to produce not only beautiful chandeliers to adorn the house, but the heaviest possible. This was because the heavier the chandeliers a factory produces, the more it gets, as its output is calculated by the ton. So factories make chandeliers weighing hundreds of pounds and fulfill the plan. But who needs such a plan?[17]

5. *"New products have often been given an arbitrary and excessive weight by Soviet statisticians, but the attempts to replace this by one of our own devising is necessarily imperfect. What, for ex-*

ample, is the correct '1926–7' weight for excavators if none were made in 1926–7?"[18]

6. Changes and manipulation of the value of the ruble lead to gross distortions. Devaluation, which has occurred many times in Soviet economic history, is reflected several years after the event. But the great distortion arises from any supply-demand system of pricing. Prior to 1961, a ruble was officially worth 25 cents for government purchases and for export of industrial goods, but varied from 2 to 12 cents for the purchase of consumer goods. Tourists paid 10 cents for a ruble, but on the black market it was worth 2½ to 3 cents.[19]

One interviewer posed the question to Mr. Khrushchev:

How do you determine the costs of production in your plans? True, this is beyond the scope of simple statistics, these are already the fundamentals of economics. Do your prices correspond to the costs of production?

The cost of production, as you know, consists of many elements. Our domestic prices do not always and in all cases correspond to the costs of production. In our home trade there do not exist the two aspects as you understand them. We sell some goods at prices exceeding their cost of production. But some goods are sold below the cost of production. They are sold at a loss but their production is necessary from the point of view of the development of our country's economic potential. The state uses the funds it receives in the form of extra charges to subsidize the manufacture of goods with a high cost of production. Moreover, they help in the accumulation of funds for the development of our national economy.[20]

Pricing creates a marked distortion in the Soviet income-distribution picture. Industrial products were, substantially, priced close to a 25-cent (old) ruble value, consumer goods at an average 7½-cent ruble. Thus when the USSR produces a billion rubles of goods, of which 500 million is in consumer goods, the ratio is not 50–50 but 77–23.

Professor G. Warren Nutter of the University of Virginia adds:

7. "Whatever the faults of data on output of individual industries, they are more reliable than official aggregative measures, such as the official Soviet index of industrial production. Although the details underlying this index have not been made public, Western specialists are generally agreed that, from what they know about the construction and behavior of the index, it exaggerates industrial growth." [21]

8. Soviet figures are faced with ideological blocks which prohibit consideration of such values as interest, land, mineral resources, and services not directly connected with industrial production. Mr. Khrushchev points out:

Of course, the economic conceptions which underlie Soviet statistics and bourgeois statistics are different. Soviet statistics, for example, clearly distinguish between the sphere of material production and that of nonproductive branches and between the concepts "production" and "services." In the USSR the volume of the total social product does not include the value of "services" in nonproductive branches of the national economy, whereas in United States statistics the "gross national product" embraces all services irrespective of whether they are connected with production or not. Similarly, while defining the volume and structure of the national income not as a mere sum of all kinds of income, as is the practice in bourgeois statistics, but as a sum of primary incomes received in the sphere of material production. As far as production costs are concerned, statistics in capitalist countries are obliged, for instance, to take into account the existence of the so-called "commercial secret."

It can therefore be seen that Soviet statistical data provide at least the same opportunities for the study of industrial development in the USSR as American statistical data provide for the study of industrial development in the U.S.A., as well as for a comparative study of their development. [22]

9. Placing figures outside of the economic context creates a spe-

cial type of distortion. Broadcasts point out that the USSR produces more sugar and wool than the United States. Or that there are more strikes in the United States (there are practically none in the USSR). This is seen as the sign of the downfall of capitalism, rather than as a basic freedom.

Failing to note that the United States long ago substituted synthetics for most natural fabrics, Alexei N. Kosygin, now Vice Premier, proudly announces in *Pravda*, January 29, 1959:

"The Soviet Union ranks first in the world in output of woolen and linen fabrics. . . . In output of woolen fabrics we shall exceed the United States by 80 per cent."

10. "But the distortion of the information reported to the Soviet authorities is the lesser of the impediments to statistical adequacy. A much more serious problem for us is the distortion of the facts about the Soviet economy reported by the Soviet authorities in their publications. This is a very different kind of distortion which takes the form not of numerical falsification, but of a concerted effort to mislead the reader by withholding and suppressing data, by partial and selective release, by deliberate ambiguity in description, and by biased choice of bases for comparison. The reasons for this systematic Soviet effort to deprive and to deceive are twofold: first, an almost compulsive preoccupation with preserving military secrecy which, in Soviet practice, is defined much more comprehensively than almost anywhere else in the world, and second, a vital political and ideological stake in presenting a special kind of image of the Soviet economy both to its own citizens and to the world at large."

But now says Khrushchev, our statistics are better than yours.

I should point out that for a number of indexes Soviet statistical publications are more informative than those of the American statistics.[23]

Here is a typical informative note by Khrushchev that leaves one wondering, How much did they produce?

In the past two years we achieved considerable success in developing our national economy. Today Soviet industry is

398

working much better and is producing far more goods than it was two years ago. In 1957, industrial output was 22 per cent higher than in 1955, the year preceding the Twentieth Congress of the CPSU. In those two years steel production increased by 5,800,000 tons, coal by 72 million tons, oil by 27,500,000 tons, cement by 6,400,000 tons and electric power by 39,000 million kilowatt-hours.

So that you may be better able to judge the significance of these figures I must add that the increase in output for the past two years exceeded the total volume of production in pre-Revolutionary Russia for the year 1913: steel by almost 50 per cent, coal by 150 per cent, oil by almost 200 per cent, cement by more than 300 per cent and electric power by 1,900 per cent.[24]

And here is one analysis of some of Mr. Khrushchev's figures: "Regardless of what the situation may be with 'bourgeois statistics,' Khrushchev must have made some adjustment in the data for the state farms to 'make the situation look better than it is.' It is a little difficult to average 14.5 and 14.0 and obtain 9.9, the average labor used to produce milk for 1956–1957, or to average 64 and 76 and obtain 52.0 as the labor used for beef. The man-hour data for the years 1956 and 1957 were published by I. Benediktov, formerly Minister of State Farms, who would hardly have any reason to exaggerate the amount of labor used. While the evidence is not quite as clear for the collective farms, since we have data only for one year and expressed in days rather than hours, it appears that Khrushchev found it necessary to make a few adjustments in the data to prevent the ratio of labor used on collective farms from reaching a level of 20 to 25, instead of 16, times the U.S. level."[25]

Enthusiasm is no index:

Comrade Deputies, the year 1957 is drawing to a close. We are on the brink of the new year of 1958. The year 1957 was a good year! And I think that 1958 will be even better!

The outgoing year brought the peoples of the Soviet Union great success in industry, in agriculture, in raising cultural and living standards, brilliant achievements in science and engineering, success in strengthening the international position of our country and in further enhancing its prestige.[26]

But in the year 1958, the USSR scrapped its sixth Five-Year Plan and created a new Seven-Year Plan with 1965 goals in most categories roughly at the point where 1960 goals had been set.

Said Alexei I. Kirichenko, ill-fated member of the Presidium:

"The failings in a plan are almost never admitted by the administration in power. It is only when a new management takes over that we hear. Even the lumber industry, notorious for many years, as you will recall, cheered us all last year. . . .

"We all know the state of agricultural production a few years back. The country was short on grain and experienced an acute shortage of meat, milk, butter, sugar, vegetables and other food products of prime necessity." [27]

The statistical picture is framed by a goal of "catching up with the United States."

Today our country is ahead of the U.S.A. both in annual rates and in annual physical growth of production. We go forward four times as fast, and we add more to our output each year. Consequently, it is now much easier to overtake the Americans. . . .

If we reckon per head of population, it will probably take us another five years after completing the Seven-Year Plan to catch up and surpass the United States in industrial production. Consequently, by that time—or even earlier—the Soviet Union will rank first in the world both for physical volume of production and production per head of population. That will be a world historic victory for socialism in its peaceful competition with capitalism in the international arena.[28]

"Setting the goal of catching up on a per capita basis with the most opulent country in the world, and specifying a target date [10 to 12 years hence] for the attainment of that goal, is a very clever

400

move. It attracts the world's attention in as vivid a fashion as any to the dynamic nature of the Soviet economy, and by implication to the lagging pace of capitalism. It focuses on 'peaceful competition' [though nothing in the Seven-Year Plan indicates any reduction in the volume of resources devoted to military use]. It raises spirits and mobilizes energies at home by means of a vision of the American standard of living at the end of another big push for a decade or so. In short, it is to create momentum on which the USSR, and Khrushchev himself, can capitalize externally and internally.

"It seems to have escaped general notice, in part thanks to the studied silence on this point by the Soviet press itself, that the present 'catch up and overtake' campaign is a repetition of a very similar campaign launched by Stalin just twenty years earlier."

And:

" 'The time has come to take practical measures to solve the basic economic task of the USSR: to catch up with and overtake . . . economically the most developed capitalist countries of Europe and the U.S.A. . . . Then and then only will the significance of the new era in the development of the USSR unfold itself, the era of transition from a socialist to a communist society.' "

And:

" 'Only in the event that we overtake economically the main capitalist countries shall we be able to regard our country as fully saturated with consumer goods, and we shall [then] be able to go over from the first to the second phase of communism. What do we need in order to overtake the economically most powerful capitalist countries? . . . a determined and unremitting desire to move ahead and a readiness to bear sacrifices . . . and, lastly, time . . . ten to fifteen years.'

"These are not Khrushchev's words at the Twenty-first Party Congress in 1959. They are the words of Molotov and Stalin speaking at the Eighteenth Congress in March 1939, and their purposes clearly were then, as their successor's are now, to instill an impression of

strength and invincibility abroad, and to spur production efforts at home." [29]

Bourgeois lackeys like to exaggerate the imaginary advantages of the so-called system of free enterprise. Listening to them, one may think that this system is mankind's ultimate dream, and there is or can be nothing better. But then why cannot they name even one capitalist country which has attained in such a short period of time such significant achievements in economic development as have the countries which took the socialist road? [30]

Although the number of visitors to the USSR is limited and the areas open to visit are restricted, it would place too great a strain on world credulity to say that Soviet citizens are as well off materially as those of Western nations.

However, Khrushchev consistently stresses several substitute theses: (1) that the rate of growth indicates the Soviet Union will overtake the United States in standard of living, and (2) that in some respects it has passed United States levels.

And Khrushchev denies all criticism:

Hostile propaganda is obviously in a tight spot, one absurdity succeeding another in its evaluation of socialist economic developments. It either howls about "crisis" in some economic branch of our country or, compelled to speak about Soviet economic successes, the achievements of Soviet science and technology, switches to warnings about the "danger" to the West of the rapid growth of the Soviet economy and culture. And people in the capitalist countries are coming to see the falsehood of bourgeois information about the Soviet Union and the other socialist countries. They are coming to realize how far these countries have advanced in their development.[31]

Our people would be still better off today if out of forty years we had not spent almost two decades on wars imposed upon us, and on postwar economic rehabilitation.

Do you know that during the war the German fascist invaders burned or otherwise destroyed 1,710 towns and settlements and upwards of 70,000 villages and hamlets, leaving about 25 million people homeless? We lost many millions of people and suffered material damage amounting to nearly $500,000 million. But for these fearful losses and destruction, we would probably have caught up with the United States by now both in volume of output and in living standard.[32]

Khrushchev has selected as indexes of Soviet ability to meet and surpass U.S. standards a group of commodities that have down-to-earth meaning in the underdeveloped world and even in the Soviet Union—commodities with which the United States long ago was surfeited: meat, milk, and butter.

In these items there has been a chronic shortage in the USSR. And occasionally sugar and woolens have been added to the list.

But even the campaign for more meat, milk, and butter is not a serious contest. It is a "slogan"—a goal established essentially for propaganda purposes, a goal which even 1965 Plan quotas will not reach.

The U.S. long since has discovered means of producing more food than it can eat or use with only 9 per cent of the population on the farms. In the USSR more than 40 per cent work at farming and do not produce enough to furnish even a fair diet for the people.

"Apart from the question of differing attitudes of the two populations toward fats in their diets, this comparison overlooks the fact that butter production in the United States is supplemented by an output of margarine 3 per cent greater than the production of butter itself, whereas in the Soviet Union the output of margarine is only 70 per cent of butter output.

"Another such prestige output which they have elevated to the status of a symbol is the output of sugar. Soviet propagandists are fond of comparing sugar output in the two countries. For instance, in one of the standard statistical handbooks for agitators, the per capita production of sugar in the two countries is shown as 17 kilograms in the Soviet Union and 12 kilograms in the United States. This figure appears to be accurate enough as far as it goes, but what it fails to mention is that while Soviet sugar output is augmented by imports only to the extent of about 2 per cent, U.S. domestic output is far overshadowed by imports so that per capita consumption is more nearly 45 kilograms than 12." [33]

"The United States, because of rapid technological development, has been steadily preoccupied with the problem of farm surpluses and excess capacity in agriculture, except during World War II and the years immediately thereafter, when maximum output was essential. Control of farm surpluses and other aspects of farm relief, therefore, have been the principal concern of U.S. policy." [34]

This Mr. Khrushchev understands and derides:

Governments, particularly the United States, are trying to cut crop areas and reduce harvests by every means. This is at a time when millions of people in vast areas of Southeast Asia and Africa are starving, and when in the metropolitan countries too large a section of the population is seriously undernourished. . . .

All have more than sufficient reason to be dissatisfied with the United States, which has disorganized the world market by . . . dumping agricultural produce.[35]

However, the USSR still has to cope with grain-growing problems.

But it was precisely in the production of grain that the most serious lagging was allowed to occur which entailed stagnation in some other important branches of agriculture, in livestock breeding in particular. The quantity of marketable grain was utterly insufficient. Difficulties in the supply of bread arose in larger towns.[36]

On the whole we cover the necessary requirements of the country for grain, in the sense that the country is provided with bread, that we have needed State reserves and conduct, within certain limits, expert operations in grain.[37]

The Propaganda Front (II)

Although in 1949 Khrushchev was proud to announce:

Toilers of agriculture honorably fulfill their obligations before the homeland and Comrade Stalin. From year to year the collective farms and state farms fulfill ahead of time the plans for delivery to the State of grain, meat and other agricultural products.[38]

In 1958 he admitted:

As a result of major defects in the management of collective farms and the state farms and a certain distortion of the Leninist policy in building up the collective farms, the development of agriculture was held back. It is easy to be convinced of this if we were to consider the results of the development of agriculture during the years of 1948–1953. In these years the over-all harvests and procurements of cereals did not, in essence, increase. The production of milk did not increase either, and the average annual meat production was below the level attained by the country before the war. There thus arose a certain discrepancy between the development of industry and of agriculture between the actual requirements by the state of cereals and other products and of their actual production. This lack of balance boded dangerous consequences.[39]

In 1956 Khrushchev had revealed that the problem was acute:

We can and must solve this problem in the very near future.[40]

In 1957:

Already, this year we will get as much butter, and even perhaps a little more, than the United States produced last year. This means that regarding bulk we will have as much butter, or even more, than the United States. But as our population is greater than that of the United States, we must pull our socks up. Regarding the per capita production of milk, we can not only catch up with, but even surpass, the United States as early as 1958.[41]

And:

We do not intend to blow up the capitalist world with bombs. If we catch up with the United States in the per capita production of meat, butter, and milk we will have hit the pillar of capitalism with the most powerful torpedo yet seen.[42]

Notwithstanding Mr. Khrushchev's pride in socialism, the Soviet Union's 1960 statistical yearbook reports that private gardens of farmers and workers produce almost half the meat, milk, and vegetables, 82 per cent of the eggs, and 70 per cent of the potatoes for Russia's table.

And:

It will be interesting now to see what the imperialists of the U.S.A. have to say when they read that the USSR is undertaking to surpass them in the near future in per capita production of meat, milk and butter. Now the more zealous defenders of capitalism will invent all sorts of cock-and-bull stories about this matter. They will think of something. Well, let them howl to themselves. The folk saying goes: "The wind carries away the dog's barking." [43]

"This particular propaganda drive has a number of interesting aspects. First, in announcing the goal of overtaking the United States, Khrushchev revealed to the Russian population the very great disparity between the per capita outputs of livestock products in the two nations, especially in the case of meat. The following figures on annual per capita production for 1956 were given: meat, USSR, 32.3, and United States, 102.3 kilograms; milk, USSR, 245, and United States, 343 kilograms; and factory butter, USSR, 2.8, and United States, 3.8 kilograms.

"Second, despite Khrushchev's great confidence, neither the milk nor butter goals were achieved in 1958. The per capita output of

406

factory butter in 1958 was 3.2 kilograms and total production per capita was 3.8 kilograms. The per capita production of milk accepting the official figures was less than 280 kilograms or significantly less than the U.S. level.

"Third, in announcing the program Khrushchev indicated that he had disregarded the advice of the economists who had said that it would not be possible to surpass the United States in per capita livestock production before 1976."

And in presenting his Seven-Year Plan thesis, Khrushchev said: [44]

Our country has advanced to first place in the world in total output of milk and butter. Within the next few years we shall not only overtake but considerably surpass the United States of America in the per capita output of these products. At the same time much work will have to be done to utilize all potentialities and possibilities so as to increase meat production 2.5 to 3 fold, to top the Seven-Year Plan assignment considerably and implement the call of the country's leading collective and state farms to overtake the United States in per capita output of livestock products.

High rates of growth in agricultural production such as these are based on the tremendous advantages of the socialist system of economy, and the increased might of our industry, which is supplying all the necessary material and technical facilities for large-scale mechanized agriculture.[45]

In an April 24, 1959, Minsk radio broadcast:

"On many collective farms, milk yields of cows during the first quarter of 1959 not only failed to increase, but even declined in comparison with the level of last year. On collective and state farms of the Brest Oblast the average output of milk per cow declined by 61 kilograms and the total output of milk decreased by 7 per cent. In the Mogilev Oblast, the average output of milk per cow declined by 54 kilograms and the total production of milk decreased by 12 per cent. In the Gomel Oblast the corresponding figures were 67

MEAT PRODUCTION—USSR and U.S.[47]

(slaughter weight in million metric tons)

	USSR	U.S.	USSR output as a percentage of U.S. output
1913	4.94	8.50	58.1
1940	3.88	11.40	34.0
1950	4.87	13.61	35.8
1955	6.32	16.24	38.9
1956	6.60	17.22	38.3
1957	7.37	16.70	44.1
1958	7.85	16.34	48.0

Note: Soviet population exceeds U.S. population by 19 per cent.

MILK PRODUCTION—USSR and U.S.[48]

Net Output

(in million metric tons)

	USSR	U.S.	USSR as a percentage of U.S.
1913	25.4	29.4	86.7
1940	27.6	48.2	57.3
1950	26.5	51.4	51.6
1955	33.3	54.3	61.3
1956	38.9	55.5	70.1
1957	43.9	55.6	79.0
1958	46.5	55.3	84.1

kilograms and 9 per cent. There has been particularly bad lagging behind in milk production on collective and state farms of the Pruxhany, Gomel, Zhlebin, Kormya, Mezyr, Lyaban, Pukhowichi, Robrulsk, and Ospipovichi rayons, where the average output of milk per cow in three months declined, in comparison with the corresponding period of 1958, 100 or more kilograms.

"This lagging behind in milk production was one of the main reasons for the failure to carry out the plan for the sale of milk to the state. Collective and state farms of the Mogilev Oblast implemented the quarterly plan for the sale of milk to the state to the extent of only 61.8 per cent and the Six-Month Plan—by April tenth—to the extent of only 19.5 per cent.

"Collective and state farms of the Molodechno Oblast carried out 77.1 per cent of the quarterly plan and 25 per cent of the Six-Month Plan. Collective and state farms of the Brest, Vitebsk, Gomel, and Grodno oblasts also failed to carry out their plan for milk supply to the state by a large margin." [46]

In May 1960, before the Supreme Soviet, Khrushchev again admits:

We lag far behind the United States in the per capita output of meat products. Under the Seven-Year Plan we are not scheduled to catch up with the United States.

By January 1961, Khrushchev was admittedly frustrated by the fact that farm production did not meet statistics. He told a meeting of the Central Committee:

Unless we put things in order, our plans will be fulfilled statistically, but we shall be short of food. You cannot make *blinchiki* [pancakes] out of statistics, you know.

The Battle of Living Standards

"The highest living standard in the world," is Khrushchev's promise to the Soviet people. This he offers as the ultimate proof of the efficiency of the socialist system. This is, for the Russians, quite a promise.

In the USSR it is no secret that the U.S. standard is considerably higher. In a country where owning a bicycle is a status symbol, almost everyone knows that most Americans own cars; where each family shares a room, the people have been told that most American workers live in small cottages of their own. The refrain was sung by Stalin: "The basis for the Stakhanov movement was first and foremost the radical improvement in the material welfare of the workers. Life has improved, comrades. Life has become more joyous. And when life is joyous, work goes well."

Just twenty-four years later, Mr. Khrushchev repeats:

The situation is altogether different now, as you know. . . . Everywhere you hear the cheerful song "Life is better, life is more joyous." [49]

The plain fact is that with a per capita income variously estimated at $310 to $600 a year, the Soviet Union ranks—under the best estimates—with the Bahama Islands, Argentina, Israel, and Czechoslovakia. The estimates that put the USSR figure at $500 to $599 quote the United States at $2,000 to $2,099; Canada at $1,400 to $1,499; Finland at $600 to $699; West Germany at $700 to $799; Norway at $800 to $899; Sweden at $1,100 to $1,199; France and the United Kingdom at $900 to $999.

The Russians rank even lower in the line in a study by Professor Philip M. Hauser, of the University of Chicago.*

North America	$1,100	USSR	$310
Oceania	560	Africa	75
Europe	380	Asia	50
	South America	17	

But this is not the whole picture as we shall see. Substantially more of the Soviet citizen's income is taken by the state (to support heavy industry) than in any other country. This is reflected in the pricing system, which includes an average 45.8 per cent turnover (sales) tax above normal retail profits and serves to hold down consumption practically to food, government-subsidized shelter, and a bare minimum of clothing and other items.

---

*Because statistics in this book are obtained from various sources and compiled under various definitions, similar statistics are not always comparable.

Bertram Wolfe, who has spent much effort in the study of the Soviet system, notes:

"There is no obvious reason why the Soviet living standards should not be substantially higher, particularly insofar as food is concerned. The fact that it has had such serious deficiencies in the past was due to ill-conceived policies which sought to exact agricultural deliveries at arbitrarily low prices."

But Khrushchev proclaims:

We are carrying our communist ideas to the people not with the force of weapons, not by war, which causes only hatred as it destroys people and all things of value they created. We are carrying the ideas of communism to the consciousness of the people by our example, by our socialist system established by the people, a system which insures a creative life for the people and the abundance of material wealth for man. And the time is not far away when also those who now oppose communism will say: "What a fool I have been in believing fables about communism. I did not know what it was. This is exactly what I and other people need." [50]

Thus the gauge of peaceful competition has been set by Mr. Khrushchev: which system provides more for its people—socialism or capitalism.

When everyone sees that people in socialist countries live well, enjoy equal rights, have good houses—and we have now set ourselves the task of solving the housing problem within the next ten or twelve years—are well fed, have the shortest working day because they are the owners of their plants and factories and are exploited by no one; when people see that science develops faster and more successfully in these countries, that everyone can have a higher education and finds application for his abilities in any sphere of mental

411

or physical labor, that people enjoy material benefit; when they see that as a result of a higher productivity of labor and the shorter working day, man will have increasingly more free time to develop his talents and take up art according to his inclination, then only an idiot, pardon the word, will oppose this.[51]

The cardinal task in the immediate period ahead is to ensure, without diverting attention from the development of heavy industry, the bedrock of the Soviet economy, swift advancement in agriculture and a steep increase in output of consumer goods. The task is to give the population, within the next two or three years, a plentiful supply of manufactures and foodstuffs, and substantially raise the people's living standards.[52]

The most recent Soviet statistical yearbook reported that by 1958 capital-goods production had increased to 570 per cent of its 1940 level, while consumer-goods production had reached only 270 per cent. The Seven-Year Plan (1959–1965) calls for an average annual increase of 9.4 per cent in the production of capital goods, as against 7.4 per cent for consumer goods.[53] But a 1959 study by Soviet Academician Stanislav Strumilin indicates that the national product has been overstated by approximately 300 per cent and growth rates by 50 per cent.

The de-emphasis on production of consumer goods remains a basic policy according to Soviet statements.

Notwithstanding this, Khrushchev continues to make much of the smaller but steady increases in this field of consumer goods.

The imperialists are afraid of peaceful competition with the Soviet Union, for the capitalist system clearly cannot withstand such competition. More and more frequently the American bourgeois press is voicing fears that the rapid rate of the Soviet Union's development and the rise in the living standards of the people have a magnetic influence on the working folk in the capitalist countries. Indicative in this respect is an article in the *New York Herald Tribune* of April 11 [1954], which makes noteworthy admissions.

"While we still lull ourselves with outworn legends about the 'backward Russians,'" says the paper, "the giant Soviet empire is consolidating her economic strength at a much faster rate than Western Europe. . . ."

The switch is on to consumer goods. Believe it or not, it is probably the most menacing development of this half of the twentieth century. "The grim and inescapable fact" (we add: grim for the imperialists) "is that there has been enormous industrial and technical progress in the Soviet Union since the war; stupendous by Russian standards and enormous even by our own." [54]

We prepared for discussion at the session the question of increasing by 25 to 30 billion rubles expenditures for the expansion of industry manufacturing consumer goods so as to emerge to first place in Europe during this Seven-Year Plan period and to catch up with the United States five years later. What lofty aims from the attainment of which not a single people, not a single individual in the world, would suffer.[55]

Some foreign tourists and journalists, on the basis of superficial observations and motivated by ill will, are shouting about the real or fictitious shortcomings in our standard of living. Well, we know about the present shortcomings. We make no secret of them. However, more farsighted observers who see and soberly judge the other aspects of the matter can be met increasingly often. They see the speed with which our country's economy is growing and the people's living standards rising, our measures aimed at doing away with existing shortcomings, and the excellent prospects facing our country.[56]

Occasionally there is a slip, a handbook for lecturers notes: "When speaking of the living standard in capitalist countries, the lecturer used confused formulations. . . . Thus, for example, the author said at a certain point that even in the most developed capitalist countries millions of working people live miserably. This is a very correct statement as it is the faithful picture of the situation in the capitalist countries. But when he compares the living standard in the socialist countries with that in the most developed capitalist countries he asserts textually: 'The living standard of the population in the United States, Britain, or Germany has not as yet been reached by the socialist countries.' " [57]

Occasionally even Khrushchev turns frank:

The standard of living of the Russian worker is lower than that of the French worker.[58]

The Russian people are, of course, aware of the disparity between advances in technical fields and what they receive in the form of consumer goods.

"We have mastered the sputniks. We have mastered the atomic icebreaker. We have mastered the greatest atomic-power stations in the world. Let us now take the trouble to produce a down pillow or a pair of pliers that will draw a nail." [59]

An interesting clue to the mood of the ordinary Soviet citizen was provided by *Komsomolskaya Pravda*, the Moscow youth newspaper, when it printed an anonymous letter June 11, 1960. "What have these sputniks and rockets given a simple mortal like me?" its author asks, and then continues:

"Doesn't it seem to you that enthusiasm for these sputniks and the cosmos is altogether untimely, more exactly, too early? I want to say that earthly matters have us by the throat: housing and nurseries are in short supply; goods are expensive. And these rockets, I have no doubt, devour so much resources that all would be dismayed if they knew their price. . . . Rockets, rockets, rockets! Who needs them now! The devil take them and the moon, but give me something better on the table. After that one can really play with the moon." [60]

What is the standard of living of the Russian workman? How does it compare with that of the working man in the United States?

414

The Propaganda Front (II)

In a radio address reported in *Pravda* on January 28, 1959, Mr. Khrushchev noted:

As a result of higher money wages, pensions and allowances, and a reduction of prices in public catering establishments, the real per-worker incomes of factory and office workers will rise 40 per cent at the end of the seven-year period. We plan to raise the minimum wages of low paid workers from 270–350 rubles to 500–600 rubles a month. Real incomes of collective farmers will also grow by no less than 40 per cent, chiefly through the expansion of collective-farm production.

The radio address continued, but *Pravda* omitted the remark:

By 1965 the average earnings will be increased 26 per cent to 990 rubles.

These wages were set on September 8, 1956, in a joint decree issued by the Soviet Government and the Central Committee of the CPSU. The basic minimum wages for factory workers was raised to 300 rubles, and for collective farmers living in rural areas to 270 rubles. This decree was to become effective on January 1, 1957.

At the Twenty-first Party Congress Khrushchev again reported that

. . . it is envisaged to raise the minimum wages for low-paid workers and employees from 270–350 rubles to 500–600 rubles per month.

In 1958 there was still a category of workers and employees who earned 270 rubles a month.

The same decree established that minimum monthly income on which income taxes could be levied should be raised from 260 to 370 rubles.

This raise is planned for 1965.

Equivalent buying power in the United States: $27 to $35 and $50 to $60 a month. In 1960 minimum wages in the United States were $1 per hour or $195 per month for equivalent time. Minimum wages are expected to rise 15 per cent in 1962, 25 per cent by 1965. Thus the Soviet minimum wage is 13½ cents per hour, the average wage

415

about 40 cents. This compares with Puerto Rico's minimum, raised from 48 to 64 cents in 1960.

Khrushchev continues proudly:

These are big sums, comrades. Only a socialist state can allot such funds for improving living standards. It is no accident that many visitors to our country from the capitalist world—often not communists at all, but fair-minded people— are amazed to see how much is being done for man in our country.[61]

In the Soviet system, wages are, for the most part, based on a piecework basis.

"[The wages] are paid in accordance with a tariff system, which helps to fix wages depending on the conditions of labor and the qualification of the worker concerned, the importance of the branch of industry and enterprise and its geographical location.

"The tariff system consists of three related elements: rates of tariff, which determine the level of payment per hour or day, tariff scales, which determine the correlation in payment for labor in a given branch of industry between workers of different qualifications [grades], and tariff qualification tables, which help to assign workers and work to different grades [in accordance with the complexity of the work]." [62]

In terms of purchasing power, the old ruble had an average worth of 6 to 10 cents—a few cents more for the lower-paid, who buy principally bread and cabbage, which are relatively cheaper. Thus, the minimum wage in the Soviet Union in 1959 was $27 to $35 a month, the average wage $79.60 a month—in terms of American purchasing power, using a generous 10-cent ruble. Comparable figures in the U.S. for equivalent time: minimum wage $240; average for men $436.83; for women $267.08.

For more than five years now the great majority of workers have received neither a blanket pay increase nor a blanket cut in prices such as took place annually during the 1948-54 period. On the contrary, recently millions of workers have been subject to a new wage system based on higher work quotas, which in not a few cases have resulted in pay cuts.

Soviet apologists claim that rent is relatively cheaper in the Soviet Union: Rent takes 5 per cent of the average income. But the benefits derived are almost proportional—the new model living quarters in the Soviet Union are substandard according to New York City's code of 1901 and could command little more in rent in any Western nation. Rent is paid by area, but the more modern apartments, which pay the same rent as older buildings, go to Party workers and other special classes.

The difficulty in comparing living standards is magnified because the choices made for the people by Soviet authorities are so different from the American standards. A 10-cent phone call in the Soviet Unions costs 15 kopeks, or 3 cents figuring a 10-cent ruble. But a $50 bed and mattress costs 1,552 rubles, or $155.20 figuring a 10-cent ruble.

There is little consistency between prices filed by the government in the Soviet system and the free market price created in the United States. The accompanying chart shows how many United States pennies are required to buy the same amount as one ruble in the purchase of various items—in effect, the dollar value of a ruble in terms of purchasing power.

Mr. Khrushchev had a good reason for keeping prices high:

When I spoke at the construction site of the Bratsk hydro-power station, one of the listeners asked me about the reduction of prices. Of course I explained things to him. But I would like to add a few words on that matter. What will happen if we venture to reduce sharply the prices of all goods at once? There may be queues in the shops, because we cannot yet secure the production of sufficient quantities of all goods. We cannot permit this because such a situation would encourage the development of speculation, which we have been fighting and will continue to fight firmly.[63]

417

WHAT THE RUBLE IS WORTH IN TERMS OF
WHAT THE RUBLE BUYS

	USSR Official Price in Old Rubles 1958[a]	U.S. Prices in New York City Stores in Dollars 1960	Value of One Old Ruble in U.S. Cents, to Buy Equivalent Products
FOOD[b]			
Rye Bread.............	1.24	.51	41.12
White Bread...........	2.35	.46	19.57
Butter................	28.00	1.43	5.11
Margarine.............	14.00	.33	2.36
Eggs (10).............	7.50	.50	6.67
Milk (quart)...........	2.20	.27	12.24
Apples...............	20.00	.33–.64	1.65–3.20
Lemons (each)..........	3.50	.05	1.43
Oranges..............	15.00–20.00	.22	1.10–1.47
Prunes...............	17.90	.55	3.08
Fish (average).........	11.00	1.10	10.00
Chicken...............	16.50	1.10	6.67
Beef (stewing)..........	12.00	1.54–1.76	12.8–14.7
Frankfurter sausage......	16.50	.88	5.33
Mutton (medium grade)...	13.00	.95	7.30
Pork.................	19.50	1.08	5.50
Cabbage.............	1.50–2.00	.11	7.33-5.50
Carrots...............	3.50	.28	8.00
Cucumbers (each)........	3.00	.05–.15	1.67–5.00
Onions................	3.00–4.00	.22	8.00–5.50
Potatoes.............	1.00	.06	6.00

[a]**Source:** Soviet prices from *Comparisons of the United States and Soviet Economies,* Joint Economic Committee, U.S. Congress, Washington, D.C., 1959.

[b]Unless otherwise noted, food prices are given in terms of one kilogram. The kilogram is taken at 2.2 pounds, and American prices are adjusted for this quantity.

The Propaganda Front (II)

	USSR Official Price in Old Rubles 1958	U.S. Prices in New York City Stores in Dollars 1960	Value of One Old Ruble in U.S. Cents, to Buy Equivalent Products
FOOD			
Ice-cream cone (each)....	1.90	10	5.23
Sugar................	10.00	.22	2.20
Coffee................	40.00	1.43	3.57
Tea..................	70.00	3.30	4.71
Beer (small bottle).......	3.00–3.50	.25	8.33–7.14
Champagne (bottle)......	30.00	3.50	11.67
Cigarettes (25).........	2.20	.34	15.46
Noon meal at work......	5.00–6.00	1.00	20.00–16.67
CLOTHING			
Blanket, wool mixture.....	100.00	6.00	6.00
Cotton print, cheap (meter)c	6.50	.30	4.62
Rayon-crepe fabric (meter).	57.00–62.00	70	1.23–1.13
Silk dress fabric (meter)...	11.00–125.00	1.00	1 00–.8
Dress, cotton print........	200.00	3.00	1.50
Dress, wool.............	475.00	11.00	2.32
Man's all-wool suit.......	2000.00	50.00	2.50
Man's felt hat...........	69.00	7.00	10.17
Man's overcoat..........	720.00	40.00	5.55
Poplin shirt.............	50.00	2.50	5.00
Nylon (kapron) hose......	14.00–30.00	.50–1.00	3.57–3.33
Wool socks.............	11.00	1.00	9.09
Boys' leather shoes.......	85.00	6.00	7.06
Canvas shoes...........	27.00	4.00	1.48
Shoes (adequate)........	200.00	6.00	3.00

cOne meter = 39.37 inches.

419

	USSR Official Price in Old Rubles 1958	U.S. Prices in New York City Stores in Dollars 1960	Value of One Old Ruble in U.S. Cents, to Buy Equivalent Products
DURABLE GOODS			
Auto: Pobeda or Volga...	30,000.00	1500[d]	5.00
Alarm clock..............	30.00–50.00	3.00	10.00–6.00
Aluminum frying pan......	7.50–8.50	2.00	2.67–2.35
Bicycle.................	450.00–600.00	40.00	8.89–6.67
Family divan............	1300.00	100.00	7.69
Fountain pen............	17.50	1.00	5.71
Pillows.................	35.00	4.00	1.14
Popular wrist watch......	500.00	15.00	3.00
Radio..................	400.00	20.00	5.00
Radio, hi-fi.............	2100.00	70.00	3.00
Record player..........	250.00–300.00	25.00	10.–8.33
Refrigerator (Zil).........	2000.00	200.00	10.00
Television (14-inch).......	2400.00	150.00	6.25
Vacuum cleaner........	425.00	40.00	9.41
Washing machine........	2250.00	200.00	8.89
PERSONAL CARE			
Haircut................	.90–1.50	1.50	16.66–10.00
Lipstick................	4.50–6.00	.50	11.11–8.25
Shoeshine..............	1.00	.15	15.00
Toilet soap.............	2.20	.10	.45
RECREATION			
Film (roll)..............	5.80	40	6.89
Football...............	35.00	5.00	14.14
Gasoline...............	3.00	.30	10.00
Movie admission.........	3.00–5.00	.75–1.00	25.00–20.00
Newspaper.............	.20	.05–.10	25.00–50.00
Postage (domestic).......	.60	04	6.67
Record (12 inch).........	7.90	3.50	44.30
Theater seats...........	5.00–25.00	3.60–8.80	7.20–35.20

Note: In general, prices are for items of moderate quality. However, no adjustment is made for difference in standards: i.e., packaging of American foods, variety of choice, styling, etc.
[d]Price in West Germany.

The food ruble (meat, fish, tea, milk) buys approximately what 6 cents would in the U.S. For butter, sugar, fruits, the ruble is worth 3 cents. For a shirt or nylons, it is worth 2 cents, a suit 3 cents, shoes 4 cents.

It does better on musical instruments than cooking utensils, better on television sets than bicycles. On the average the consumer's ruble buys 7½ cents worth of merchandise.

One analyst notes:

"Having the power to do so, the Soviet government proceeds to overprice the goods sold to the consumer by approximately the amount by which it wishes to underprice the goods it sells to itself, namely capital goods and military matériel. This Herculean task of 'compensation,' as some Soviet economists prefer to call it, is canceled out by the turnover tax. Its use has made it possible over the years to depress the share of consumer goods in total industrial output from 60 per cent in the late 1920's to less than 30 per cent at present." [64]

Government-operated social services are perhaps more extensive in the Soviet Union than in the U.S. But in the U.S., public services in the field of health, education, welfare, and recreation are supplemented by the total of the services offered by voluntary agencies and health insurance and is probably not lower than what a Soviet citizen can expect.

The teaching of Marxism-Leninism is not an abstract theory, and not a fantastic biblical story of life in paradise in the other world. It is a profoundly viable and true teaching, the correctness of which is daily confirmed by the practice of our building of communism and the experience of the hundreds of millions of people of the socialist countries, where everything is placed at the service of the people, and where free people create their own happiness by their work. This example and experience are highly appreciated by the peoples struggling for their independence, peace, and a better life on earth.[65]

"A turbine operator in Russia earns about 1,200 rubles a month as a salary. At the average rate of 10 rubles to a dollar, this means that he is earning about $120 a month. In addition he could earn a bonus that would increase this to $140 to $160 a month. An American worker with the same sort of a job earns about three times as much. On the average the Russian worker receives about 800 rubles a month.

"A graduate engineer receives about 2,500 rubles a month. The director of a plant receives 4,000 rubles or $400 a month. With bonus, his salary may be about $500 a month." [66]

A wide variation in earnings exists in the Soviet Union not only between workers in different sectors of the national economy, but also among production workers in particular industries.

	1960 Monthly earnings (in old rubles) [67]
Scientist (academician)	8,000–15,000
Minister (head of Government ministry or department)	7,000
Opera star	5,000–20,000
Professor (science)	6,000–10,000
Professor (medicine)	4,000– 6,000
Docent (assistant professor)	3,000– 5,000
Plant manager	3,000–10,000
Engineer	1,000– 3,000
Physician, head	950– 1,800
Physician, staff	850– 1,000
Teacher, high school	850– 1,500
Teacher, primary school	600– 900
Technician	800– 2,000
Worker, skilled	1,000– 2,500
Worker, semiskilled	600– 900
Worker, unskilled	270– 500

The Propaganda Front (II)

In contrast, this is the gross weekly earnings of production workers in the U.S. in January 1960: [68]

Field	Weekly	Hourly
Manufacturing	$ 92.29	$2.29
Durable goods	100.86	2.46
Nondurable goods	80.77	2.05
Ordnance and accessories	107.42	2.62
Textile-mill products	64.48	1.60
Chemical products	102.09	2.46
Mining	111.11	2.73
Wholesale and retail trade	91.43	2.28

The government, workers, and trade unions in the Soviet Union act in concord, hand in hand, in order to accomplish in the best possible way and as early as possible the task of steadily raising the living standards of the people. Only in a socialist system can the reduction of the work day and the raising of wages be regarded as a paramount task for the state. Can a capitalist country plan a 40 per cent increase in the workers' income over seven years as we do? No, it cannot. And what capitalist government can secure a reduction of the work week to 30–35 hours while increasing wages? There is no such capitalist government.[69]

HOW THE LOT OF SOVIET WORKMEN HAS IMPROVED
Worktime required
to buy week's supply of selected foods in Moscow [70]
1959 as a percentage of 1928

Eggs 290%
Milk 253%
Rye bread 118%
Sugar 110%
Beef 100%
Potatoes 85%
Butter 80%
All foods combined 108%

Monthly Labor Review, April 1960, p. 361.

Only under socialism can a rapid and genuinely mass movement forward be started in all fields of social and personal life, a lusty increase of material production, an increase of the well-being of the working people, and an unparalleled flourishing of science and culture. Only the socialist revolution has made it possible for the Soviet Union to change from a backward and semi-illiterate country into a leading industrial power, which has set itself the very real task: in a historically brief period to rank first in the world in insuring material and cultural standards for the life of its citizens.[71]

"Official Soviet price and wage data indicate that the average Soviet worker had to work about 8 per cent longer in 1959 than he did in 1928 in order to buy for his family the same average weekly supply of seven essential foods—bread, potatoes, beef, butter, eggs, milk, and sugar. In particular, he had to work about 18 per cent longer for a pound of bread, about 10 per cent longer for sugar, about 153 per cent longer for milk, and 190 per cent longer for eggs. Beef was just as 'cheap' as in 1928, and potatoes and butter were slightly 'cheaper.' Comparable data for 1928 are not available for other consumer goods; however, other data clearly indicate that prices for these goods, especially clothing, also rose after 1928 at a higher rate than money earnings." [72]

"In 1959, a Soviet worker, if the sole supporter of a family of four, would have had to work 28.49 hours, or 62 per cent of the legal 46-hour work week of most workers, to buy enough of the seven foods listed for his family. An earlier study showed that in 1953 the average Soviet worker had to work approximately 38.17 hours for the same amount of food, or 79.5 per cent of the then prevailing legal 48-hour work week of most workers. The relatively high cost of food in the Soviet Union helps explain the exceptionally high percentage of the labor force who are women (47 per cent of the labor force in January 1960 were women, compared with 35 per cent in the United States)." [73]

"Since 1954, there have been only occasional price cuts, mostly on luxury and semi-luxury goods; for example, on July 1, 1959,

prices were cut on bicycles, cameras, women's rayon stockings, wines, and children's toys, and on March 1, 1960, on electric sewing machines, silk clothing, radios, motor scooters, accordions, safety razor blades, and certain other items. There have also been some price increases; for example, in 1958, for vodka, wines, automobiles, and machine-made carpets."[74]

These are 1959 prices of typical consumer goods in Moscow—when they are available—in terms of man hours.

WORKTIME TO BUY CONSUMER ITEMS [a]
(August 1959)

Item	New York hours and minutes	Moscow hours and minutes	Moscow worktime as percentage of New York worktime
Beef, rib roast, 1 lb.	21m	1h 22m	400%
Bread, rye, 1 lb.	6m	9m	150%
Butter, salted, 1 lb.	21m	3h 4m	900%
Eggs, second grade, 1 doz.	17m	2h 24m	800%
Milk, 1 qt.	8m	31m	400%
Potatoes, 1 lb.	2m	7m	350%
Sugar, 1 lb.	3m	1h 4m	2,100%
Tea, 1 oz.	6m	33m	600%
Vodka, 1 pt.	1h 22m	6h 19m	450%
Dress, street, rayon	4h 36m	73h 30m	1,600%
Shirt, men's, cotton	56m	15h —	1,600%
Shoes, men's, oxfords	7h —	61h —	850%
Shoes, women's, oxfords	5h 10m	57h 30m	1,100%
Stockings, nylon	37m	8h —	1,300%
Suit, men's wool	23h —	275h —	1,100%
Cigarettes, 1 pkg.	7m	27m	400%
Soap, toilet	3m	32m	1,050%

[a]**Source:** U.S. Bureau of Labor Statistics, figures compiled by National Industrial Conference Board, June 3, 1960.

The average Moscow worker must spend 1 hour and 4 minutes on the job to earn enough to purchase a pound of sugar, which his counterpart in New York City can buy after 3 minutes of labor.

APPROXIMATE WORKTIME REQUIRED TO BUY SELECTED COMMODITIES AT STATE-FIXED PRICES IN MOSCOW AND AT RETAIL-STORE PRICES IN NEW YORK CITY, AUGUST 15, 1959 [75]

Commodity	Moscow price (in rubles)	New York City price (in dollars)
Foods:		
Beef, rib roast, 1 pound	5.45	.757
Bread, rye, 1 pound	.59	.215
Butter, salted, 1 pound	12.27	.741
Eggs, Second grade, per dozen	9.60	.629
Milk, at grocery, 1 quart	2.08	.273
Potatoes, 1 pound	.45	.060
Sugar, 1 pound	4.27	.110
Tea, 1¾ ounces	3.80	.200
Men's clothing:		
Shirt, cotton	60.00	2.03
Shoes, leather oxfords, pair	245.00	15.10
Suit, wool, single-breasted, medium-price range	1,100.00	50.41
Women's clothing:		
Dress, street, rayon	294.00	10.00
Shoes, leather oxfords, middle of price range	230.00	11.21
Stockings, nylon	32.00	1.35
Other commodities		
Soap, toilet, 3½ ounces	2.10	.105
Cigarettes, package of 20	1.80	.25
Vodka, pint	25.28	2.98

If the Russian worker gives a friend the shirt off his back it is, indeed, a generous gesture, for a cotton shirt represents almost two eight-hour days of his labor. By contrast, the American worker

WORKTIME REQUIRED TO BUY SELECTED COMMODITIES, MOSCOW AS A PERCENTAGE OF NEW YORK CITY, 1959 [76]

	Approximate worktime		Moscow work-time as a percentage of New York City worktime
Unit	Moscow	New York City	
Pound.........	82 min........	21 min.........	400
Pound.........	9 min.........	6 min..........	150
Pound.........	184 min.......	20.5 min........	900
Dozen.........	144 min.......	17.4 min........	800
Quart.........	31 min........	7.5 min.........	400
Pound.........	7 min.........	2 min..........	350
Pound.........	64 min........	3 min..........	2,100
Ounce.........	33 min........	5.5 min.........	600
Each..........	15 hr.........	56 min.........	1,600
Each..........	275 hr........	23	
Pair..........	61 hr.........	7 hr..........	850
Each..........	73 hr. 30 min...	4 hr. 36 min.....	1,600
Pair..........	57 hr. 30 min...	5 hr. 10 min.....	1,100
Pair..........	8 hr.........	37 min.........	1,300
Each..........	31.5 min.......	3 min..........	1,050
Package.......	27 min........	7 min..........	400
Pint..........	6 hr. 19 min....	1 hr. 22 min.....	450

earns enough in less than an hour to purchase a cotton shirt.

Even the solace afforded by vodka is harder to obtain in Moscow than in New York. The Muscovite spends 6 hours and 19 minutes on the job to earn a pint of the liquor; the New Yorker 1 hour and 22 minutes.

The NICB chart compares the worktime required to buy seventeen selected consumer goods in New York City and Moscow. Worktime figures for New York City are based on earnings of $2.17 per hour for production workers in manufacturing. For Moscow, worktime is based on estimated average gross earnings of 4 rubles per hour for manufacturing workers.[77]

Disregarding the price factor, what can the ordinary Soviet citizen buy with his ruble?

Soviet consumers get one-third as much goods, or one-fourth as much per capita as the United States.

Bourgeois lackeys like to exaggerate the imaginary ad-

APPROXIMATE WORKTIME REQUIRED TO BUY SELECTED FOODS AT STATE-FIXED PRICES IN MOSCOW, APRIL 1, 1928, APRIL 1, 1953, AND AUGUST 15, 1959 [78]

Food	Prices (in rubles)		
	1928	1953	1959
Rye bread, 1 kilogram.............	0.080	1.35	1.30
Potatoes, 1 kilogram................	.085	.75	1.00
Beef, 1 kilogram...................	.870	12.60	12.00
Butter, 1 kilogram.................	2.430	26.75	27.00
Sugar, 1 kilogram.................	.620	9.09	9.40
Milk, 1 liter......................	.063	2.20	2.20
Eggs, per 10.....................	.200	6.88	8.00
All 7 foods......................	....	....	....

428

vantages of the so-called system of free enterprise. Listening to them, one may think that this system is mankind's ultimate dream, and there is or can be nothing better. But then why cannot they name even one capitalist country which has attained in such a short period of time such significant achievements in economic development as have the countries which took the socialist road?[79]

"Recently *Pravda* published reports concerning a visit by workers' correspondents to Kirov shops. The picture that emerges from this report is disgraceful. The premises of a number of shops appeared to be in an unsanitary state. They refused to wrap the goods sold to shoppers. For instance, if a person wants to buy flour he must bring his own wrapping material. The assistants are inattentive, and some are even rude to the shoppers. In their dictionaries there are no such simple expressions as 'Please' and 'Would you be so kind.'

"Such facts occur not only in Kirov. The working people waste much time in shopping. Often the queues form only because of

WORKTIME REQUIRED TO BUY WEEK'S SUPPLY OF SELECTED FOODS IN MOSCOW, 1959, AS A PERCENTAGE OF 1928 [80]

Quantity consumed per week by a family of 4	Approximate worktime				
	In hours			1953 as percentage of 1928	1959 as percentage of 1928
	1928	1953	1959		
9.84 kilograms...	2.71	4.52	3.20	167	118
12.16 kilograms..	3.56	3.10	3.04	87	85
3.68 kilograms...	11.04	15.77	11.04	143	100
.44 kilogram.....	3.69	4.00	2.97	108	80
1.80 kilograms...	3.85	5.57	4.23	145	110
4.96 liters.......	1.08	3.71	2.73	344	253
6.40 eggs.......	.44	1.50	1.28	341	290
....	26.37	38.17	28.49	145	108

429

the lack of administrative ability of the shop personnel. Cases of fraud, overcharging, and giving short weight to shoppers still exist." [81]

Mr. Khrushchev tells this story:

Recently we met a woman who was walking with her small child. We stopped and asked her: "How are you doing?"

She answered: "Things are not going bad," and she added, "We are very glad that you came to us and that I had the pleasure to meet you." She stopped again and added: "In connection with your coming to us, shoes, fabrics and milk were thrown into our stores."

"They threw it into your stores?"

"Yes, they threw them in."

"And how is the situation with fresh fish since you live at the shore?"

"We have plenty of herring," she answered, "but there are no other fish available." [82]

Two other visitors report:

"While taking a stroll around town one night before going to bed, I noticed a crowd of about twenty-five people on the sidewalk in front of a darkened furniture store.

" 'What's going on?' I asked one of the men.

" 'We're waiting to buy chairs,' he replied.

"I looked through the window. Piled high were plain, straight-backed wooden chairs such as one might find in a cheap restaurant.

" 'You mean you're going to wait in line all night long?' I asked in amazement.

" 'Of course,' he answered.

"And early the next morning when I drove by, the crowd had grown to about seventy-five people." [83]

Soviet citizens are told they have much to look forward to.

We will insure the production of consumer goods at a higher rate. It will be soon, we shall see, not very much time will pass. We will jump the obstacle of the highest capitalist country which is the United States. Then, my dears, what will you have to say? We will then see who eats the most.[84]

But at present, in the same speech Khrushchev says:

Many low-quality goods are still being produced by the enterprises of the sovnarkhozes, manufacturing cooperatives and local councils. . . .

There is no justification for the fact that the enterprises of local councils of industry have stopped producing such essential consumer goods as hardware, spades, pig-iron utensils, castings, and wearing apparel. . . .

We cannot but be troubled by the fact that often dwellings are put into use before they have been completed, and while they still have numerous defects. Some builders forget that they build for the people. . . . There are numerous cases of houses without sewers, water facilities, or even electric lights.

Some trading organizations have caused shortages in the supply of the most essential goods to some towns and workers' settlements, especially supplies of vegetables, potatoes, and fruit. Supplies of agricultural produce could have been improved considerably had there been proper organization of delivery, processing, and storage. Trading enterprises have little refrigeration equipment. The supply of goods and foodstuffs to kolkhoz markets is still disorganized in our republic. All sorts of second-hand dealers and speculators take advantage of this. . . .

Production of all-year supplies of fresh tomatoes, cucumbers, and greenstuffs is not organized. The growth of catering facilities in our republic is insufficient. In Tashkent, for example, at Cholanzar and at other mass housing sites, into which many families have already moved, there is not one canteen, not one snack bar, although the attention of the administrative workers of the city has been drawn to this

431

situation more than once. Labor-consuming processes are not mechanized sufficiently at public catering enterprises. Little care is given to improving the taste of food or providing greater variety . . .

The planned development of all branches of the national economy enables us to see the broad prospects of the development of our country. Some people are wont to assess the standard of life in this or that country by the scale of production of motor cars. They take the statistics of production of motor cars in our country, in the United States, or some other country and compare these figures.

But it is precisely in this that we do not intend to compete with America, because we consider that human energy is spent none too wisely on the production of automobiles there. We fully satisfy the requirements in cars. In the future our automobile production will develop in this way: We shall increase the output of cars, establishing a wide network of car rental garages. I cannot tell you at present whether these garages will be owned by the state or the unions, or whether they will belong to other public organizations. But the system will be as follows: When anyone needs a car he will go to a garage, rent a car and go wherever he wants. He will use the car as he needs it. After using the car he will return it to the garage and will have no further care.

With such a system we shall need approximately ten to fifteen times fewer cars than if we tried to provide everyone with a car of his own. We shall better satisfy people's demand for cars. People are not tramps; they work, and when people work, the car stands idle. But even when idle, the car grows old. Therefore, we consider that it is irrational to have too many cars. A proprietary, capitalist way of using cars does not suit us. We shall introduce the socialist method in the service of the populace.[85]

The *Wall Street Journal* of September 2, 1960, quotes Joseph Stalin, *circa* 1930: "When we put the Soviet Union on an automobile and the muzhik [peasant] on a tractor, then let the worthy capitalists, who boast so loudly of their 'civilization,' try to overtake us."

But Khrushchev, still working on meat, butter, and milk, notes:

We will turn out a lot of cars, but not now. We want to establish a system for the use of automobiles that will differ from the one in capitalist countries, where people reason on the principle: "The car may be lousy but it's my own." We will make more rational use of automobiles than the Americans do. We will develop public taxi pools on an even broader scale; people will get cars from them for necessary trips. Why should a man have to worry about where to park his car, why should he have to bother with it?[86]

Our growth should not be measured by the number of cars. We are not as yet seeking to compete in this respect as we do not consider the number of cars to be the main indication of the growth of well-being of the people. So the increase in the number of cars on the streets of Moscow is not, in our opinion, most characteristic of the growth of our economy, of our development.[87]

"The principle of 'a car for anyone who can afford it' is inappropriate for a country trying to build socialism. . . . Why? Because the incomes of workers in the socialist sector are fixed and have been fixed at a level which at present does not allow them to buy motorcars. If the system of 'a car for everyone who can afford it' were valid, it would mean that only people who draw their incomes from the private sector, or even from illegal sources, could buy cars. The same applies to houses, furs—in fact, to everything which the family budget of even a better-placed employee cannot include." [88]

Production of many important foodstuffs and manufactured goods still lags behind the growing demand in the country. Some towns and communities are still not receiving a sufficient supply of such foodstuffs as meat, milk, butter and fruit,

433

for example, and in some instances even the supply of potatoes and vegetables is irregular.[89]

An Ashkhabad radio broadcast reports:

"It is mainly the enterprises producing foodstuffs and consumer goods which fail to fulfill the plan." [90]

And one in Tashkent is heard:

"It is hoped that in the next few years supplies of good drinking water will be brought to collective farms. Electrification is still lagging in villages. . . . In many towns and rayons [districts] the sale of milk, vegetables, potatoes, and fruit is still very inadequate. . . .

"At present the organization of public catering is extremely poor. . . . Serious shortcomings still exist in communications services in the countryside. There are often long delays in the delivery of letters. One cannot buy any stationery or postage stamps from the postman at remote places. . . .

"There are still shortcomings in medical services in the countryside which must be eliminated; there are not enough nursing homes and institutions for preschool children at collective farms. . . .

"A popular campaign must be organized for better hygiene, for a healthy way of life, for clean homes. More health resorts must be set up, red tape and bureaucracy must be combated firmly in the work of welfare organs. . . .

"Very few lecturers visit villages. There are not enough films dubbed in Uzbek and Kara-Kalpak languages. In Fergana, Andizhan, and Surkhan Darin oblasts the number of village libraries and clubs has decreased. Book trade in villages is absolutely unsatisfactory. Uzbekistan is still lagging in radiofication, especially in rural areas. Many collective-farm radio centers do not function well, and there is no proper control over them. . . . Many broadcasts are poor in content and cannot win popularity." [91]

Chemistry now enables us to produce many high-quality, inexpensive goods. You have probably all noticed that people have begun to dress better now, although not yet as well as one would wish. Our clothes are still rather dull.[92]

The Propaganda Front (II)

During the past few years, production of consumer goods has considerably increased. The production of textiles, clothing and other goods has increased. The people are becoming better fed and clad but it is necessary to admit in this respect that there are certain difficulties which it is necessary to overcome. We are facing an important task; to increase production of footwear, textiles, clothing and other consumer goods in order, in the coming five to seven years, to insure the need of the Soviet people for these goods.[93]

Using synthetic resins and plastics, we can produce a large quantity of various good quality consumer goods. At the same time, their quality will be higher than that of goods made of natural raw materials and will be less expensive. Consequently, the population will be able to buy these goods at lower prices.[94]

We also know that our production of a number of consumer goods items still lags, both in quantity and—especially—in quality. The production costs and prices of many of these goods are still high. A great deal of work has to be done for the further improvement of production and its specialization, integrated mechanization and automation, raising work standards in order to achieve a substantial rise in labor productivity, and—on this basis—a further rise in wages.[95]

Challenging the United States to competition to produce more meat, butter, clothes, and footwear, to build more good housing, to manufacture more television and radio sets, vacuum cleaners, and other goods and articles necessary to man, the Soviet people are confident in their victory.[96]

COMPARATIVE PRODUCTION

	USSR	USA
Automobiles (1959)	.12 million	4.26 million
Washing Machines (1959)	.54 million	47.10 million
(1965 goal)	16 million	
Refrigerators (1959)	.36 million	50 million
(1965 goal)	10 million	

435

And Khrushchev promises better quality:

In the coming years the production of consumer goods will increase considerably. It is necessary to improve in every possible way the quality of these goods, to manufacture high-quality goods and attractive clothing and footwear. Our people not only want to have all the prime necessities of life, they also want to wear attractive and good-quality clothes. Has our industry done everything to meet these demands? No, far from it.[97]

"It is sometimes impossible to obtain a new book or to subscribe to a children's magazine." [98]

"Moscow's spokesmen always bridle at any suggestion that economic discontent is a factor in Kremlin policy. They point to the statistics to show that consumer well-being is at an all-time high, with real wages, production and housing construction growing steadily. Premier Khrushchev's speech appeared to argue at one point that the shortages plaguing consumers were mainly of such secondary commodities as pianos.

"The skeptics reply that Soviet consumers cannot eat, drink or wear statistics. Some of these observers, who have been in the Soviet Union recently, report that early in March no fresh milk could be bought in Moscow even though the statistics show milk production now rivaling that of the United States." [99]

This basic difference between the two systems is made clear by a definition of the capitalistic system presented by John Chamberlain in his book *The Roots of Capitalism:*

"The test of an economic system lies in the choice it offers, the alternatives that are open to the people living under it. When the choices are limited by coercion of one sort or another, the system must fall short of meeting the test in greater or less degree. The virtue of a free system—i.e., competitive capitalism—is that it allows energy to flow uncoerced into a thousand and one different forms, expanding goods, services, and jobs in myriad, unpredictable ways. Every day, under such a system, a consumer's

436

*plebiscite (the phrase is von Mise's) is held, the vote being counted
in whatever money unit is the handiest. With his votes the consumer directs production, forcing or luring energy, brains, and
capital to obey."* [100]

What problem worries people living in towns most at
present? It is the housing problem. The party and the
government have outlined a great house-building program
which is being successfully carried out. One must admit
that at many villages the housing situation among collective
farmers is also far from brilliant. Some collective farms
which have opportunities for it do not yet build sufficient
numbers of cultural and other premises and dwellings for
collective farmers. The life of collective farmers must be
organized in a more civilized way.[101]

COMPARATIVE HOUSING STATISTICS [102]

U.S.—1957	370 sq. ft. per person	1480 sq. ft. for 4
USSR—1961 "new homes"		162 sq. ft. for 4
	(1 kitchen and 1 bath for each 3 families; cement walls)	
1965 goal	129 sq. ft. per person	516 sq. ft. for 4

You, I take it, are aware of the recent decision of the
Party and the Government to satisfy the housing needs in the
next ten or twelve years. We aim at providing a flat for every
family—a flat, not just a room. I cannot say how good all
the flats will be. It may be that not all of them will have
the conveniences that would fully satisfy all the people. For
this a longer period, of course, is needed. But at any rate we
shall abolish the housing shortage and create normal conditions with regard to urban and rural housing. Possibly in
the countryside this will be accomplished much earlier.[103]

A recent visitor describes a typical Russian flat:
*"The 'apartment' consisted of one room, about fifteen by thirty
feet. Two iron beds were crammed on one side; another bed, an
unpainted wooden table, and a chest of drawers jammed the
other. One corner, enclosed by a curtain, served as a closet and*

437

dressing room. Near the top of one wall, a solitary window framed a bleak view.

" 'My mother, father, and I moved in twenty-five years ago, when I was a child,' said Ivan, 'and we're here still.'

" 'What about baths?' I asked.

" 'We go to the public bath down the street.' " [104]

Although well aware of the local housing situation, Khrushchev, in his famed "kitchen debate" with Richard Nixon at the House Exhibit in the 1959 Soviet Exhibition, in Moscow, says with a straight face:

You think the Russian people will be dumfounded to see this? But I tell you all our modern homes have equipment of this sort, and to get a flat you have only to be a Soviet visitor, not a citizen.[105]

"Our editorial office has been receiving a lot of justified complaints from our working people about the poor repair of housing. Here, for instance, is what the working people living at No. 6 Barykadna Street in Dnepropetrovsk write in this regard: 'Not long ago the roof of our house was repaired, but after the first rain fell the ceiling became wet and stucco in various places deteriorated. This is because they are repairing our roof with rags and tar, which they have been doing every year for seven consecutive years.' " [106]

. . . additional housing whose total floor space will exceed one-quarter of all the housing available in our capital before the Revolution. In the current seven-year period we will build about 15 million apartments in towns and 7 million houses in the countryside. That is roughly equivalent to some 50 new towns as large as San Francisco. An important point is that our country has the world's lowest rent—a mere 4 or 5 per cent of the family budget.

We are seeing to it that there are more comfortable homes and that Soviet people get more and better consumer goods. And we are as good as our word. In the last six years

438

Soviet agriculture has trebled meat sales to the urban population, and more than doubled those of milk.[107]

"The results of housing construction are very alarming. The annual plan for commissioning housing has been fulfilled only to the extent of 23.3 per cent. . . . Capital construction and the commissioning of production capacities are progressing slowly in the light and food products industries. . . . Construction of cultural and public-service buildings, medical and children's establishments, and water-supply and sewerage systems is also progressing unsatisfactorily. An acute shortage of construction materials is felt in many economic regions of the republic. . . . The low quality of construction, the poor use of technical equipment, and serious shortcomings in the organization of work at construction projects are linked with the low level of construction management." [108]

Russians could see an American house at the 1959 exhibition. Tass reported:

"All New York papers today publish photographs and articles enthusiastically describing the 'typical house' of the 'typical American working man and his family,' which will be shown at the American exhibition in Moscow this summer. In fact, however, such a house can be described as much typical of American workers as, say, the Taj Mahal is typical of Bombay textile workers or Buckingham Palace British miners. This allegedly typical house [costing $13,000] is meant to show the Soviet people how American workers live." [109]

The Facts:

Average construction cost of a one-family house	$13,025
Average family personal income	6,130
Average down payment on a house with a V.A.-guaranteed mortgage	1,050

U.S. *Statistical Abstract,* 1958

Visit our country and see how we build. I have visited several French cities and seen your construction, I have invited your mayors to come to the Soviet Union. Let them come and see how we do our building. I think they will see much of interest to them. We are using more industrial methods, and we shall willingly share our experience with you.[110]

"In Stalinsk in 1959 over 70 per cent of dwelling houses were accepted as only satisfactory, and even the satisfactory evaluation was accorded, in many cases, with difficulty. This is shown convincingly by the fact that in many houses given this evaluation the sanitary and technical installations were lacking. Similar shortcomings were revealed in Krivoy Rog, Kostroma, Tula Kazan, and some other towns." [111]

The capitalists are worse off, says Khrushchev:

Let us take so vital a matter as housing. Housing is one of the most acute social problems of mankind. In the United States, for example, as stated in the *Democratic Facts Book* issued by the National Committee of the Democratic Party, 15 million people live in slums, 13 million dwellings (one-quarter of the total) do not conform to standard, and 7 million urban dwellings are so dilapidated as to be unfit for human habitation. The shortage of housing, the high rents which swallow up 25 to 30 per cent of the family budget, are a constant curse to the working people in the capitalist world.[112]

We know that we have an acute shortage of housing. We do not want to be content to make comparisons with the past or with the wealthy capitalist countries where millions of houseless people have no shelter and where tens of millions live in slums.[113]

"The inevitable hallmark of the big towns of bourgeois countries are the slums, the so-called working-class districts on the outskirts of the town which represent a heap of dark, damp, in the majority of cases, cellar-dwellings, in a semi-dilapidated condition, where usually the poor live and curse their fate. The revolution in the USSR has swept away the slums. . . . Their place is taken by well-built and bright workers' houses and in many cases the working-class districts of our towns are better built than the central districts."—Stalin.[114]

And Khrushchev continues to describe the burdens of the working people of the United States, quoting George Meany, president of the AFL-CIO:

Do you know, he [George Meany] said, that according to the last survey, in December 1956 13 million families were living in houses not conforming to the accepted standards. Thirteen million families! And the census showed that these figures had remained practically unchanged since 1950.

"We are short of many thousands of classrooms," Meany said. "Many children of our trade-union members today study in buildings which are not much better than mere chicken coops, in old, neglected buildings with a big fire risk . . . and then people wonder why we do not have enough scientists, engineers, and technicians to equal the Soviet Union.

"We must get America back to work . . ." George Meany exclaims. This is the only possible answer to the economic crisis that is confronting our country today.[115]

But he fails to mention that these standards are not met by 95 per cent of Soviet houses.

"All is quiet at 9 Asula Street, Tallinn, which is the construction site of an apartment house belonging to the Tallinn Plywood and Furniture Factory. Under the roof of the old fashioned two-storied building all has been quiet for a month already. These massive walls and narrow window openings make a closed-in impression, as do all other houses in Asula Street.

"We enter. Somewhere under the floor there is a sound. Who is there? Future tenant Karl Hurden looks out through a hole in the floor and announces he is building a cellar for himself, grumbling that the foundation walls ought to have been higher—you cannot burrow the cellar into the ground, because of water.

"Only desultory work is done at the house. The factory trade-union committee has repeatedly broached the problem of building materials with the management, but the reaction has been slack. Plastering is delayed because the installation of central heating, water pipes, drains, electric cables, etc., is delayed. It is only a couple of days ago that doors and windows were ordered from the Kose Rayon industrial combine, therefore the proper finishing coat of the front is bound to be delayed.

"The collective contract provides for the turning over for use of the apartment house by the forty-first anniversary of the October Revolution. At the present pace of work this item of the bargain will obviously remain unfulfilled." [116]

The Seven-Year Plan has many advantages: the period is long enough so that any projection can be made; the end totals are sufficiently sizable to offer major incentive; the time elapsing is sufficient to provide alibis for failure.

The free workers of this free socialist society are capable of accomplishing wonders and blazing a trail to the bright future of mankind, communism.[117]

Our economic plans are being successfully fulfilled year after year. Compared with 1913, gross industrial output has grown 36-fold; output of means of production has increased 83-fold and of the engineering and metal-working industries 240-fold.[118]

Promised by 1965: 62 per cent more consumer goods, including 50 per cent more fabrics and clothing, twice as many household appliances (of which washing machines will increase 900 per cent, refrigerators 600 per cent), and improvements in quality.[119]

Forecasts are based on promises:

We already have the first promising signs. For example, the collective and state farms of Ryazan Region have pledged that already this year they will produce 3.8 times more meat than in 1958, while Stavropol Territory and Rostov Region committed themselves to step up meat output 2.5 and 2 times respectively. Throughout Moscow Region the commitment for 1959 is to increase meat output to 70 centners (hundredweights) per 100 hectares of farmland and sell the state twice as much meat as in 1958. Krasnodar Territory undertook to produce 84 centners of meat per 100 hectares of farmland this year and to increase the output of meat in the collective and state farms by more than 150 per cent.[120]

But at the end of 1959 a Moscow broadcast announced:

"As is known, livestock breeding has been one of the lagging branches of agriculture for a long time. . . . There are many kolkhozes and sovkhozes which produce small quantities of animal products per 100 hectares. Furthermore, on kolkhozes and sovkhozes in the Turkmenian, Kirghiz, Azerbaijan, and Tadshik SSR's in 10 months of this year milk yields per cow have decreased as compared with the corresponding period of last year." [121]

In announcing the goals of the new Seven-Year Plan (1959-65), it has been admitted that there is no chance of catching up with the United States in meat production by 1965. The meat-production goal for 1965 has been set at 16 million tons, substantially less than the 22 million tons required for the 1956 population of 200 million. And the 1961 special Central Committee meeting revealed an agricultural failure of prime magnitude.[122]

It is planned that in 1965 gross industrial output should be about 80 per cent greater than in 1958. In group "A" [output of means of production] there is to be an increase of 85–88 per cent, and in group "B" [output of consumer goods], 62–65 per cent. This is a very big increase. The growth of the volume of industrial output in the next seven years will be equal to the increase in output achieved in the past twenty years.[123]

The figures indicate, incidentally, that 26 per cent of the total production increase is to be devoted to consumer goods. This approximates the current ratio.

Khrushchev promises a brighter future, however. His thesis on the Seven-Year Plan, 1959–1965, predicts:

The Seven-Year Plan is a concrete proposal made by the Soviet Union to the capitalist world to compete on peaceful economic grounds, because the Soviet Union opposes competing in the arms race, which is being carried out by imperialist circles of Western powers. One cannot scare the Soviet people with saber rattling. The selfless labor of workers, collective farmers, scientists, and the fighting efficiency of the Soviet Army and the strengthening of the might of the whole of the socialist camp is the guarantee that imperialist plans to violate peace will be brought to naught.[124]

And:

Our Seven-Year Plan envisages a considerable rise in the living standards of the Soviet people. The working people of the Soviet Union will have in 1965 the world's shortest workday and the shortest work week concurrently with a considerable increase in their real incomes. Of apartments alone, we intend to build about 15 million which equals approximately the living area of seventy-five such big cities as Leipzig.[125]

The national income will increase by 62–65 per cent in 1965 as compared to 1958. With its growth a further increase in public consumption will be effected. It will increase by 60–63 per cent in the next seven years. The real incomes of factory and office workers in the next seven years, per working person, will increase on the average by 40 per cent as a result of the increase in wages, pensions, and grants as well as further price reduction in public catering. The real incomes of collective farmers, too, on the basis of the growth of agricultural production and higher laborer productivity, will increase for the same period by not less than 40 per cent, mostly due to the expansion of the common output of the collective farmers.[126]

We have now worked out and begun a titanic Seven-Year Plan of economic development. I shall name just one figure to give you an idea of its scale; our capital investments alone will amount to approximately $75,000 million in these seven years. Fulfillment of this plan will bring us close to the level of the economic development in the United States.[127]

A 40 per cent rise in real income would bring living standards to roughly 35 per cent of the 1960 United States levels.

Huge funds are allocated to build houses, cultural institutions and establishments providing general amenities. From 375,000 million to 380,000 million rubles of state funds alone will be invested in housing and public building as against 214,000 million rubles in the preceding seven years; more than 80,000 million rubles will be for building schools, hospitals and other cultural and medical establishments as against 46,000 million rubles. Large funds will be invested in the building of boarding-schools and child-welfare establishments.[128]

The drive for utmost thrift is of special importance in our country, where intramural accumulation at the various enterprises is the main source of extended socialist reproduction. The Party has always emphasized the need to operate the economy in the most rational manner. Today, when a 1 per cent reduction in production expenses stands for the colossal figure exceeding 12,000 million rubles—and at the end of the seven-year period it is going to be 21,000 million rubles annually*—the effort to cut production costs, to be thrifty in everything, is of greatest importance.[129]

It should be taken into account that the people's needs as regards the means of existence are not unlimited. Man cannot, for instance, consume more bread or other food than his body requires. There are also certain limits of clothing and housing. Of course, when we speak of satisfying the needs of the people, we have in mind not the whims and desires for luxuries.[130]

---

* Indicating a gross national product of 1,200 billion rubles in 1958, 2,100 billion anticipated in 1965. At 10 rubles to the dollar; respectively 120 billion and 210 billion, versus U.S. 1960 gross national product of 503 billion, and anticipated 1965 gross national product of 740–800 billion.

The enigma of Soviet statistics was briefly unraveled, at least in part, by Alec Nove and Alfred Zauberman and detailed in an article in Soviet Studies in October 1959. They wrote:

"For many years Western students have tried—with considerable effort and ingenuity—to find out the Soviet Union's own valuation of her income and product in current rubles. A precise answer has now been provided by a Soviet source giving at last—for the first time in more than a quarter of a century—a current-price national-income magnitude. Considering the status of the source, it may be taken to carry the imprint of authority.

". . . the aggregate . . . is indicated in a note by G. Polyak published in the May 1959 issue of Vestnik statisiki. It deals with the budget/national income correlation . . . and states that in 1957 budgetary expenditure, when corrected for some specified duplications, equaled 56 per cent of national income. Since budget figures are known, the simplest arithmetic yields the national income of 1100 millard (thousand million) rubles."

NATIONAL INCOME—SOVIET UNION, 1957 [131]
(In billion rubles, rounded)

Accumulation Fund

Investment in national economy, within State Plan		211.
Addition to circulating funds and investment, collective farms		41.
Accumulation in productive and nonproductive funds	61.	
Less net depreciation	35.	26.
		278.

Consumption Fund

Population consumption	781.	
Institution consumption	41.	
		822.

1100.[132]

446

Actual material consumption for this year was computed at 731 billion rubles, plus 50 billion rubles for nonmaterial, remunerated services—roughly 36 per cent of the gross national product. Of this sum, 277 billion rubles (about 12½ per cent of the gross national product) was returned to the government through the turnover tax.

Based on recent performance, these seem realistic projections. But many of the pronouncements made by Mr. Khrushchev regarding the Soviet Union and the United States are unrealistic and seem designed purely for internal consumption and for propaganda purposes in the underdeveloped countries. Discussing the growth rates in the present plan, he said these

. . . will enable our country in the course of approximately five years after 1965 to catch up with and to surpass the per capita output level in the United States. So by that time, and possibly even earlier, the Soviet Union will gain first place in the world both as regards the absolute output and the output of goods per capita, which will insure for the population the highest living standard in the world. That will be the world historic victory of socialism in its peaceful competition with capitalism.[133]

"If the estimates in this report are reasonably accurate, the projected 1970 Soviet gross national product will even fall short of the 1957 gross national output of the United States, and far short of expected 1970 output [$400 billion for the USSR as against $740 billion for the United States]. In the industrial sector, however, the gap will be considerably narrowed. Assuming the Soviets maintain an industrial growth rate of 9 per cent per year, their 1970 output will approximate the 1957 United States industrial production. If the United States maintains an industrial growth rate of about 4 per cent per year, Soviet industrial production in 1970 will equal some 60 per cent of U.S. industrial production for that year, compared to 40 per cent in 1957. However, if we exclude consumer goods such as automobiles, refrigerators, washing machines, TV, and so forth, they will probably have exceeded the United States by that date.

447

"Contrary to Mr. Khrushchev's prediction, the CEIR [Corporation for Economic and Industrial Research] 1970 projection for per capita gross national product shows $3,600 for the United States and only $1,600 for the USSR. Moreover, the latter will be well below the projected West European per capita output of $2,100. The world-historic victory Mr. Khrushchev anticipates lies, if at all, in the more distant future. The Soviet people can expect relatively little amelioration of their standard of living, given the uses made of their gross national product by the USSR." [134]

SUMMARY DATA ON THE CEIR PROJECTIONS FOR THE USSR:

	USSR 1957	USSR 1970	U.S. 1960
Gross national product ..	$175 billion	$400 billion	$505 billion
Population	204 million	254 million	182 million
Labor force	89 million	109 million	67 million
Per capita gross national product	$858	$1,570	$2,800

But a plan is not always fulfilled:

In February 1956 the Twentieth Congress of the Communist Party adopted directives for an ambitious sixth Five-Year Plan for 1956–1960. Within a year, it was apparent that the plan was not workable. A secret report by an investigating commission led by N. K. Baibakov, and the head of the Committee for Current Economic Planning, M. Z. Saburov, indicated that materials and supplies would not be available to meet the plan. Targets for 1957 were lowered. Then in April 1957 the 260-billion-ruble internal debt was deferred for twenty years with interest payments frozen. At this point Khrushchev submitted a new decentralized management-organization plan, substituting regional centralization for national centralization.

It is naturally very difficult to manage an industry on a nation-wide scale from one center, from a ministry in Moscow. A minister had to be greater than God because he had to know everything and see everything that is done for example in Sakhalin, Kamchatka, Baku, or Armenia. That is im-

448

possible. Now we have transferred the solution of these problems of operating plants to the localities and this has been all to the good.[135]

Now the management of enterprises and construction sites is concentrated in the economic areas and is carried on by the economic councils set up in those areas. The combination of centralized planning with democratic methods of management is the key to more efficient use of the advantages of the socialist system of economy.[136]

The Five-Year Plan presented to the Twentieth Congress in 1956 was essentially a Khrushchev plan, opposed by the "anti-party" group, and served to purge the Malenkov, Molotov, Kaganovitch, Shepilov group. It was simply too ambitious. Even after being scaled down in 1957, it showed many bottlenecks that disorganized and slowed the entire economy. Preparation of a new plan was begun in September 1957 with the rationalization that new resource discoveries and technological developments required reshuffling. At the same time, management was decentralized and reshuffled.

Although the new plan was given an extra coat of propaganda, it actually toned down growth rates, but covered them up with a longer-term plan and a five-year "perspective plan."

The new 1965 goal for meat was set at one-third the quota originally proposed for 1957, the goal for milk less than the one set for 1960. The ultimate aim was first place in per capita production by 1972. Khrushchev took personal responsibility for the plan.

Khrushchev chooses to ignore this record of recent years:

The successful carrying out of the Five-Year Plans by the Soviet Union has demonstrated to the entire world the advantages of the socialist system of economy over the capitalist system. It has helped to change the balance of forces between capitalism and socialism on the world scale to the advantage of socialism. Of the greatest international significance are the national-economy plans carried out in our times in the Soviet Union, the CPR, and in all the countries of the socialist camp. The realization of the Seven-Year Plan of the develop-

449

ment of national economy for 1959 to 1965 will be another important stage in the peaceful economic competition of the two systems—socialist and capitalist.[137]

But:

In drafting the Seven-Year Plan, we proceeded from the necessity for gaining time in the peaceful economic competition with the capitalist countries, and we envisage a maximum acceleration of the development of the economy, particularly of the decisive branches of production which are conducive of the further upsurge of the entire national economy.[138]

The chief obvious weakness in the Seven-Year Plan is the labor factor. To come even close to achieving his goals, Khrushchev must draft 12 million additional workers into his industrial labor force.

The increase in the working-age population is expected to supply 5.6 million. The years ahead will reflect the low wartime birth rate. Recent additions have run around 2 million, but in 1959, only 1.3 million youth joined the labor force. By cutting back two years of schooling, 2 million 15- and 16-year-olds will enter the labor market.

Although farms are expected to increase production by 70 per cent, 5 million farmers are expected to go into factories.

The army, non-working women, school yards, and street corners are expected to make up the difference.

The problem is complicated by the promise to reduce the work week from 46 to 41 hours in 1960, to 40 hours by 1962, and to 35 hours by 1964. But these promises have been made before and are not taken too seriously by Soviet workers.

If the plan is operational and the labor force is increased 21 per cent during the seven-year period, labor productivity will still have to increase by 50 per cent to meet the output goal. For this, the planners count on greater automation and mechanization.

At the present time we are developing at forced pace our chemical industry, which will enable us to produce more mineral fertilizers and insecticides, the broad application of which will make it possible to increase greatly the harvest

450

yields of agricultural crops, to increase the output per person employed in agriculture.

This we regard as a great reserve of ours. There also are some other big reserves we have for the further improvement of agriculture production.[139]

There can be no doubt that our workers, collective farmers, and intellectuals, who are working for themselves, for their society, will display the creative energy and initiative needed to exceed the productivity levels of the American worker and farmers who live in an exploiter society.[140]

Now when the socialist sector has become the principal source of the country's supply of all products, when our people are solving the historic task of the transition to communism, the problems of raising labor productivity are coming to the fore—and this not only in industry but also in agriculture. The reduction of labor expenditure per unit of production acquires first-grade importance at the present stage of communist construction.[141]

Soviet labor productivity is scheduled to increase 45 to 50 per cent over the seven-year period.[142] *But according to Soviet Academician Stanislav Strumilin, to achieve its goals in seven years, an 80 per cent increase in labor productivity would be required.*[143]

Soviet labor productivity is lowest in the field of agriculture, and here lies its greatest reservoir of manpower.

COMPARISON OF LABOR PRODUCTIVITY IN SOVIET COLLECTIVE AND STATE FARMS WITH AMERICAN FARMS[144]
(Unit—U.S. Labor Input = 1)

Commodity	In Collectives	In State Farms
Grain	7.3	1.8
Potatoes	5.1	4.2
Sugarbeets	6.2	4.2
Cotton (irrigated in USSR)	2.3	1.6
Milk	3.1	2.1
Beef	14.2	6.6
Pork	16.3	6.8

But by its very nature, socialism cannot provide the variety of products, the multitude of choices, the satisfactions of ownership, and the consequent do-it-yourself motivation that adds so much to American life. Khrushchev aims for an economy of bare necessities adapted from the American scene—meat, butter, milk, "a flat" for each family. His public services are designed to provide medical aid to keep workers healthy and nurseries to free mothers for labor. The $7 billion[145] the United States spends on roads is not needed in an economy that makes 124,000 motor vehicles a year.

Thus, even in its wildest flights of imagination the Soviet Union could not hope to reach the American standard of living in this century.

Beyond the production figures is another factor, which Khrushchev chooses to ignore. More than 58 per cent of American nonfarm families (and an even larger percentage of farm families) own their own homes, 59 per cent own cars, 98 per cent have refrigerators, 89 per cent have television sets, 21 per cent have freezers, 71 per cent have vacuum cleaners, 91 per cent have electric washers, 16 per cent have electric or gas dryers, 12 per cent have air conditioners.[146] Most American women can and do stay home to produce care and comfort for their families. All this creates a standard of life and comfort that statistics cannot measure.

For the Soviet worker the cry for more production has been backed by carrot and by whip for forty years, by Lenin, by Stalin, by Khrushchev.

The promises continue, and in small measure, rewards are given and taken away. But there is no real secret about the ultimate goal: greater Soviet power.

The Battle of Growth

"No single item of Soviet propaganda has been so vital—and so widely believed—as their claim to a high growth rate which must inevitably lead to their surpassing the United States in industrial output and standard of living. The Communist Party is attempting to project to the world an image of an ardent, energetic, and tech-

nically competent competitor closing fast on—and preparing to
supersede—a front runner who has lost the capacity to deal with
his problems and prefers to go down in the style to which he has
become accustomed rather than to maintain his position." [147]

Ignoring the fact that the Soviet Union produces only 21 per cent
of the world's total industrial product, Khrushchev announces:

Of decisive importance is the fact that the speed of development of the socialist economy is significantly higher than
the speed of development of the capitalist economy. It is
hardly a year ago that we found that the countries of the socialist world system—comprising 25 per cent of the earth's
population—are responsible for about one-third of the world's
industrial production. Since that time the economy of the socialist countries has made uninterrupted progress, while the
economy of the capitalist countries, as a result of the crisis in
the heartland of capitalism, the United States, is shaken by
fever, as it were.[148]

Despite the "cold war" policy, our country's development
has always been much higher than in capitalist countries.
This is convincingly shown by facts. The time is not far off
when we shall outstrip the most advanced capitalist states
and leave them behind in per capita output. Everything now
adds up to this: When this is achieved the indisputable superiority of the socialist system will be even more obvious.[149]

It is well known that pre-Revolutionary Russia's total industrial output was one-eighth, and in per capita terms from onefourteenth to one-thirteenth of the United States amount. In
1958 we were producing roughly half of the amount of industrial products turned out by the United States, or slightly
less than one-half in terms of per capita output. In other
words, our country has reduced its lag in comparison with
the United States four times in the volume of output and
more than six times in per capita production.[150]

*"There is also another sense in which Soviet economic growth, as
an end in itself, can affect the power balance on the current inter-*

national scene. The Soviet leaders have made an international symbol out of their ambition to catch up with America in per capita production by 1970. The impact of this symbol could be quite powerful. Not even Khrushchev expects seriously to achieve such parity of output in any meaningful sense by 1970. He could hardly be that unrealistic. But the exact timing of the 'triumph' may be of no consequence, so long as the relative trends continue in the Soviet favor. It is not the sudden tipping of the scales, but the steady and progressive diminution of the United States lead that would tend to be most demoralizing to the West and that would give an immense boost to Soviet prestige." [151]

After the fulfillment of the Seven-Year Plan [in 1965] it will take us some five years, or possibly even less, to surpass the United States not only for total volume of production but also per capita output.[152]

The dates vary, but the theme remains the same:

In 1965 the absolute output of some of the most important types of goods in the Soviet Union will surpass, and the output of other types of goods will approach, the present level of industrial output in the United States. By that time, the per capita output of the most important products of agriculture as a whole will surpass the present standard of the United States.[153]

In the course of the next fifteen years the USSR will take first place in the world not only in the general volume of production but also in the output of products per capita. In our country there will be created a material-technical base of communism which at the same time will signify the great victory of the Soviet Union in the peaceful economic competition against the more developed capitalist countries.[154]

"Such rapid Soviet economic progress would exercise fascination and appeal in the vast parts of the world where speedy economic development has become virtually a prerequisite to political survival. The spectacle of a Soviet economy successfully pursuing

454

rapid economic growth with a sense of utmost urgency is bound to hold strong attractions for the less-developed countries and would lend conviction to the Soviet claim that, in the age of industrialism, its own style of planned economy is superior to the market economy of the West and that its example constitutes a relevant model of economic development for all of the underdeveloped world." [155]

We do not have a paradise—nor communism in our country—as yet. But we do have a mighty economic upsurge, and the Soviet people are forging ahead with confidence on their way to communism, and we can assure you that we are overtaking you and we shall surpass you in economic development. This is quite logical. When the French people made their bourgeois revolution, while we still lived under feudalism, you moved ahead of our country. In 1917 our people carried through a socialist revolution, while you went on living under capitalism. In the years of Soviet rule our country has made a giant stride in its development. And the day is not far off when we shall have passed the most developed capitalist countries in the volume of production.[156]

The world socialist system has the advantage of superior rates of economic growth. The annual industrial-production increase for the entire socialist camp has in the past five years [1954–1958] averaged 11 per cent, whereas in the capitalist world it was under 3 per cent.

In the world socialist system all countries unite and coordinate their productive efforts, whereas irreconcilable antagonisms dominate relations between the capitalist countries. Coordination of national economic plans is the form in which the productive efforts of the socialist countries are pooled in the current stage. International division of labor, particularly its highest forms—specialization and cooperation—are to play a big part in the economic development of the socialist camp. This offers new additional opportunities of expanding production in the socialist camp, and in each individual socialist country. By itself no country could develop at the rapid pace

455

at which it develops within the system of socialist countries.[157]

Socialism exerts a tremendous, continuously growing influence on the course of world history, changing the face of the earth. Reality bears out the great Marxist truth which says that socialism makes rapid social progress possible. What can modern capitalism counter to that? Between 1937 and 1956, a period in which the socialist countries increased their production more than fourfold, the capitalist world could do no more than double its production despite all the measures to "prime" the economic situation, including a reckless arms race.[158]

And Khrushchev can cite capitalist publications to bolster his arguments.

Many bourgeois politicians are frankly saying that they are frightened by the rate of growth of Soviet industry, frightened by the influence of the Soviet example to the workers of the world. And you and I know very well how convincing our example is to the minds of the workers of all countries.[159]

Our socialist homeland is making a powerful new advance. The Soviet Union's successes in peaceful construction are inspiring cheer and confidence in the hearts of our friends and fierce anger and hatred in our enemies. The imperialists are starting to figure out what year the Soviet Union's economic level of development and per capita production in our country will surpass the highest indexes of the most advanced capitalist countries. They no longer doubt that it will happen. And the prospect frightens them.[160]

The *Des Moines Register* warns Western leaders to take the Seven-Year Plan seriously, because the USSR has "proved its capacity for making great economic advances—faster than those of the United States." A *New York Times* editor admits: "The Soviet Union is now breathing down our necks, economically speaking. They are only two jumps behind us —a decade or so behind us—in productive capacity." This is a sober deduction. We are well inclined to agree with it.[161]

The right-wing French *L'Aurore* writes that the Soviet Union "has set the dates when the dreams of Marxist revolutionaries will become reality. It is starting out on unprecedented ventures." *The Wall Street Journal* says that the plan may have so great an impact on some countries that they will "choose communism," and that "there is not much the United States can do about it." Well said.[162]

Some people frequently dream that socialist Russia is the same as it was before the Revolution. But let's compare the rates at which the Soviet Union has been developing since we overthrew the old, rotten system, and the rates of development in the United States during the same period. Compared with the 1913 level, output in the Soviet Union has increased 36-fold, and only fourfold in your country. Why does our economy and culture develop more rapidly than yours? [163]

The slogan of catching up with highly developed capitalist countries was not born today. As long ago as the first years of the Soviet regime, when the people were engaged in the restoration of the national economy, this idea was insistently expressed at workers' meetings and on the pages of our papers. At that time, bourgeois observers and journalists only laughed at this. The thought that we could catch up with flourishing America struck them as stupid and groundless fantasy.[164]

"Due to the Revolution, Russia in its political structure has caught up with the advanced countries in the course of a few months. But this is not enough. War is implacable; it puts the question with merciless sharpness; either perish or overtake the advanced countries and surpass them also economically . . . either full steam ahead or perish. This is how history has put the question." [165]

457

Stalin said it in 1931:

"We are fifty to a hundred years behind the advanced countries. We must make good this distance in ten years. Either we do it or they will crush us.[166]

Molotov said it in 1939:

"The time has come to take practical measures to solve the basic economic task of the USSR: to catch up with and overtake . . . economically the most developed capitalist countries of Europe and the United States of America. . . . Then and then only will the significance of the new era in the development of the USSR unfold itself, the era of transition from a socialist to a communist society." [167]

And Khrushchev said it in 1957:

In peaceful competition, it is no less important to gain victories for the socialist economy, and crush the rich ones who have waxed fat through exploitation of the working classes and regard the capitalist system as second to none. The United States of America is the embodiment of the capitalist system's strength. Here, then, is where it is important for the Soviet people to show the imperialist beasts of prey that we can beat them in economic competition.[168]

The superiority of the USSR in the speed of the growth of production will create a real basis for insuring that within a period of say, five years following 1965, the level of U.S. production per capita should be equaled and overtaken. Thus, by that time, perhaps even sooner, the USSR will have captured first place in the world both in absolute volume of production and per capita production, which will insure the world's highest standard of living. This will be the world's historic victory of socialism in peaceful competition with capitalism.[169]

Within ten to twelve years our country will take first place in the world for per capita production. The Soviet Union will become a country with the highest standards and the shortest working day in the world.[170]

458

The Propaganda Front (II)

Regarding competition with the United States, Khrushchev says:

We are competing with America, but we do not regard America as a standard of economic development. For, though it has a highly developed economy, the U.S.A. is dominated by the vice-ridden capitalist mode of production and distribution. While it has a profusion of every kind of goods, it also has millions of unemployed, and millions with inadequate incomes, who cannot satisfy even their most elementary needs. The communists do not want to imitate that order of things. On the contrary, we want to put an end to that injustice. And if America's production level is taken as a measuring rod for our own economic progress, it is only in order to compare this country with capitalism's leading power. When we win in this economic competition with the U.S.A., we shall only have completed the initial phase of communist construction. The economic level reached in this phase will not be the end of our road, but only a midway station at which we shall overtake capitalism's most developed country, leave it behind and push ahead.[171]

How does Khrushchev reach his figure on overtaking the United States? By semi-official count, the USSR figures its 1955 gross national product at 47.6 per cent of that of the United States. If their industrial output grows at the rate of 8.6 per cent per year, and that of the United States at 2 per cent, they would reach the present American industrial output in 1965, and overtake the United States current level by 1970.

In his words:

What are the immediate prospects in the economic development of the two world systems?

The time span in which the USSR will accomplish its basic economic task depends above all on the initial relation between the production levels in the USSR and the U.S.A. What can be said on that score?

The volume of Soviet industrial production is about half

of America's volume, and that of Soviet agricultural production is 20 to 25 per cent lower;

U.S. industrial output per head of population is more than double that of the USSR, and agricultural output about 40 per cent higher.

How soon can we close this gap, draw level, and then surpass the U.S.A. in these indexes?

Rates of production growth are decisive. And the advantage in rates rests with the socialist economic system. Our mean annual industrial rates of growth since the Revolution have been 3 to 5 times higher than those of the developed capitalist countries.[172]

"It now appears that the various Soviet claims are constructed on an extremely inadequate statistical base. Thus it seems from the evidence of Soviet Academician Stanislav Strumilin that the conclusion that Soviet industrial output is over half that of the United States is based on a ten-commodity sample, although, as he points out, 'no reason is given why these ten products can replace the dynamics of the level of total industrial production of the countries being compared.' There are good grounds for supposing that the gap between American and Soviet industrial production is greater than this, and for treating the claims for the future (notably 'the highest standard of living in the world') with considerable skepticism, even while not denying the fact of rapid growth rates." [173]

People in the West no longer dispute that we shall catch up with the United States in per capita output. The argument is only about the time, the period in which the Soviet Union will catch up with the United States. We say that this will happen in 1970. Some bourgeois economists say that the Soviet Union will be unable to carry out such a task in this period. Let us not waste time arguing. We are convinced that we shall successfully carry out the plans that have been mapped out.[174]

For several years Western writers accepted the Soviet growth-rate statistics with only a small discount.

Herbert Levine, of the *New Leader*, notes that on the comparative rates of industrial growth, "For example, if Soviet industry grows at an average annual rate of 9 per cent and that of the United States at 3 per cent [a very likely situation], then Soviet industrial output will equal ours in fourteen years." [175]

A. B. Aristov, chief Soviet planner, is more specific.

"The Soviet Union will catch up with and then surpass the United States no later than 1970 in the output of basic types of industrial products in total volume of production and in per capita production. By that time we shall have a higher standard of living and a higher level of technology than any capitalist country. . . ."

The Soviet Union intends to surpass the United States economically. The United States production level is the ceiling capitalist economy has been able to achieve. We all know that favorable historical and natural conditions have done their part in this. To surpass America's level is to surpass capitalism's supreme achievement.[176]

Even more convincing, Khrushchev indicates, will be the relative production of the Soviet bloc and the capitalist countries:

Comrades, an economic competition between the USSR and the U.S.A., between the entire world socialist system and the world capitalist system, is in progress on the international scene.

The state of contemporary capitalism is characterized not only by the highly developed countries, but by countries whose productive level is immeasurably lower. The level of production in the capitalist system as a whole lags far behind that of the United States. There is a big, constantly widening gap between the various capitalist countries in rates of economic growth.

At the same time, all the countries of the world socialist system are making rapid economic and cultural progress.

High rates are a general objective law of socialism, now confirmed by the experience of all the countries of the socialist camp. In 1958, industrial output in the socialist countries was five times that of 1937. Through 1950–1958 the Chinese People's Republic raised its industrial output approximately tenfold. Compared with prewar, industrial production in 1958 increased more than 450 per cent in Poland, 230 per cent in Czechoslovakia, more than 150 per cent in the German Democratic Republic, nearly 300 per cent in Rumania, over 300 per cent in Hungary, about 800 per cent in Bulgaria and 1,700 per cent in Albania. The Korean People's Democratic Republic increased industrial output 3.5-fold over 1949.[177]

According to Khrushchev's reasoning, Albania is fast catching up with the Soviet Union.

Calculations show that in 1965 the countries of socialism will produce more than half of the entire world industrial output. Thus, during that short time an absolute superiority of the world system of socialism will be secured over the capitalist system in material output, which is the decisive sphere of human life.[178]

COMPARISON OF GROSS NATIONAL PRODUCT
(in billions, 1958 dollars)[179]

	USSR	U.S.	Western Europe
1950	117-120*	352	20
1955	158*	435	36
1957	175-179*	452.5	40
1958	190*	441.7	43
1959	205*	479.5	42
1960 est.	220*	503	40
1965 est.	286	633	45
1970 est.	370	740.90	50
	400-420		

*A 1958 analysis by Soviet Academician Stanislav Strumilin, revealed in November 1960, indicated that these estimates may include considerable duplication in counting products.

The Propaganda Front (II)

China, too, is producing:

It is not the Soviet Union alone which is faced with the problem of winning as much time as possible in its economic competition with capitalism. It may be recalled, for example, that the Communist Party of China has in 1957 set the target of surpassing Britain in output of key industrial items in the next fifteen years. The mass movement to make the "big leap" which has spread in that country, shows that the Chinese people will achieve that target in a far shorter period. The Republic of Czechoslovakia intends by 1965 to raise industrial output 90 to 95 per cent over 1957 and the Polish People's Republic 80 per cent over 1958. The people of Bulgaria intend to fulfill their five-year plan in three to four years.[180]

"Soviet production is still well below that of the United States, but is increasing far more rapidly and—what should not be forgotten—far more steadily than is that of the United States. Moreover the increasing Soviet output consists to a much larger degree of goods which serve to further the national power of the Soviet Union than does the product-and-services mixture of the United States economy. As a result the standard of living of the American people is far higher than that of the Soviet people, but the efficiency of Soviet utilization of resources for power purposes is far greater than our own. Any long continuation of these trends must pose the most serious questions about the future of our society and our way of life." [181]

"The professional Soviet literature on 'catching up' with the United States suggests the objective in the next decade is to equal or surpass American production in certain key sectors related to military potential (e.g., steel) rather than to exceed American levels of gross national product or to exceed American consumption levels on the American pattern." [182]

This is far different from Khrushchev's continual boasts.

GROWTH RATES FOR INDUSTRY IN CZARIST RUSSIA, USSR, AND U.S.

Output, labor productivity, and output per capita,
selected concurrent periods
(In per cents)
Average annual growth rate

	Output		Output per unit of labor			Output per head of population	
	Russia or USSR[a]	U.S.	USSR per person engaged[b]	Per person engaged[b]	Per man-hour	Russia or USSR	U.S.
				U.S.			
1870–1913	5.3	5.1	[c]	[c]	[c]	3.7	2.9
1913–55	3.9[d]	3.7	1.2	2.2	2.2	3.3	2.4
1913–28	.1	3.7	.7	2.7	3.6	0.5	2.3
1928–55	6.1[d]	3.7	1.6	1.9	2.2	5.3	2.5
1928–40	7.4[d]	1.8	.5	1.1	2.4	5.9	1.0
1940–55	5.1	5.2	2.4	2.5	2.0	5.1	3.6
1928–37	10.9	1.3	1.1	.7	2.4	9.9	0.5
1950–55	7.7	4.5	3.9	2.7	2.2	5.9	2.8

[a]For Soviet Union, measured by index for all civilian industrial products.
[b]Persons engaged measured in full-time equivalents.
[c]Not available.
[d]Adjusted to exclude territorial gains.

Khrushchev is a man in a hurry. He hopes to see the USSR dominant during his lifetime.

The fundamental problem of the forthcoming seven-year period is the problem of the accelerated development of the national economy on the road to communism, the problem of the maximum gaining of time in the peaceful economic competition of socialism with capitalism. Supremacy in the speed of development has always been and remains the decisive supremacy of the socialist system of economy.[183]

The factor of time in this matter is more valuable than direct material expenditure—because more time cannot be compensated for by any money. In our peaceful competition with the capitalist countries we must gain ten to fifteen years.[184]

What is Russia's lag in industrial strength?

A study of 37 basic industries in the USSR made by G. Warren Nutter, of the University of Virginia, and reported in the American Economic Review of May 1957, indicates that the median lag in total output was 28 years in 1913, 36 years in 1937 and 36 years in 1955. In per capita output the median lag was 56 years. For consumer goods per capita output was 60 years behind, for all other goods, 56 years.

USSR PRODUCTION LAG COMPARED WITH U.S. [185]

	1959 Production USSR*	Year in which U.S. reached this level
Gross national product ..	$220 billion	1930
Steel	66 million tons	1940
Petroleum	142.7 " "	1929
Shoes	389 " pairs	1936
Radios	4 million	1929
Television sets	1.3 "	1949
Electric power	264 billion KWH	1943
Trucks and buses	370,500	1923
Automobiles	124,500	1910
Refrigerators	426,000	1928
Meat	9.5 million tons	1907
Milk	110 billion pounds	1941

*Soviet figures.

What are the real prospects of the Soviet Union during the next ten years?

The United States Central Intelligence Agency estimated that the Soviet gross national product will grow 80 per cent by 1970, an average of 6 per cent per year. This should bring the total to 420 billion compared with a 1960 U.S. figure of 503 billion and an anticipated 1970 figure of 740 billion. On a per capita basis, this must be adjusted to a 20 per cent population differential.

Soviet growth in industrial output multiplied between five and six times during the period 1913–1955. Machinery and equipment increased sixteen fold, intermediate industrial products nine times, and consumer goods three times. The average annual growth rate was 4.2 to 5.6 per cent for machinery and equipment, 5.5 per cent for intermediate goods, 2.6 per cent for consumer goods, and 4.2 per cent for industry as a whole. Newly acquired territories accounted for 11 per cent of the growth. Without this additional territory the average growth rate would have been 3.9 per cent.

The over-all growth rate for the 1900–1913 period was 5.3 per cent a year.

But annual growth in output per worker increased only 1.2 per cent per year compared with the United States figure of 2.2 per cent, and 2.7 per cent when adjustment is made for shorter hours. However, during the 1950–1955 period, Soviet productivity has accelerated and the United States figure has retarded.

The comparative United States growth rate has been less. Just how much depends on when you start and when you finish. An interesting table drawn up by the McGraw-Hill Publishing Company indicates why. Put your finger on the point where the two axes intersect and you have the average rate of growth for the period covered.

Following this procedure, you can find growth rates ranging all the way from −2.3 per cent, between 1957 and 1958, to +8.7 per cent, between 1949 and 1950, along with almost any other rate you would choose for various years and sequences of several years over the postwar period.

"For example, if you want to demonstrate that the postwar growth rate through 1953 was less than 4 per cent per year, you take off from 1946, include a drop of 0.1 per cent between 1946 and 1947, and come up with a growth rate for the 1946–1953 period of 3.9 per cent. But if you want to show it was quite high, you take off a year later, from 1947 [which drops out that dismal −0.1 per cent for 1947] and come up with a fine growth rate of 4.6 per cent for the 1947–1953 years." [186]

ANNUAL AVERAGE GROWTH RATES OF THE U.S. ECONOMY, 1946–1959*

(per cent increases, starting year to terminal year,
of GNP, in 1954 dollars)

Start-ing Year	TERMINAL YEAR													
	1946	1947	1948	1949	1950	1951	1952	1953	1954	1955	1956	1957	1958	1959
1946	X	−0.1	−1.9	−1.2	3.0	3.9	3.8	3.9	3.2	3.7	3.6	3.4	2.9	3.2
1947	X	X	3.8	1.8	4.1	4.9	4.6	4.6	3.7	4.2	4.0	3.8	3.2	3.5
1948	X	X	X	−0.1	4.2	5.3	4.8	4.7	3.6	4.3	4.0	3.8	3.1	3.4
1949	X	X	X	X	8.7	8.1	6.5	6.0	4.4	5.0	4.6	4.2	3.5	3.8
1950	X	X	X	X	X	7.4	5.4	5.1	3.4	4.3	3.9	3.6	2.9	3.3
1951	X	X	X	X	X	X	3.4	3.9	2.0	3.5	3.2	3.0	2.2	2.8
1952	X	X	X	X	X	X	X	4.4	1.3	3.6	3.2	2.9	2.0	2.6
1953	X	X	X	X	X	X	X	X	−1.6	3.2	2.8	2.6	1.6	2.4
1954	X	X	X	X	X	X	X	X	X	8.1	5.1	4.0	2.4	3.2
1955	X	X	X	X	X	X	X	X	X	X	2.1	2.0	0.5	2.0
1956	X	X	X	X	X	X	X	X	X	X	X	1.8	−0.2	2.0
1957	X	X	X	X	X	X	X	X	X	X	X	X	−2.3	2.0
1958	X	X	X	X	X	X	X	X	X	X	X	X	X	7.0
1959														

*Compound rates of growth.

Postwar growth rate has been 3.5 per cent per year, substantially more than the 2 per cent per year between 1909 and 1930.

The lackeys of the bourgeoisie love to boast about the alleged advantages of the so-called system of free enterprise. If you listen to them, the picture you get is that this system is the limit of man's dreams, that there is nothing better, nor could there be. But why is it that they cannot name a single capitalist country which, within such a short period of time, has made such progress in the development of its economy as the countries which have taken the road of socialism? Take, for example, countries that are neighbors of Bulgaria—Greece and Turkey. Statistics objectively reflect the fact that People's Bulgaria who has embarked on the road of socialist development, has achieved much greater success in promoting her economy and culture than her capitalist neighbors.[190]

WORLD PER CAPITA DISTRIBUTION OF GROSS NATIONAL PRODUCT 1957 and 1970 [187]
(in 1957 dollars)

Country or region	Population (in millions)	1957	1970 Est.	Approximate per cent increase
Noncommunist countries:				
United States	176	2,570	3,593	40
Canada	17	1,899	2,548	35
Western Europe	344	1,154	2,079	80
Japan	91	308	532	70
India	392	69	101[a]	50[a]
Other	817	170	234[a]	40[a]
Communist countries:				
USSR	204	858	1,563	80
European satellites ..	96	729	1,453	100
China	630	63	94[a]	50[a]
Asian satellites	23	45	68[a]	50[a]

CEIR summary estimates for Western Europe in 1970 are shown below: [188]

Western Europe	1957	1970
Gross national product	$397,000,000,000	$800,000,000,000
Population	344,000,000	383,000,000
Labor force	154,000,000	172,000,000
Per capita gross national product	1,154	2,100

[a]The 1970 per capita projections for these countries, whose output or population estimates, or both, are subject to a wide margin of error, are considered extremely speculative.

468

WORLD-WIDE PROJECTIONS [189]

The foregoing projections, and those for other countries and regions are shown below.

World distribution of gross national product, 1957 and 1970

| Country or region | Gross national product | | | |
| | Total amount (in billions of 1957 dollars) | | Per cent of world total | |
	1957	1970 est.	1957	1970 est.
Noncommunist:				
United States	440	733	32.6	29
Canada	32	53	2.4	2
Western Europe	397	796	29.5	31
Japan	28	58	2.1	2
India	27	50[a]	1.9	2
Other	139	250[a]	10.3	10
Total	1,063	1,940	78.8	76
Communist:				
USSR	175	397	13.0	15
European satellites	70	159	5.2	6
China	40	75[a]	3.0	3
Asian satellites	1	2[a]	—	—
Total	286	633	21.2	24
World Total	1,349	2,573	100.0	100

[a]Orders of magnitude only.

And here is the growth picture on a world-wide scale:

TOTAL OUTPUT OF GOODS AND SERVICES PER PERSON*

	Increase in 1959 (in per cents)
WESTERN EUROPE	5.1
Italy	6.1
Sweden	5.9
France	5.7
Germany	4.4
Netherlands	3.3
Britain	2.8
Belgium and Luxembourg	2.2
UNITED STATES	4.9†
SOVIET RUSSIA	4.1

Note: Production figures based on 1953 = 100, and reflect output in the first three months of 1960, except in the case of Russia, where latest available figures are used.

---

*Source: U.S. News & World Report, July 11, 1960.
†After a recessionary 1948.

How does the USSR with 40 to 50 per cent of the United States gross national product manage to grow as fast as it does?

The answer lies in 25 factors—some of which aid growth, some of which distort the statistic, and some of which merely explain the fact.

1. *The primary factor is the Soviet Government's ability to hold down consumption to about a fourth of what Soviet workers produce. The balance goes for military hardware and basic industry which increases productive capacity. This in turn is reinvested in other facilities producing producers (rather than consumer goods).*

"Less than 25 per cent of the Soviet gross national production goes into consumer goods. In contrast, about 70 per cent of our country's gross national product goes into consumer goods and services." [191]

But planning is not always enough.

Z. T. Serdyuk, a Moldavian, complains of the ". . . important problem of assuring the necessary materials for an extensive program of capital construction on the collective farms. The facts show there are serious shortcomings here. Rural deliveries of lumber, cement and other building materials which we are unable to produce in this unforested republic remain at a low level." [192]

And Mr. Khrushchev complains:

More order must be introduced into the planning of machine-tool production and supply. At present our planning of machine-tool production is largely unspecific. We must plan the output of the respective economic areas and even of specific industrial establishments. . . . Consequently it is not a matter of merely planning the number of machine-tools to be put out according to types, but of specifying machines for specific plants and specific processes.[193]

2. Total control and planning permits full use of labor force and resources without regard to labor demands or previous condition of ownership.

You are well aware how the Soviet people acted in building their socialist economy. We denied ourselves a great deal and restricted ourselves with regard to food, clothing and production of consumer goods, and each ruble saved was invested in the construction of factories and mills for heavy industry, in erecting power stations. We made great haste in this matter, because we knew that if, within a brief historical period, we did not create our own powerful industry, our own large-scale mechanized agriculture, our own skilled personnel, or if we lagged behind in the development of science and technology, the imperialists would crush us and would destroy the country in which for the first time, workers and peasants, the working people, had come to power. And we emerged victorious.[194]

The powerful socialist industry, which is the basis of all national economy, is in the hands of the Soviet state and in the hands of the people. We have state ownership of land. All economic levers of economic management remain in the hands of the state. Finally, and this is decisive, the Communist Party directs the entire socialist building. It directs the development of agriculture and industry along a single path—the path of building a communist society.[195]

Under socialism the contradiction of production rising and the consumption of the principal masses of population remaining at a standstill is unthinkable. Growth of production in a socialist society is planned for the very purpose of increasing the sum total of material benefits for ever fuller satisfaction of the needs of all the members of society. It should be stressed that although the level of production both in a socialist and a capitalist country, such as in the USSR and the United States, can be identical, the ensuing social consequences will differ as heaven and earth. Herein lies the superiority of socialism, under which production is not subjected to the aims of deriving profits but to the maximum satisfaction of the needs of all the members of the society.[196]

3. The lower base from which the rise is made lends to the distortion. Speaking in terms of a thirty-year span, Richard M. Nixon has noted:[197]

"The third fallacy is suggested by the behavior of the absolute gap between our economies. Just before World War II the total production of goods and services in the USSR was less than half that in the United States. To be exact, it was 44 per cent. Twenty years later, in 1959, the total production of goods and services in the Soviet Union is still just about 44 per cent of the United States.

"In terms of currency, the United States lead is substantially larger than the entire value of Soviet production. Mr. Khrushchev boasts that he will catch and pass us in seven or ten years. By any projection that can be applied, there is no possibility that the Soviet economy will overtake our own at any time in this century." [198]

4. Soviet statistics of production are determined on an index of ten basic products in which "wealth in the ground" is fundamental.

472

This product is, and always has been there for the taking, but was underdeveloped only because of inadequacies of the system. The heavy exploitation of these resources, plus a total disregard for the computation of other elements of national product [services are entirely ignored] enables the Soviets to convince themselves and others of vast progress.

5. The statistical base in the USSR is much lower than in the U.S.A. A 1 per cent increase in total gross national product is $125 million in the Soviet Union, $500 million in the U.S.A. A 100 per cent increase in production between 1950 and 1959 was $100 billion. In the U.S.A., a 70 per cent increase meant $199 billion.

This means, for example, for the increase in electric power:

(millions of kilowatts of capacity)

	U.S.	USSR
1957	146.2	48.4
1965	245.0	108.0
Actual increase	98.8	59.6
Per cent increase	67.6	123.1

Khrushchev understands this when he talks percentages within the Soviet Union,

Of course, one must be just and say that in the Ukraine the level of output of animal produce, of meat and milk, is higher than in other republics. Therefore, to the Ukrainians every percent comes harder than, for example in Byelorussia, where the level of production was lower. As the saying goes, there are percents and percents.[199]

6. The difference in stages of development is a major factor. A 100 per cent increase in motor-vehicle production in the USSR is equivalent to ½ of 1 per cent in the United States. A 100 per cent increase in United States production of automobiles in a single year would be unthinkable.

At present in the U.S.A. the level of production is, of course, higher than in the Soviet Union, and that is quite understandable, for the United States of America embarked upon the path of industrial development considerably earlier than Russia. But now, after the October Revolution and the triumph of socialism, this gap between our countries is narrowing and the time is not far off when the Soviet Union will be in advance of the U.S.A. in economy and we shall ensure higher living standards for our people. And this will convince all people still more of the advantages of the socialist system over the capitalist system.[200]

Obviously Russia began its industrial revolution long before 1917.

The peaceful economic competition between us and the United States could be visualized, if you please, as a long-distance race. The United States is still running ahead of us, and this is not surprising. They had an earlier start. To speak figuratively, it already runs under great tension, as if its breath were running short. A young and strong runner, the socialist Soviet Union, is slowly catching up with it and will soon leave it behind.[201]

Russia is now roughly at the level of the United States development in the first decade of the twentieth century when the United States growth rate was roughly 7 to 9 per cent per year. But it came to maturity at a more advanced level of technology.

Thus West Germany, Japan, and most of Europe have been recovering at growth rates of 9 to 23 per cent.

7. It should be remembered that since 1939 the Soviet Union has added 700,000 square kilometers—a developed area greater than France—to its territory, 20 million to its population by conquest, "liberated" 10 per cent of the factories of Western Germany, at least 15 per cent of the factories of East Germany, almost all of the billions of dollars invested by Japan in Manchuria, and whatever reparations it could obtain from the satellite bloc, amounting to several billions of dollars during the last few years. Altogether the Soviet Union received some 20 billion in these reparations between 1945 and 1956, much of it in industrial machinery.[203]

474

The Propaganda Front (II)

GROWTH RATES FOR INDUSTRY IN SOVIET UNION AND UNITED STATES

Output and output per capita, selected "comparable" periods[a]

(average annual growth rate[202])

Period for USSR	Output		Output per head of population		Period for
	USSR	U.S.	USSR	U.S.	U.S.
1913–15	3.9[b]	5.0	3.3	3.0	1877–1919
		4.8	———	3.0	1885–1927
1928–55	6.1[b]	5.6	5.3	3.5	1877–1904
		5.3	———	3.3	1885–1912
1928–40	7.4[b]	7.0	5.9	4.7	1877–89
		4.5	———	2.6	1885–97
		6.3	———	4.8	1939–51
1950–55	7.7	8.0	5.9	5.9	1908–13

[a]Periods are comparable for growth in output only, not output per capita.
[b]Adjusted to exclude territorial gains.

Of Russia's growth, 11 per cent is attributable to annexation, a large but unmeasurable fraction to reparations and expropriation.

8. The industrial labor force has been increased by enlisting women and children, by conquest, by force. Thus 60 per cent of the growth in output is attributable to expanded employment, only 40 per cent to increased labor productivity. Each person engaged in labor increased his productivity at an annual rate of 1.2 per cent compared with 2.7 per cent in the United States.[204]

To achieve a sevenfold increase of industrial production between 1928 and 1956, the number of industrial-production workers in Soviet industry was increased nearly fivefold, or by 14,684,000 workers. The United States, on the other hand, attained more than a sevenfold increase in the output of manufactured goods between 1935 and 1956 by less than doubling the number of production workers in manufacturing.[205]

Part of the increase in the Soviet labor force was achieved by increasing the working population to 95 per cent of the men and

62 per cent of the women over sixteen, and recently by cutting back two years of schooling, the eighth and ninth years.

"In the United States, growth in industrial output has come mainly from improved labor productivity: Over 1913–55, output multiplied 4.5 times while employment multiplied only 1.8 times and man-hours only 1.5 times. In the Soviet Union, on the other hand, growth in output has come mainly from expanded employment, as we have seen. The contrast is sharp: Improved labor productivity accounted for 67 per cent of the growth in output in the United States, but for only 40 per cent in the Soviet Union. Labor productivity grew at 2.2 per cent a year in the United States (2.7 per cent based on man-hours) as contrasted with 1.2 per cent in the Soviet Union," a study by G. Warren Nutter indicates.

9. The productivity of labor in the USSR had been tremendously underutilized. A man working at 35 per cent efficiency can be brought up to 50 per cent efficiency much more easily than a man working at 70 per cent to 100 per cent efficiency. In 1955, 43 per cent of the population was down on the farm compared with 12 per cent in the United States. Even now 1½ to 2 million workers still gather wood and low-grade fuel in the country.

It goes without saying that the lag in our agriculture as compared with yours in the sphere of mechanization and labor productivity is a temporary thing. The socialist system of agriculture makes it possible to overcome this lag within a short time and attain a labor productivity higher than on your farms. It offers boundless scope for developing production since it knows neither crises nor competition. In our country there is not and cannot be any danger of some farms being ruined. In our country we have a sufficiently high standard of agricultural skilled personnel, and an engineering industry capable of manufacturing machinery needed for agriculture. We strive to accomplish integrated mechanization of all agricultural production processes by applying perfect machines and by utilizing the labor force in a more rational way and thus insuring greater output per person employed.

We have remarkable machine operators who have attained higher labor productivity than on your best farms in cultivating corn, cotton, sugar beet, and other crops.[206]

Soviet labor productivity is universally lower than in the United States, the degree of difference varying greatly by economic sector. A recent article published in the USSR compares Soviet and U.S. productivity:

	USSR labor productivity as percentage of U.S.
Industry	50
Construction	59
Transportation	33
Agriculture	20–25

The annual rate of growth of labor productivity was at its lowest in 1953 and 1958 (6 per cent) and at its highest in 1955 (8 per cent). The highest rate occurred immediately after World War II, from 1947 through 1950, when it fluctuated between 12 and 15 per cent. The relatively high rates of Soviet growth, as compared with the United States, reflect the relatively low level of productivity in the Soviet Union. According to a 1959 Soviet study, total output per production worker for the whole national economy in 1957 was 2.5 to 3 times as great in the United States as in the USSR, and for industry, 2 times as great.

At present, productivity of labor in U.S. industry is approximately 2 to 2.5 times higher than ours, and about three times higher in agriculture. We are in a position to catch up with and overtake the U.S.A. in productivity in the not too distant future. . . .[207]

10. There is no reason why Russia should not long ago have become an industrial power. She has resources, power, markets, manpower. She is the only temperate-climate area underdeveloped except China.

Are we, people of a free socialist state, people of socialist labor, less able than the Americans? Have we less knowledge than they of how to till the soil, breed cows, milk them, fatten pigs, prepare good jellied meat or make a roast? We, Soviet people, have everything—intelligence, hands, and natural riches. Why then should we produce less goods than they? Who can accept this? Who said that the Soviet man must eat half of what an American eats? I believe that, should it be necessary—unless the stomach would refuse to accept it—we can well secure for every Soviet man five American rations![208]

11. Soviet production is keyed to producing higher statistics rather than more goods. We have already seen how the fact that both workers and managers are compensated on the basis of quotas and overfulfillment of their quotas distorts their output. Thus work is concentrated on producing heavy machinery where production is computed by weight, narrower fabrics where production is measured in linear yards, smaller items when production is measured in numbers. Sheeting and pipes are made thicker. Difficult orders are refused. Product modernization and style changes are avoided, etc. New products receive value ratings to satisfy the need for statistical satisfaction. Production is "borrowed" from one period to another.

Our engineering industry still produces many obsolete models of machine-tools and machines. A number of surface-grinding machines produced by the Kirov works at Vitebsk are obsolete in their design. Pumps produced by the Stalin works in Bobruysk perform poorly, are designed poorly, and are poorly finished. The Komintern works in Vitebsk is producing a gear-planning machine for conic pinions which was designed nearly forty years ago.[209]

And here are some of the complaints of factory managers: ". . . it is very important for saving metal that the standards for reinforcing rods be strictly observed. Experience shows that almost all the rolled metal reaching reinforced concretes has excessively high allowances. . . . Metallurgical plants deliver rolled metal by weight and thus, in terms of linear meters, give substantially less reinforcing steel than they should . . . metal losses in Moscow alone amount to approximately 15,000 tons a year." [210]

"So far our country has been producing pipe with excessively thick walls, which leads to the unproductive expenditure of an enormous amount of metal. This is caused by the lack of standardized technical norms and technical conditions for the use of pipe . . . and also by the obsolete, All-Union State Standards." [211]

12. The scoring of industrial production for comparison purposes is fantastically difficult. The Soviet Union has no price system. The same items cost as much as 40 per cent more from one source as from another. Quality standards do not exist in the sense they do in a manufacturer-customer relationship. Vice-Premier Kosygin complains:

"In the area of retail prices . . . measures will also be adopted to regulate prices and eliminate price disparities. For example, we have different prices on identical goods manufactured by state industry and by producers' cooperatives. Frequently goods manufactured by the producers' cooperatives are of inferior quality yet are sold at higher prices."

"We must first of all eliminate the disparities in prices for identical types of products and the unwarranted diversity in profitability. A situation in which some types of metals, machines and fuel are produced at a loss while others yield a handsome profit cannot be considered normal. . . . Profitability of production of individual machines for the coal industry ranges from a 16 per cent loss to a 45 per cent profit." [212]

"This is what happens at certain enterprises. At the Roshal Machine-Building Plant under the Leningrad Economic Council a temporary price of 110,000 rubles was established in 1956 for a paper pulp mill. At the present time the production cost of this machine is 68,000 rubles. Nevertheless the temporary price is still in effect. Many similar examples could be cited from other branches of industry. Such a practice leads to artificial inflation of profit and distorts the indicators of production volume and level of labor productivity. It also leads to the necessity of increasing *appropriations for capital construction and thereby holds back the introduction of new machinery and equipment."* [213]

13. There is, of course, no competition or standard of quality. Thus everything produced is given an arbitrary value regardless of its usefulness or salability in the capitalist sense.

Says the "customer":

"We believe it is time to insist that the metallurgists deliver metal to the shipyard in cut forms free of rust." [214]

14. With no demand limitations Soviet factories work at full capacity with a minimum of pattern changes, and almost entirely regardless of specific needs, or of time and place utility.

Take for instance the Podolsk Works of Moscow Oblast Sovnarkhoz. The sewing machines it sends to market are antiquated in design and do not meet the demands of the buyers. The widely known household refrigerator Saratov-2 is also outdated in its technical and use qualities, while the Saratov Works is not hurrying to introduce the manufacture of a new, improved design.[215]

Says the "customer":

"Comrade Trifonov, the Deputy Minister of Trade, gave some unpleasant figures. Customers do not want to buy serge, but even now it accounts for 60 per cent of all the all-wool and half-wool fabrics being put out. . . . The Krasnodar mills turned out nearly 90,000 meters of 'Argon' tricot, which is commanding no sale at all. The Tambov Economic Council produced dark-colored cloths that were not in demand, instead of light-colored ones that were." [216]

In spite of the existence of large staffs of inspectors our industries sometimes put out low-quality articles to the detriment of the national economy. According to information released by the Central Statistical Board, industrial spoilage in 1955 and 1956 amounted to approximately 6,000 million rubles; and this in spite of the fact that there are more than 400,000 technical inspectors in the Union and republican industries.[217]

And:

"Some plant directors, in an effort to avoid responsibility, are refusing to accept orders and consequently it has become extremely difficult in 1959 to place orders for new equipment. There are great interruptions in deliveries of machinery to the chemical industry."[218]

Industry continues to manufacture heavy, uneconomical, towed implements of low productivity, even when new mounted implements have been designed for the same job.[219]

15. There is no evaluation as to the ability to use and distribute the output in terms of consumer needs. It is quite a simple thing to produce milk on the farm—quite another to deliver it fresh on the shelf of a city store.

"During 1959, Soviet consumer goods output rose 10.3 per cent but retail sales were up only 7.2 per cent. The result, familiar to any capitalist, was a rise in inventories, estimated by the Soviets at eleven percent. Thus, while the rise in Russia's consumer goods production, under Khrushchev's prodding, has been impressive statistically, much of it has turned out to be items that nobody wants—tasteless canned food, ill-fitting dresses, old-fashioned lampshades with tassels—or else things that people want badly but can't afford."[220]

And:

"Severe charges were leveled at transport officials. It was pointed out that ready products remain for a prolonged period at the enterprises, while vehicles often leave the enterprises' area empty."[221]

16. There is no discounting of uneconomic or overvalued units, which are automatically eliminated under capitalism as "business failures."

"One hundred seventy-nine billion rubles were invested in 320,000 uncompleted building projects on January 1, 1959. The large proportion of incomplete construction was the result of serious defects in the work of economic agencies, primarily the planning agencies, and particularly of the former heads of the USSR State Planning Committee, in providing technical and economic justification of new construction." [222]

And:

A. B. Aristov—Khrushchev's expert on automation—goes even further and says:

"There are roughly eighty steel rolling mills in the plants of the RFSR, of which only three are modern ones, while the rest of them—seventy-seven—are antiquated machines built in the nineteenth and even in the eighteenth centuries. Labor productivity in some of them is twenty to thirty times lower than in the modern ones. In some of them, unfortunately, rolling cages are still being used to roll roofing iron according to the old Ural manner—which entails heavy physical strain." [223]

17. The growth rate has enjoyed some advantages from the youth and backwardness of Soviet industry.

Some of its plants have been built only recently. The growth-generating capacity has yet to be affected by a rising burden of maintenance, wear and tear and obsolescence. Maintenance expenses are minimized with the objective of greater immediate production.

"I must emphasize that too little up-to-date equipment is being used in tire production. The machine-building plants have been producing equipment of obsolete design." [224]

18. *Capital investment has been concentrated in enterprises which produce results quickly. Transport, housing, hydroelectric plants have been sidetracked for projects which lend themselves to more immediate production statistics: mining, petroleum, lumber, steel plants.*

"In estimating the effectiveness of capital investments, one should always consider which is better—somewhat lower production costs with large capital investments or somewhat higher costs with smaller capital investments and reduced plant construction time. By pursuing relatively lower costs we may be freezing large investments in enterprise that cannot contribute to expanded production for a long time." [225]

Given present conditions, the main thing is to win time, to reduce the construction time, and to obtain more electric power with the least expense. At the same time, from the viewpoint of the state, it is expedient to accept deliberately a certain rise in kilowatt-hour costs with a view to winning time and to obtain in a short span of time a maximum increase in the electric power output. [226]

This way of looking at the problem is due to the fact that we must in a short time invest more funds in the development of heavy industry, especially in the chemical industry, iron and steel and nonferrous metallurgy, and other branches. In this context we have to analyze the question as to how one could get more and quicker electric power in a given economic area with the same outlay. If we do so, then we arrive at the conclusion that, at present, one has to arrest to some extent the development of the construction of some hydroelectric power stations in order to give priority for some years—maybe for seven or eight years—to the construction of thermal power stations. [227]

As a result of Khrushchev's statement and the new policy on hydro stations, the work on Krasnoyarsk which had been started in 1955 was stopped and the inactivity was to last for "at least ten years." This new policy apparently held also for the smaller Saratov station to be built on the Volga. In fact, as the specific plans for electrification came out, it became clear that the hydro-capacity to be introduced in the Seven-Year Plan was to be largely as a result of the completion of projects already well under way.

The need arises to postpone somewhat the periods for the construction of hydroelectric stations. Why? The hydroelectric stations now under construction require a great deal of labor and much time and money. True, a hydro-electric station is cheap to run; once it is built, it yields only profits. But the time factor must be considered. We must gain time in the competition with capitalism so as to over-take the U.S.A. in per capita production in the shortest possible time.[228]

Even safety devices are de-emphasized:

"Questions concerning safety techniques and industrial sanitary services have not been settled until now in the mines of Karaganda. This leads to a high number of accidents. There are also serious shortcomings in the everyday life of workers at the mines which has as its result a large turnover of the labor force."[229]

And:

"It seems to us that a procedure should be worked out and introduced for the designing and introduction of new equipment which would take the requirements of industrial safety into strict account."[230]

19. Wealth already in the ground has been developed heavily and this has been "creamed" without long-term considerations of conservation.

Says Mr. Aristov:

"The United States is in the best position of all capitalist countries insofar as mineral wealth is concerned. But even the United States resources can in no way stand comparison with our motherland's natural wealth. If we take the known world deposits of the sixteen most important minerals, the USSR holds first place in thirteen. . . . The time has now come when we are beginning to put into effect major measures for the utilization of the country's eastern areas. Forty per cent of all capital invest-ments over the next seven years have been assigned to these purposes . . ."[231]

20. Underveloped land has been available, the best of which has been utilized.

484

The Propaganda Front (II)

In 1954 Khrushchev pointed out:

We have much empty land, and it needs to be used in a businesslike way. Is this a bad task, comrades? The Soviet people will eat better, live better, and this, obviously, is the most important thing for us. Such a task has been posed by our Party, our Government, and it is for this that our Communist Party is struggling.[232]

"The area sown to crops in the USSR is reported to have increased from 371.6 million acres in 1940, to 410.5 million in 1954, and 483.1 million in 1958. A part of this increase, of course, reflects territorial changes. By way of comparison, the U.S. Department of Agriculture estimates that the total cropland available for crops in this country in 1954 was 465 million acres. Acres of cropland are not necessarily a good measure of agricultural potential as soil, topography, climate, technology, and the availability of new land that can be brought into production through drainage and irrigation are also important.

"Soil scientists have reported that the USSR has great soil resources and that much of the land now under cultivation has a high natural fertility."[233]

21. Growth is accelerated by concentration on a few simple, basic industries. More complicated projects are left for the future.

An end should be put, comrades, to the deleterious system of diffusing funds over numerous construction projects; capital investments and material and labor resources should be concentrated on the major projects and on projects scheduled for early commissioning. We must not begin new construction projects without sufficient preparation, without complete designs, the necessary building facilities and other conditions guaranteeing rapid building. It is very important for our planning and economic bodies to be careful and thrifty when making investments in the national economy.[234]

485

In scientific investment, concentration has been directed towards a few industries useful for military and propaganda purposes.

"This concentration of capital investment in industry produces some impressive results and striking contrasts. First-rate technological performances in aircraft, the missile industry, ordnance in general, some parts of the machine-tool industry, and others stand in contrast to remnants of the plant and equipment taken over from the Czarist regime. There are wood-burning locomotives and peat-fueled thermoelectric plants, both of which however, can still deliver goods and energy to an ultramodern military electronics plant." [235]

22. *The heavy cost of science and engineering—research, development and design is eliminated by the simple device of borrowing from the more advanced technologies of the West. Thus most Soviet automobiles are copies of American ones. Except in highly publicized sputniks, jet aircraft, in the oil industry, and a few other scattered instances Soviet science has produced few major technological advances. Research in medicine and physiology, where knowledge is freely diffused from the West, is de-emphasized while the best minds are directed toward sciences of military and political value.*

Said Lenin:

"While the revolution in Germany is slow in 'coming forth,' our task is to study the state capitalism of the Germans, to spare no effort in copying it and not shrink from adopting dictatorial methods to hasten the copying of it. Our task is to do this even more thoroughly than Peter [the Great] hastened the copying of Western culture by barbarian Russia, and he did not hesitate to use barbarous methods in fighting against barbarism." [236]

"The Bolsheviks, though seeking to build a new and different type of economy, had considerable experience on which to draw— Russian, British, German, American, French, Japanese among others. It could and did call upon the technical and engineering skills and assistance of the more industrially developed countries. It secured substantial credits from other lands to help its capital development and accumulation." [237]

Mr. Khrushchev admits:

Mankind is now living in a wonderful time. It is a time when science and technology, economy and culture are flourishing, when, indeed, the fantastic is becoming reality.[238]

Your country has attained a high level of industrial development. The rapid development of industry in the United States of America astounded the whole world and aroused admiration and even envy in other countries.

Under revolutionary conditions, on a new social basis, we utilized everything valuable that you had created and we proved that your achievements could not only be equaled but also surpassed.[239]

"A $42 million synthetic rubber factory now is rising in Dnepropetrovsk, an industrial center in Russia's Ukraine. Major components of the factory were imported intact from Britain.

"In Italy, technicians of Montecatini are at work on components of three chemical plants. Some time next year, the three plants will be assembled in Russia to supply raw materials for a growing plastics industry. These transactions point up the rising flow of Western technology into Russia as the Reds rush their industrialization drive. Modern machinery makes up a big share of Russia's imports, which rose to $5.1 billion last year, up 16.7 per cent from 1958." [240]

23. The Soviet Union has, during the past fifteen-year period, had an abnormally small number of unproductive children and aged to support. The number over sixty years of age will increase from 6.7 per cent of the population in 1940 and 8.2 per cent in 1959 to 11.9 per cent in 1975. The percentage under fifteen years of age will remain low: 35.2 per cent in 1940, 29.2 per cent in 1959, 28.3 per cent in 1975.

24. "There is a fundamental difference between the Soviet society and that of the United States. Americans are free to produce and consume what they like and possess what they can afford. An enormous portion of their national capital is represented in the American home. Most of our millions of homes are, in effect,

miniature factories, heavily equipped with capital equipment such as refrigerators, television sets and cars, able to produce a better life as a capital dividend. None of this is revealed as capital plant in comparing growth rates. But in a very real sense a refrigerator, a washing machine, a television set produce consumer good." [241]

25. "Our whole perspective on the rate of recovery and industrial expansion in post-World War II Russia is altered if we stop to consider the faster rate of recovery and expansion of, let us say, Germany and Japan, during the same period." [242]

In industrial output, this is the picture:

INCREASE IN PRODUCTION RATE
compared with a year before [243]
(in per cents)

WESTERN EUROPE	12.6
Italy	16.3
Netherlands	14.7
Britain	13.2
Germany	12.3
France	11.9
Sweden	9.0
Belgium and Luxembourg	8.8
SOVIET RUSSIA	11.0
UNITED STATES	7.8

Although the increase in the Soviet's industrial output will obviously not begin to challenge America's per capita production in the foreseeable future, one phase of it does present a challenge. Eighty-five per cent of Soviet investment is in items that have military and trade potential. Although over-all Soviet industrial growth is at the rate of 6 per cent per year, her expansion of hardware and basic industry increases at the rate of 10 to 12 per cent per year.

"The particular directions, or industries, into which these resources have gone is the important point, more important than general rates of gross-national-product growth or productivity changes. Thirty years ago consumption accounted for about 60 per cent of Soviet industrial output; it is now about 27 per cent. Capital investment and armaments absorb the remaining 73 per cent. Since 1928 half of the country's total investment has gone into industry, and of this, 85 per cent goes into producers' rather than consumers' goods industries. The Soviet production of industrial equipment equaled about 65 per cent of U.S. industrial equipment output. However, their industrial equipment on hand is roughly equal to 40 per cent of U.S. installed industrial equipment; 30 years ago it was only 8 per cent. Again, this shows the concentrated effort of Soviet investment.

"Their concentration has produced an immense armament industry of diversified character, and a capital goods industry equal in some lines such as machine tool production, to that of the United States." [244]

The total effect of the Soviet system is similar to total all-embracing monopoly capitalism with control and management vested in the Communist Party. Notwithstanding verbalisms regarding ownership by the people and for the people, workers have no actual control of capital assets, nor do they receive even as large a portion of their own total production as do most employees of capitalist monopolists.

CHAPTER **13**

Contradictions in Communism

"I'm not talking about the immediate future. I'm talking about thirty or forty or fifty years hence. That's not too long a time as history goes. It seems reasonable to me that friction with its Chinese ally might ultimately turn Russia toward the West."

—Winston Churchill [1]

Marx and Lenin saw plainly the contradictions (i.e., conflicts) within the capitalist system. Communist theory is based on the assumption of struggle among rival groups and ideas (contradictions) from which one system (in modern times, communism) will emerge dominant.

In the nineteenth century and the beginning of the twentieth, when these ideas were formulated, the struggle between capital and labor, and between imperialist nations for colonies, was a struggle for power, markets, and resources. This struggle, as Marx and Lenin saw it, would lead to an international war for colonies and to a class war within each nation.

The early socialists and communists expected that once the revolution began, it would spread like wildfire through the whole world—at first through industrialized Europe and then through still-backward Asia. The socialist world would then unite modern economic strength with inexhaustible population and raw-material resources. This as has been noted, was how Lenin saw it:

"In the last analysis, the outcome of the struggle will be

determined by the fact that Russia, India, and China, etc., constitute the overwhelming majority of the population of the globe.[2]

And Stalin noted:

"If the proposition is true that the more developed proletariat
of the West cannot finish the world bourgeoisie without the support
of the peasant East, which is less developed but abounds in raw
materials and fuel, the proposition is equally true that more
developed Central Russia cannot complete the revolution without
the support of the border regions of Russia, which are less
developed but which abound in essential resources."[3]

But revolution did not spread. Stalin's Russia withdrew into its
shell—intent on building "socialism in one country." The upheavals
in Europe were suppressed. India was slowly advancing toward
independence along the path of nonviolence under the leadership
of Mohandas K. Gandhi, whom the communists despised as a
"bourgeois" and denounced as a tool of British "imperialism."

If socialism did not spread, the Soviet Union did. Russia emerged
from World War II as an imperial power, with Eastern Europe
firmly in the hands of its army and police.

There is one major exception to this pattern of Soviet expansion:
China occupies a special place in the communist empire. The
most populated country in the world is not a "satellite" in the
sense applied to the European "people's democracies." She was
never conquered by Soviet troops. And the communist rulers of
continental China ascended to power after a quarter of a century
of revolutionary struggle. They fought for a democratic China in
the ranks of Chiang Kai-shek's Kuomintang; they fought the
Kuomintang after having been excluded from Kuomintang ranks;
they fought the Japanese invaders, even while Russia remained
neutral. They owed very little to Moscow when, on October 1, 1949,
they proclaimed the establishment of the "People's Republic of
China." It was only after the proclamation of the Republic that the
Soviet Union recognized them. It was only to the communist regime
in power that the Soviet Union promised and delivered help.

There was even suspicion that Stalin attempted to establish a
puppet government in Manchuria in 1949, that the Korean war was

491

designed to weaken China, to increase Soviet dominance and possibly cut off the Russian-held treaty ports and railroad. Vladivostok is only seventy miles north of Korea. If Soviet-dominated North Korea had assumed power over South Korea, China would have been outflanked and could never have been a competitive problem. When the United States resisted, the whole balance of power changed in the Far East.

By reason of its size, its inexhaustible manpower, its natural resources, its potential economic and military strength, China is the only country of the socialist camp that can now raise its voice in opposition without being immediately silenced by an order from Moscow. And despite the periodic reaffirmations of unity, there are indications that Moscow and Peking do not see world problems in the same light.

China's mores, culture, objectives, and national aspirations are quite different from those of Russia. Younger in communist ideology, it is more orthodox, more dogmatic, more aggressive, more intransigent. Its needs are greater and its urges stronger. It is less advanced and thus has much more to expect from the modern world. By Chinese standards, Russia is the goal to equal and surpass, the "have" country, almost bourgeois in its outlook, uncultured and already decadent in its "fear of the atomic bomb." Some Chinese remember Kublai Khan (1216–1294) who collected tribute from all of Russia and most of his world. And perhaps, too, the 2 billion Chinese of the twenty-first century will expect to dominate the world of their day.

Russia must view China with suspicion and fear: here is a nation with three times Russia's population and a substantially larger rate of increase. China is creating a new population as big as Turkey's each year. Her 680 million people grow 2 per cent a year; Russia's 214 million people increase at the rate of 1.81 per cent a year. The result: by 1975 China will have 1 billion people to feed on the 10 per cent of her area that can be cultivated. Russia will be comparatively empty with a 281 million population.

Contradictions in Communism

Where can the Chinese go? For decades, they have overflowed into any other countries that would have them—a whole world of Overseas Chinese, many retaining loyalty to Peiping. Adjacent to China, there are few places to go that are not almost as hard-pressed as the Chinese mainland. Some 12 million Chinese live in Southeast Asia, comprising 6 per cent of the area's population, most of its merchants, skilled laborers, and much of its professional class. Chinese are prominent in the rice trade, banking, tin, mining, rubber. In some countries Chinese are already numerically dominant— 80 per cent of Singapore, 40 per cent of Malaya, 25 per cent of Borneo, 16 per cent of Thailand, 8 per cent of South Vietnam. And they do not assimilate. To the south, there was Tibet (already absorbed by China), there are the tiny border states, protectorates of India, and then the land mass of Southeast Asia, Burma, India, Pakistan. Westward, there is Outer Mongolia, a Russian satellite, and Russia itself. Of the two directions, the underdeveloped west obviously offers more space and more opportunity.

China is already moving in a westerly direction. Her biggest development is at Lanchow, 1,000 miles inland, the gateway to her west. Population here has jumped from 200,000 to 24 million in ten years; 188 industrial plants have been built. In three years 1,400,000 Chinese have moved into Inner Mongolia. Farther west, Outer Mongolia is receiving aid from China as well as from Russia, which has considered it virtually a Soviet principality since 1920.

Is it to counter this westward move that Khrushchev is moving East? Within a few years he has invested 3 billion rubles to develop the "virgin lands" of Siberia and Central Asia. Slavic populations are being settled in these areas—while in Sinkiang, its Western Province, China is reliably reported to be replacing the population of Turkmens with peasants and workers of Chinese stock.

It is necessary to recall that in the eastern area there are concentrated up to 75 per cent of all coal reserves, up to 80 per cent of the hydroelectric power, four-fifths of the timber wealth, the main reserve of our nonferrous and rare metals, and enormous resources of chemical raw materials, iron ore, and building materials.[4]

China's aggressiveness is contrary to Khrushchev's plans.

We deeply regret the incidents which took place recently on the frontier of two states both of which are our friends. The Chinese People's Republic, to which we are bound by indestructible bounds of fraternal friendship, and the Indian Republic, with which we have successfully been developing friendly relations. We are especially grieved by the fact that as a result of these incidents casualties occurred on both sides. Nothing can compensate the parents and families for the losses they suffered. We would be glad if the incidents on the Chinese-Indian frontier were not repeated and if the existing unsettled frontier questions could be solved by means of friendly negotiations to the mutual satisfaction of both sides.[5]

Chinese expansionism toward the south is not the only "embarrassment" Peking creates for Moscow. Khrushchev's entire policy of peaceful coexistence, of conquest without war, his claim to absolute leadership of the Communist world are challenged by the communist rulers of China.

This conflict (although denied by Khrushchev) is apparent. It is logical, based as it is on profound divergences of interests. It is expressed in communist dialect, involves communist dogma.

Foremost is the question of war and peace: Khrushchev says that war would be a world calamity. The Chinese Party organ People's Daily *speaks of "modern revisionists" (clearly indicating it meant the Russians) who sought to whitewash United States imperialism because they were "frightened out of their wits by the imperialist blackmail of nuclear war, exaggerated the consequences of the destructiveness of nuclear war and begged imperialism for peace at any cost."*[6]

This is strong language, particularly when we realize that the word *revisionist* is almost obscene in communist semantics.

494

According to Peking, the result of nuclear conflict "would certainly not be extinction. On the ruins of imperialism the victorious people would create a civilization a thousand times better than capitalism." [7]

Rejecting Khrushchev's preaching that "socialism" can triumph peacefully, Peking's authoritative journal *Red Flag* called on communists to "stick to the principles of Marxism-Leninism" and prepare for "a just war to end the unjust war" for which "Eisenhower and his ilk are actively making ready." Nuclear war is not something for communists to fear, said *Red Flag*, for "on the debris of a dead imperialism, the victorious people will create with extreme rapidity a civilization thousands of times higher than the capitalist system." [8]

Khrushchev himself had in the past expressed similar thoughts:

As a result of World War I, Soviet Russia became a socialist country. As a result of World War II, twelve other countries became socialist countries. As a result of a third world war, should it ever be launched by the imperialists, capitalism will be eliminated. We are convinced of this. [9]

In fact China has nothing to lose from a nuclear war but its surplus population; Russia has already created a vested interest in peace—her newly established industry. A nuclear war would leave the capitalist world in ruins, the Soviet bloc only a shell, but China—even with a 50 per cent loss of population—the biggest country in the world, on a par with the greatest ruins of industrialized civilization. Moreover, the tension of inevitable war is a rationale for excessive demands and sacrifice on the part of the population. So China chooses to accept the Leninist dogma of inevitable war, and to espouse an aggressive, expansionist policy.

The Soviet Union has much to fear from China, must, in fact, appease her and control her aggressiveness. In a few years, China must get the atom bomb. One such bomb dropped on the U.S. Seventh Fleet must lead to retaliation, and in atomic war, the target is clearly the main base.

Khrushchev's policy of peaceful coexistence involves negotiations with the West—with the United States in particular. The Chinese consistently warned that agreements with the capitalists would "tie the hands" of the communists. And they wanted to have their hands free, to promote revolution, for as *Red Flag* wrote:

"The imperialist system will not crumble by itself. It will be pushed over by the proletarian revolution." [10]

While the Chinese see the victory of communism through war and/or revolution—Khrushchev promises conquest without war, with the help of China but under the leadership of the Soviet Union:

Indeed, when the USSR becomes the leading industrial power in the world, when the Chinese People's Republic becomes a mighty industrial power and all the socialist countries together will produce more than half of the world industrial output, the world situation will change radically. The successes of the countries of the socialist camp will doubtlessly serve to strengthen the forces of peace throughout the world. By that time the countries working for lasting peace will no doubt be joined by new countries that have thrown off colonial oppression. The idea that war is inadmissible will take still firmer root in the minds of men. This new balance of forces will be so patently evident that even the most die-hard imperialists will clearly see the futility of starting a war against the socialist camp. Backed by the might of the socialist camp the peaceful nations will then be able to compel militant imperialist groups to abandon their plans of a new world war.

In this way, a real possibility of excluding world war from the life of society will take shape even before the universal triumph of socialism, with capitalism still existing in some parts of the world. [11]

In November 1957, the Chinese seemed to accept the leadership of the Soviet Union. On the occasion of the fortieth-anniversary celebration of the Russian Revolution, a declaration stressing the "leading role" of the Soviet Union in the communist camp was accepted by all Parties of the communist-bloc countries. Only Yugoslavia refused to sign.

But a few months later, in the spring of 1958, the Chinese embarked on a policy inconsistent with Soviet views on the way to achieve communism: the communes. They proceeded to organize almost 27,000 units aimed at becoming self-sufficient through a combination of small-scale industry and agriculture. An estimated 500 million peasants were to live and work under strict military discipline, women being freed for work by child nurseries. The communes, the Chinese said, are "the basic social unit of communist society"—a short-cut to communism, by-passing the Soviet Union's stage of socialism.

The Soviet Union, on the other hand, holds that the path to communism lies in the high development of industry, ample production, and unequal rewards as an incentive to increased output. They do not make any claim to achieve communism at any specific date.

The reasons for this new Chinese policy were probably not entirely ideological: Soviet industrial assistance to China had been curtailed after the 1956 explosions in Hungary and Poland and the subsequent revision of Soviet economic policy in its European Empire. China had to rely on what it had—manpower.

The Russians did not at first conceal their shock and displeasure at China's great leap forward toward total communism. The extreme regimentation was a shock to all civilized people. In the Soviet Union, the new Chinese policy was greeted with less than enthusiasm:

Trying to anticipate the results of fully matured communism by rushing to set up communes, said Pravda, is like trying to teach higher mathematics to a four-year-old child.[12]

Khrushchev was skeptical of communes on the basis of 1917 experiences. He considered the Soviet Union too poor for egalitarianism.

Soon after the conclusion of the civil war we began in our country to set up not agricultural cooperatives but communes. People were found who argued roughly this way: if we are to strive for communism, then let us set up communes. Many people, it seems, still had a poor understanding of what communism is and how it is to be built. Well, they organized communes, though neither the material nor political conditions for it—I mean the consciousness of the peasant masses—existed then. The situation then arose in which all wanted to live well but at the same time, to contribute as little labor effort as possible to the common cause. Or as one may put it: to work according to possibility, but to receive according to requirements. Nothing came of many of these communes.[13]

But, to keep the peace, he has to admit that China uses different "methods":

Comrades, each country has its peculiarities and each country solves various questions of socialist construction according to these peculiarities. This applies to Czechs and Slovaks and the Czechoslovakia on the whole, to Yugoslavia, to Bulgarians, to Albanians, and especially to China. China is a very large and unique country, and a very complicated one. I would say that China never directly copies or repeats anything; it does everything on the basis of Marxist-Leninist teaching, but everything in China is done in a Chinese way. Is this a matter for an argument? No, we are glad that the Chinese, our friends, are successfully solving the rebuilding of their society on socialist foundations, taking into consideration China's specific peculiarities.[14]

And . . .

We are in full and complete agreement with the fraternal Communist Party of China, though its methods of building socialism are in many ways dissimilar to ours. We know that China has its peculiarities in historical development, in the size of its population, the level of production, and national culture. Therefore, it would be a mistake to ignore these peculiarities and to imitate what is good for one country but does not suit another.[15]

What might have been a showdown regarding the two paths to communism was deftly avoided when the Twenty-first Congress of the Communist Party of the Soviet Union met in Moscow in 1959. Mao Tse-tung was the only leader of a communist-bloc country who did not appear at the congress. Chou En-lai, speaking for the Chinese Communist Party, noted the "indestructible solidarity" and glossed over the ideological differences. Two days after the congress ended, a new and additional nine-year, 5-billion-ruble barter agreement for Chinese industrialization was announced. China was to receive 78 plants—steel, chemicals, coal, oil and power.

The repeated assertions of "indestructible solidarity" did not put an end to the divergences between Russia and China on the conduct of international affairs. Prior to the aborted summit conference in Paris, the Peking spokesmen unleashed a new barrage against "revisionism," indicating that the Chinese are ready to consider "transition [from capitalism] to communism by nonpeaceful means."

Khrushchev's behavior in Paris is attributed—in part at least—to Chinese pressure to adopt a more "militant" line toward the "capitalists" headed by the United States. After the break-up of the Paris summit, Peking continued its line—there is no agreement possible with the imperialists—only revisionists forget Lenin's teachings that war is inevitable. To which Khrushchev answered in effect in his speech at the June 1960 conference of the Communist leadership in Bucharest: only madmen can think of war in the nuclear age. Verbally, at least, the Chinese seemed to knuckle under their powerful neighbor. The Peking Party press, after ignoring Khrushchev's Bucharest speech, began to admit that coexistence with capitalism is possible.

But Bucharest did not end the controversy. Tensions increased. Soviet technicians went home. Soviet news virtually disappeared from the Chinese press. Amity periodicals ceased publication. S. Tirenko, a Soviet ideologist, even questioned China's ability to build socialism successfully if it "were to find itself in an isolated position —not able to rely on the cooperation and mutual aid of all other socialist countries." The inference is, of course, that unless China acknowledges the Soviet's ideological leadership, she can count on no technical help. And Khrushchev rallied the satellites to a United Nations meeting for support.

A subsequent meeting of the Communist "summit" in Moscow lasted for more than three weeks in November 1960. A 20,000-word joint statement was issued, but the disagreement appeared to remain.

Thus, if one is to judge only by statements and writings on communist theory, Khrushchev has defeated the "doctrinaire" opposition to his general political line: Lenin's thesis on the inevitability of war has been superseded by Khrushchev's doctrine of peaceful co-existence.

But in practice, the revival of the militant struggle against "imperialism"—whether the pretext is Laos, Congo or Cuba, the attacking of an American plane over the high seas, the artificial transformation of minor incidents into major crises—corresponds to the policy recommended by Peking.

China's position on the international scene is determined by its relative isolation—its absence from the United Nations, its non-participation in the summit meetings of the "Bigs," its continued demand to "recover" Taiwan (Formosa). On all these matters, Khrushchev makes himself the spokesman for Peking:

1. Taiwan:

Taiwan can certainly be liberated and brought back to the embrace of its great homeland, the People's Republic of China.[16]

And in a letter to President Eisenhower . . .

There can be no stable peace in the Far East until the American naval forces are withdrawn from the Taiwan Strait, until the United States soldiers are recalled home from Taiwan. We are convinced that this view is shared not only by the Soviet Union and the other socialist states, but by all the other nations which highly prize the cause of peace in the Far East and throughout the world.[17]

There is only one Chinese state and it is in China, not elsewhere, while Taiwan and the other Chinese islands where the Chiang Kai-shekists have entrenched themselves are a part of China. . . . Will anyone deny that China is striving to liberate its territory which has been turned into a foreign war base that is a constant threat to the peaceful life of the Chinese people? [18]

And . . .

The United States—trampling underfoot all the rules of behavior of civilized nations—has grossly interfered in China's affairs and its trying to have it all its own way by force of arms in another people's house, having thus created a great threat to peace in the Far East.[19]

And . . .

The strivings of the Chinese people and of the Chinese People's Republic Government to reincorporate in the Chinese state Taiwan and the other islands which belong to China but are occupied by foreign troops are understandable to the Soviet Union. In this question we fully support and shall support the Chinese People's Republic Government until it has achieved the settlement of this question because the legal and moral right is on its side.[20]

The place of Communist China on the world scene:

True enough, the United States does not recognize China, but China will not cease to exist because of that and will suffer no harm at all. The great People's China does exist, not only exists but is also successfully developing.[21]

501

And . . .

Now the U.S.A. and several other Western countries do not recognize the Chinese People's Republic, a great country with a population of more than 650,000,000. But this does not alter the fact that the Chinese People's Republic exists and is amassing mighty forces. To put it graphically, all the people of People's China have but to sneeze and a storm will arise in some of the countries that at present do not recognize the Chinese People's Republic.[22]

In the case of a major conflict, China would need Soviet assistance. Without the atomic bomb, Communist China is not a modern military power. And "there are . . . persistent reports to the effect that Khrushchev is not eager to promote the entry of Communist China into the atomic club.

"Intelligence reports from London state that Soviet Russia has given no nuclear weapons to the Red Chinese and is anxious to keep the Chinese from getting any H-bombs or A-bombs."[23]

Khrushchev indirectly confirms these reports.

In your letter of February 8, 1960, you touch upon the question of the undesirability of any expansion of the so-called atomic club, which may be brought about if the powers which now have nuclear weapons hand them over to other countries. Your initiative in this question which is so important for peace undoubtedly merits the greatest support possible. I fully understand your concern when you say that the handing of means of nuclear destruction to other countries by the atomic powers can intensify many times all factors which cause uncertainty in the present international situation.[24]

The Chinese know their weakness. They also know that they can rely only on themselves. According to reports filtering from China,

502

Chinese scientists who already operate the nuclear reactor are working frantically on the production of an atomic bomb.

Until the day China enters the atomic club, its war potential is limited:

China has 2.5 million men under arms, a militia of 250 million, 3,200 aircraft including 2,450 jet fighters, plenty of pilots. But its technology is of World War II vintage, it is short of fuel, its pilots only three-quarters trained. . . .

Red Chinese industry "produces small arms and ammunition; and, with Soviet help . . . Soviet-type artillery, jet aircraft, tanks and submarines. Some of the component parts for these items are presently supplied by the USSR but the Chinese Communists have not advanced beyond the 'assembly stage' in which the Soviet-made parts were put together in Chinese factories." The Red Chinese, however, are manufacturing an increasing amount of electronic and engineering equipment, vehicles, artillery, and small arms. In mid-1960 there was considerable discussion of the importance of creating a modern weapons technology, indicating a continuing reluctance on the part of the Soviet Union to provide know-how—particularly in the field of nuclear weapons.

"China's ambitions are now backed by only one resource—manpower. This she is ready, willing and able to export wherever she can. Colonies of fecund Chinese have been established in metropolitan centers of Asia, Africa and Latin America." [25]

While Khrushchev has been trying to cultivate the friendship of De Gaulle, China has been feeding arms and funds to Algeria, taking the line that Algerian resistance sets an example for other African nations. China regards herself, in fact, as the leader of the anti-colonial movement. It was China that first supplied troops—even loans—for Korea, Laos, Guinea and other African nations. Russian and Chinese agents compete for influence in several African countries, in most of Southeast Asia, and in Cuba. There are more Chinese "technicians" from technology-impoverished China than from affluent Russia in many areas. Almost as many delegations—more than 100 in 1960—visit Peking as Moscow, and China sends twice as many broadcasts into the areas. Now twenty-six noncommunist nations have diplomatic relations with China, forty-five others have trade ties. Hardly able to feed her people or to build her industry or to supply rice to pay for rubber purchased from Ceylon, China arranged loans to Yemen, Burma, and Cambodia in 1956. Peking's foreign aid is already one third of her rich neighbor's.

By the end of 1960 the Soviet Union was meeting the Chinese challenge with aggressiveness of her own. Military aid went to Algiers, to Laos, to Mali, to Guinea, to Cuba, in full measure—overshadowing the offers of the poorer Chinese.

As a matter of fact, the whole area of Soviet aid to China, shadowy as it is, seems to reflect Russia's willingness to give verbal support, but a reluctance to go far beyond this. Import and export figures seem to indicate that little Soviet credit has been given to China—in fact, the balance of exports seems to be in China's favor. In his address to the Twentieth Congress, Khrushchev seems to indicate aid to China is paid for in goods.

Our country is helping the Chinese People's Republic to build, within one five-year period alone, 156 enterprises and 21 separate shops by supplying industrial equipment to a total value of 5,600,000 rubles.

In exchange for these deliveries the Soviet Union is receiving goods from China and other people's democracies—goods in which it is interested, supplies and consumers' goods which these countries customarily export.

We shall continue to give one another all-round assistance in economic, technological, scientific and cultural development. We regard this as our fraternal duty to the camp of socialism. The stronger the entire socialist camp, the more reliable will be the guarantee of the freedom, independence and economic and cultural progress of each of the countries making up this great camp.[26]

Although Soviet technicians saturated Chinese industry during the fifties, these were, apparently, a part of Soviet exports to be

504

Contradictions in Communism

USSR TRADE WITH CHINA*
(in million rubles)

	Exports	Imports	Soviet Credit to China
1938	44.1	68.5	—
1955	2993.4	2574.0	419.4
1956	2932.1	3050.9	124.8
1957	2176.4	2952.5	(776.1)
1958	2536.0	3525.0	(11.0)

*Source: United Nations: Economic Survey. See also *Statistical Yearbook*, 1951, p. 389.
( ) indicates debit balance.

paid for. The departure of Soviet technicians was reported in mid-1960 and never denied. There were other indications of a fissure in the socialist camp: the withdrawal of magazines carrying articles about Sino-Soviet friendship, a coolness in the Chinese press, and a lessening of Khrushchev's posture of amity.

When the agricultural disaster of 1960 forced China to buy grain, she turned to Australia and Canada, not the Soviet Union. Regardless of the fact or fiction of Sino-Soviet friction, many forecasters foresee an entirely new world alignment in the 1970's. As the division of the world's "haves" and "have nots" widens, the Soviet Union will become—comparatively—a have nation, while some in the socialist camp will still be have nots. The present gap between China and Albania (annual per capita income $25–$75) and the Soviet Union and other bloc nations (annual per capita income $300–$500) creates differences in outlook, attitudes and needs. When the per capita incomes are doubled demands for Soviet aid will increase. Some see a shift in Soviet attitudes as a result of this distinction and a new joining of the USSR with the industrial West— perhaps in a truly universal aid program.

Khrushchev claims no contradiction:

The contradictions existing in a socialist society, a society cemented by great moral-political unity, when there are no longer any exploiting classes and when only the friendly classes of working people—workers and peasants—remain, are different in principle. In the main these are contradictions and difficulties of growth resulting from the rapid development of socialist economy, from the growth of the material and cultural demands of the people, and from the contradictions between what is new and what is old, what is advanced and what is backward. These are the contradictions between the growing needs of members of a socialist society and still insufficient material-technical basis for their satisfaction. Such contradictions can be successfully overcome, as is shown in the forty years of experience of the Soviet state, by the socialist society itself, through a rapid and constant development of the material-technical basis of socialism and communism and through a heightening of the socialist consciousness of working people.

But a *New York Times* expert on Russia remarks:

"I am thinking of a point made by Prime Minister Nehru of India a number of years ago, on which he said that anyone who thought that the fundamental conflict in the world was between communism and anticommunism was crazy. The real division of the world was between the haves and the have-nots. Now on a world scale, Russia is increasingly becoming a have nation, as we are, and they are going to become more so in the future. But there is a great have-not nation appearing on the scene, accelerating very rapidly in its achievement of national power if not in national prosperity, and that of course is communist China. Communist China's rapid increase in power is so fantastic that the Russians feel the same way as they look at the Chinese rate of growth, as we do when we look at the Russian rate of growth. And it's not inconceivable, the constellation of forces will be such that the United States and the Soviet Union will feel that they have common interests vis-à-vis any challenge of communist China, that may even override the secular religious evangelism of whoever leads Russia at that time. There are prospectives for changing the situation, but they are not prospectives likely to become reality for the next three, six months or year or two." [27]

CHAPTER 14

Summary

Reading the words of Nikita Khrushchev alone, one is easily convinced that he is a social reformer bent on creating a better world for its impoverished masses, and that he will succeed. Viewed in the light of facts and deeds, it becomes apparent that what his "communism" offers is a supreme exploitation of the working people for a mirage of an oppressionless, "withered-away" state, a regime of the whip, of denial and sacrifice, of stoicism—all rationalized with a promise of a higher standard of living in the future. The words of N. S. Khrushchev radiate success, confidence, and hope. The facts belie them. In an age when the world has learned how to conquer the problems of production, the communist-dominated man still struggles to achieve a measure of milk, butter, and meat. In an age of sputniks, the communist places his hopes for achievement on the possession of a bicycle. Of these the Soviet Union manufactures fewer than the United States produces Cadillacs—and the bicycles are in oversupply. In an age when men can live on the labor of machines, Khrushchev's people struggle for as little as 1⅓ (old) rubles an hour—the price of a handkerchief, an ice-cream cone, or half a cucumber.

If we are tempted to believe that production-wise the communists are "catching up," we need only see how they live compared with other nations which we consider "underdeveloped."

Khrushchev's brand of peaceful coexistence is a variety of the war of nerves. He pursues it relentlessly in Berlin and Africa, in Cuba and the Middle East—careful always to make no single provocation unbearable, but determined to leave the adversary no rest.

Khrushchev seems to believe that he can wear the West down by this war of nerves alone. The Chinese doubt it. They see no victory without war, for they do not have the means to compete peacefully, nor do they believe that the Soviet Union has the means for successful "peaceful competition."

It is in disintegrating colonialism that Khrushchev places his greatest hope, the "emerging nations" of Africa, Asia, Latin America—even the underdeveloped nations of Europe—Greece, Portugal, Spain, Italy. It is to the leaders of these nations that he offers the symbolism of Russia emerging from underdevelopment to an abundance of milk, butter, and meat, without the aid of the West. For those who do not have enough to eat, the slogans have immediate reality. But the leaders of most nations have been able to see that Russia has little to offer, in ideology, technology, or material aid, compared with the nations of the West. It is only to the uneducated, the misinformed and the uninformed that he can have some appeal.

The Khrushchev design is clear and outspoken, in line with a long Party tradition: a world federation of Soviet states "in a single world socialist economic system" [1] ruled by the Communist Party under the acknowledged leadership of Moscow. Called "dictatorship of the proletariat" or "commonwealth of nations" or "the socialist camp" it is still imperialism directed by a new elite.

The political contest for this power is fought on many fronts and with many devices. Nuclear war is one, but only one, and the last resort if capitalist nations "resist." [2]

Into this competition, Khrushchev comes with great advantages, not the least of which is knowing that he is fighting and what he is fighting for. He has monolithic command, complete control over a population of 212 million and substantial control over 800 million others, with a seemingly logical authoritarian ideology to sell, a flexible morality that justifies almost any means, and great confidence. His military establishment could pulverize the wealth of the world and this provides a major weapon of diplomatic blackmail.

His corps of image makers have kept him on the front pages of the world's press, creating a picture of success and morality. They have been able to convince a substantial portion of the world's population that his threats are "peace"; that his poverty is "progress"; that his prison world is "freedom"; that his dictatorship is "democracy"; and that his promises of trade and long-term credits are "aid." Khrushchev has all the advantages of an arsonist in a flammable world: he can set fires where he will, while the Western nations, with values to protect, must rush to put them out. On this planet where two-thirds of the people are poor and colored, there are many tensions—and little love for the white man, the Yankee, or the "rich"—particularly in those areas that have lived through centuries of arrogant colonialism.

But Khrushchev has many disadvantages to conceal and overcome. He is "selling" a system that is manifestly autocratic, oppressive, and inefficient. Although his economic power is growing, he still cannot afford to join in substantial aid to underdeveloped nations. The economy of which he is master provides an average personal income of less than $10 a week in terms of purchasing power, all in spite of the fact that 67 per cent of its women and its children of fifteen and sixteen are in the labor force, a level comparable with that of subtropical pre-Castro Cuba's. He rules a nation where only 4 per cent of the population has any voice in government, and these only the right to applaud; where the workers are exploited so that they receive hardly a quarter of what they produce; where, despite much touting, only 7 per cent of those entering school can expect to get a college degree, and most of these earn it on a part-time or correspondence-school basis. In his super-welfare state, full-time schooling is limited to eight years, and social services remain approximately at the level of charity clinics in the Western world. Position, party membership, privileges, and adequate housing are largely restricted to the new aristocracy. This "system," which offers the dream of a Utopia of plenty for all— in a nation with vast resources, a temperate climate, a large population, a good industrial base even in Czarist times—after forty-three years still struggles unsuccessfully to provide an even moderately decent diet for its people. This nation, which can produce sputniks still counts with an abacus, still builds "model" apartments with one room for a family (kitchen and bath shared among three families) and sometimes without running water.[3] This is, obviously, not a nation which can produce an exemplary life or living standard for its people.

But Khrushchev by his political acumen, by his strength of purpose, by his ability to deny his people the good of modern technology, can, and does, challenge the powers of the world. By concentrating resources, by limiting objectives, by creating the image of success, by division, diversion, distraction, Khrushchev has won many battles. He has real power to cajole and blackmail, to subvert and inflame, to infiltrate and destroy—and perhaps once, carelessly, to start the fire that will destroy civilization.

Increasingly as the months pass by, Khrushchev, even more than the West, must weigh the probability of China's eventual possession of the bomb. Many years may pass before China can be a direct threat to the world or to the Soviet plan for world domination. China with a bomb would be an uninhibited hoyden in this world, especially if attached to the Soviet Union. Would China attack Taiwan and start a series of events that must force Russia to join her or repudiate her?

In the era that begins in 1961, the world situation remains dominated by Soviet initiative and threats—in Asia, Africa and Latin America. Intent—it seems—on avoiding a nuclear war, Khrushchev still carries his drive for conquest to the fringes of the Western world.

The Congo experience apparently convinced Khrushchev that the United Nations is a major obstacle on this road. Failing in an effort to control the U.N., he made a major effort to destroy it or render it ineffective. With the new administration in Washington, he made a bid for a new approach, prepared to change his methods. But there was no sign that he was prepared to change his objective:

"The victory . . . of communism," he declares, "is no longer far off." [4]

And on January 22, 1961, Tass quoted an optimistic Khrushchev:

"Coexistence of states with different social systems represents a form of class struggle between socialism and capitalism in which socialism, in view of its inherent advantages, inevitably triumphs."

If words can win the world, here is the man who plans to do it.

NOTES

Notes

To conserve space, both the notes and the text use abbreviations common in the field of Kremlinology.

USSR is, of course, Union of Soviet Socialist Republics.
CPSU is the Communist Party of the Soviet Union.
GDR is the German Democratic Republic.
CPR is the Chinese People's Republic.
CEIR is the Corporation for Economic and Industrial Research, Inc., a private organization that has done much study in the field.
RSFSR is Ruskaya Socialisticheskaya Federationaya Sovietskaya Respublica (Great Russian Republic).
SPD is the Sozialdemocratische Partei Deutschlands.

Khrushchev's speeches and interviews are taken from *Pravda* (which prints them one day to a month later), from Tass releases, and from several authorized collections.

Part I: The Scene
1. *QUEST FOR WORLD DOMINATION*

[1] Allen W. Dulles, "The Communist Attack upon Parliamentary Government," *Soviet Total War,* p. 423. Committee on Un-American Activities, U.S. House of Representatives, Washington, 1956.

[2] *Current Soviet Policies III; The Documentary Record of the Extraordinary 21st Congress, CPSU.* New York: Columbia University press, 1960.

[3] J. V. Stalin, "On Problems of Leninism" (1920), *Problems of Leninism,* p. 135. Moscow: Foreign Languages Publishing House, 1948.

[4] At Jakarta University, Indonesia; Moscow broadcast, Feb. 22, 1960.

[5] *Pravda,* Feb. 1, 1959.

[6] Leon Trotsky, signed N. Trotsky, *Nashi Politicheskye Zadachi,* Geneva, 1904; quoted in Isaac Deutscher, *The Prophet Armed,* p. 90. New York: Oxford University Press, 1954.

2. *THE FIRST SECRETARY*

[1] Quoted in Edward Crankshaw, *Khrushchev's Russia,* London: Penguin Books, Ltd., 1959.

[2] At Twentieth Century-Fox Studios, Hollywood, California, Sept. 19, 1959.

[3] George Pálóczi-Horváth, *Khru-*

shchev, the Road to Power. London: Secker and Warburg, 1960.
4 Secret Speech to 20th Congress, CPSU, Feb. 25, 1956.
5 "Khrushchev's Foreign Policy," *Socialist Courier,* New York, Apr., 1959.
6 Secret Speech to 20th Congress, CPSU, Feb. 25, 1956.
7 William K. Medlin, "Khrushchev, a Political Profile," *Russian Review,* Oct., 1958–July, 1959.
8 Sharaf R. Rashidov, First Secretary, Uzbek Communist Party, Jan. 14, 1960, at USSR Supreme Soviet.

Part II: Objectives

3. *CONQUEST WITHOUT WAR*

1 To 20th Congress, CPSU, Feb. 14, 1956.
2 In Kaprun, Austria; *The Washington Post and Times Herald,* July 6, 1960.
3 V. I. Lenin, "Partiyanskaia voina" (Oct. 13, 1906), *Sochineniya,* Vol. X, pp. 80-81.
4 Bukharin, "Speech at 4th Congress of Communist International" (Nov. 18, 1922), p. 171.
5 Lenin, "The Crisis Has Matured" (Oct. 12, 1917), *Selected Works,* Vol. VI, p. 227. New York: International Publishers, 1943.
6 To 7th Congress, MSZMP (Hungarian Socialist Workers' Party); Tass, Dec. 1, 1959.
7 *The USSR and Eastern Europe.* A Study prepared by a Columbia-Harvard Research Group for the Committee on Foreign Relations, United States Senate. Washington, D.C., 1960, p. 6.
8 In Tatabanya, Hungary; *Pravda,* Apr. 9, 1958.
9 In Leipzig, GDR, Aug. 9, 1957.
10 At Kremlin reception, Nov. 26, 1956. (Denied by USSR delegation to UN, Oct. 5, 1957.)
11 To Civic Authorities, Los Angeles, Sept. 19, 1959.
12 See note 8.
13 To All-Union Conference of Cotton Growers; Moscow broadcast, Feb. 22, 1958.
14 At National Press Club, Washington, D.C., Sept. 16, 1959.
15 To Plenary Session of the Party Central Committee; *Pravda,* May 10, 1958.
16 To Iverach McDonald; *The Times,* London, Jan. 31, 1958.
17 To Arab ambassadors during visit of French Premier Guy Mollet; *Populaire de Paris,* June 26, 1956.
18 At Hungarian Academy of Sciences; Moscow broadcast, Apr. 10, 1958.
19 To graduates of military academies; Moscow broadcast, Nov. 15, 1958.
20 To Tomoo Hirooka of *Asahi Shimbun,* Tokyo; Tass, June 29, 1957.
21 *Foreign Affairs,* Oct. 1959, Vol. XXXVIII, No. 1, p. 8.
22 To Serge Groussard; *Le Figaro,* Paris, Mar. 19, 1958.
23 To 13th Komsomol Congress; Moscow broadcast, Apr. 18, 1958.
24 See note 8.
25 On the chemical industry; Moscow broadcast, May 10, 1958.
26 To 5th Congress, Socialist Unity Party, GDR, July 11, 1958.
27 At Baltic Shipworks; Moscow broadcast, Nov. 4, 1958.
28 To 40th Jubilee Session, USSR, Supreme Soviet; Moscow broadcast, Nov. 6, 1957.
29 At Csepel Iron and Steel Works, Hungary, Apr. 9, 1958.

[30] At Soviet-Polish Friendship Meeting, Leningrad, Nov. 4, 1958.

[31] In Tula, USSR; *Pravda,* Feb. 18, 1959.

[32] See note 15.

[33] To 9th All-German Conference of Trade-Union and Plant Officials, Leipzig, GDR; Tass, Mar. 26, 1959.

[34] On returning from India, Burma, and Afghanistan; *Pravda,* Dec. 30, 1955.

[35] In Ryasan; *Pravda,* Feb. 1, 1959.

[36] To USSR Supreme Soviet; Tass, Dec. 21, 1957.

[37] See note 27.

[38] To Tula Oblast Party Committee and Soviet; Moscow broadcast, Feb. 12, 1959.

[39] "Control Figures for the Economic Development of the USSR for 1959–1965," to 21st Extraordinary Congress, CPSU, Jan. 27, 1959, p. 78.

[40] *Ibid.* The theme is part of a whole series of "inevitable triumph" speeches made during 1958, 1959 and early 1960 to create a bandwagon psychology.

[41] At Czech CKD-Stalingrad Works; Prague broadcast, July 11, 1957.

[42] To William Randolph Hearst, Jr.; *Pravda,* Nov. 29, 1957.

[43] Seven-Year-Plan thesis; Moscow broadcast, Nov. 14, 1958.

[44] Awarding Order of Lenin to Uzbeks; *Pravda,* Jan. 14, 1957.

[45] Lenin, *Sochineniya,* 4th Edition, Vol. XXIII, p. 413.

[46] To 3rd Congress, Workers Party of Rumania; *Pravda,* June 22, 1960.

[47] At Budapest Opera House; broadcast, Apr. 3, 1958.

[48] George F. Kennan, *Russia, the Atom and the West,* New York: Harper & Brothers, 1958.

[49] At Hungarian Academy of Sciences, Apr. 9, 1958.

[50] At reception, Albania, Apr. 15, 1957.

[51] To Polish delegation at Baltic Works meeting, Leningrad, Nov. 3, 1958.

[52] To James Reston; *The New York Times,* Oct. 7, 1957.

[53] To CBS correspondents, May 28, 1957.

[54] See note 28.

[55] To 9th Session, USSR Supreme Soviet (4th Convocation), Dec. 21, 1957.

[56] To U.S. Senators; Tass, Sept. 19, 1959.

[57] Lt. Col. V. Yarovikov; *Red Star,* Moscow, Mar. 6, 1959.

[58] J. Edgar Hoover, "Struggle on a New Plane," *Soviet Total War,* Vol. I, p. 10. Washington, D.C., Sept 23, 1956.

[59] Lenin, "Tactics of the Russian Communist Party" (Report to 3rd Congress of Communist International, July 5, 1921), *Selected Works* (New York), Vol. I, p. 242.

[60] At departure of China's premier Lai; *Time,* Nov. 21, 1960, p. 26.

4. *PEACEFUL COEXISTENCE*

[1] *The USSR and Eastern Europe.*

[2] To 3rd Congress, Workers' Party of Rumania; *Pravda,* June 22, 1960.

[3] In Tatabanya, Hungary, Apr. 8, 1958.

[4] See note 2.

[5] Prague Castle; Prague broadcast, July 12, 1957.

[6] "On Peaceful Coexistence," *Foreign Affairs,* Oct. 1959, Vol. XXXVIII, No. 1, pp. 1-18.

7 Lenin, "Report to the Central Committee, 8th Party Congress, CPSU" (1919), *Selected Works* (New York), Vol. VIII, p. 37.

8 Lenin, "War and Peace" (Mar. 7, 1918), *Selected Works* (New York), Vol. VII, p. 302.

9 Lenin, "Report to Moscow Party Nuclei Secretaries" (Nov. 26, 1920), *Works*, 3rd Edition, Vol. XXV, p. 512.

10 George F. Kennan, in *Foreign Affairs*, Jan. 1960, Vol. XXXVIII, No. 6, p. 173.

11 To USSR Supreme Soviet; Moscow broadcast, Oct. 31, 1959.

12 See note 5.

13 Secret Speech (Feb. 25, 1956); *Soviet Conduct in World Affairs*, p. 47.

14 At Hrabuvka Airdrome; Prague broadcast, July 13, 1957.

15 Stalin, *Economic Problems of Socialism in the USSR*, p. 15. Moscow: Foreign Languages Publishing House, 1952.

16 Seven-Year-Plan thesis; Moscow broadcast, Nov. 14, 1958.

17 In France, June 5, 1960.

18 Boris I. Nicolaevsky, "Khrushchev and Mao, *Socialist Courier*, Oct., 1959."

19 Harry Schwartz, Soviet Affairs expert of *The New York Times*, on "Open End" television interview, Apr. 10, 1960.

20 To graduates of military academies; Moscow broadcast, Nov. 15, 1958.

21 At Twentieth Century-Fox Studios, Sept. 19, 1959.

22 Karl von Clausewitz, *On War*, 1818.

23 V. I. Lenin, "Collapse of the Second International" (Summer, 1915), *Selected Works*, Vol. V, pp. 178–180. London: Lawrence and Wishart, Ltd., 1936.

24 Lenin, "Military Program of Proletarian Revolution" (1917), *Selected Works* (New York), Vol. XIX, pp. 362-366.

25 In Moscow; *Pravda*, Feb. 25, 1958.

26 To 3rd Congress, Workers' Party of Rumania, Bucharest, June 22, 1960.

27 To A. E. Johann, West German writer, Sept. 20, 1958.

28 To Kalinin constituency; Moscow broadcast, Feb. 24, 1959.

29 To Iverach McDonald of *The Times*, London; Tass, Feb. 15, 1958.

30 At Polish embassy reception; Tass, July 22, 1959.

31 At Palace of Sports, Moscow, Sept. 28, 1959.

32 To 9th All-German Conference of Trade-Union and Plant Officials, Leipzig, GDR; Tass, Mar. 25, 1959.

33 To Turner Catledge; *The New York Times*, May 10, 1957.

34 To CBS correspondents, May 28, 1957.

35 See note 31.

36 "Control Figures for the Economic Development of the USSR for 1959–1965," p. 99. To the 21st Congress, CPSU, Moscow, Jan. 27, 1959.

37 *Kommunist*, Nov. 12, 1957, p. 28.

38 See note 33.

39 At reception of Polish People's Republic, Apr. 21, 1958.

40 To James Reston; *The New York Times*, Oct. 7, 1957.

41 At Albanian Embassy, Apr. 15, 1957.

42 In Bangalore, India; *Pravda*, Nov. 28, 1955.

43 To William Randolph Hearst, Jr.; *Pravda*, Nov. 22, 1957.

44 Marshal S. Biryuziv, *Zembedelsko Zname*, Sofia, Feb. 22, 1959.

45 Marshal Malinovsky, to USSR Supreme Soviet, Jan. 16, 1960.

46 Walter Lippmann, *The Communist World and Ours*, p. 13. Boston; Little, Brown and Company, 1959.

47 To Jubilee Session, USSR Supreme Soviet, Nov. 6, 1957.

48 *The USSR and Eastern Europe.*

5. BREAKING THROUGH THE WALL

1 To 17th Congress, RSFSR; *Pravda*, Jan. 16, 1937.

2 To 18th Congress, CPSU, Mar., 1939.

3 Hubert H. Humphrey, *Khrushchev, on the Shifting Balance of World Forces.* Special study by the Legislative Reference Service, Library of Congress, Washington, D.C., Sept. 1959.

4 To Serge Groussard; *Le Figaro*, Paris, Mar. 19, 1958.

5 In People's Chamber, during visit to GDR, Aug. 8, 1957.

6 Lenin, "Left-Wing Childishness and Petty Bourgeois Mentality" (1918), *Selected Works* (New York), Vol. VII, p. 365.

7 *Ibid.*, p. 365.

8 To 5th Congress, Socialist Unity Party of Germany, July 9, 1958.

9 To Chancellor Adenauer; Tass, Feb. 1, 1960.

10 See note 9.

11 To USSR Supreme Soviet; Moscow broadcast, Jan. 14, 1960.

12 To 9th All-German Conference of Trade-Union and Plant Officials, at Leipzig, GDR; Tass, Mar. 26, 1959.

13 To SPD editors; Tass, May 8, 1959.

14 Harry S. Truman, *Memoirs.* Vol. I, p. 214. New York: Doubleday & Company, 1955.

15 To 9th All-German Conference of Trade-Union and Plant Officials at Leipzig, GDR; East Berlin broadcast, Mar. 7, 1959.

16 In People's Chamber of the GDR, Aug. 8, 1957.

17 To E. Pickering; *Daily Express*, London, Dec. 19, 1957.

18 East German News Service, Deutschlandsender, Aug. 13, 1957.

19 *World Almanac*, 1960, p. 355.

20 *Ibid.*, p. 356.

21 To 21st Congress, CPSU; Moscow broadcast, Jan. 28, 1959.

22 To 21st Congress, CPSU; Moscow broadcast Feb. 5, 1959.

23 To agricultural workers, Byelorussian Republic; *Pravda*, Jan. 26, 1958.

24 See note 23.

25 In People's Chamber of the GDR, Aug. 8, 1957.

26 To USSR Supreme Soviet; Tass, Dec. 21, 1957.

27 Moscow broadcast, May 15, 1959.

28 In *Foreign Affairs*, Oct. 1959; quoted in *Pravda*, Sept. 6, 1959.

29 Hugh S. Cummings, Jr., Department of State Bulletin, Vol. XL, p. 871.

30 Concluding speech at 21st Congress, CPSU; Moscow broadcast, Feb. 5, 1959.

31 *Op. cit.* Hugh S. Cummings, Jr., pp. 869-70.

32 To Electrochemical Works at Bitterfeld, East Germany; Moscow broadcast, July 22, 1958.

33 At meeting of the working peo-

ple of Leipzig, GDR, Aug. 9, 1957.

34 *Ibid.*

35 At Tirana textile combine, Albania; Moscow broadcast, May 27, 1959.

36 A century ago Engels wrote: ". . . the Germans . . . will become free and will take bloody revenge on the Slavic barbarians." *Russian Menace,* p. 67.

37 See also comments on the Hungarian revolution.

38 To James Reston of *The New York Times;* Tass, Oct. 11, 1957.

39 At reception in Polish embassy; *Pravda,* Apr. 21, 1957.

40 To Premier Mollet of France; Tass, June 21, 1956.

41 To a delegation of French Socialists; *Der Monat,* June 1957.

42 To CBS correspondents, May 28, 1957.

43 To 5th Congress, Socialist Unity Party of Germany, July 8, 1958.

44 To Chancellor Adenauer in Moscow; Moscow broadcast, Sept. 11, 1955.

45 *The New York Times,* Mar. 14, 1960.

46 See note 38.

47 On return from trip to India, Burma and Afghanistan; *Pravda,* Dec. 30, 1955.

48 At luncheon in Rheims, France; Moscow broadcast, Mar. 29, 1960.

49 To French-Soviet Friendship Group of French Parliament; Tass, Mar. 26, 1960.

50 To Chancellor Adenauer; Tass, Aug. 26, 1959.

51 To *Pravda* editorial board concerning events in France.

52 See note 34.

53 At political meeting, Rangoon, Burma; *Pravda,* Dec. 7, 1955.

54 See note 53.

55 See note 30.

56 East German radio broadcast, Aug. 8, 1957.

57 See note 56.

58 At Friendship Meeting of Polish People's Republic and the Soviet Union, Nov. 19, 1958.

59 See note 32.

60 See note 33.

61 "On Peaceful Coexistence," *Foreign Affairs;* quoted in *Pravda,* Sept. 6, 1959.

62 To A. E. Johann, West German writer, Sept. 20, 1958.

63 *The New York Times,* Nov. 20, 1958.

64 Kremlin press conference; Tass, Mar. 10, 1959.

65 To Kalinin constituency, Moscow; Moscow broadcast, Feb. 24, 1959.

66 To National Press Club; Moscow broadcast, Sept. 16, 1959.

67 Kremlin press conference, Nov. 27, 1958.

68 At 40th Anniversary of the Azerbaijan Communist Party; *The New York World-Telegram and The Sun,* Apr. 26, 1960, p. 4.

69 To Axel Springer of *Die Welt,* Bonn; *Pravda,* Feb. 8, 1958.

70 *New York World-Telegram and The Sun,* Apr. 21, 1960, p. 2.

71 To 21st Congress, CPSU; Moscow broadcast, Feb. 5, 1959.

72 To 7th Congress, MSZMP (Hungarian Socialist Workers' Party); Tass, Dec. 1, 1959.

73 At anniversary rally, Azerbaijan, Apr. 25, 1960; *The New York Times,* Apr. 26, 1960, p. 20.

74 To All-German Conference of Trade-Union and Plant Officials, Leipzig, GDR; East German broadcast, Mar. 7, 1959.

75 At Czechoslovakian Embassy, Moscow; Tass, in *The New York Times,* May 10, 1960, p. 14.

76 Kremlin press conference; Tass, Nov. 27, 1958.

77 At Berlin rally; East German broadcast, Mar. 9, 1959.

78 Kremlin press conference; Tass, Mar. 19, 1959.

79 At Berlin rally; East German broadcast, Mar. 9, 1959.

80 *The New York Times,* Apr. 3, 1960.

81 Moscow press conference; *The New York Times,* June 4, 1960.

82 At Soviet-GDR Friendship Meeting at the Kremlin; Moscow broadcast, June 19, 1959.

83 See note 82.

84 See note 82.

85 Polish-USSR rally; Moscow broadcast, Nov. 10, 1958.

86 See note 68.

87 *The New York Times,* Apr. 5, 1960.

88 At Berlin rally; GDR broadcast, Mar. 9, 1959.

89 At Stalinallee meeting, Berlin; GDR broadcast, Mar. 7, 1959.

90 See note 21.

91 David Lilienthal, on "Open End" television interview, Apr. 10, 1960.

92 See note 91.

93 See note 91.

94 Maurice Hindus, *Crisis in the Kremlin,* p. 89. New York: Doubleday, 1953.

95 Stalin, "Revolutionary Movement in the East," *Sochineniya,* Vol. VII, p. 228.

96 *The USSR and Eastern Europe,* p. 11.

97 To Tomoo Hirooka of *Asahi Shimbun,* Tokyo; Tass, June 29, 1957.

98 Moscow broadcast to Japan, Aug. 6, 1958.

99 Lenin, "Speech to Moscow Nuclei Secretaries," Nov. 26, 1920, *Selected Works* (New York), Vol. VIII, p. 284.

100 Moscow broadcast, Aug. 6, 1958.

101 See note 97.

102 See note 97.

103 See note 97.

104 See note 97.

105 *The New York Times,* June 16, 1960.

106 See note 97.

6. *NEUTRALIZING THE UNDERDEVELOPED COUNTRIES*

1 Lenin, "Imperialism, the Highest Stage of Capitalism" (1916), *Selected Works* (New York), Vol. V, p. 81.

2 Lenin, "Tactics of the Russian Communist Party (Bolshevik)" (1921), *Selected Works* (New York), Vol. IX, pp. 228, 229.

3 Stalin, *Marxism and the National Question,* p. 113. New York: International Publishers, 1942.

4 Stalin, "New Features of the National Question" (1921), *Marxism and the National Question,* p. 115.

5 Stalin, "New Features of the National Question"; quoted in *Pravda,* May 8, 1921.

6 Stalin, "The Amalgamation of Soviet Republics," *Marxism and the National Question,* p. 124.

7 In Calcutta, India; *Pravda,* Dec. 1, 1955.

8 To Indonesian Parliament; Tass, Feb. 26, 1960.

9 At Friendship Meeting with UAR, May 15, 1958.

10 At Kremlin luncheon for Nasser; *Pravda,* May 1, 1958.

11 To 21st Congress, CPSU; Moscow broadcast, Jan. 28, 1959.

12 To USSR Supreme Soviet; Tass, Apr. 26, 1954.

13 *The Soviet Empire: Prison House of Nations and Races.* A study prepared by the Legislative Reference Service of the Library of Congress, Washington, D.C., 1958.

14 Infiltration into Outer Mongolia began under Stalin who sent technicians and emigrants. Outer Mongolians now study in Moscow and Peking in about equal numbers. The area appears to be headed for conflict of influences between Russia and China.

15 For an analysis of Soviet-bloc relations see Z. K. Brzezinski, *The Soviet Bloc.* Cambridge, Mass.: Harvard University Press, 1960.

16 To 20th Congress, CPSU; Tass, Feb. 14, 1956.

17 At Jogjakarta University, Indonesia; Moscow broadcast, Feb. 22, 1960.

18 The power of the new nations was exhibited in the 1960 elections to the Security Council, when they forced the election of Liberia for one year to replace Portugal.

19 The trinary principle—one representative from the East, the West and neutral countries— was proposed for each Committee.

20 See Elliot R. Goodman, *The Soviet Design for a World State,* p. 485. New York: Columbia University Press, 1960.

21 Konni Zilliacus, *A New Birth of Freedom?* p. 104. London, 1956.

22 See note 16.

23 Ernest Block, "Communism in the (Underdeveloped) Countries," *Problems of Communism,* July–August, 1958, Vol. VII, No. 4, p. 32.

24 To 21st Congress, CPSU; Moscow broadcast, Jan. 27, 1959.

25 To Giuseppe Palocci of *Il Tempo,* Italy; Tass, Apr. 2, 1958.

26 Edward L. Dale, Jr., "The Case for Optimism," *The Yale Review,* June, 1960, Vol. XLIX, p. 487.

27 Mao Tse-tung, *On the People's Democratic Dictatorship,* Hong Kong, 1949; quoted in Henry Wei, *China and Soviet Russia,* p. 264. New York: Van Nostrand, 1956.

28 Pre-election speech; Moscow broadcast, Mar. 14, 1958.

29 *The USSR and Eastern Europe.*

30 See note 11.

31 Soviet trade with Latin America accounts for less than 2% of the Latin American total.

32 To Jubilee Session, USSR Supreme Soviet; Moscow broadcast, Nov. 6, 1957.

33 At Luzhniki Stadium; Moscow broadcast, Mar. 5, 1960.

34 Stalin, *Sochineniya,* p. 415. Moscow: Government Political Publishing Co., 1949.

35 To Indian journalists; *Pravda,* Aug. 5, 1958.

36 At Ordzhonikidze Baltic Shipworks, Moscow broadcast, Nov. 4, 1958.

37 To Serge Groussard of *Le Figaro,* Paris; *Pravda,* Mar. 27, 1958.

[38] To James Reston; *The New York Times,* Oct. 7, 1957.

[39] At reception by Vice-President of UAR, Marshal Abdul Hakim Amer, Oct. 21, 1958.

[40] To graduates of military academies; Moscow broadcast, Nov. 15, 1958.

[41] See note 8.

[42] Speech after trip to India, Burma and Afghanistan, Dec. 30, 1955.

[43] In Tirana, Albania; *Pravda,* May 31, 1959.

[44] To agricultural workers, Byelorussian Republic, Jan. 22, 1958.

[45] See note 11.

[46] See note 37.

[47] "Control Figures for the Economic Development of the USSR for 1959–65," report p. 96. To the 21st Congress, CPSU, Moscow, 1959.

[48] To 5th Congress, Socialist Unity Party, GDR, July 11, 1958.

[49] At Soviet-Czechoslovak Friendship Meeting; Moscow broadcast, July 12, 1958.

[50] A long account appears in *Pravda,* Nov. 4, 1960.

[51] Report of the Mutual Security Administration, Washington, D.C., 1960.

[52] Compare with votes on Soviet proposals in the U.N.

[53] At UN General Assembly, Sept. 18, 1959.

[54] See note 53.

[55] See note 53.

[56] Henry G. Aubrey, in *Comparisons of the United States and Soviet Economies,* pp. 445-446. A hearing before the Joint Economic Committee of the Congress of the United States. Washington, D.C., 1959.

[57] *Ibid.*

[58] *Ibid.*

[59] Durga Das, *The Hindustan Times,* New Delhi, India.

[60] *Comparisons of the United States and Soviet Economies.*

[61] To USSR Supreme Soviet; Moscow broadcast, Jan. 14, 1960.

[62] As measured by appropriations, the ends appear to be, in order, domination of the Middle East, Southeast Asia and the bordering countries.

[63] At luncheon for Nasser; Tass, Apr. 30, 1958.

[64] Telegram to Berlin by German Ambassador, Nov. 26, 1940, on conditions by the Soviet Union on acceptance of a treaty with Hitler.

[65] To Muhammad Hassanayu Haykal of *Al-Ahram,* Egypt; *Pravda,* Nov. 25, 1957.

[66] Parker T. Hart, Department of State Bulletin, May 18, 1959, Vol. XI, p. 716.

[67] At Palace of Culture of the Electrochemical Works of Bitterfeld, East Germany; Moscow broadcast, July 22, 1958.

[68] At Kremlin reception for Marshal Abdul Hakim Amer, UAR, Oct. 23, 1958.

[69] See note 63.

[70] At Polish Embassy reception; Tass, July 22, 1958.

[71] See note 70; *The New York Times,* Nov. 19, 1956.

[72] To James Reston of *The New York Times;* Tass, Oct. 11, 1957.

[73] Awarding Order of Lenin to Uzbeks; *Pravda,* Jan. 14, 1957.

[74] See note 73.

[75] Awarding Order of Lenin to Young Communist League leaders; *Pravda,* Nov. 10, 1956.

523

76 To French Socialist Party (SFIO), Oct. 16, 1957.
77 See note 73.
78 See note 65.
79 Khrushchev has made much of the point that a war in the Middle East would inevitably drag in all the NATO powers.
80 A. Mikoyan on "Meet the Press" television interview; *The New York Times,* Jan. 19, 1959.
81 To President Eisenhower; *Pravda,* July 20, 1958.
82 Moscow broadcast, July 28, 1958.
83 A. Mikoyan, in Arabia; Moscow broadcast, July 21, 1958.
84 At luncheon in Srinagar with Y. K. Singh, Chief of State of Kashmir; *Pravda,* Dec. 11, 1955.
85 In Smolensk; *Pravda,* Aug. 24, 1958.
86 At reception at Embassy of Polish People's Republic on 14th Anniversary of Day of National Renascence, July 22, 1958.
87 To Polish People's Delegation leaving Moscow, Nov. 11, 1958.
88 See note 11.
89 Revival of anti-Semitism in the Soviet Union has been linked with anti-Zionism, but its causes lie much deeper in the Russian tradition and in the resentment of Jewish intellectual leadership during the early days of the Party.
90 See note 42.
91 See note 11.
92 See note 63.
93 See note 42.
94 At meeting of the Tula Oblast Party Committee and the Oblast Soviet; Moscow broadcast, Feb. 18, 1959.
95 To USSR Supreme Soviet; Tass, Dec. 21, 1957.
96 See note 84.
97 To Indian Parliament; Tass, Feb. 11, 1960.
98 At dinner in New Delhi, India; Tass, Feb. 12, 1960.
99 *Recent History of the Countries of the Far East,* p. 172. Moscow: Foreign Languages Publishing House, 1954.
100 *Small Soviet Encyclopedia,* 2nd Edition, 1939, Vol. II, p. 930.
101 A. M. Dyakov, *India and Pakistan,* p. 15. Moscow, 1950.
102 See note 35.
103 In Bhilai, India; Tass, Feb. 15, 1960.
104 See note 42.
105 See note 61.
106 See note 65.
107 Mutual Security Program, Fiscal Year 1961.
108 See note 65.
109 See note 19.
110 To Serge Groussard of *Le Figaro,* Paris; *Pravda,* Mar. 27, 1958.
111 See note 19.
112 *The New York Times,* May 18, 1960.
113 To Brazilian journalists; Tass, Dec. 5, 1957.
114 See note 28.
115 To Manuel Mejia of *Excelsior,* Mexico City; Moscow broadcast, Feb. 22, 1958.

7. *ABSORBING THE SATELLITES*

1 Lenin, "Polozhenie i zadachi sosialisticheskogo internationala" (Nov. 1, 1914), *Sochineniya,* Vol. XVIII, p. 70.
2 *Pravda,* June 10, 1950.
3 Prague, Czechoslovakia, July 11, 1957.
4 Z. K. Brzezinski, *The Soviet*

Bloc, p. 112, Harvard University Press, Cambridge, Mass. 1960.

[5] P. S. Wandycz, "The Soviet System of Alliances in East Central Europe," *Journal of Central European Affairs,* July, 1956, XXI, No. 2.

[6] To 21st Congress, CPSU; Moscow broadcast, Jan. 28, 1959.

[7] *Kommunist,* No. 14, 1955, p. 127.

[8] See note 6.

[9] At Soviet-Czechoslovakian Friendship Meeting, July 12, 1958.

[10] To 5th Congress of Socialist Unity Party of Germany, July 8, 1958.

[11] Hugh Seton-Watson, *Imre Nagy on Communism,* p. xxii. New York: Frederick A. Praeger, 1957.

[12] To President Eisenhower; Tass, Aug. 5, 1958.

[13] To 7th Congress of Bulgarian Communist Party; Bulgarian broadcast, June 4, 1958.

[14] Pre-election speech; Moscow broadcast, Mar. 14, 1958.

[15] Kremlin press conference; Tass, Mar. 19, 1959.

[16] Molotov, "Foreign Policy of Soviet Union." To the USSR 5th Session, Supreme Soviet; *Pravda,* Nov. 1, 1939.

[17] At Polish Embassy; Tass, Apr. 20, 1957.

[18] To Tomoo Hirooka of *Asahi Shimbun,* Tokyo; Tass, June 29, 1957.

[19] To 7th Congress, Bulgarian Communist Party, Bulgarian broadcast, June 11, 1958.

[20] To Z. Bronjarek of *Trybuna Ludu,* Warsaw; *Pravda,* Mar. 12, 1958.

[21] *U.S. Foreign Policy Study* by Maxwell Graduate School, Syracuse University, for Committee on Foreign Relations, U.S. Senate, Washington, D.C., 1959, p. 23.

[22] In Minsk; *Pravda,* Jan. 26, 1958.

[23] In Budapest, Hungary; Moscow broadcast, Apr. 5, 1958.

[24] To 9th session, USSR Supreme Soviet, Dec. 21, 1957.

[25] In Prague, Czechoslovakia, July 16, 1957.

[26] See note 25.

[27] See note 18.

[28] J. Wszelski, "Communist Economic Strategy," *The Role of East Central Europe,* Washington, 1959.

[29] *Scanteia,* Bucharest, Jan. 31, 1954.

[30] To Jubilee Session, USSR Supreme Soviet; Moscow broadcast, Nov. 6, 1957.

[31] At Csepel Iron and Steel Works, Hungary, Apr. 9, 1958.

[32] At Palace of Culture, Bitterfeld Electrochemical Works, GDR, July 9, 1958.

[33] See note 25.

[34] *The USSR and Eastern Europe.*

[35] In Leipzig, GDR, Mar. 7, 1959.

[36] See note 35.

[37] See note 6.

[38] See note 6.

[39] Robert Loring Allen, in *Comparisons of the United States and Soviet Economies.*

[40] See note 9.

[41] Allen, *op. cit.*

[42] To 20th Congress, CPSU; Tass, Feb. 14, 1956.

[43] See note 9.

[44] In Leipzig, GDR; Mar. 26, 1959.

[45] See note 44.

[46] "Program of Communist International," *Handbook of Marx-*

ism, Sect. 4, p. 991. New York: International Publishers, 1935.

47 See note 44.

48 See note 44.

49 Lenin, "Proposals Submitted by the Central Committee of the Russian Social-Democratic Labor Party to the 2nd Socialist Conference" (April, 1916), *Selected Works* (London), Vol. V, p. 236.

50 See note 44.

51 In the Ukraine; *Pravda Ukrainy,* Oct. 30, 1949.

52 *The New York Times,* June 2, 1955.

53 *For a Lasting Peace, For a People's Democracy,* May 27, 1955.

54 See note 13.

55 Speech in Sofia, Bulgaria, June 3, 1955.

56 Secret Speech to 20th Congress, CPSU, Feb. 25, 1956.

57 See note 56.

58 In Czechoslovakia; Prague broadcast, July 11, 1957.

59 See note 13.

60 See note 13.

61 Brzezinski, *op. cit,* p. 304.

62 *Ibid.,* p. 319.

63 To East Germany Party Congress; East Berlin broadcast, July 11, 1958.

64 See note 10.

65 See note 13.

66 See note 13.

67 At Polish-USSR rally; Moscow broadcast, Nov. 10, 1958.

68 At 5th Congress, Socialist Unity Party of Germany, GDR, July 12, 1958.

69 In Moscow; *Pravda,* July 13, 1958.

70 See note 13.

71 See note 9.

72 *Current Digest of the Soviet Press,* Vol. X, No. 16, 1958. Joint Committee on Slavic Studies. A final version of the program appears in *Jugoslavia's Way,* translated by S. Preibechlvich, New York, 1958.

73 See note 6.

74 See note 6.

75 See note 13.

76 See note 63.

77 See note 30.

78 Seven-Year-Plan thesis; Moscow broadcast, Nov. 14, 1958.

79 At Soviet-Polish Friendship Meeting, Nov. 4, 1958.

80 See note 6.

81 See note 13.

82 See note 23.

83 At Bulgarian Embassy; *Pravda,* Feb. 20, 1957.

84 To William Randolph Hearst, Jr., Nov. 22, 1957.

85 To Bertrand Russell, Mar. 5, 1958.

86 See note 31.

87 *Facts About Hungary,* compiled by Imre Kovacs. New York: Waldron Press, 1958.

88 In Budapest, Hungary; Moscow broadcast, Apr. 5, 1958.

89 To agricultural workers of Byelorussian Republic, Jan. 22, 1958.

90 At meeting in Tatabanya, Hungary; *Pravda,* Apr. 8, 1958.

91 At meeting in Cegléd, Hungary, Apr. 7, 1958.

92 See note 91.

93 At Ganz-Mavag Works, Hungary; Tass, Dec. 2, 1959.

94 See note 31.

95 At Budapest Opera House; Budapest broadcast, Apr. 3, 1958.

96 See note 89.

97 On return from Hungary, Apr. 10, 1958.

98 See note 95.

99 United Nations, *Report of the Committee on the Problem of Hungary,* New York, 1957.

Supplement No. 18 (UN Document A/3592), p. 9.
100 S. Schwartz, "Khrushchev in America," *Socialist Courier,* Oct. 1959.
101 At meeting in Tatabanya, Hungary; *Pravda,* Apr. 9, 1958.
102 To representatives of CBS; Tass, June 3, 1957.

Part III: Methods

8. *THE POWER FRONT*

1 To 21st Congress, CPSU, Jan. 27, 1959.
2 Stalin, "The Tasks of Business Executives," *Problems of Leninism,* p. 356.
3 Lenin, "Report of the 8th Congress of Soviets" (Dec. 22, 1920), *Selected Works* (New York), Vol. VIII, pp. 276-277.
4 Lenin, *Selected Works* (New York), Vol. X, p. 328.
5 Stalin, *Problems of Leninism,* p. 399.
6 In New Delhi, India; Tass, Feb. 12, 1960.
7 At meeting of Young Communists; *Pravda,* Jan. 8, 1955.
8 To Plenary Session, Party Central Committee; *Pravda,* Feb. 3, 1955.
9 Seven-Year-Plan thesis; Moscow broadcast, Nov. 14, 1958.
10 *Study on Foreign Relations,* U.S. Senate, Washington, Aug. 1959, p. 13.
11 To 7th Session of Supreme Soviet; *Pravda,* May 8, 1957.
12 On chemical industry; Moscow broadcast, May 10, 1958.
13 To Jubilee Session, USSR Supreme Soviet; Moscow broadcast, Nov. 6, 1957.
14 At meeting of electors, Kalinin constituency, Mar. 14, 1958.

15 Lenin, "A Great Beginning," *Selected Works.*
16 At Csepel Iron and Steel Works, Hungary, Apr. 9, 1958.
17 See note 13.
18 *The Wall Street Journal,* June 10, 1960, p. 17.
19 To graduates of military academies; Moscow broadcast, Nov. 15, 1958.
20 *The Wall Street Journal,* June 10, 1960, p. 16.
21 To All-Union Conference of Power Industry Construction; Moscow broadcast, Dec. 13, 1959.
22 *Kommunist,* No. 1, 1959, p. 83.
23 Edwin Vennard, in *Comparisons of the United States and Soviet Economies,* p. 478.
24 To 21st Congress, CPSU, Jan. 27, 1959.
25 Sokolova, *Voprosy Ekonomiki,* 1958, No. 5, p. 65.
26 See note 13.
27 To delegation to 5th Congress, Socialist Unity Party of Germany, in Halle, GDR, July 8, 1957.
28 *Statistical Yearbook.* New York: United Nations, 1959.
29 At Bitterfeld Electrochemical Works, GDR, July 9, 1958.
30 See note 29.
31 In Cegléd, Hungary; Moscow broadcast, Apr. 8, 1958.
32 To Party Central Committee Plenary Session; *Pravda,* July 2, 1959.
33 To 21st Congress, CPSU, Jan. 28, 1959.
34 See note 33.
35 *The New York Times,* July 3, 1959, p. 1.
36 "Work of District Committee," *Partinoye Stroitelstvo* ("Party Construction"), No. 13–14 (July, 1945), p. 11.

527

37 At Ganz-Mavag Works, Hungary, Dec. 2, 1959.
38 Stalin, "Interview with American Worker Delegation" (Sept. 9, 1927), *Voprosy Leninizma,* 9th Edition, p. 287, Moscow, 1932.
39 Stalin, "The Results of the First Five-Year Plan" (Jan. 7, 1933), *Problems of Leninism,* p. 404.
40 To William Randolph Hearst, Jr.; reported in *The Washington Post and Times Herald,* Nov. 24, 1957.
41 To 1st Session, USSR Supreme Soviet, Apr. 26, 1957.
42 *Pravda,* Nov. 30, 1959.
43 *The Washington Post and Times Herald,* July 10, 1960.
44 Report to Central Committee at 20th Congress, CPSU, Feb. 14, 1956.
45 To agricultural workers, Byelorussian Republic, Jan. 22, 1958.
46 To William Randolph Hearst, Jr.; *Pravda,* Nov. 29, 1957.
47 To CBS correspondents, May 28, 1957.
48 In Pittsburgh, Sept. 24, 1959.
49 Letter to President Eisenhower; Tass, June 5, 1958.
50 At Economic Club of New York, Sept. 17, 1959.
51 See note 50.
52 See note 48.
53 See note 48.
54 *U.S.–Soviet Trade,* p. 203. Cleveland: Trade Research Associates, 1960.
55 See note 48.
56 In Krasnoyarsk; Moscow broadcast, Oct. 11, 1959.
57 To French Peace Council; Tass, Mar. 23, 1960.
58 See note 50.
59 In Birmingham, England; *Pravda,* Apr. 24, 1956.
60 See note 50.

61 See note 48.
62 To E. Pickering of the *Daily Express,* London; *Pravda,* Dec. 24, 1957.
63 *Le Monde Hebdomadaire,* Mar. 24–30, No. 597, 1960.
64 See note 63.
65 To Paris Chamber of Commerce; Tass, Mar. 25, 1960.
66 See note 57.
67 Aubrey, *op. cit.*
68 To Al Baker; *The Wall Street Journal,* May 23, 1960.
69 *Digest of Investment Advices,* New York, Sept. 8, 1960, No. 294, p. 1.
70 James R. Schlesinger, *The Political Economy of National Security,* p. 69. New York; Frederick A. Praeger, 1960.
71 To Soviet journalists; Tass, Nov. 17, 1959.
72 Mao Tse-tung, "Problems of War and Strategy" (Nov. 6, 1938), in *(Hsuanchi) Selected Works of Mao Tse-tung,* Vol. II, p. 505. Peking, 1952.
73 Lenin, *Selected Works* (New York), Vol. III, p. 313.
74 "Theses of the 6th World Congress of the Communist International" (1928), *International Press Correspondence,* Nov. 28, No. 84, p. 1590.
75 Stalin, "Report of the Work of the Central Committee to the 17th Congress, CPSU" (Jan. 26, 1934), *Problems of Leninism,* p. 467.
76 In Kiev, May 26, 1938.
77 At Moscow mass meeting, Sept. 28, 1959.
78 In Azerbaijan, Apr. 25, 1960; *The New York Times,* Apr. 26, p. 20.
79 To West German editors; *Pravda,* May 9, 1959.
80 To Henry Shapiro of the

United Press; Tass, Nov. 18, 1957.

81 To USSR Supreme Soviet; Moscow broadcast, Jan. 14, 1960.

82 *International Security, the Military Aspect,* Special Studies II of The Rockefeller Brothers Fund, pp. 16, 17. New York: Doubleday & Company, 1958.

83 In Tatabanya, Hungary; *Pravda,* Apr. 9, 1958.

84 See note 46.

85 See note 80.

86 Kremlin press conference; Tass, Mar. 19, 1959.

87 To President Eisenhower; *Pravda,* July 20, 1958.

88 At meeting of the Political Consultative Committee of the Warsaw Treaty; *Pravda,* May 27, 1958.

89 *International Security, the Military Aspect,* p. 17.

90 *Ibid.*

91 In response to questions on national defense, office of the Secretary of Defense, Mar. 25, 1960.

92 On the U-2 plane incident; *The New York Times,* May 19, 1960.

93 See note 91.

94 See note 80.

95 W. W. Rostow, "Summary and Policy Implications," *Comparisons of the United States and Soviet Economies,* p. 27.

96 *The USSR and Eastern Europe.*

97 In Rangoon, Burma; *Pravda,* Dec. 7, 1955.

98 To Turner Catledge; *The New York Times,* May 10, 1957.

99 At Jogjakarta University, Indonesia; Moscow broadcast, Feb. 22, 1960.

100 To Peter Dempson of the *To-ronto Telegram;* Tass, Nov. 2, 1957.

101 To USSR Supreme Soviet; Moscow broadcast, Jan. 14, 1960.

102 To 3rd Congress, Workers' Party of Rumania, Bucharest, June 22, 1960.

103 Paris news conference; *The New York Times,* May 19, 1960.

104 Humphrey, *op. cit.*

105 Paris news conference, May 18, 1960.

106 In Azerbaijan; *The New York Times,* Apr. 26, 1960, p. 20.

107 Schlesinger, *op. cit.,* p. 47.

108 *Problems of Communism,* Mar.-Apr., 1958, Vol. VII, No. 2, p. 42.

109 DeWitt Nicholas, "Basic Comparative Data on Soviet and American Education," *Comparative Education Review,* June, 1958, p. 11.

110 In San Francisco, Sept. 27, 1959; *The New York Times,* Sept. 20, p. 19.

111 *Soviet Commitment to Education,* Report of First Official Education Mission to USSR, U.S. Department of Health, Education and Welfare, Washington, D.C., 1959.

112 At Hungarian Academy of Sciences; *Izvestia,* Apr. 10, 1958, p. 2.

113 See note 112.

114 See note 50.

115 To Central Statistical Board of the USSR Council of Ministers; Moscow broadcast, Feb. 3, 1960.

116 Benjamin A. Javits, in *Comparisons of the United States and Soviet Economies,* p. 351.

117 In Washington, D.C., Sept. 27, 1959.

118 On education; Moscow broadcast, Sept. 21, 1958.
119 W. W. Eshelman, in *Comparisons of the United States and Soviet Economies,* p. 513.
120 David Granick, *ibid.,* p. 143.
121 To 1st Session, USSR Supreme Soviet, Apr. 1954.
122 "Control Figures for the Economic Development of the USSR for 1959–1965," p. 71. To 21st Congress, CPSU, Jan. 27, 1959.
123 Tass, Mar. 20, 1954.
124 Stalin, quoted by Maurice Hindus, *Crisis in the Kremlin,* p. 202. Garden City, N.Y.: Doubleday & Company, 1953.
125 See note 118.
126 Seven-Year-Plan thesis; Moscow broadcast, Nov. 14, 1958.
127 See note 118.
128 *Pravda,* Jan. 15, 1960.
129 See note 118.
130 To 13th Komsomol Congress; Moscow broadcast, Apr. 18, 1958.
131 See note 118.
132 See note 118.
133 Joseph S. Berliner, in *Comparisons of the United States and Soviet Economies.*
134 Moscow broadcast, Apr. 10, 1957.
135 See note 118.
136 M. A. Laurentyev, Novosibirsk province; *Pravda,* Feb. 11, 1959.
137 See note 118.
138 See note 130.
139 See note 130.
140 In Smolensk; Moscow broadcast, Aug. 24, 1958.
141 See note 118.
142 To All-Union Conference of Young Builders; *Pravda,* Apr. 13, 1956.
143 See note 118.
144 See note 130.

145 See note 118.
146 See note 121.
147 To Young Communist League members; *Pravda,* June 7, 1956.

9. THE DIPLOMATIC FRONT

1 Textbooks on psychological warfare can, with some adaptation, be applied to world political operations, but the techniques are, of course, quite different.
2 For an analogy to Pavlovian principles see *The New York Times Magazine,* July 17, 1960.
3 I. P. Pavlov, *Conditioned Reflexes,* pp. 395–397. New York: International Publishers, 1927.
4 At Bucharest, Rumania, June 22, 1960.
5 Pavlov, *op. cit.,* p. 321.
6 Lenin, "Left-Wing Communism," *Selected Works* (New York), Vol. X, p. 138.
7 W. W. Rostow, *op. cit.*
8 To Henry Shapiro of the United Press; Tass, Nov. 18, 1957.
9 To Chancellor Adenauer; Tass, Aug. 26, 1959.
10 To William Randolph Hearst, Jr., Nov. 22, 1957.
11 To James Reston of *The New York Times;* Tass, Oct. 11, 1957.
12 See note 9.
13 To graduates of military academies; Moscow broadcast, Nov. 15, 1958.
14 At meeting of Political Consultative Committee of the Warsaw Treaty, May 24, 1958.
15 To 21st Congress, CPSU; Moscow broadcast, Feb. 5, 1959.
16 At Berlin rally; East German broadcast, Mar. 9, 1959.

17 To CBS correspondents, May 28, 1957.

18 See note 10.

19 *The New York Times,* May 20, 1960.

20 Mao Tse-tung, *Selected Works,* Vol. II, p. 189.

21 At political meeting, Rangoon, Burma; *Pravda,* Dec. 7, 1955.

22 At National Press Club, Washington, D.C., Sept. 16, 1959.

23 At White House dinner, Washington, D.C., Sept. 15, 1959.

24 See "We Are Winning" speeches: at meeting of electors, Kalinin, Mar. 14, 1958; and Moscow election speech, *Pravda,* Mar. 7, 1954; and in Cegléd, Hungary, Moscow broadcast, Apr. 8, 1958.

25 Between Jan. 1 and Sept. 30, 1960, Khrushchev received more prominence on page 1 of *The New York Times* than Dwight D. Eisenhower.

26 An interesting summary of such techniques was compiled as a thesis by Merl E. Bonney, "Techniques of Appeal and Social Control." Menasha, Wisconsin.

27 Lenin, *Selected Works* (New York), Vol. VIII, p. 279.

28 To Henry Shapiro; United Press, Nov. 14, 1957.

29 In Warsaw; *Pravda,* May 27, 1958.

30 *International Security, the Military Aspect,* p. 41.

31 See note 28.

32 At Czechoslovakian Embassy; Tass, May 9, 1960.

33 Kremlin press conference; Tass, Mar. 19, 1960.

34 See note 21.

35 See note 21.

36 To Twickenham Council for the Abolition of Nuclear Weapons; *International Life,* Feb. 15, 1958.

37 To a group of British pacifists, Feb. 15, 1958.

38 See note 28.

39 At Bulgarian Embassy, Feb. 18, 1957.

40 In Albania, May 27, 1959.

41 In Karce, Albania; Moscow broadcast, May 20, 1959.

42 In Austria; *The New York Times,* July 7, 1960, pp. 1, 14.

43 To Peter Dempson of the *Toronto Telegram;* Tass, Nov. 2, 1957.

44 On the U-2 plane incident; *The New York Times,* May 13, 1960, p. 4.

45 W. W. Rostow, "Summary and Policy Implications," *Comparisons of the United States and Soviet Economies,* p. 27.

46 Lenin, "Left-Wing Communism," *op. cit.*

47 See note 14.

48 "Report of the Central Committee, CPSU," Moscow, 1956, pp. 27–28. To 20th Congress, CPSU.

49 "Speeches and Interviews on World Problems," Moscow, 1958, p. 24. At Jubilee Session USSR Supreme Soviet.

50 To Indian journalists; *Pravda,* Aug. 5, 1958.

51 See note 48.

52 To Muhammad Hassanayu Haykal of *Al-Ahram,* Egypt; *Pravda,* Nov. 25, 1957.

53 At Rheims, France, Mar. 29, 1960.

54 To Paris Chamber of Commerce, Mar. 25, 1960.

55 See note 53.

56 To Peace Fighters' Rally, Paris, Feb. 23, 1960.

57 At Paris airport; *The New York Times,* Mar. 24, 1960, p. 6.

58 At Diplomatic Press Associ-

ation luncheon in France; Moscow broadcast, Mar. 25, 1960.

59 Concerning events in France; Moscow broadcast, Sept. 21, 1958.

60 *Great Soviet Encyclopedia,* 1952, Vol. XI, pp. 604, 605.

61 To Paris Municipal Council; Tass, Mar. 25, 1960.

62 E. V. Tarle, *History of Diplomacy,* Vol. III, pp. 708, 709. Moscow: Government Political Publishing Co., 1945.

63 Lenin, "Left-Wing Communism," *op. cit.*

64 "Theses and Resolutions of the 6th World Congress of Communist International," *International Press Correspondence,* Nov. 28, 1928, Vol. VIII, No. 84, pp. 1576, 1577.

65 *Ibid.*

66 At UN General Assembly, Sept. 18, 1959.

67 To 3rd Congress, Workers' Party of Rumania; *Pravda,* June 22, 1960.

68 On "Open End" television interview, Apr. 10, 1960.

69 *Sovetskii Soyuz y borba za mir,* p. 23.

70 "On the Interdependence of War and Politics," speech to the Soviet Fleet, Jan. 8, 1958.

71 Seven-Year-Plan thesis; Moscow broadcast, Nov. 14, 1958.

72 To USSR Supreme Soviet; Moscow broadcast, Jan. 14, 1960.

73 See note 72.

74 See note 72.

75 See note 72.

76 See note 72.

77 To Paris Chamber of Commerce; Tass, Mar. 25, 1960.

78 See note 58.

79 Letter to C. Rajagopalachari, Dec. 3, 1957.

80 See note 72.

81 Based on official figures. Unofficial figures are considerably higher.

82 World Almanac. Various years.

83 To agricultural workers, Byelorussian Republic; *Pravda,* Jan. 26, 1958.

84 See note 43.

85 Pre-election speech; Moscow broadcast, Mar. 14, 1958.

86 See note 11.

87 To President Eisenhower; Tass, June 16, 1958.

88 In Paris; Tass, Mar. 25, 1960.

89 *Soviet Documents on Foreign Policy,* Vol. III, p. 84. Oxford, 1953.

30 To USSR Supreme Soviet; Moscow broadcast, Oct. 31, 1959.

91 At Dnepropetrovsk machine-building works; Moscow broadcast, July 30, 1959.

92 To 21st Congress, CPSU; Moscow broadcast, Jan. 27, 1959.

93 To CBS correspondents, May 28, 1957.

94 See note 43.

95 To Tomoo Hirooka; *Asahi Shimbun,* Tokyo, June 18, 1957.

96 At meeting of the Political Consultative Committee of the Warsaw Treaty, May 24, 1958.

97 *Neues Deutschland,* Mar. 8, 1960.

98 Thomas C. Schelling, *Disarmament or Arms Control* mimeo, 1959.

99 Election speech; Moscow broadcast, Mar. 1, 1958.

100 To Indian Parliament; *Pravda,* Nov. 22, 1955.

101 To 21st Congress, CPSU; Moscow broadcast, Jan. 28, 1959.

102 Lenin, *Selected Works,* Vol. X, p. 26.

103 See note 10.

104 On return from Hungarian

People's Republic, Apr. 10, 1958.

[105] In Bangalore, India, *Pravda*, Nov. 28, 1955.

[106] See note 15.

[107] Meeting with U.S. Senators; Tass, Sept. 19, 1959.

[108] At Soviet-Czechoslovakian Friendship Meeting; Moscow broadcast, July 12, 1958.

[109] At the Economic Club of New York, Sept. 17, 1959.

[110] At anniversary rally, Azerbaijan; *The New York Times,* Apr. 26, 1960, p. 20.

[111] 6th World Congress of Communist International, 1928.

[112] See note 66.

[113] *The New York Times,* June 4, 1960.

[114] See note 113.

[115] *International Security, the Military Aspect,* p. 50.

[116] See note 66.

[117] To magazine *Horizon;* Tass, Jan. 30, 1960.

[118] In Calcutta, India; Moscow broadcast, Mar. 2, 1960.

[119] See note 71.

[120] See note 66.

[121] See note 36.

[122] To Prime Minister Macmillan; Tass, Apr. 7, 1958.

[123] See note 95.

[124] To Walthanstow, England, branch of Campaign for Nuclear Disarmament; Tass, June 4, 1958.

[125] To USSR Supreme Soviet; Moscow broadcast, Jan. 14, 1960.

[126] *International Security, the Military Aspect,* p. 53.

[127] To members of French Peace Council; Tass, Mar. 23, 1960.

[128] A. M. Rosenthal; *The New York Times,* June 11, 1960, p. 8.

[129] Robert Strausz-Hupe, et al.,

Protracted Conflict, pp. 10, 959. New York: Harper & Brothers, 1960.

[130] Stalin, quoted in Dallin, *The Real Soviet,* p. 71. New Haven: Yale University Press, 1947.

[131] To Iraqi delegation at the Kremlin; Tass, Mar. 16, 1959.

[132] In village of Veshenskaya, Rostov Oblast; Moscow broadcast, Aug. 31, 1959.

[133] See note 21.

[134] To USSR Supreme Soviet; Moscow broadcast, Oct. 31, 1959.

[135] In Tirana, Albania; Albanian broadcast, May 31, 1959.

[136] See note 134.

[137] See note 134.

[138] *The USSR and Eastern Europe,* p. 62.

[139] See note 134.

[140] At anniversary rally in Azerbaijan; *The New York Times,* Apr. 26, 1960.

[141] Lenin, "Left-Wing Communism," *op. cit.,* p. 112.

[142] Reply to Bertrand Russell, Dec. 7, 1957.

[143] See note 71.

10. *SUBVERSION*

[1] Alfred G. Meyer, *Leninism,* p. 19. Cambridge, Mass.: Harvard University Press, 1957.

[2] "For a Close Tie of Literature and Art with the Life of the People," *Kommunist,* 1958, No. 12, p. 17.

[3] In Tatabanya, Hungary; *Pravda,* Apr. 9, 1958.

[4] In Leipzig, GDR; East German broadcast, Aug. 12, 1957.

[5] To 20th Congress, CPSU, Feb. 24, 25, 1956.

[6] *Izvestia,* Dec. 26, 1917.

[7] Quoted by William H. Cham-

berlain, "Old Struggle, New Tactics," *The Russian Review,* Jan. 1960, Vol. XIX.

8 To 20th Congress, CPSU; Tass, Feb. 1, 1956.

9 On the chemical industry; Moscow broadcast, May 10, 1958.

10 The Comintern and the Cominform were explicitly designed as international revolutionary units. The work is now carried on through other units, notably the Soviet Agitprop.

11 Lenin, *Selected Works* (New York), Vol. V, p. 141.

12 *International Affairs,* Moscow, Jan. 1956, p. 2.

13 Stalin, "On the Death of Lenin," *Sochineniya,* Vol. VI, pp. 50, 51. Moscow: Government Political Publishing Co., 1947.

14 Stalin, *Problems of Leninism,* p. 113.

15 "Program of Communist International; Dictatorship of the Proletariat in the USSR" (Adopted 1928 by the 6th Congress of the Comintern), *Handbook of Marxism,* Sec. 2, Pt. 5, p. 1020. New York: International Publishers, 1935.

16 Stalin, *Oktiabrskaiarevolutsiia i taktika russkikh kommunistov* (1924 to present), p. 104.

17 Stalin, *Ob osnovakh Leninizma* (1924 to present), p. 54.

18 To 9th All-German Conference of Trade-Union and Plant Officials, Leipzig, GDR; Tass, Mar. 26, 1959.

19 To working people of Berlin, Aug. 13, 1957.

20 To Jubilee Session, USSR Supreme Soviet; Moscow broadcast, Nov. 6, 1957.

21 To 7th Session, USSR Supreme Soviet; *Pravda,* May 8, 1957.

22 To Central Committee of the Italian Communist Party, May 31, 1958.

23 Lenin, to 2nd Congress of Communist International; *Pravda,* July 21, 1920. Washington, D.C., 1920.

24 See note 20.

25 In village of Veshenskaya; Moscow broadcast, Aug. 31, 1959.

26 To 21st Congress, CPSU, Jan. 27, 1959.

27 Stalin, "The International Situation and Defense of the USSR," *Sochineniya,* Moscow; Gospolitizdat, 1949.

28 "Stalinist Friendship of Nationalities," on Stalin's seventieth birthday; *Pravda,* Dec. 21, 1949.

29 See note 26.

30 Vyshinsky, "Communism and the Motherland," *Problems of Philosophy,* No. 2, 1948.

31 To Henry Shapiro of the United Press; Tass, Nov. 18, 1957.

32 To G. Palocci of *Il Tempo,* Italy; Tass, Apr. 2, 1958.

33 See note 26.

34 See note 26.

35 See note 26.

36 Seven-Year-Plan thesis, to 21st Congress, CPSU; *Pravda,* Nov. 14, 1958.

37 To 20th Congress, CPSU, Feb. 14, 1956.

38 Stalin, "On the Program of the Comintern" (July 5, 1928), *Sochineniya,* Vol. XI, p. 152.

39 See note 26.

40 See note 37.

41 To Iverach McDonald of *The Times,* London; Tass, Feb. 15, 1958.

42 Lenin, "Tasks of the Youth Leagues" (Oct. 20, 1920), *Selected Works* (New York), Vol. IX, p. 475.

43 Lenin, "Left-Wing Communism, an Infantile Disorder" (1920),

Selected Works (New York), Vol. X, pp. 139-140.

44 Lenin, "Where to Begin?" (1901) *Selected Works* (New York), Vol. II, pp. 21-22.

45 In Krasnoyarsk; Moscow broadcast, Oct. 11, 1959.

46 To 7th Congress, Bulgarian Communist Party; Bulgarian broadcast, June 4, 1958.

47 Lenin, "Farewell Letter to Swiss Workers," *Selected Works* (New York), Vol. VI, p. 16.

48 *History of the Communist Party of the Soviet Union (Bolsheviks)*, p. 206. Edited by a commission of the Central Committee of the CPSU. Moscow: Foreign Languages Publishing House, 1949.

49 To Indian journalists; Tass, Aug. 4, 1958.

50 To Brazilian journalists, V. Martorelli and T. Fleuri; Tass, Dec. 5, 1957.

51 See note 26.

52 To Indian journalists, July 29, 1958.

53 To voters in Moscow; *Pravda,* Feb. 25, 1958.

54 To Diplomatic Press Association luncheon; Moscow broadcast, Mar. 25, 1960.

55 To USSR Supreme Soviet; Moscow broadcast, Oct. 31, 1959.

56 Pre-election speech; Moscow broadcast, Mar. 14, 1958.

57 About trip to India, Burma, and Afghanistan; *Pravda,* Dec. 30, 1955.

11. *THE PROPAGANDA FRONT (I)*

1 Mikhail Kalinin, to 14th Congress, CPSU (1925). Stenographic Report of 14th Party Congress, p. 321. Moscow: Gosudarstvennoye Izdatelstvo, 1926.

2 At 43rd Anniversary Celebration; *The New York Times,* Nov. 8, 1960.

3 To 20th Congress, CPSU; Tass, Feb. 14, 1956.

4 To Economic Club of New York, Sept. 17, 1959.

5 At Diplomatic Press Association luncheon; Moscow broadcast, Mar. 25, 1960.

6 To Jubilee Session, USSR Supreme Soviet, Nov. 6, 1957.

7 To 7th Congress, Bulgarian Communist Party, June 3, 1958.

8 At Ganz-Mavag Works, Hungary; Tass, Dec. 2, 1959.

9 In Novosibirsk; Moscow broadcast, Oct. 14, 1959.

10 To voters in Moscow; *Pravda* Feb. 25, 1958.

11 See note 3.

12 See note 3.

13 Report to the chemical industry; Moscow broadcast, May 10, 1958.

14 Tass, Mar. 20, 1954.

15 Moscow press conference, Aug. 5, 1959.

16 In Plowel, Poland; *Izvestia,* July 21, 1959.

17 Moscow press conference, Aug. 8, 1959.

18 To French socialists; *Der Monat,* June, 1957.

19 *Nepszadsog,* June 14, 1959.

20 To Turner Catledge; *The New York Times,* May 10, 1957.

21 To CBS correspondents, May 28, 1957.

22 At Twentieth Century-Fox Studios, Sept. 19, 1959.

23 In Pittsburgh, Sept. 24, 1959.

24 To 21st Congress, CPSU; Moscow broadcast, Jan. 28, 1959.

25 See note 6.

26 See note 24.

27 *Survey of Current Business,* U.S. Department of Commerce.

28 Seven-Year-Plan thesis, to 21st Congress, CPSU, Nov. 14, 1958.

29 Edmund Nash, "Purchasing Power of Workers in the USSR," *Monthly Labor Review,* Apr., 1960, p. 363.

30 See note 24.

31 Lenin, *Collected Works,* 4th Edition, Vol XXIV, p. 5.

32 Stalin, *Problems of Leninism,* p. 363.

33 See note 24.

34 To Serge Groussard, of *Le Figaro,* Paris; Moscow broadcast, Mar. 27, 1958.

35 At Rangoon University, Burma; *Pravda,* Dec. 8, 1955.

36 See note 24.

37 Boris I. Nicolaevsky, "Crimes of the Stalin Era," *New Leader.*

38 See note 24.

39 Estimate, John Price Jones Agency, New York.

40 *U.S. Statistical Abstract,* 1960, p. 870.

41 Pre-election speech; Moscow broadcast, Mar. 14, 1958.

42 See note 41.

43 See note 41.

44 In Kiev; Moscow broadcast, Apr. 28, 1958.

45 *The New York Times,* Aug. 15, 1960, p. 2.

46 *The New York Times,* Aug. 18, 1960.

47 On education; Moscow broadcast, Sept. 21, 1958.

48 Scherbakov, explanation of labor-reserve system; *Pravda,* Jan. 22, 1941.

49 Jay Lovestone, in *Comparisons of The United States and Soviet Economies.*

50 Lenin, *Selected Works* (New York), Vol. II, p. 280.

51 To 13th Komsomol Congress; Moscow broadcast, Apr. 18, 1958.

52 To agricultural workers, Byelorussian Republic; Moscow broadcast, Jan. 25, 1958.

53 See note 24.

54 See note 6.

55 In Tirana, Albania: Moscow broadcast, May 31, 1959.

56 See note 24.

57 *America's Needs and Resources,* p. 39. Deerhurst and Associates, 1955.

58 U.S. Department of Labor, *Monthly Labor Review,* Sept. 1960.

59 In Katowice, Poland; Warsaw broadcast, July 6, 1959.

60 See note 41.

61 To 21st Congress, CPSU; Moscow broadcast, 1959.

62 Moscow broadcast, Jan. 14, 1959.

63 *Health Insurance Data,* p. 8. New York: Health Insurance Institute, 1959.

64 Thomas Hammond and Erich Lessing, "A Firsthand Look at the Soviet Union," *National Geographic Magazine,* Sept. 1959, Vol. CXVI, p. 405.

65 *The New York Times,* July 21, 1959, pp. 1, 8.

66 At Washington, D.C., television interview, Sept. 27, 1959.

67 For an example, see *Komsomolskaya Pravda,* Apr. 14, 1959.

68 Alma-Ata broadcast, July 25, 1959.

69 John F. Kantner, in *Comparisons of the United States and Soviet Economies,* p. 56.

70 To Eric Ridder, *Journal of Commerce,* Mar. 27, 1958.

71 *Statistical Handbook of the USSR,* p. 97. National Industrial Conference Board, 1957.

72 *Pick's Currency Yearbook,* p. 372. New York, 1960.

73 "Control Figures for the Economic Development of the USSR for 1959-1965," p. 70. To 21st Congress, CPSU, Jan. 27, 1959.

74 At conference on farm personnel; *Pravda,* Apr. 10, 1957.

75 See note 68.

76 See note 8.

77 See note 28.

78 See note 28.

79 See note 28.

80 To James Reston of *The New York Times;* Tass, Oct. 11, 1957.

81 *Krymskaya Pravda,* May 24, 1959.

82 See note 80.

83 *Molodoi Kommunist,* Oct. 1959.

84 To Young Communist League members; *Komsomolskaya Pravda,* June 7, 1956.

85 At meeting of the Kalinin constituency; Moscow broadcast, Feb. 24, 1959.

86 See note 24.

87 See note 52.

88 To 13th Komsomol Congress; Moscow broadcast, Apr. 18, 1958.

89 See note 13.

90 To 9th All-German Conference of Trade-Union and Plant Officials, Leipzig, GDR; East Berlin broadcast, Mar. 7, 1959.

91 See note 24.

92 See note 24.

93 See note 24.

94 Resolution on propaganda adopted by Central Committee, CPSU; *Pravda,* Jan. 10, 1960.

95 To Henry Shapiro of the United Press; Tass, Nov. 18, 1957.

96 To 7th Komsomol Congress; Moscow broadcast, Nov. 14, 1957.

97 To Iverach McDonald of *The Times,* London; Tass, Feb. 15, 1958.

98 See note 24.

99 See note 51.

100 In Vladivostok; Moscow broadcast, Oct. 8, 1959.

101 At luncheon with Robert F. Wagner, Mayor of New York, Sept. 17, 1959.

102 At Economic Club of New York, Sept. 17, 1959.

103 To leaders of U.S. Congress and Members of the Senate Foreign Relations Committee, Sept. 16, 1959.

104 Harry Hodgkinson, *Doubletalk, the Language of Communism,* p. 5. London: George Allen—Unwin, Ltd., 1955.

105 See Chapter 4.

106 To Members of French Peace Council; Tass, Mar. 23, 1960.

107 At Hrabuvka Airdrome; Prague broadcast, July 13, 1957.

108 Lenin, *Collected Works* (New York), Vol. XIX, pp. 362, 366.

109 Stalin, "Report to 15th Congress" (Dec. 2, 1927), *Sochineniya,* Vol. X, pp. 288, 289.

110 Tass, Dec. 21, 1957.

111 To agricultural workers, Byelorussian Republic, Jan. 22, 1958.

112 World Survey, *Manchester Guardian Weekly,* Apr. 17, 1950.

113 At luncheon in honor of Finnish President, Dr. Urho Kekkonen, May 23, 1958.

114 In Tatabanya, Hungary; *Pravda,* Apr. 9, 1958.

115 See note 114.

[116] To Tass correspondent, Oct. 3, 1958.

[117] To President Eisenhower; Tass, Sept. 8, 1958.

[118] In Jakarta, Indonesia; Tass, Feb. 29, 1960.

[119] Stalin, "Lenin," *Sochineniya,* Vol. VI, pp. 58-59.

[120] Stalin, "Recho khoziaistvennom stroitelstve" (Mar. 31, 1920), *Sochineniya,* Vol. XXV, p. 119.

[121] To Tomoo Hirooka of *Asahi Shimbun,* Tokyo; *Pravda,* Jan. 18, 1957.

[122] At Csepel Iron Works, Hungary; *Pravda,* Apr. 1, 1958.

[123] Pre-election speech, Moscow; *Pravda,* Mar. 15, 1958.

[124] In Kiev; Moscow broadcast, Apr. 28, 1958.

[125] Franz-Josef Strauss, "Soviet Aims and German Unity," *Foreign Affairs,* Vol. XXXVII, Apr., 1959, p. 373.

[126] See note 117.

[127] Pre-election speech, Kalinin; Moscow broadcast, Feb. 24, 1958.

[128] To a delegation of French Socialists; quoted by Pierre Lochak in *Der Monat,* June, 1957.

[129] To Indian Parliament; Tass, Feb. 11, 1960.

[130] Stalin, "Thirty Years of Proletarian Dictatorship," *Sochineniya,* Vol. IV, p. 389.

[131] Lenin, "Trade Union and Mistakes of Trotsky and Bukharin," *Selected Works* (New York), Vol. IX, p. 70.

[132] See note 24.

[133] See note 40.

[134] See note 122.

[135] See note 6.

[136] Kremlin press conference; *Pravda,* Nov. 28, 1958.

[137] Lenin, "The Autocracy Is Tottering," *Sochineniya,* Vol. VI, p. 314.

[138] To newsmen aboard Lille-Rouen train; Tass, Mar. 31. 1960.

[139] See note 20.

[140] In Moscow; *Pravda,* Dec. 26, 1958.

[141] In Des Moines, Iowa; *The New York Times,* Sept. 23, 1959, p. 29.

[142] To U.S. Senators; Tass, Sept. 19, 1959.

[143] Kazakh radio teletype to Kazakh local press, Nov. 18, 1959.

[144] See note 80.

[145] At a Soviet-Czechoslovakian Friendship Meeting in Ostrava, Czechoslovakia, July 13, 1957.

[146] *Pravda,* Jan. 27, 1960.

[147] At meeting on return of Soviet Party and Government Delegation from Hungarian People's Republic, Apr. 10, 1958.

[148] *The Washington Post and Times Herald,* Nov. 1959.

[149] *Le Monde Hebdomadaire,* Mar. 24-30, 1960, No. 597.

[150] *New York World-Telegram and The Sun,* Mar. 25, 1960.

[151] To CBS correspondents, May 28, 1957.

[152] *The New York Times,* Aug. 8, 1960, p. 30.

[153] At Economic Club of New York, Sept. 17, 1959.

[154] S. Schwartz, "Khrushchev in America," *Socialist Courier,* Oct. 1959; quoted in *Pravda,* Sept. 21, 1959.

[155] See note 4.

[156] In Krasnoyarsk; Moscow broadcast, Oct. 11, 1959.

[157] See note 3.

[158] See note 24.

[159] To French trade unionists; Tass, Apr. 1, 1960.

160 To graduates of military academies, Nov. 14, 1958.
161 In Moscow; *Pravda,* July 24, 1959.

12. *THE PROPAGANDA FRONT (II)*

1 Report on chemical industry; Moscow broadcast, May 10, 1958.
2 In Tatabanya, Hungary, Apr. 8, 1958.
3 In Peking, China; New China News Agency, Sept. 30, 1959.
4 Oleg Holfding, "State Planning and Forced Industrialization," *Problems of Communism,* Nov.-Dec. 1959, Vol. VIII, No. 6, pp. 38-46.
5 Stalin, "Report to the 13th Congress, CPSU" (1924), *Sochineniya,* Vol. VI, pp. 214-215.
6 To Eric Ridder, *Journal of Commerce,* Mar. 27, 1958.
7 Report on agriculture, CPSU Central Committee, Oct. 15, 1958.
8 G. M. Malenkov, to USSR Supreme Soviet, Aug. 8, 1953.
9 Robert W. Campbell, in *Comparisons of the United States and Soviet Economies,* p. 3.
10 P. G. Podyachikh, *The All-Union Census, 1939.* Moscow: State Statistical Publishing House, 1953.
11 S. G. Strumilin, *Ocherki Sostsialisticheskoi Ekonomiki SSSR;* quoted in *The New York Times,* Sept. 10, 1960.
12 To 19th Congress, CPSU; *Pravda,* Oct. 13, 1951.
13 To USSR Supreme Soviet; Moscow broadcast, Mar. 28, 1958.
14 Moscow broadcast, Mar. 27, 1958.

15 At Sugar-Beet Conference; Moscow broadcast, Nov. 1, 1958.
16 Hans Heymann, Jr., in *Comparisons of the United States and Soviet Economies,* p. 2.
17 Humphrey, *op. cit.*
18 Alec Nove, *Communist Economic Strategy,* p. 40. New York: National Planning Association, 1959.
19 *Pick's Currency Yearbook,* New York, 1960. Gives black-market value of the ruble at 27 to the dollar.
20 See note 6.
21 G. Warren Nutter, in *Comparisons of the United States and Soviet Economies,* p. 97.
22 See note 6.
23 See note 6.
24 To *Trybuna Ludu,* Warsaw, Poland, Mar. 10, 1958.
25 D. Gale Johnson and Arcadius Kahan, in *Comparisons of the United States and Soviet Economies.*
26 To 9th Session, USSR Supreme Soviet, 4th Convocation, Dec. 21, 1957.
27 A. I. Kirichenko; *Pravda,* Feb. 1, 1959, pp. 4, 5.
28 "Control Figures for the Economic Development of the USSR for 1959–1965," p. 77. To 21st Extraordinary Congress, CPSU, Jan. 27, 1959.
29 Gregory Grossman, "Communism in a Hurry: The Time Factor in Soviet Economics," *Problems of Communism,* May–June, 1959, Vol. VIII, No. 3.
30 To 7th Congress, Bulgarian Communist Party; Bulgarian broadcast, June 4, 1958.
31 At Soviet–Czechoslovakian Friendship Meeting in Leningrad, July 4, 1958.

[32] On television, Washington, D.C., Sept. 27, 1959.

[33] Robert W. Campbell, *op. cit.*, p. 25.

[34] Lazar Volin, *ibid.*

[35] To 20th Congress, CPSU; *Pravda*, Feb. 15, 1956.

[36] See note 7.

[37] To Plenum Session of the Central Committee, Sept. 3, 1953.

[38] *Pravda Ukrainy*, Oct. 30, 1949.

[39] On agriculture; Moscow broadcast, Dec. 16, 1958.

[40] At celebration by builders of Lenin Central Moscow Stadium; *Pravda*, Aug. 1, 1956.

[41] In Leningrad; *Pravda*, May 24, 1957.

[42] See note 41.

[43] See note 41.

[44] *Comparisons of the United States and Soviet Economies.*

[45] "Report to 21st Congress, CPSU," Jan. 27, 1959; *Current Soviet Policies III*. New York: Columbia University Press, 1960.

[46] Minsk broadcast, Apr. 24, 1959.

[47] Sources: USSR—D. Gale Johnson and Arcadius Kahan, "Soviet Agriculture: Structure and Growth," *Comparisons of the United States and Soviet Economies*, p. 223. *Pravda*, Feb. 26, 1956; U.S.—Dept. of Agriculture, "Livestock and Meat Statistics," *Statistical Bulletin*, 1957, No. 230, July, 1958, p. 140.

[48] *Comparisons of the United States and Soviet Economies*, p. 223.

[49] To farm women, Ryazan; *Pravda*, Oct. 17, 1959.

[50] To 9th All-Union Conference of Cotton Growers; Moscow broadcast, Feb. 22, 1958.

[51] To Iverach McDonald of *The Times*, London; *Pravda*, Feb. 15, 1958.

[52] To 1st Session, USSR Supreme Soviet, Apr. 26, 1954.

[53] *Monthly Labor Review*, Apr., 1960, p. 359.

[54] See note 52.

[55] At Czechoslovakian Embassy, Moscow; Tass, *The New York Times.*

[56] In Szczecin, Poland; Warsaw broadcast, July 17, 1959.

[57] "All Care for the Ideological Purity of Lectures"; Munco, Rumania, Aug. 9, 1958.

[58] To French socialists, reported by Robert Coutant, *Populaire de Paris*, June 23-24, 1956.

[59] Hubert H. Humphrey, *op, cit.*, p. 9; quoting *Pravda.*

[60] *The New York Times*, June 20, 1960.

[61] See note 28.

[62] N. Mikhailov, *The Land of the Soviets*, p. 183. Moscow: Foreign Languages Publishing House, 1957.

[63] In Krasnoyarsk; Moscow broadcast, Oct. 11, 1957.

[64] Leon M. Herman, "Taxes and the Soviet Citizen," *Problems of Communism*, Sept.-Oct., 1957, Vol. VII, No. 5.

[65] At Luzhniki Stadium; Moscow broadcast, Mar. 5, 1960.

[66] Campbell, *op. cit.*, p. 482.

[67] *Monthly Labor Review*, Apr., 1960, p. 362.

[68] *Ibid.*

[69] To Z. Bronjarek of *Tribunu Ludu*, Warsaw; *Pravda*, Mar. 12, 1958.

[70] *Monthly Labor Review*, Apr., 1960, p. 361.

[71] Seven-Year-Plan thesis, to 21st Congress, CPSU; Moscow broadcast, Nov. 14, 1958.

[72] *Monthly Labor Review*, Apr., 1960, p. 357.

73 *Ibid.,* p. 360.

74 *Ibid.*

75 *Monthly Labor Review,* Apr., 1960, No. 175.

76 *Ibid.*

77 Bureau of Labor Statistics, *Road Maps of Industry,* June 3, 1960, No. 175.

78 See note 75.

79 See note 30.

80 See note 75.

81 *Pravda,* Sept. 27, 1958.

82 *Pravda,* Oct. 8, 1959.

83 Hammond and Lessing, *op. cit.,* p. 357.

84 Moscow broadcast, Apr. 10, 1959.

85 See note 29.

86 In Vladivostok, Oct. 6, 1959.

87 To William Randolph Hearst Jr.; *Pravda,* Nov. 29, 1957.

88 Aleksander Bochenski, *Slowo Povszechne,* Nov. 13, 1959.

89 *Pravda,* Feb. 15, 1956.

90 Moscow broadcast, Nov. 17, 1959.

91 Tashkent broadcast, May 22, 1959.

92 Seven-Year-Plan thesis, to 21st Congress, CPSU; Moscow broadcast, Nov. 14, 1958.

93 Pre-election speech; Moscow broadcast, Mar. 14, 1958.

94 See note 1.

95 To Jubilee Session, USSR Supreme Soviet; Moscow broadcast, Nov. 6, 1957.

96 See note 87.

97 See note 93.

98 V. Ye Semchastrez, Young Communist League, Jan. 30, 1960.

99 *The New York Times,* May 8, 1960.

100 John Chamberlain, *The Roots of Capitalism.* New York: Van Nostrand, 1959.

101 In Kursk; Moscow broadcast, Apr. 26, 1958.

102 Edwin Vennard, in *Comparisons of the United States and Soviet Economies,* p. 483. This study gives current housing at 79 sq. ft. per capita. This figure has been updated to 1960 in view of current claims.

103 *The Washington Post and Times Herald,* Sept. 12, 1960. p. 13.

104 Hammond and Lessing, *op. cit.,* p. 363.

105 To Henry Shapiro of the United Press; Tass, Nov. 18, 1957.

106 Dnepropetrovsk broadcast, Aug. 29, 1958.

107 In Washington, D.C., Sept. 27, 1959.

108 Alma-Ata broadcast, July 22, 1959.

109 Tass, Apr. 9, 1959.

110 See note 6.

111 Moscow broadcast, Mar. 12, 1960.

112 Seven-Year-Plan thesis, to 21st Congress, CPSU, p. 59.

113 See note 95.

114 Stalin, "Report to 17th Congress, CPSU," (Jan. 28, 1934), *Problems of Leninism,* p. 507.

115 To electors of Kalinin constituency, Moscow, Mar. 14, 1958.

116 *Rahva Haal,* July 19, 1958.

117 In Novosibirsk; Moscow broadcast, Oct. 14, 1959.

118 Seven-Year-Plan thesis, to 21st Congress, CPSU.

119 Early in 1961 it was apparent that quotas for consumer goods were being made secondary to industrial goals in all fields except housing.

120 "Report to 21st Congress," *Current Soviet Policies III,* p. 41.

121 Moscow broadcast, Nov. 17, 1957.

122 *Comparisons of the United*

541

States and Soviet Economies, p. 221.

123 See note 118.

124 See note 118.

125 In Leipzig, GDR; Tass, Mar. 4, 1959.

126 See note 45.

127 To Economic Club of New York, Sept. 17, 1959.

128 Seven-Year-Plan thesis.

129 See note 128.

130 See note 128.

131 Alec Nove and Alfred Zauberman, "A Disclosure of 1956 Ruble Income," *Soviet Studies,* Vol. XI, p. 195. London, Oct., 1959.

132 Gross National Product was estimated at 2200.

133 *Worldwide and Domestic Economic Problems and Their Impact on the Foreign Policy of the United States.* A study by the Corporation for Economic and Industrial Research, Inc., for the Committee on Foreign Relations, U.S. Senate, Washington, 1959, p. 27.

134 *Ibid.*

135 See note 51.

136 See note 70.

137 Seven-Year-Plan thesis.

138 To graduates of military academies; Moscow broadcast, Nov. 15, 1958.

139 In Des Moines, Iowa, Sept. 22, 1959; *The New York Times,* Sept. 23, 1959, p. 29.

140 Seven-Year-Plan thesis.

141 See note 95.

142 F. Koslov, at 21st Congress, CPSU, *Current Soviet Policies III,* p. 155.

143 *The Times,* London, Dec. 31, 1958.

144 *U.S. Statistical Abstract,* 1960, p. 870.

145 *Ibid.,* p. 822.

146 Recent regulations have permitted Soviet citizens to build their own homes provided they could obtain materials and build without "exploiting" labor of others.

147 Rostow, *op. cit.*

148 To East German Communist Party Congress; Berlin broadcast, July 11, 1958.

149 *Monthly Labor Review,* Apr., 1960.

150 At opening of U.S. exhibition in Moscow; *Pravda,* July 25, 1959.

151 Heyman, Jr., *op. cit.,* p. 10.

152 See note 92.

153 See note 92.

154 See note 92.

155 Heyman, Jr., *op. cit.*

156 To French-Soviet Friendship Group of French Parliament; Tass, Mar. 26, 1960.

157 "Report to 21st Congress," *Current Soviet Policies III.*

158 From report "Forty Years of the Great October Socialist Revolution," to Jubilee Session, USSR Supreme Soviet, Nov. 6, 1957.

159 "For a Close Tie of Literature and Art with the Life of the People," *Kommunist,* Nov. 12, 1957, p. 11.

160 To the Party Central Committee Plenary Session; *Pravda,* Mar. 21, 1954.

161 "Control Figures for the Economic Development of the USSR for 1959–1965," p. 85.

162 *Ibid.*

163 See note 127.

164 In Szczecin, Poland; *Pravda,* July 18, 1959.

165 Lenin, "The Threatening Catastrophe and How to Fight It," *Selected Works* (Moscow), Vol. II, p. 98.

166 Stalin, "Tasks of the Business Managers," *Sochineniya,* Vol.

II, p. 366. Moscow: Cooperative Publishing Society of Foreign Workers, 1936.

167 Molotov, quoted in *Problems in Communism*, May-June, 1959, Vol. VIII, No. 3, p. 2.

168 In Leningrad; *Pravda*, May 24, 1957.

169 See note 139.

170 See note 3.

171 See note 28.

172 "Report to 21st Congress," *Current Soviet Policies III*.

173 Nore, *Communist Economic Strategy*, p. 39.

174 In Kiev; Moscow broadcast, May 12, 1959.

175 Herbert Levine, *The New Leader*, June 1, 1959, p. 12. June 1, 1959, p. 12.

176 See note 28.

177 "Report to 21st Congress," *Current Soviet Policies III*.

178 See note 92.

179 *U.S. News & World Report*, July 11, 1960.

180 See note 48.

181 Rostow, *op. cit.;* quoted by *The New York Times*.

182 Rostow, *op. cit.*

183 See note 92.

184 In Kuibyshev; Moscow broadcast, Aug. 10, 1958.

185 *U.S. News & World Report*, May 2, 1940, p. 62.

186 G. Warren Nutter, in *Comparisons of the United States and Soviet Economies*, p. 117.

187 *The U.S. Economy and the Mutual Security Program*, pp. 59, 60. Washington, Apr. 1959.

188 *Ibid.*

189 *Ibid.*

190 To 7th Congress, Bulgarian Communist Party, June 3, 1958.

191 Humphrey, *op. cit.*, p. 567.

192 Z. T. Serdyuk at the 21st Congress, CPSU, *Current Soviet*

Policies III, p. 104. New York: Columbia University Press, 1960. Quoted in *Pravda*, Jan. 31, 1959, p. 6.

193 *Improvement of Industrial Management in the USSR*, Soviet News Booklet, No. 10, p. 9. London, 1959.

194 To 5th Congress, Socialist Unity Party of Germany, GDR, July 11, 1958.

195 To USSR Supreme Soviet; Moscow broadcast, Mar. 27, 1958.

196 "Report to 21st Congress," *Current Soviet Policies III*.

197 Richard M. Nixon, in a campaign address; *The New York Times*, June 22, 1960.

198 By most professional estimates, the gap in total production increases in absolute terms.

199 In Surabaya, Indonesia; *Pravda*, Feb. 24, 1960.

200 See note 88.

201 "Report to 21st Congress," *Current Soviet Policies III*.

202 See note 122.

203 Brzezinksi, *op. cit.*, pp. 124-128.

204 *Comparisons of the United States and Soviet Economies*, p. 112.

205 John F. Kantner, *ibid.*

206 To Des Moines Chamber of Commerce; Moscow broadcast, Sept. 23, 1959.

207 See note 206.

208 In Novosibirsk; Moscow broadcast, Oct. 14, 1959.

209 Minsk broadcast, Aug. 27, 1959.

210 U. I. Ustinov, "Report to 21st Congress," p. 74.

211 N. V. Podgorny, "Report to 21st Congress," p. 73.

212 Kosygin, "Report to 21st Congress, CPSU," *Current Soviet Policies III*, p. 79.

213 Kosygin, *ibid.,* p. 79.

214 U. I. Gorbunov, "Report to 21st Congress," p. 102.

215 Moscow broadcast, Oct. 18, 1959.

216 *British-Soviet Newsletter,* July 11, 1959.

217 *Improvement of Industrial Management in the USSR,* p. 330.

218 A. I. Khvorostukhn, Tula Province, "Report to 21st Congress, CPSU," *Current Soviet Policies III,* p. 84.

219 See note 195.

220 *The Wall Street Journal,* June 21, 1960, p. 1.

221 Stalingrad broadcast, Nov. 20, 1959.

222 A. F. Zasyadko; *Pravda,* Feb. 3, 1957, pp. 8, 9.

223 Humphrey, *op. cit.*

224 A. M. Rybakoia; *Pravda,* Feb. 1, 1959, p. 3.

225 See note 222.

226 At dedication of Kuibyshev hydroelectric station, Aug. 18, 1958.

227 See note 226.

228 See note 196.

229 D. A. Kunayev, at 10th Party Congress, Kazakhstan Communist Party; *Kazakhstanskaya Pravda,* Mar. 11, 1960.

230 V. V. Grishin, All-Union Central Council of Trade Unions, at 21st Congress, CPSU; *Pravda,* Feb. 3, 1959, p. 143.

231 A. B. Aristov, "Report to 21st Congress, CPSU," *Current Soviet Policies III,* p. 121.

232 *To New Advances, Youth!* p. 11, Moscow, 1956.

233 Charles B. Shuman, in *Comparisons of the United States and Soviet Economies,* p. 496.

234 "Report to 21st Congress, CPSU," *Current Soviet Policies III.*

235 *Worldwide and Domestic Economic Problems and Their Impact on the Foreign Policy of the United States.* A Study for the Committee on Foreign Relations, United States Senate, Washington, D.C., 1959, p. 41.

236 Lenin, "Left-Wing Childishness and Petty Bourgeois Mentality" (1918), *Selected Works* (New York), Vol. VII, pp. 365-366.

237 Humphrey, *op. cit.*

238 Reply to letters and telegrams on eve of departure on U.S. tour, Sept. 1959.

239 In Pittsburgh, Sept. 24, 1959.

240 *The Wall Street Journal,* June 8, 1960, p. 1.

241 Richard M. Nixon; *The New York Times,* June 22, 1960, p. 22.

242 Bertram D. Wolfe, "Facts and Polemics," *Problems of Communism,* Jan.–Feb. 1960, Vol. IX, No. 1.

243 *U.S. News & World Report,* July 11, 1960.

244 *U.S. Foreign Policy.* A study by CEIR. Washington, Nov. 11, 1959, p. 47.

13. *CONTRADICTIONS IN COMMUNISM*

1 Winston Churchill, 1955; quoted by William Randolph Hearst, Jr.

2 Lenin, "Better Fewer, But Better" (1923), *Selected Works* (New York), Vol. IX, p. 400.

3 Stalin, "The Policy of the Soviet Government on the National Question in Russia" (1920), *Marxism and the National Question,* p. 76.

4 To 20th Congress, CPSU; *Pravda,* Feb. 15, 1956.

5 To USSR Supreme Soviet; Moscow broadcast, Oct. 31, 1959.

[6] *People's Daily,* Peking; quoted in *The Washington Post and Times Herald,* June 26, 1960.

[7] *U.S. News & World Report,* July 11, 1960, p. 58.

[8] *Red Flag;* quoted in *Time,* May 2, 1960.

[9] In Dnepropetrovsk; Moscow broadcast, July 30, 1957.

[10] See note 8.

[11] To 21st Congress, CPSU; Jan. 27, 1959.

[12] *Time,* June 27, 1960, p. 20.

[13] To Plawce producers' cooperative, Poznań, Poland; Moscow broadcast, July 21, 1959.

[14] Prague broadcast, July 11, 1957.

[15] See note 11.

[16] In China; Chinese Communist news service, NCNA, Sept. 30, 1954.

[17] Letter to President Eisenhower, Sept. 19, 1958; *Pravda,* Sept. 20, 1958. Rejected and returned Sept. 21.

[18] Tass, Sept. 8, 1958.

[19] See note 17.

[20] To USSR Supreme Soviet; Moscow broadcast, Oct. 31, 1959.

[21] Pre-election speech; Moscow broadcast, Mar. 14, 1958.

[22] In Kishinev; *Pravda,* May 15, 1959.

[23] *U.S. News & World Report,* May 2, 1960, p. 32.

[24] To Hans Richter, president of the European Federation Against Atomic Armament, and Canon L. John Collins, vice-president; Moscow broadcast, Mar. 18, 1960.

[25] C. L. Sulzberger; *The New York Times,* June 27, 1960.

[26] To Jubilee Session, USSR Supreme Soviet, Nov. 6, 1957.

[27] Harry Schwartz of *The New York Times,* Apr. 10, 1960.

14. *SUMMARY*

[1] *Pravda,* Mar. 27, 1959.

[2] Report on Nov., 1960, Party conclave; *The New York Times,* Jan. 18, 1961.

[3] Associated Press, Dec. 30, 1960.

[4] See note 2.